THE STAND

Jesus in the Book of Daniel

"Therefore, take up the full armor of God,
that you all may be able
to withstand during the evil day,
and having done all things,
to remain standing."
Ephesians 6:13

"Therefore be submitted unto God:
Take your stand against the devil,
and he will flee from you."
James 4:7

"He shall be made to stand,
for God is able to
make him stand."
Romans 14:4

SCOTT BURGESS

TEACH Services, Inc.
PUBLISHING
www.TEACHServices.com • (800) 367-1844

World rights reserved. This book or any portion thereof may not be copied or reproduced in any form or manner whatever, except as provided by law, without the written permission of the publisher, except by a reviewer who may quote brief passages in a review.

The author assumes full responsibility for the accuracy of all facts and quotations as cited in this book. The opinions expressed in this book are the author's personal views and interpretations, and do not necessarily reflect those of the publisher.

This book is provided with the understanding that the publisher is not engaged in giving spiritual, legal, medical, or other professional advice. If authoritative advice is needed, the reader should seek the counsel of a competent professional.

Copyright © 2020 Scott Burgess
Copyright © 2020 TEACH Services, Inc.
ISBN-13: 978-1-4796-1136-2 (Paperback)
ISBN-13: 978-1-4796-1137-9 (ePub)
Library of Congress Control Number: 2020905751

Except where noted with the letters KJV (King James Version), all Bible verses are the author's own translation of the Hebrew and Aramaic Old Testament and the Majority Text Greek New Testament.

Published by

www.TEACHServices.com • (800) 367-1844

TABLE OF CONTENTS

PRELIMINARY MATTER. v
    LIST OF TABLES vi
    ACKNOWLEDGMENTS. vii
    READER REACTIONS viii
    INTRODUCTION. xi
    ABBREVIATIONS xiii

1: GOD'S INVESTIGATION—TEN DAYS. 17
    DANIEL 1: TEN HANDS WISER—STANDING
        BEFORE THE KING. 18
    DANIEL, PART 1: THE KEY POINTS 27

2: GOD'S JUDGMENT—SEVEN TIMES 33
    DANIEL 2: WITHOUT HANDS—THE REVEALER
        AND HIS STONE. 34
    DANIEL 3: THE KING'S HAND—THE IMAGE
        AND THE FURNACE. 52
    DANIEL 4: GOD'S HAND—HUMBLED 7 TIMES. 64
    DANIEL 5: GOD'S HAND—WEIGHED 7 TIMES 84
    DANIEL 6: THE LIONS' HAND—THE PROHIBITION
        AND THE DEN. 103
    DANIEL 7: THE HORN'S HAND—THE JUDGE
        AND HIS JUDGMENT 115
    DANIEL, PART 2: THE KEY POINTS 159

3: GOD'S ATONEMENT—SEVENTY TIMES SEVEN **169**
   DANIEL 8 AND 9: GOD'S HAND—DELIVERANCE
      BY MESSIAH'S ATONING SACRIFICE 170
   DANIEL 10–12: RAISED HANDS—MESSIAH
      APPLIES ATONEMENT IN JUDGMENT 229
   DANIEL, PART 3: THE KEY POINTS 328

CONCLUDING MATTER **335**
   BIBLIOGRAPHY 336
   THE WEDDING: JESUS STANDS FOR HIS BRIDE
      IN THE BOOK OF REVELATION 343
   ABOUT THE AUTHOR 344

PRELIMINARY MATTER

LIST OF TABLES

Table 1: Chiastic Arrangement of Daniel 1 28
Table 2: Relation of Sanctuary Weights One to Another 92
Table 3: God's Standard of Righteousness and Belshazzar's
Shortfall 94
Table 4: Jesus and the Holy Spirit in Daniel 2–7 157
Table 5: Simplified Chiastic Structure of Daniel 2–7 158
Table 6: Panel Structure of Daniel 2 and 7 159
Table 7: Panel Structure of Daniel 3 and 6 161
Table 8: Panel Structure of Daniel 4 and 5 161
Table 9: The Number Seven in Daniel 2–7 162
Table 10: The Numbers Four, Seven, and Ten in Daniel 2–7,
Sorted by Chapter with Chiastic Matches Indicated 163
Table 11: Other Key Numbers in Daniel 2–7, Sorted by Number . . 165
Table 12: Scriptural Significance of Ram 177
Table 13: Eastward Movement and Rebellion Against God
in Genesis 178
Table 14: Scriptural Significance of "Male Goat of the Goats"
and "Buck" 180
Table 15: Use of Hebrew *tamid* in Scripture 188
Table 16: Symbolism of Jesus' Description in Daniel 10:5–6 243
Table 17: *Chamad* ("desire," "esteem") in Scripture 270
Table 18: Family Tree for Egypt, Libya, and Ethiopia (Genesis 10) . 292
Table 19: Chronology of Events in the Exodus 319
Table 20: Simplified Structure of Daniel 8–12 328
Table 21: Detailed Structure of Daniel 8–12 330

ACKNOWLEDGMENTS

The author is grateful to the following individuals (listed alphabetically) for their role in bringing this project to completion:

NAME	HELP PROVIDED
Karen Burgess: My wife and mother of our children	Provided photo for front cover.
Dr. Richard Davidson: Old Testament Professor, Seventh-day Adventist Theological Seminary at Andrews University	Reviewed and identified several exegetical and semantic points, with suggestions for improvement and/or sources to consult.
Edwin de Kock: Historicist author, retired English professor	Provided answers to sundry historical questions, recommended a proofreader.
Charles and Sharon Ferguson: Pastor-and-wife team	Gave encouragement in getting started with this project.
Holly Joers: Active, soul-winning member of the Seventh-day Adventist Church	Gave encouragement to employ TEACH Services Inc as publisher.
Brenda Nieves: English teacher, Ouachita Hills College	Supplied sundry formatting/style pointers.
Magda Rodriguez: President of Ouachita Hills College, Ph.D. candidate	Granted me time to work on the manuscript.
David Sydnor: Book reviewer, former pastor	Proofread manuscript thoroughly and swiftly.
Dr. Alberto Treiyer: Pastor, scholar, and historicist author	Encouraged me to make the historical portions of this book as strong as possible.
Dr. Karl Tsatalbasidis: Pastor, teacher, and author	Suggested title "The Stand" based on sermon I presented.
Anonymous	Reviewed closing material of book, provided assistance in publicizing the book.

READER REACTIONS

Pastor Charles Ferguson, D.Min., Carolina Conference of Seventh-day Adventists
THE STAND: Jesus in the Book of Daniel by Scott Burgess is a breath of fresh air to the much visited book of Daniel. *THE STAND* is an inductive approach to understanding Daniel. As such rather than imposing upon Daniel Burgess's version of truth, Burgess lets Daniel speak for himself. Burgess approaches Daniel with the tools of a trained and disciplined biblical theologian; first, understanding the words in the original languages penned by Daniel himself. Then, gaining vital insights from word allusions found in other biblical books, as well as recognizing the literary chiastic structures carefully crafted by the inspired prophet, and finally visiting insights from history. As an inductive study, *THE STAND* affirms the historicist position through discovery. Once I got into *THE STAND* I could not put it down. It was gripping. The author is succinct, yet thorough. I recommend Scott Burgess's *THE STAND: Jesus in the Book of Daniel* to both theologian and layman without qualification.

Edwin de Kock, M.A., Dip. Theo.
As its title suggests, *THE STAND: Jesus in the Book of Daniel* by Scott Burgess does not limit itself to interpreting the predictions in that work. It is profoundly Christ-centered, in both its historical and prophetic parts, dealing with both the explicit appearances of the Saviour and where He or His principles are implicitly involved. But the author does not by any means neglect the prophecies. Carefully he analyzes and matches each of them with real events throughout the centuries. He is demonstrably a

Historicist, emphatically rejecting both Catholic Preterism and Futurism together with its derivative, Protestant Dispensationalism. In this, he draws on the most up-to-date and varied research as well as the time-tested work of Uriah Smith. While I differ on some points (e.g., the identification of the kings of the north and south in Daniel 11, about which Seventh-day Adventists scholars still have many divergent ideas), I agree with most of his conclusions. The minutiae of his commentary are all thought-provoking, ranging from the interesting to the profound. A most impressive feature is that Scott Burgess has made and uses his own translation of both the Hebrew and Aramaic portions of Daniel in its entirety. For students of prophecy and related matters, *THE STAND* will prove a most valuable resource.

Karl Tsatalbasidis, Ph.D.
Daniel's name means "God is my judge," and when reading the book of Daniel, one cannot help but notice the theme of judgment, especially in chapters 7 and 8. Yet, the theme of judgment in the book of Daniel is more pervasive than what we find in those chapters. By paying close attention to the Hebrew and Aramaic, Scott Burgess has discovered the importance and widespread use of the word "stand" as a key concept that runs like a golden thread throughout the major chapters of Daniel. From chapter 1, where Daniel and his friends stand before the king, to when he is told to stand in his lot in chapter 12, *The Stand* gives fresh exegetical insights into the judgment, a theme that should occupy our time and attention in this important hour of earth's history.

David Sydnor
"When the books of Daniel and Revelation are better understood, believers will have an entirely different religious experience. They will be given such glimpses of the open gates of heaven that heart and mind will be impressed with the character that all must develop in order to realize the blessedness which is to be the reward of the pure in heart" (White, *TM*, p. 114).

This admonition has held weight for me since I first read it. Therefore, I am interested when I become aware of significant efforts to expand on the resources that have been produced over the course of the Advent movement regarding these two Bible books. The first question that always comes to mind is, "In what way does the author hope to add to what is already a rich heritage of contributions in the past?" Before committing myself to a detailed review of this manuscript, I asked the author if he felt his work offered a perspective unique enough to justify another commentary on Daniel. He felt it did, and after reviewing it, I wholeheartedly agree. It would be asking too much for me to agree with every position taken on the most difficult passages of unfulfilled prophecy, and it is not necessary. This work contains a rich array of insights at several different levels that provided me with satisfaction both scholarly and devotionally. It is difficult for me to believe that anyone looking to add depth to their experience will not find it a valuable resource. I therefore recommend it to all.

INTRODUCTION

The Bible was written for everybody and meant to be understood by everybody. To that end, the present work employs Scripture's own simple method of exegesis: "precept must be upon precept, precept upon precept; line upon line, line upon line; here a little, and there a little" (Isa. 28:10, KJV). Besides explaining each passage of Daniel, the present work also teaches the reader *how to uncover these truths for oneself*, walking the reader through the author's own thought process. Once one masters how to apply this skill prayerfully, *any* Scripture may be understood, no matter how difficult.

This commentary covers the entire book of Daniel. The translation followed is that of the author, who has been trained in the biblical languages and passionately studies the Scriptures daily in the original languages. Except where noted with the letters KJV (King James Version), all Bible verses are the author's own translation of the Hebrew and Aramaic Old Testament and the Majority Text Greek New Testament.

Two related themes are traced in this book: "standing" in judgment, as well as God's "hand," which strengthens us to do so. To draw attention to the theme of standing, each instance of the Hebrew *'amad* and its Aramaic counterpart *qum* appear in bold in the translation at the beginning of each chapter. To draw attention to the theme of God's hand, each chapter title employs the word "hand(s)."

The name Daniel signifies "God is my Judge," and the book of Daniel is about standing in the judgment, whether in historic references to Daniel and his companions or prophesying of God's last-day people who are to stand before the Judge of all things, "not having spot, or wrinkle, or any such thing ... holy and without blemish" (Eph. 5:27, KJV).

This work follows the historicist method of prophetic interpretation, permitting history to confirm the prophecies of Daniel. The preterist, futurist, and idealist schools of interpretation are all rejected, as they spiritualize away concrete realities readily verified in history, and each fails to identify the enemy of God and His people that the book of Daniel plainly identifies.

This work is unique in its emphasis upon the use of numbers that saturate the book of Daniel. Certain passages *cannot* be fully appreciated without due attention to the numbers employed. This is not to be confused with numerology (e.g., the Jewish *Kaballah*), which gives to biblical numbers mystical meanings not supported by the text.

The author has intentionally gone contrary to the rule of spelling out numbers, instead printing them numerically (e.g., "7," "62," "490"). Exceptions to this are "thousands" and "million," ordinal numbers ("first," "second," etc.), the word "one" when used of an individual (e.g., "The one who lives like Abraham lives by faith"), and when numbers are used to begin a sentence. In a work so saturated with numbers, it is easier to write in this fashion, and it is easier for the reader to locate numbers on a given page. Further, standard style manuals disagree on rules for spelling out numbers.

May the reader prayerfully take up the study of this end-time book of books, and may this commentary shed light on the prophecies therein, that the reader may take hold of God's hand and **stand** in the end-time judgment, on fire to prepare other souls to **stand** for the Messiah and Judge—the Lord Jesus.

Scott Burgess
June 2019

ABBREVIATIONS

BOOKS OF THE BIBLE AND 1 MACCABEES

ABBREVIATION	BOOK	ABBREVIATION	BOOK
1 Macc.	1 Maccabees	Jonah	Jonah
Gen.	Genesis	Mic.	Micah
Exod.	Exodus	Nah.	Nahum
Lev.	Leviticus	Hab.	Habakkuk
Num.	Numbers	Zeph.	Zephaniah
Deut.	Deuteronomy	Hag.	Haggai
Josh.	Joshua	Zech.	Zechariah
Judges	Judges	Mal.	Malachi
Ruth	Ruth	Matt.	Matthew
1 Sam.; 2 Sam.	1 or 2 Samuel	Mark	Mark
1 Kings; 2 Kings	1 or 2 Kings	Luke	Luke
1 Chron.; 2 Chron.	1 or 2 Chronicles	John	John
Ezra	Ezra	Acts	Acts
Neh.	Nehemiah	Rom.	Romans
Esther	Esther	1 Cor.; 2 Cor.	1 or 2 Corinthians
Job	Job	Gal.	Galatians
Ps.	Psalms	Eph.	Ephesians
Prov.	Proverbs	Phil.	Philippians
Eccles.	Ecclesiastes	Col.	Colossians
Song of Sol.	Song of Songs	1 Thess.; 2 Thess.	1 or 2 Thessalonians
Isa.	Isaiah	1 Tim.; 2 Tim.	1 or 2 Timothy
Jer.	Jeremiah	Titus	Titus

ABBREVIATION	BOOK	ABBREVIATION	BOOK
Lam.	Lamentations	Philemon	Philemon
Ezek.	Ezekiel	Heb.	Hebrews
Dan.	Daniel	James	James
Hosea	Hosea	1 Peter; 2 Peter	1 or 2 Peter
Joel	Joel	1 John; 2 John; 3 John	1, 2 or 3 John
Amos	Amos	Jude	Jude
Obad.	Obadiah	Rev.	Revelation

BIBLES CITED

ABBREVIATION	BIBLE
ASV	*Revised Version, American Standard Edition*
CEB	*Common English Bible*
CJB	*Complete Jewish Bible*
EBR	*Rotherham's Emphasized Bible*
ERV	*English Revised Version*
ESV	*The Holy Bible, English Standard Version*
GWN	*God's Word Translation*
JPS 1917	*JPS Holy Scriptures 1917 (English)*
KJV	*King James Version*
LEE	*Isaac Leeser (Jewish Bible)*
LXX	*Septuaginta (Old Greek Jewish Scriptures)*
NAB	*New American Bible, revised edition*
NASU	*The New American Standard Bible, 1995 Update*
NET	*The NET Bible*
NIV	*The New International Version*
NJB	*New Jerusalem Bible*
NJPS	*Jewish Publication Society of America Tanakh*
NKJV	*The New King James Version*
NLT	*New Living Translation*
RSV	*Revised Standard Version of the Bible*
YLT	*Young's Literal Translation of the Holy Bible*

REFERENCE WORKS

ABBREVIATION	AUTHOR/EDITOR	TITLE
ANLEX	Friberg, Friberg, and Miller	*Analytical Lexicon of the Greek New Testament*
Antiquities	Flavius Josephus	*Complete Works of Flavius Josephus: Antiquities of the Jews*
BDB	Brown, Driver, and Briggs	*The Brown-Driver-Briggs Hebrew and English Lexicon*
CTBH	Ellen G. White	*Christian Temperance and Bible Hygiene*
DA	Ellen G. White	*The Desire of Ages*
FE	Ellen G. White	*Fundamentals of Christian Education*
GC	Ellen G. White	*The Great Controversy*
LSJ	Liddell, Scott, Jones, and McKenzie	*A Greek-English Lexicon*
xMR	Ellen G. White	*Manuscript Releases, vol. x* [x can be from 1 to 21]
PFF	LeRoy Edwin Froom	*The Prophetic Faith of Our Fathers*, 4 vols.
PK	Ellen G. White	*Prophets and Kings*
PP	Ellen G. White	*Patriarchs and Prophets*
RH	Ellen G. White	*The Review and Herald* (Seventh-day Adventist periodical)
1SAT	Ellen G. White	*Sermons and Talks*, Vol. 1
SC2	Will Durant	*The Story of Civilization, Part II: The Life of Greece*
SDABC4	Francis D. Nichol	*The Seventh-day Adventist Bible Commentary*, Vol. 4
666	Edwin de Kock	*The Truth About 666 and the Story of the Great Apostasy*
SL	Ellen G. White	*The Sanctified Life*
ST	Ellen G. White	*The Signs of the Times* (Seventh-day Adventist periodical)
TM	Ellen G. White	*Testimonies to Ministers and Gospel Workers*
TWOT	Laird, Archer, and Waltke	*Theological Wordbook of the Old Testament*
YI	Ellen G. White	*The Youth's Instructor* (Seventh-day Adventist periodical)
Wars	Flavius Josephus	*Complete Works of Flavius Josephus: Wars of the Jews*

1:
GOD'S INVESTIGATION—
TEN DAYS

DANIEL 1: TEN HANDS WISER—STANDING BEFORE THE KING

Seventy-Year Captivity Begins: Year 3 of Jehoiakim

1 ¹In year 3 of the reign of Jehoiakim king of Judah, Nebuchadnezzar king of Babylon came to Jerusalem and laid siege against it. ²*Adonai* gave into his hand Jehoiakim king of Judah, along with a portion of the vessels of the house of God. He brought them to the land of Shinar, to the house of his god; the vessels he brought to the treasure house of his god.

Royal Seed Selected for Judgment

³Then the king told Ashpenaz, chief of his officials, to bring some of the sons of Israel, from the seed of royalty and nobility, ⁴youths in whom was no blemish, of good appearance; those skillful in all wisdom, possessing knowledge, and exercising discernment in thought; in whom was strength to **stand** in the palace[1] of the king, so as to teach them the literature and language of the Kasdim. ⁵So the king appointed them a portion day by day from the king's delicacies and his banqueting wine, to enable them to grow 3 years, so that at the end thereof, they might **stand** before the king.

---

[1] In religious contexts, this is the same word translated "temple." This is important, for Daniel's stance before king Nebuchadnezzar models how we are to stand before God in His temple during the day of judgment.

⁶Now there were among them, from the sons of Judah, Daniel, Hananiah, Mishael, and Azariah. ⁷The ruler of the officials determined names for them: for Daniel, he determined Belteshazzar; for Hananiah, Shadrach; for Mishael, Meshach; and for Azariah, Abed-Nego.

Daniel Determines Not to Defile Himself

⁸However, Daniel determined in his heart that he would not defile himself with the king's delicacies, nor with the king's banqueting wine, so he sought [permission] from the ruler of the officials that he might not defile himself. ⁹God granted Daniel to be regarded with noble character and compassion by the ruler of the officials. ¹⁰The ruler of the officials said to Daniel, "I fear my lord the king, who has appointed your food and your banqueting drink; for why should he see your faces more drawn than the youth which are of your age group? Thus you would incriminate my head before the king."

The 10-Day Test

¹¹So Daniel said to the guardian whom the ruler of the officials had appointed over Daniel, Hananiah, Mishael, and Azariah, ¹²"Please, test your servants 10 days: give us some of what grows from seed that we may eat, and water that we may drink. ¹³Let our appearances be seen before you, along with the appearance of the youths who eat the king's delicacies. Then as you see fit, deal with your servants." ¹⁴So he listened to them concerning this matter and tested them 10 days.

¹⁵At the end of 10 days, their appearances were seen to be better and fatter of flesh than all the youths who were eating the king's delicacies. ¹⁶So the guardian continued removing their delicacies and their banqueting wine and giving them that which grows from seed. ¹⁷As for these 4 youths, God gave them ability to think and skill in all literature and wisdom, but Daniel he gave discernment in every vision and [all] dreams.

Four Faithful Hebrews Stand Before King in Judgment

¹⁸Now at the end of the days, when the king had said to bring them in, the ruler of the officials brought them in before Nebuchadnezzar. ¹⁹The king spoke with them, and among them all, there was not found any like Daniel, Hananiah, Mishael, and Azariah; therefore they **stood** before the king. ²⁰And every matter of wisdom [and] discernment which the king sought from them, he found them 10 hands above all the magicians [and] astrologers which were in his entire kingdom.

Seventy-Year Captivity Ends: Year 1 of King Cyrus

²¹So Daniel continued until year 1 of King Cyrus.

COMMENTARY: DANIEL 1

Seventy-Year Captivity Begins: Year 3 of Jehoiakim

The book of Daniel opens as the heathen king Nebuchadnezzar besieges Jerusalem in 605 BC. Ironically, *Adonai* Himself has given the people of Jerusalem into Nebuchadnezzar's hand, permitting His own temple to be defiled. Why would their loving God do this? Let Scripture answer:

> 2 Chron. 36:15–17: *Yahweh* God of their fathers sent to them by the hand of His messengers, rising early and sending because He had compassion on His people and on His dwelling place; but they jeered at God's messengers, despising His words, misusing His prophets, until the wrath of *Yahweh* rose against His people—until there was no remedy. Therefore He brought against them the king of the Kasdim, who killed their young men with the sword in the house of their sanctuary, and had no compassion upon young man or virgin, elderly or decrepit: He gave all into his hand.

Nebuchadnezzar is appointed by *Adonai* as His instrument of judgment, serving as both king and judge. As the rest of Daniel makes clear, it is Jesus who is ultimately the King and Judge of all, but God often uses human agents, including heathens, to work out His plans. He raises up the kings He chooses (see Dan. 2:21), even calling Cyrus His messiah, that is, His anointed one (Isa. 45:1–5). Nebuchadnezzar's role as judge is of supreme interest, for judgment is the overarching theme throughout Daniel, whose name signifies "God is my Judge"—or better yet, for those who surrender all to God, "God is my Vindicator."

Royal Seed Selected for Judgment

Nebuchadnezzar appoints Ashpenaz to select choice young men of the Jewish captivity, those who would be able to stand before the king. As the book of Daniel unfolds, it becomes clear that one's ability to *stand* in the judgment is key. The good news is that God Himself develops our characters so that we can be assured we are fit to stand. It is evident that, taken collectively, God's people were unable to stand in judgment in 605 BC; hence Nebuchadnezzar's successful conquest. Nevertheless, a remnant of this group of captives, distinguished by fidelity to God's requirements, *was* able to stand.

Any proper judgment, whether in this world or the heavenly realm, involves an examination of evidence. Hence the select Hebrew youth are to be trained for 3 years, then examined at the end thereof to see if they are worthy of the trust the king has placed in them. Are they able to stand in his presence?

Unbeknownst to the Babylonians, God has factored in His own investigation. In verse 5, the youth are faced with the choice of whether to partake freely of the king's fare or diligently consider what he has set before them, curbing their appetite lest they be ensnared (see Prov. 23:1–3). Will their faithfulness to God's Word lead them to forsake the king's food? While an idol is nothing in this world, eating food offered to an idol could lead onlookers to conclude that those eating such food *approve* of idol worship and therefore become sin against them and God (see 1 Cor. 8:4, 7–13).[2] In fact, the story of Balaam reveals that knowingly eating such food can indeed lead one to engage in idolatry itself (see Num. 25:2). Further, the use of alcohol, forbidden by God (see Prov. 23:29–35), and stimulating food (that would almost certainly be unclean per Leviticus 11) would dishonor God and injure their physical and mental power.[3]

The captors change the names of the Hebrew youth. In the Bible, name changes coincide with changes in character, especially changes that put one's life into harmony with God's everlasting covenant. Specifically, it deals with making mankind righteous by exercising faith in God's promise (see Gen. 15:6) and involves a death to the old nature, the person of the flesh, as symbolized by the circumcision of the flesh (see Gen. 17:7, 13, 19). *Yahweh* counsels Abram to "walk before Me, and be perfect" (Gen. 17:1). Immediately following this command/promise, He asserts that He will make His covenant with him, promising him that he will be a father of many nations, even changing his name from Abram ("exalted father") to Abraham ("father of a multitude"), showing that his seed will partake of the covenant blessings.

Another prime example of a name change occurs when Jacob wrestles with the Angel of *Yahweh* (Jesus), pleading that He not forsake him, but rather bless him. In consequence, the Angel changes his name from Jacob ("heel grabber," often rendered "supplanter"), to Israel, which means both "God prevails" and "ruler of God" (Gen. 32:28). He is no longer rebellious Jacob, but Israel, who has partaken of *Yahweh's* righteousness by exercising faith in His everlasting covenant.

---

[2] "But a portion having been offered to idols, the food from the king's table was consecrated to idolatry; and one partaking of it would be regarded as offering homage to the gods of Babylon. In such homage, loyalty to Jehovah forbade Daniel and his companions to join. Even a mere pretense of eating the food or drinking the wine would be a denial of their faith. To do this would be to array themselves with heathenism and to dishonor the principles of the law of God" (White, *PK*, p. 481).

[3] "Among the viands placed before the king were swine's flesh and other meats which were declared unclean by the law of Moses, and which the Hebrews had been expressly forbidden to eat" (White, *SL*, p. 19).

Therefore, in Daniel 1:6–7, the Hebrew names, which point to *Yahweh's* character and work in the life,[4] are changed into Babylonian names, which direct their attention to false idol gods. The captors' intent is to fashion these promising youth into Babylonians at heart.[5]

Daniel Determines Not to Defile Himself

What was not accounted for by the Babylonian captors was the devotion of Daniel and his friends to the God of their youth. "Daniel determined in his heart that he would not defile himself." Comparison of verse 7 and verse 8 makes it apparent that Daniel recognized the Babylonian king's intent to change their character. Nevertheless, God worked through Daniel's winsome character to bring him into favor with the ruler of the officials, opening the way to be able to stand true to principle.

One marvels that a teenager could adhere so strongly to principle.[6] The year of his birth coincided with the introduction of Josiah's reforms.[7] Hence, in his formative years, Daniel's parents were raising him with a mindset greatly influenced by the rediscovered Word of God (see 2 Chron. 34:15–33).[8] There will be a faithful remnant at the end of earth's history, so Daniel 1 is an admonition to parents to be faithful to their

---

[4] Daniel: "God is my Judge"; Hananiah: "*Yah*[*weh*] is gracious"; Mishael: "Who is like God?"; Azariah: "*Yah*[*weh*] helps."

[5] "The king did not compel the Hebrew youth to renounce their faith in favor of idolatry, but he hoped to bring this about gradually. By giving them names significant of idolatry, by bringing them daily into close association with idolatrous customs, and under the influence of the seductive rites of heathen worship, he hoped to induce them to renounce the religion of their nation and to unite with the worship of the Babylonians" (White, *PK*, p. 481).

[6] 4T, p. 570: "Daniel was but eighteen years old when brought into a heathen court in service to the king of Babylon."

[7] Josiah's reign was 641–609 BC. His reforms began in year 18 of his reign (see 2 Kings 22:3), which would be 624 or 623 BC, depending on whether his first year of reign was the year of accession to the throne or his first full year of reign. Hence, in the conquest of Jerusalem in 605 BC, Daniel was indeed but 18 years old.

[8] "Daniel and his associates had been trained by their parents to habits of strict temperance. ... This education was to Daniel and his companions the means of their preservation amidst the demoralizing influences of the court of Babylon" (White, *PK*, p. 482).

charge, so that in the final days of the judgment, *their* children may stand as did Daniel.

The 10-Day Test

While the ruler of the officials fears for his own life should the youth begin to look lean and unhealthy, Daniel turns the tables and proposes a test: let him and his companions be permitted a simple plant-based diet and water for 10 days, then compare their health with those who eat the king's fare.

This test is notable for several reasons:

1. It permits God to visibly demonstrate the superiority of his ways via the superior health of the faithful youth.
2. It hearkens back to Eden, where the great test of loyalty to God hinged on self-control in the area of appetite (see Gen. 2:17; 3:1–24). It demonstrates that God's grace is sufficient to overcome any temptation or trial, contrary to Satan's charge that unfavorable circumstances make perfect obedience impossible (see Job 1:9–11; 2:4, 5).
3. It points forward to Jesus' victory over appetite and Satan at the beginning of his ministry (see Matt. 4; Luke 4).
4. In Scripture, the number 10 is associated with investigative judgment. The premier example is God's 10 Commandment law (see Exod. 20:1–17), for Ecclesiastes 12:13–14 asserts that this is the basis of the judgment by which our characters are investigated. Likewise, Abraham pled that judgment be averted if God's investigation of Sodom revealed only 10 faithful people (see Gen. 18:21, 32).
5. After 10 days, they are investigated. This prepares them to stand before the king's judgment, 10 hands above all.

At the end of 10 days, the guardian is convinced, so he continues providing the requested diet.

Four Faithful Hebrews Stand Before King in Judgment

Having proved their adherence to principle in that which was apparently least (diet), God blesses them extraordinarily in that which was greatest—standing before the king who was to judge them after 3 years. The linkage between this final judgment and the former 10-day test is established by the assertion that they performed "10 hands above" all of the king's wise men.

To fully appreciate the remainder of Daniel and Revelation, one must note carefully that they "stood before the king." The remainder of Daniel and Revelation portray what it means to stand in the judgment, as well as the provision that God, in His great love for fallen mankind, has made to save us to the uttermost, that we "may be able to withstand during the evil day, and having done all things, to remain standing" (Eph. 6:13). The only parties to stand in the end-time judgment are the righteous and the Judge Himself:

> Ps. 76:7–9: Who will **stand** before you when you are angry? From the heavens, you caused deliverance to be heard. The earth became afraid, and quiet, when God arose for judgment, to save all the humble of earth.
>
> Ps. 130:3: If you keep record of deviant behavior, *Yah Adonai*, who will **stand**?
>
> Dan. 12:1: At that time, Michael shall **stand**, the great Ruler who **stands** over the sons of your people … at that time, your people will be delivered, everyone who is found written in the scroll.
>
> Ps. 106:30: Then Phinehas **stood** and intervened, and the plague was restrained [Phinehas typifies Michael when he stands at the close of human probation, protecting his people from receiving the 7 last plagues as they fall].
>
> Acts 7:56: Behold, I see the heavens opened, and the Son of man **standing** at the right hand of God [Jesus stands at the conclusion of the Jewish nation's probationary period of 70 weeks (see comments on Daniel 9)].

The events of Daniel 1 typify, on a small scale, the judgment "at the end of the days" that all must face, "for all of us will **stand** before Messiah's judgment seat" (Rom. 14:10). The phrase "at the end of the days" appears also in Daniel 12:13, referring to the commencement of the end-time judgment.

Seventy-Year Captivity Ends: Year 1 of King Cyrus

The chapter concludes by noting that Daniel continued until year 1 of King Cyrus, significant as it marks the end of Judah's 70-year captivity. In Isaiah 45:1, Scripture refers to Cyrus as "messiah" ("anointed"), a title shared by Jesus. Cyrus and Jesus were both called of God to provide deliverance for God's people. While the Jews were captive in Babylon, Jerusalem kept Sabbath for 70 years, while Cyrus's decree in year 1 of his reign marked the release of the Jews, and hence the terminus of the 70 years of captivity (see 2 Chron. 36:21–23).[9]

Hence, Daniel 1 opens with God's rebellious people being judged with a period of captivity in an effort to reform them, and the chapter closes with the end of this judgment period. Thus, we have a framework whereby to understand the rest of the book of Daniel: God's judgment of His professed followers includes His redemptive efforts currently underway to save us, climaxing when He renders His final verdict.

---

[9] "Upon [Darius'] death, within about two years of the fall of Babylon, Cyrus succeeded to the throne, and the beginning of his reign marked the completion of the seventy years since the first company of Hebrews had been taken by Nebuchadnezzar from their Judean home to Babylon" (White, *PK*, pp. 556, 557).

DANIEL, PART 1: THE KEY POINTS

DANIEL 1: JESUS

Jesus is the focus of all Scriptures, and they testify of Him (see John 5:39). One might question where Jesus is in Daniel 1. Verse 2 refers to *Adonai*, highlighting God as Judge. *Adonai* first appears in Genesis 15:2 and 8, referring to God as the One who judges who is worthy of the covenant blessings, and its next use is in Genesis 18:3 and 27–32, in which God investigates matters to render an appropriate verdict. In Exodus 5:21, the Israelite overseers come to Moses and Aaron in their Egyptian bondage and request that *Yahweh* judge the two of them; in verse 22, Moses submits this petition before *Yahweh*, addressing him as *Adonai*. In reference to the end time judgment, Malachi 3:1–5 states that *Adon* (a variant of *Adonai*) comes to His temple to commence the work of judgment. Since the Son of man comes before the Ancient of Days when the judgment commences (see Dan. 7:13), and "the Father judges no one, but has delegated all judgment to the Son" (John 5:22), we conclude that Jesus *is Adonai*.

In verse 17, God rewards the youth with great wisdom, and to Daniel He gives understanding of visions and dreams. Jesus distributes gifts according to everyone's work (see Rev. 22:12), and rewards follow judgment (see Eccles. 12:13, 14). Again, it is plain that the great Judge in Daniel 1 is Jesus.

DANIEL 1: THE STAND

In verse 5, the youth are selected for the express purpose of standing before the king at the end of 3 years' training; in verse 19, their faithfulness to God enables them to stand before the king who served as judge.

This story typifies an experience all will have: either we remain faithful to God, standing firm during the end time judgment, looking for and hastening Jesus's return, or we stand with all the wicked before the judgment seat of God to hear the sentence of doom (see Rev. 20:12).

DANIEL 1: THE 10 HANDS

In verse 20, Daniel and his friends are found "10 hands above" Nebuchadnezzar's magicians and astrologers. While this does imply that they are 10 times better, "hand(s)" permeate the rest of the book of Daniel and, as will be seen later, are associated with one's spirit, whether godly or carnal. Hence, the spirit of the faithful youth was superior to that of Nebuchadnezzar's magicians and astrologers.

DANIEL 1: WHY DOES GOD NEED A JUDGMENT?

Solomon notes that God "alone knows the heart of the sons of Adam" (2 Chron. 6:30). He already knows who is fit for heaven by the exercise of a living faith in Him. On the other hand, heavenly angels who have been watching the sin drama on earth for the last 6,000 years, as well as unfallen beings in other parts of the universe (see Heb. 1:2), need evidence to be convinced, for faith is recognized by "the evidence of activities not seen" (11:1). To this end, God permits a demonstration before the entire universe to provide the evidence necessary to convince everyone of His ability to save to the uttermost. This is why Jesus informs His followers that, when dragged before church bodies and even kings to answer for their faith, "it will turn into a testimonial for you" (Luke 21:12, 13).

DANIEL 1: APPLICATION TO THE LAST DAYS—DIET AS TEST

The story of Israel's wilderness wanderings typifies events for those living in the last days, and all of Scripture is written for our instruction (see 1 Cor. 10:6, 11; Rom. 15:4). This suggests that all of Scripture, including Daniel 1, should be examined in light of its applicability to those of us living in the last days.

Daniel and his friends not only *refused* food offered to idols, alcohol, and that which was unclean; they requested a *replacement*—a plant-based diet. This replacement principle is brought out in Jesus' parable of the unclean spirit (see Matt. 12:43–45). The diet adopted was that given to Adam and Eve before sin entered this world (see Gen. 1:29), reiterated and possibly augmented after the fall (see Gen. 3:18).

After the flood, God permitted the eating of clean meat with blood properly drained (see Gen. 9:3, 4), since all vegetation had been devastated. It must be emphasized that Genesis 9:3 is not a *command*, but a necessary *provision* until plants became available once again. It is akin to the scriptural teaching on divorce: the writings of Moses set forth guidelines concerning divorce, yet centuries later, Jesus plainly taught, "Moses because of the hardness of your hearts suffered you to put away your wives: but from the beginning it was not so" (Matt. 19:8, KJV). Similar remarks can be made concerning slavery in Scripture. God would not have His people settle for what may be permissible, but search out, aim for, and achieve His ideal. "Seek, and ye shall find" (Matt. 7:7, KJV).

God's plan is to restore His image in His people. We need to cooperate with Him in the accomplishment of this miraculous work, for we need every faculty in peak condition to discern spiritual truth. The plant-based diet of the faithful youth in the judgment setting of Daniel 1 implies that those of us living in the end-time judgment are to follow a plant-based diet if we would honor God, standing 10 hands above the world.

DANIEL 1: APPLICATION TO THE LAST DAYS— THE 10-DAY TEST

The most obvious allusion to the end-time judgment in Daniel 1 is that Nebuchadnezzar sits as judge of the Jewish captives "at the end of the days". This phrase appears again in Daniel 12:13, referring to the beginning of the end-time judgment. To better appreciate the application of

Daniel 1 to the end-time judgment, Table 1 presents the chiastic structure of Daniel 1, highlighting the 10-day test:

Table 1: Chiastic Arrangement of Daniel 1

VERSE(S)	EVENT		VERSE(S)
14	**DANIEL AND 3 HEBREW FRIENDS TESTED 10-DAYS**		14
13	Appearances to be examined, compared with others	Appearances are examined, compared with others.	15
11, 12	Seed-based food and water requested	Seed-based food continues to be given.	16
8–10	Daniel determines not to defile himself	Daniel given discernment in every vision and [all] dreams.	17
3–7	A: King tells chief of officials to bring sons of Israel.	C': At end of days	18–20
	B: Youth of royalty, have wisdom, exercise discernment.	A': Ruler of officials brings them just as king had said	
	C: To grow for 3 years. At end thereof,	E': 4 youth identified by Hebrew names	
	D: They are to stand before the king.	D': They stand before the king.	
	E: 4 youths identified by Hebrew names.	B': In wisdom and discernment, 10 hands above those in kingdom.	
1, 2	**Seventy years' captivity begins in year 3 of Jehoiakim.**	**Seventy years' captivity ends in year 1 of King Cyrus.**	21

How does this typify events after Daniel's day? Revelation reveals a trial of 10 prophetic days, corresponding to the persecution begun under Emperors Diocletian and Maximian in AD 303, ending with the Edict of Milan in February of AD 313 under Constantine and Licinius.[10] In the

---

[10] See Revelation 2:10. The link between Daniel 1 and Revelation 2:10 hints at the literal-day-for-a-prophetic-year principle to be employed later in these books. There is another hint of this year-day principle in Daniel 1 as well: the conclusion of the "3 years" of verse 5 is referred to as the "end of the days" in verse 18.

end times, there is a trial, not of a specific length, but dealing with the number 10 as well. Our study of Daniel and Revelation (see the present author's book *THE WEDDING: Jesus Stands for His Bride in the Book of Revelation*) will show that God's people will be tested on their fidelity to His 10 Commandments, after which they are strengthened by His seal so that when they are "brought before kings and governors for My name's sake, it will turn into a testimonial for you" (Luke 21:12, 13) to win others to righteousness.

2: GOD'S JUDGMENT—SEVEN TIMES

DANIEL 2: WITHOUT HANDS—
THE REVEALER AND HIS STONE

Introduction: King Nebuchadnezzar Has a Dream

2 ¹In year 2 of the reign of Nebuchadnezzar, Nebuchadnezzar dreamed dreams; his spirit was troubled so that his sleep was turned against him. ²So the king said to call for the magicians, astrologers, necromancers, and Kasdim that they might disclose to the king his dreams. So they came and **stood** before the king. ³Then the king said to them, "I have dreamed a dream, and my spirit is troubled to know the dream."

⁴So the Kasdim spoke to the king [from this point on, the text is Aramaic]:

Investigation: The King Seeks to Know His Dream

"Your majesty, live forever! Tell the dream to your servant, that we may declare the interpretation." ⁵The king answered the Kasdim, "My decree is certain [or, "The matter is gone from me"¹¹]: If you do not make known to me the dream and its interpretation, you will be turned into pieces, and

---

¹¹ BDB and TWOT indicate that the word *'azda'* is a Persian loan word signifying that the king's declaration is "firm" (i.e., it has "gone [forth]"). However, Theodotion's Greek text reads, "The king answered the Chaldeans, 'The word departed from me.'" Similarly, verse 8 of Theodotion reads, "The thing/matter departed from me." BDB states that Theodotion does not read *'azda,'* but *'azad,* the same as the Aramaic *'azal* in verse 17, which means, "go away." Hence, Theodotion understood the Aramaic of verse 8, and perhaps verse 5, to mean that the king forgot his dream. In verse 13, "the decree went forth" uses entirely different words. Whatever the language difficulties, the present commentary provides evidence that Nebuchadnezzar did forget his dream.

your houses made a refuse heap. ⁶But if the dream and its interpretation you do declare, you will receive gifts, reward, and great honor directly from me. Therefore, declare to me the dream and its interpretation!"

⁷They answered a second time, "Let the king tell the dream to his servants, and we will declare the interpretation." ⁸The king answered, "I know for sure that you are buying time, because you have seen that my decree is firm [or, 'the matter is gone from me']. ⁹So, if the dream you do not make known to me, there is but 1 decree for you, for a false, corrupt word you have agreed to speak before me until the time changes! Therefore tell me the dream that I may know that you can declare its interpretation to me."

¹⁰The Kasdim answered before the king, "There is not a man upon the dry land that is able to declare the king's matter, therefore no king, chief, or official, has asked a matter like this of any magician, astrologer, or Kasday. ¹¹What the king asks is a difficult matter; there is no one else who can declare it to the king except the gods whose dwelling is not with flesh."

¹²For this reason, the king got angry, so greatly infuriated, that he gave word to destroy all the wise men of Babylon. ¹³The decree went forth that the wise men were about to be executed, and they sought Daniel and his companions to be executed.

Intercession with the King and with God

¹⁴To this, Daniel replied with prudence and discretion to Arioch, chief of the king's guards, who had gone out to execute the wise men of Babylon. ¹⁵He answered Arioch, the king's official, "Why this urgent decree direct from the king?" Then Arioch made known to Daniel the matter. ¹⁶So Daniel went in and besought the king to give him a set time, that he might declare the interpretation to the king.

¹⁷So Daniel went to his house, and unto his companions Hananiah, Mishael, and Azariah he made known the matter ¹⁸in order to seek great compassion direct from the God of the heavens concerning this secret, that they not destroy Daniel and his companions along with the rest of

the wise men of Babylon. ¹⁹Then unto Daniel, in a vision at night, the secret was revealed; accordingly, Daniel blessed the God of the heavens. ²⁰Daniel responded, "Blessed be the name of God from eternity past unto eternity future, for wisdom and might are His. ²¹He is the one who changes times and appointed times [or "seasons"]; removes kings and **sets up** kings; gives wisdom to the wise and knowledge to those who possess discernment. ²²He is the one who reveals the deep things, the things which are hidden; He knows what is in the darkness, and the light abides with Him. ²³Unto You, God of my fathers, I give thanks and praise, for wisdom and might You have given me. Now You made known that which we sought of You, for the king's matter You have made known to us."

Daniel Brought Before King Nebuchadnezzar

²⁴Therefore this Daniel went to Arioch, whom the king had appointed to destroy the wise men of Babylon; he went, and thus he said to him, "Do not destroy the wise men of Babylon! Bring me before the king, and I will declare the interpretation to the king."

²⁵Then Arioch brought Daniel in haste before the king, and thus he said to him, "I have found a man among the sons of the captivity of Judah who will make known the interpretation to the king!"

²⁶The king said to Daniel, whose name was Belteshazzar, "Are you able to make known to me the dream which I saw, and its interpretation?" ²⁷Daniel answered before the king, "The secret which the king asks, the wise men, the astrologers, the magicians, and the diviners[12] are not able to declare to the king. ²⁸However, there is a God in the heavens—He reveals secrets. He has made known to King Nebuchadnezzar what will occur in the last days. This is your dream and the visions of your head upon your bed:

---

[12] The Aramaic word *gezar*, translated "diviners," refers to the action of cutting, as with the stone cut out of the mountain in verses 34 and 45. Here in verse 27, it refers to those who prognosticated by examining excised animal body parts such as livers.

The King's Dream

²⁹"Your majesty, your thoughts upon your bed came up concerning what would occur hereafter. The Revealer of secrets has made known to you what will occur. ³⁰As for me, not by wisdom which is in me beyond anyone living was this secret revealed to me; rather, they [or "He," referring collectively to the Godhead] will make known the interpretation to the king in order that you may know the thoughts of your heart.

³¹"Your majesty was watching, and behold, 1 great image. That image, great and of extraordinary splendor, **was standing** before you, and its appearance[13] was awe-inspiring. ³²The head of this image was fine gold, its chest and arms were silver, its belly and thighs were bronze, ³³its calves were iron, its feet were partly iron and partly clay. ³⁴You were watching until a stone, which had been cut out without hands, struck the image upon its feet of iron and clay, and broke them in pieces; ³⁵then they were broken in pieces as 1 [unit]: the iron, the clay, the bronze, the silver, and the gold. They were like chaff of the summer threshing floors: the wind bore them away, and no trace of them was found. But the stone which struck the image became a great mountain and filled the entire earth.

The King's Dream Interpreted

³⁶"This was the dream; now its interpretation we will tell before the king: ³⁷Your majesty is a king of kings, for the God of the heavens has given you a kingdom, power, might, and honor; ³⁸wherever dwell the sons of man, the living creature of the field, and the bird of the heavens, he has given them into your hand and made you ruler over them all. You are the head of gold.

³⁹"Then in your place, another kingdom will **arise**, closer to the earth than you, then another, a third kingdom of bronze, which shall rule over all the earth.

---

[13] The Aramaic *rev* is cognate with the Hebrew *mar'eh* for the "appearance" of the youth in Daniel 1, the "appearance" of the first 70 weeks of the 2,300 evening-mornings in Daniel 8, and the "appearance" of Jesus in Daniel 10.

⁴⁰"But the fourth kingdom will be strong as iron, for as iron breaks in pieces and shatters everything, so like iron which crushes, all of these it will break in pieces and crush.

⁴¹"The feet and the toes which you saw, partly of potter's clay, and partly of iron: the kingdom will become divided, though some of the rigidity of the iron will be in it, for you have seen the iron mixed with the baked clay. ⁴²The toes of the feet, partly of iron and partly of clay: some of the end of the kingdom will be strong, while some of it will be brittle. ⁴³The iron mixed with the baked clay which you saw: they will mix themselves with the seed of man, but they will not adhere one with another, just as the iron does not mix with the clay.

The Stone Kingdom

⁴⁴"However, in the days of those kings, the God of the heavens will **establish** a kingdom which will never be destroyed, nor will the kingdom be left to another people. It will break in pieces and put an end to all of these kingdoms. It will **stand** forever, ⁴⁵for as you saw that a stone had been cut out of the mountain—but not with hands—and it broke in pieces the iron, the bronze, the clay, the silver, and the gold, the great God has made known to the king what will occur after this. The dream is certain, and its interpretation certain."

The Secret of Nebuchadnezzar's Heart Revealed

⁴⁶At this, King Nebuchadnezzar fell upon his face and made obeisance unto Daniel; he commanded a grain offering and fragrant offerings be offered unto him. ⁴⁷The king answered Daniel, "Truly your God[14] is the God of gods, the Lord of kings, and the Revealer of secrets, because you have been able to reveal this secret." ⁴⁸Then the king made Daniel great, gave him many great gifts and made him ruler over the entire province

---

[14] In Aramaic, "your" is plural, so the king is saying "The God of you [Hebrews]."

of Babylon, and chief prefect over all the wise men of Babylon. ⁴⁹Then Daniel besought the king, and he appointed over the administration of the province of Babylon Shadrach, Meshach, and Abed-nego; but Daniel [he appointed to be] at the king's gate.

COMMENTARY: DANIEL 2

Introduction: King Nebuchadnezzar Has a Dream

At the close of Daniel 1, the 4 faithful Hebrew youths stood before the king, 10 hands above all his magicians and astrologers. Now, in year 2 of Nebuchadnezzar, apparently right after his examination of the captives in Daniel 1,[15] the king calls in 4 groups of court advisors to help him know his dream. These 4 stand before him only moments before Nebuchadnezzar discerns their unfaithfulness. Why the difference? The 4 Hebrew youths withstood the most penetrating examination because of their unswerving faithfulness to God's commandments, relying solely upon His strength. That which will ultimately stand before *the* King, God himself, constitutes the message of the remainder of Daniel 2.

Nebuchadnezzar informs his advisors that he desires to know his dream. Following the phrase, "So the Kasdim spoke to the king," and their words, "Your majesty, live forever," there is a single adverb in Hebrew, which can be read as "Aramaic," "Aramaically," or "in the Aramaic tongue." While this might seem to indicate that the advisors spoke to the king in Aramaic (and they may have, since Aramaic was a *lingua franca* at that time), this would not account for why Nebuchadnezzar's words in verse 3 are recorded in Hebrew, nor why the text remains in Aramaic until the end of Daniel 7, taking in events years after the conversation recorded here in verses 4–11.

---

[15] The time from which Nebuchadnezzar ascended the throne until the new calendar year began was but a partial year and disregarded in computing the length of reign. Hence, the Hebrew youths could complete their 3 years of study during his second regnal year, just prior to the events of Daniel 2.

The simplest and most compelling reason that can be put forth for the change in language here and in Daniel 8:1 is that these breaks divide the book of Daniel into 3 distinct sections, each with its unique focus. The chiastic structure for Daniel 1 highlighted the 10-day test. The chiastic structure for Daniel 2–7 pits Nebuchadnezzar's humbling in Daniel 4 against Belshazzar's pride in Daniel 5. Finally, Dan. 8–12 focuses on Jesus as High Priest of the heavenly sanctuary during the end-time Day of Atonement.

The key number in Daniel 1 was 10, highlighting the test whereby people's *characters* are investigated and judged. In Daniel 2–7, the key number is 7, the number of God's perfection; Daniel 2–7 focuses on the development of God's righteous character within us via His everlasting covenant. Jesus' goal is to present a people "faultless before the presence of his glory with exceeding joy" (Jude 24, KJV).

Investigation: The King Seeks to Know His Dream

In the three exchanges between the king and his wise men, the king discerns that his counsellors are deceivers. He recognizes that their interpretation can be trusted *only* if they are able to miraculously relate the dream; without this confirmation, any interpretation is worthless.

In verse 5, Nebuchadnezzar states that "the thing is gone from me" (KJV). Is the "thing" his dream, meaning he has forgotten it, or is the "thing" his ultimatum, gone forth from his mouth? The numerous parallels between the stories of Daniel in Babylon and Joseph in Egypt might lead one to compare this story with Joseph's revelation of Pharaoh's dreams. In Genesis 41, Pharaoh *did* recall his dreams (though he could not understand them), but he also evidenced this by *relating* the dreams. Pharaoh's revelation of his dream more closely matches Nebuchadnezzar's revelation of his second dream in Daniel 4.

On the other hand, the entirety of verse 5 makes plain the king's distrust of his servants' evasiveness, resulting in a decree going forth that they must reveal the dream and its interpretation, or their lives and houses are forfeited. Therefore, one might suppose the king did know his dream and was simply testing his counsellors' trustworthiness. However, he makes the same request of Daniel in verse 26, whose character is unimpeachable. This suggests that the dream itself had indeed escaped him.[16]

The wise men make a chilling self-condemnatory remark in: "there is no one else who can declare it to the king except the gods whose dwelling is not with flesh." Ironically, the wise men have for once spoken the truth: God does not dwell with such shady characters, but in Daniel 3, God walks right with His faithful followers through the greatest of trials. Hence, the wise men are not able to stand before the king as did Daniel and his 3 friends, and the king issues a decree to destroy all the wise men.

Intercession with the King and with God

Daniel intercedes with Nebuchadnezzar to avert the destruction threatened against his counsellors. In verse 17, he immediately goes home to tell his companions the matter. Things are indeed urgent, for according to verse 13, the slaughter is imminent. Together they implore God regarding the secret.

"The effectual fervent prayer of a righteous man availeth much" (James 5:16, KJV). Accordingly, the dream is revealed in a vision to Daniel in verse 19. The word "reveal" is used 7 times in Daniel 2 [see vs. 19, 22, 28, 29, 30, 47 (twice)], indicating that God is the one who revealed the dream to Daniel. As will be seen, the number 7 is prominent in each chapter of Daniel 2–7.

Some practical lessons may be learned from the events surrounding God's revelation to Daniel:

---

[16] Ellen White refers to "his forgotten dream" (*CTBH*, p. 21; *YI*, December 31, 1907; *RH*, November 10, 1904). She also makes the following observations: "Nebuchadnezzar ... dreamed a dream which he could not bring to his remembrance when he awoke" (*FE*, p. 410); Nebuchadnezzar "found it impossible to recall the particulars" of his dream (*PK*, p. 491); "The Lord had in His providence given Nebuchadnezzar this dream, and had caused the particulars to be forgotten" (*SL*, p. 34).

1. Daniel's tact garners the support of Arioch, a non-believer.
2. He petitions the king himself for time. We are to come boldly to God for grace (see Heb. 4:16; Matt. 7:7).
3. He petitions God *with fellow believers*. We encourage each other when we assemble together (see Heb. 10:25).
4. Daniel gives God all credit. God honors those who ask in harmony with His will (see 1 John 5:14, 15).

Before thanking God, Daniel extols His name. God's name, *Yahweh*, is important due to its association with His everlasting covenant, which is His promise to create in us a new heart by His wisdom and might. Daniel credits God with sovereignty over time periods and times of appointment, as well as the removal and establishment of kings.

Perhaps most intriguing are the words of verse 22, in which Daniel asserts that God reveals the hidden things, exposing that which is enshrouded in darkness. This refers not merely to God's ability to elucidate difficult prophecies, but as verse 30 makes clear, the deepest secrets of each person's mind.

Daniel Brought Before King Nebuchadnezzar

In verse 26, Nebuchadnezzar asks Daniel if he is able to reveal both the dream and its interpretation. There is a certain irony at this point in the story: the wise men of Babylon assert that only the gods could reveal the dream, and further, they do not dwell with flesh, making the king's request impossible. On the other hand, Daniel asserts that while no *person* can reveal the dream, there is indeed a *God* who reveals secrets. The one who is faithful has access to God that others fail to experience!

The King's Dream

Daniel humbly points out that he has no innate ability to relate the dream, but rather attributes it to God, just as Joseph in Egypt before him (see Gen. 41:15, 16).

Before the contents and interpretation are revealed to the king, verses 29 and 30 provide great insight into the significance of the dream. Daniel states that the king had been wondering what would occur hereafter, and that God chose to respond that he might know what would occur, as well as the thoughts of his own heart. Evidently, the king's thoughts were not simply an idle curiosity concerning the future, but focused specifically on his legacy and the perpetuity of his kingdom.

Daniel begins to relate the particulars of the dream in verse 31. It concerns an image—a *great* image—which is standing. Attention is drawn to its appearance. Daniel's hymn in verses 20–23 mentions that God is the one who removes kings and causes them to stand, so we are to expect that this image represents a kingdom (or sequence of kingdoms) that God sets up and removes according to His judgment. Since the image is broken to pieces, the stone that hits it can be understood as God's judgment upon these kingdoms. Since the dream concerns the rise and fall of kingdoms, and verse 38 equates Nebuchadnezzar with his kingdom, we conclude that kings and kingdoms fall for the same reason—ignoring God while attributing success to themselves.[17]

The image is composed of a sequence of metals from head to foot whose values decrease the lower they get in their positions on the image. Of particular interest are: 1) the legs, the top half of which are bronze, while the lower half are iron; 2) the feet, which are a mixture of iron and clay; 3) a stone "cut out without hands" that strikes the image and becomes a great mountain, filling the entire earth.

The pulverized feet and metals are "like chaff of the summer threshing floors." When grain is sifted, the chaff is discarded and carried away by the wind from the threshing floor. When David built an altar to stay the progress of the plague, the site was the threshing floor of Ornan the Jebusite (see 2 Sam. 24:18–25; 1 Chron. 21:18–30), coincident with the site of Solomon's

---

[17]"*Babylon*, shattered and broken at last, passed away because in prosperity *its rulers* had regarded themselves as independent of God, and had ascribed the glory of their kingdom to human achievement" (White, *PK*, pp. 501, 502, emphasis added).

temple atop Mount Moriah (see 2 Chron. 3:1), as well as the spot where Abraham was called to sacrifice his son Isaac (see Gen. 22:1–19). Hence, we discern the following about the stone at this point:

1) The arrival of the stone serves to sift out those who cling to the kingdoms of this world.
2) Following this sifting process, the stone grows into a mountain, which is to say, a kingdom (see Dan. 2:44).
3) The stone imagery directs our attention to God's temple, as well as Abraham's living faith (not mere mental assent) in God's promise to fulfill His everlasting covenant.

The King's Dream Interpreted

In verse 36, Daniel states that "we" will reveal the dream. Back in verse 30, Daniel mentioned that the dream was revealed to him; it is a gift from God, who must get all the glory. Likewise, in verses 37 and 38, Daniel states that God has given Nebuchadnezzar his kingdom and made him ruler over mankind, beast, and bird. He is the head of gold, but not due to any inherent greatness on his part.

While verse 38 identifies the gold head as King Nebuchadnezzar, verses 39 and 40 equate the metals with the kingdoms themselves,[18] so the head of gold is also Babylon. This golden description is most appropriate, for God represents Babylon as a golden city and golden cup (see Isa. 14:4; Jer. 51:7). Further, Aeschylus (died 456 BC) wrote of Babylon as "teeming with gold," and Herodotus (died c. 424 BC) was amazed at the incredible amount of gold in the sanctuary dedicated to Marduk (see Froom, *PFF*, vol. 1, p. 41).

Flattering as this description may have been, Nebuchadnezzar is soon humbled by the revelation that he is to be succeeded by a kingdom "closer to the earth," i.e., *inferior* to his, answering to the silver of verse 32. Babylon falls to Medo-Persia in Daniel 5:28. This inferior kingdom is to be

---

[18] See also Daniel 8:20–22, in which animal horns are used for both kings and kingdoms.

replaced by a kingdom of bronze, which history makes plain was Hellas, commonly referred to as Greece.[19]

Silver for Medo-Persia is most appropriate, for its monetary system was silver. Persian kings collected tribute from subject states mostly in talents of silver. As for Greece, Alexander and his soldiers were noted for their bronze armor. Froom notes a story related by Herodotus in which Psammetichus I of Egypt (contemporary with Nebuchadnezzar's father) was told he would avenge his enemies "when he saw men of bronze coming from the sea." In fact, when he learned that "men of bronze" (Greek pirates) had landed in Egypt, he gained their cooperation, gaining control of all Egypt (see Froom, *PFF*, vol. 1, p. 42). Reference is made to the "vessels of bronze" of Hellas in Ezekiel 27:13.

Attention now focuses on the iron kingdom, which is Rome, the only kingdom that Daniel 2 describes as persecuting. The iron refers to its *strength*, which it uses to break in pieces, shatter, and crush those whom it will. Historically, the weapon associated with Rome is the iron-headed pilum, or javelin (see Froom, *PFF*, vol. 1, p. 43).

An observation is in order at this point, with which we will deal more extensively in Daniel 7 and 8: the bronze kingdom begins with the belly, then continues into both thighs. This suggests that the bronze kingdom begins as a single entity, but is later represented as dual entities. Likewise, the iron kingdom is represented as the calves of both legs, suggesting it has a division as well. Further, the bronze extends down to the bottom of the thighs of the legs, while the iron kingdom runs from the top of the calves down to the feet. While iron and bronze are distinct metals, each are part of the legs, suggesting that the bronze and iron kingdoms are very much blended with each other. As we consider the prophecies of Daniel 7 and 8 and Revelation 13 in light of history, this observation will prove enormously insightful. In short, Greece was not abruptly followed by Rome, but rather, a Greco-Roman conglomerate emerged.

---

[19] Hellas is broader in scope than is the geographic area of Greece. This distinction will become important in Daniel 7 and 8.

Curiously enough, these iron calves are supported by feet of iron and clay, which represent a divided kingdom, one divided between strong iron and brittle clay. This mingling of iron and clay is unnatural, so these symbols represent an unnatural mingling of some kind. As the preceding metals represent kingdoms, the iron continues to represent a kingdom, or in modern parlance, the state. Clay, on the other hand, is a different substance altogether, so it must correspond to something other than a state government.

To identify the clay, we turn to the Hebrew Scriptures. Created people refer to themselves as clay: "*Yahweh*, you are our Father. We are the clay, you are our potter. We are all the work of your hand" (Isa. 64:8). "You made me like clay, and unto dust you will return me" (Job 10:9). God recreates the hearts of His people as a potter does a clay vessel. "The vessel which he was making with the clay was spoiled in the hand of the potter. Again he made it another vessel ... 'Like this potter, am I not able to remake you, house of Israel?' declares *Yahweh*. 'Behold, as the clay in the potter's hand, so are you in my hand, house of Israel'" (Jer. 18:4–6). God has to recreate the hearts of His people, for in their pride, they deny their Creator. "Your backwardness! The potter will not be reckoned as clay, will he? Will the work say to its maker, 'You didn't make me?' Will the pottery say to its potter, 'You do not understand?'" (Isa. 29:16). Those whose hearts are hardened beyond reach, God will destroy like a broken potter's vessel (see Jer. 19:10, 11).

Now we are prepared to identify what is meant by iron mixed with clay: it will be a union of state (iron) and church (clay).[20] Further, as noted above, this church will be rebellious toward God, breaking covenant with him, refusing to acknowledge His claims upon it as Creator. This union of church and state, based on false religious principles that exalt mankind above the Creator, will never be successful. Why not? God can mold clay that is wet, but this clay is brittle and will be broken in pieces, just as during its history it breaks in pieces those who oppose it (see Dan. 2:40, 45).

---

[20] "The mingling of church craft and state craft is represented by the iron and the clay" (White, *IMR*, p. 51).

The effort to unite kingdoms by intermarriage of monarchs and their seed, prophesied in verse 43, is futile.

Nebuchadnezzar sees the image standing on its feet, yet when the stone kingdom strikes the image on its feet, it crumbles. In God's judgment, those in the rebellious church are to be broken like a potter's vessel that cannot be repaired.

The Stone Kingdom

The vision closes with Daniel's interpretation of the stone, which strikes the image upon the feet of iron and clay. What is this stone? Many people assert without hesitation that it is Jesus, who is the Rock. However, the stone that breaks in pieces the prior metallic kingdoms in verse 45 is equated in verse 44 with "a kingdom which will ... break in pieces and put an end to all of these kingdoms."

God's kingdom smashes the image upon its feet of iron and clay, the mixture of church craft and state craft. History reveals that the church inevitably employs the strong arm of the state to enforce its beliefs. On the other hand, God never uses force, so when He sets up His kingdom, this mixture of church and state is brought to an end. Nonetheless, how is it that the stone also breaks in pieces the prior metallic kingdoms? Did they not already end with the rise of each new kingdom? Our study of Daniel 7:12 will show that though the kingdoms represented by iron, bronze, silver, and gold did end earlier in history, nevertheless, their *principles* lived on through each succeeding kingdom.

Why is it that God's kingdom will "never be destroyed" and "stand forever?" The answer lies in the imagery of the "stone." This stone is "cut out of a mountain," so we begin by inquiring which is God's mountain. The following passages provide the most explicit answer:

> Ps. 48:1, 2, 8, 11, 14: Great is *Yahweh*, and greatly to be praised, in the city of our God, the mountain of His holiness [or, "sanctuary"], beautiful for [its] elevation, the joy of the entire earth:

Mount Zion, in the extremities of the north, the city of the great King. ... God will establish it forever. ... May Mount Zion rejoice, may the daughters of Judah be glad, on account of Your judgments. ... For this God is our God forever and ever.

Isa. 2:2–4: In the last days, the mountain of the house of *Yahweh* will be established at the top of the mountains and lifted up higher than the hills; all the nations will flow unto it. Many peoples will come and say, "Come, let us ascend the mountain of *Yahweh* to the house of the God of Jacob, that He may teach us of His ways and that we may walk in His paths. For out of Zion will go forth the Torah, the word of *Yahweh* from Jerusalem. He will judge among the nations, He will correct many peoples."

Ps. 20:1, 2: May *Yahweh* answer you in the day of distress, may the name of the God of Jacob set you on high. May He send you help from the sanctuary, from Zion may He support you.

It is plain that God's mountain is Zion. The foregoing passages equate it with God's city Jerusalem and the seat of His judgment in the last days. It is also the location of His sanctuary, from which He sends help during the "day of distress," the "time of Jacob's distress" (Jer. 30:7). In God's mountain, specifically His sanctuary, we find something that helps unravel the mystery of the stone kingdom even further. Note the following description of Lucifer prior to his fall:

Ezek. 28:14: You were the anointed cherub who covers. I set you in the mountain of God's holiness [or "sanctuary"]. You were in the midst of the stones of fire, walking back and forth.

The significance of these stones of fire in God's sanctuary becomes apparent when we consider Mount Sinai, the earthly counterpart to Mount Zion, and Ezekiel's vision of God's throne:

Exod. 20:1–17: And God spoke all these words, saying [the 10 Commandments follow in verses 2–17].

Exod. 24:10, 12: They saw the God of Israel, and under His feet what was like a sapphire stone pavement, like heaven itself in purity [or "clearness"]. ... *Yahweh* said to Moses, "Come up to me upon the mountain and stay there. I will give you the stone tablets, the Torah and the commandment which I have written in order to teach them."

Exod. 31:18: He gave Moses, when he had finished speaking with him on Mount Sinai, the 2 tablets of the testimony—tablets of stone—written with the finger of God.

Ezek. 1:26: Above the firmament that was over their heads, as the appearance of a sapphire stone, was the likeness of a throne. Upon the likeness of the throne was a likeness, as the appearance of a man, upon it above [the firmament].

Putting the pieces together, God appeared to Moses upon Mount Sinai, seated upon His throne, His feet resting on the base of His throne, His footstool, which appeared as a sapphire stone pavement. From these sapphire stones, God selected the 2 stones upon which He wrote the 10 Commandments. These were as pure as heaven, for heaven is God's throne (see Matt. 5:34; 23:22; Isa. 66:1), and His throne resides among the stones of fire in the sanctuary on God's holy mountain, the heavenly Mount Zion. In other words, the 10 Commandments were cut out of the mountain *just like the stone that hits the great image was*. Therefore, God's kingdom is founded on the 10 Commandments, the expression of His character. "Righteousness and judgment are the foundation of His throne" (Ps. 97:2).

The stone imagery points us to a specific period in earth's history, namely, the end-time judgment. This judgment is based on the 10 Commandments (see Eccles. 12:13, 14), conducted in the heavenly sanctuary, and culminates in Jesus' second coming. The kingdom is established "in the days of those kings," i.e., while those earthly kingdoms are still in power. Hence, the end-time judgment occurs *before* the second coming.

One more observation is in order before we conclude our remarks on Daniel 2. Chapters 2–7 form a wonderful chiastic structure, with Daniel 2 and 7 as counterparts. A detailed, step-by-step chiastic structure is included in this commentary in "Daniel, Part 2: The Key Points," following remarks on Daniel 7. For now, it is sufficient to note that the events of Daniel 2:44–45 match the events of Daniel 7:26–27: God begins to establish His kingdom when the judgment sits (commences), and the stone strikes the image at the conclusion of the investigative judgment (the second coming). The preceding kingdoms are forever destroyed, and the holy people are given God's kingdom, which is without end.

The Secret of Nebuchadnezzar's Heart Revealed

This makes a profound impression upon Nebuchadnezzar, but while acknowledging Daniel's God as superior, he nevertheless makes obeisance to Daniel, presenting offerings to *him*, not his God. Thus, while God has reached out in prophetic vision to this heathen king, he has yet to receive the "heart of flesh" that leads one to walk in obedience to God's requirements, characteristic of the new-covenant experience (see Ezek. 36:25–27; Jer. 31:31–34). Nevertheless, God's work of transforming the king's heart has begun, evidenced by his promotion of Daniel and his companions to high stations in Babylon. This puts them where they will continue to have access to the king, and hence be able to share the truth of God's Word with him. As seen by the end of Daniel 4, God's striving with Nebuchadnezzar is not in vain.

SUMMARY: DANIEL 2

DANIEL 2: JESUS

Jesus is the Revealer of secrets (mentioned 7 times), not only of the future, but of our *hearts*. Jesus is also King of the stone kingdom, made up of those who fully reflect His character, as revealed in His law of 10 Commandments, carved in stone. The 10 Commandments were cut from the sapphire stone pavement at the base of His throne upon which He sat at Sinai. Stones of fire are in the heavenly sanctuary upon Mount

Zion, where Jesus conducts the end-time judgment (more on this in Daniel 7 and 8). The 10 Commandments are the basis of this judgment (see Eccles. 12:13, 14).

DANIEL 2: THE STAND

God "stands" kings up (see Dan. 2:21). The image standing before Nebuchadnezzar in verse 31 represented kingdoms that attempted to stand in their own strength, i.e., on wrong principles. Therefore, when the stone hits the image on its feet, it can no longer stand, but is broken to pieces and blown away like chaff. By contrast, God's stone kingdom will stand forever (see v. 44), founded upon the principles of His 10 Commandment law.

DANIEL 2: WITHOUT HANDS

Jesus' stone kingdom is cut out "without hands" (see vs. 38, 45). This is an example of the so-called "divine passive" in which an object (in this case, a stone) receives an action (it is cut out) by an unspecified agent, implying that it is God. In other words, God establishes His own kingdom and does so "without hands." In the Bible, hands represent both humanity's strength and power (e.g., Gen. 4:11; 16:6, 9; 37:21) and God's power to exercise judgment and to save (e.g., Exod. 7:4; Ps. 10:12; 17:7; Isa. 59:1). In other words, God will establish His kingdom not by the use of force, as do earthly kingdoms, but by the exercise of judgment, saving those who willingly submit to the character principles outlined in His 10 Commandments.

DANIEL 2: APPLICATION TO THE LAST DAYS

Nebuchadnezzar's dream concerns "what will occur in the last days." Daniel 1 detailed a 10-day trial that typifies a test in the last days concerning the number 10. Daniel 2 confirms that the stone kingdom is based on the 10 Commandments. Hence, the test in the last days concerns who will compose this kingdom—those who allow Jesus to work out in their lives His character as expressed in the 10 Commandments.

DANIEL 3: THE KING'S HAND—THE IMAGE AND THE FURNACE

Babylon's King Erects Image

3 ¹King Nebuchadnezzar made an image of gold, its height 60 cubits, its width 6 cubits. He **erected** it in the plain of Dura, in the province of Babylon. ²Then King Nebuchadnezzar sent to gather the satraps, prefects, and governors, the counselors, treasurers, judges, magistrates, and all the rulers of the provinces to come to the dedication of the image which King Nebuchadnezzar had **erected**. ³So the satraps, prefects, and governors, the counselors, treasurers, judges, magistrates, and all the rulers of the provinces were gathered for the dedication of the image which King Nebuchadnezzar had **erected**. They **were standing** before the image which Nebuchadnezzar had **erected**.

State Mandates False Worship

⁴The herald began crying aloud, "To you, peoples, nations,[21] and tongues, they command: ⁵'At the time you hear the sound of the horn, the pipe, the harp, the four-stringed trigon, the psaltery—a symphony of all kinds of music—you are to fall down and make obeisance to the image of gold which

---

[21] The Aramaic word translated "nations" is *ummah*. Comparison with its identical Hebrew counterpart shows that it can be understood as "heathen tribes" (e.g., Gen. 25:16; Num. 25:15), or as a synonym for both "[Gentile] nations" (e.g., Ps. 44:14; 117:1; 149:7) or "[heathen] peoples" (e.g., Ps. 57:9; 108:3). Spoken here by a heathen himself, it seems best to translate it simply as "nations," with the reader recognizing that the nations being addressed are in fact heathen.

King Nebuchadnezzar has **erected**. ⁶Whoever does not fall down and make obeisance, in that hour he will be thrown into the furnace of blazing fire.'"

⁷So at the very time appointed, as all the peoples heard the sound of the horn, the pipe, the harp, the four-stringed trigon, the psaltery, indeed all kinds of music, all the peoples, nations, and tongues began falling down and making obeisance to the image of gold which King Nebuchadnezzar had **erected**.

Three Jews Don't Bow to Image → Turned In

⁸So at the very appointed time, certain Kasdim came forward and ate the pieces of the Jews. ⁹They addressed King Nebuchadnezzar, "Your majesty, live forever! ¹⁰Your majesty has made a decree that every man who hears the sound of the horn, the pipe, the harp, the four-stringed trigon, the psaltery—a symphony of all kinds of music—is to fall down and make obeisance to the image of gold. ¹¹And whoever does not fall down and make obeisance will be thrown into the midst of the furnace of blazing fire. ¹²There are certain Jews whom you have appointed over the administration of the province of Babylon: Shadrach, Meshach, and Abed-nego. These men have not shown deference to you, your majesty. They do not pay reverence unto your gods, nor do they make obeisance unto the image of gold which you have **erected**."

¹³At this, Nebuchadnezzar in furious anger commanded to bring Shadrach, Meshach, and Abed-nego. So they brought these men before the king. ¹⁴Nebuchadnezzar said to them, "Is it true, Shadrach, Meshach, and Abed-nego, that you do not pay reverence unto my gods, nor make obeisance unto the image of gold which I have **erected**? ¹⁵Now, if you are ready, at the time when you hear the sound of the horn, the pipe, the harp, the four-stringed trigon, the psaltery—a symphony of all kinds of music— you are to fall down and make obeisance to the image which I have made. But if you do not make obeisance, in that hour you will be thrown into the midst of the furnace of blazing fire—and who is that god who will deliver you from my hands?"

¹⁶Shadrach, Meshach, and Abed-nego answered King Nebuchadnezzar, "We do not need to return you [an answer] concerning this matter: ¹⁷If our God whom we revere exists, He is able to deliver us from the furnace of blazing fire; He will deliver [us] from your hand, your majesty. ¹⁸But if not, let it be known unto you, your majesty, that we do not pay reverence unto your gods, nor will we make obeisance unto the image of gold which you have **erected**."

The Furnace: One Factor of Seven Hotter

¹⁹Then Nebuchadnezzar was filled with fury, so that the image of his face was changed toward Shadrach, Meshach, and Abed-nego. He gave orders to heat the furnace 1 factor of 7 more than it was [typically] seen to be heated. ²⁰He ordered men—strong mighty men in his army—to bind Shadrach, Meshach, and Abed-nego and cast them into the furnace of blazing fire. ²¹Then these men were bound in their trousers, their leg-wrappings, their head-dresses, and their other garments, and were thrown into the midst of the furnace of blazing fire.

Babylonian King's Strong Men Killed

²²Therefore, due to the king's urgent command and the furnace being exceedingly hot, those men who took up Shadrach, Meshach, and Abed-nego were killed by the fiery flame, ²³but these 3 men—Shadrach, Meshach, and Abed-nego—fell, bound, into the midst of the furnace of blazing fire.

The Son of God Saves 3 Jews

²⁴Then King Nebuchadnezzar was startled, and **stood up** quickly.[22] He inquired of his counselors, "Did we not throw 3 men, bound, into the

---

[22] Or "in alarm." To make clear that this is the same word used in Daniel 2:25 and 6:19, it has been translated "quickly."

midst of the fire?" They answered the king, "Indeed, your majesty." ²⁵He responded, "Look! I see 4 men loose, walking in the midst of the fire—and there is no injury upon them! And the appearance²³ of the fourth resembles the Son of God!"

Three Jews Investigated

²⁶Then Nebuchadnezzar approached the gate²⁴ of the furnace of blazing fire and called out, "Shadrach, Meshach, and Abed-nego, servants of the Most High God: Come forth! Come!" Then Shadrach, Meshach, and Abed-nego came forth from the midst of the fire. ²⁷Being gathered together, the satraps, the prefects, the governors, and the king's counselors saw these men over whose body the fire had no dominion: the hair of their head was not singed, their trousers were not affected, nor had the smell of fire settled upon them.

Babylon's King Prohibits Speaking Against God

²⁸Nebuchadnezzar declared, "Blessed be the God of Shadrach, Meshach, and Abed-nego, who has sent His Angel and delivered His servants who trusted in Him, violated the king's word and yielded their bodies that they might not reverence nor make obeisance to any god except their God. ²⁹I issue a decree: any people, nation, or tongue that speaks inappropriately concerning the God of Shadrach, Meshach, and Abed-nego will be turned into pieces and his house made a refuse heap, for there is no other god who is able to rescue like this."

³⁰Then the king promoted Shadrach, Meshach, and Abed-nego in the province of Babylon.

---

²³ See footnote 13 concerning the Aramaic *rev*.

²⁴ Rendering the Aramaic word *tǝra‘* as "gate" makes it obvious that this is the same word used in Daniel 2:49. The irony is rich: Nebuchadnezzar appointed Daniel to sit in the king's "gate," while here he calls the faithful 3 out of the "gate."

COMMENTARY: DANIEL 3

Babylon's King Erects Image

The chapter opens[25] with remarkable irony, noting that Nebuchadnezzar erects his own golden image. In Daniel 2, God made clear to Nebuchadnezzar that He causes kings to stand, yet His kingdom will stand forevermore. By erecting the golden image, Nebuchadnezzar is defying the message God sent him concerning the metal image in Daniel 2 and seeking to perpetuate his own kingdom.

It is not insignificant that the dimensions of this image are given in verse 1. At approximately 1.5 feet per cubit, the image rests on an imposing base 9 feet wide, with its head some 90 feet above the ground. The great size mirrors Nebuchadnezzar's high estimate of himself and his kingdom. Further, the Babylonian number system is base 60 (digits 0 through 59, unlike our base 10 system with digits 0 through 9), so Nebuchadnezzar is unmistakably exalting his own Babylonian kingdom. The height is precisely 10 times greater than the base width, emphasizing Nebuchadnezzar's self-exaltation at the expense of a solid foundation. This stands in marked contrast to God's eternal stone kingdom, resting solidly on the 10 Commandments. Our familiar system of angular measure (360° for a full circular revolution) comes from Babylon, so it is worth noting that Nebuchadnezzar's golden image measures 60 cubits by 6 cubits,

---

[25] When do the events of Daniel 3 take place? A couple options present themselves, though neither are directly supported by the Hebrew Scriptures. Maxwell notes that a clay tablet translated in 1956 records that Nebuchadnezzar put down a mutiny that broke out in his army in December 594 BC. In his fourth year (593 BC), weak Judean king Zedekiah went to Nebuchadnezzar (see Jeremiah 51:59), so perhaps all of Nebuchadnezzar's underlings were called to worship the image as a token of their allegiance, lest they be put to death as was his mutinous army (*The Message of Daniel: God Cares, Volume One*, p. 49). Another possibility comes from the Greek translations (the Septuagint and Theodotion): both state that the events of Daniel 3 took place in the 18th year of Nebuchadnezzar's reign, or 586/585 BC. It may be that deciding to build the image, designing it, assembling the workers, fashioning it, standing it up, sending couriers throughout lands hundreds of miles away, and allowing time for the invited parties to arrive took more than just the few months required for the hypothesized worship service in 593 BC.

or 360 square cubits. These dimensions imply that his kingdom will run the entire circuit of history, i.e., last forever, contradicting God's express revelation in Daniel 2.

From verse 14, it is clear that Nebuchadnezzar's image is to glorify his own kingdom and religious system. In fact, the story of Daniel 3 typifies the end-time unholy union of church and state discussed in the remarks on Daniel 2. Nebuchadnezzar's demand for worship in Daniel 3 typifies the image of and to the beast in Revelation 13:14–15. This takes on more significance by noting that Daniel 7 represents Babylon, no longer by gold, but rather by the king of beasts, the lion.

State Mandates False Worship

In verse 4, Nebuchadnezzar's herald cries out to the "peoples, nations and tongues," similar to the angel in Revelation 14:6 who cries out to "every nation, tribe, tongue and people." The similarity is more than coincidental; the herald's lack of a call upon "every tribe" underscores the fact that Babylon does not recognize anyone as belonging to "tribes." What does this signify? The covenant people who trace their roots back to Abraham, Isaac, and Jacob all identify with the 12 tribes descended from Jacob. Babylon of old recognized no "tribes," for Babylon had already subjugated the inhabitants of Jerusalem in Daniel 1:1–2. Babylon in the end time will recognize no tribes—those spiritual descendants of Jacob (see Rom. 2:28, 29; Gal. 3:28, 29) who are being fully transformed by God's everlasting covenant.

Note the contrast in verse 5. Those gathered to the dedication of Nebuchadnezzar's image are to *fall down* in reverence before the image that he has *stood up*. God has already revealed in Daniel 2 that Nebuchadnezzar's kingdom will not stand. Nebuchadnezzar seeks to control his subjects' consciences, forcing them to fall down; God woos His followers to surrender their hearts to Him, so that He may enable them to stand *without* falling (see Jude 24; Rom. 14:4). In seeking to exalt himself, Nebuchadnezzar is following the path taken by Lucifer, whose self-exaltation led to his fall from heaven (see Isa. 14:12–15). We are to follow the footsteps of Jesus, who *humbled* Himself, after which God highly exalted Him (see 1 Peter 2:21; Phil. 2:8, 9).

Those who refuse to worship the image will be thrown into a furnace of blazing fire. By this decree, Nebuchadnezzar usurps the prerogative of God. In Malachi 4:1 we read that "the day is coming, burning like an oven," referring to God's ultimate destruction of those who have refused to worship according to His commandments in the lake of fire (see Revelation 20:9, 15). Only God may impose the death penalty for improper worship.

The book of Revelation pictures distinct calls for worship: the call to false worship in 13:15 and God's call to worship in spirit and truth in 14:6–12 and 18:4. The story of Daniel 3 typifies Satan's false, end-time loud cry, rallying the world with a counterfeit revival and beguiling the inhabitants with the thought that they are doing God service.[26]

Three Jews Don't Bow to Image → Turned In

At the time appointed, some Kasdim approach Nebuchadnezzar and "ate the pieces of the Jews," meaning they spoke malicious lies against them. In Daniel 2:5, Nebuchadnezzar decreed that his deceitful Kasdim were to be dismembered. Envious of the great honor bestowed on Daniel and his friends at the close of Daniel 2, the Kasdim seize the chance to be rid of these high-ranking Jews.

In verses 8–12, the accusers are Kasdim, while those accused of not complying with state-mandated worship are Jews. Moving from type to antitype, the story of Daniel 3 suggests that the target of religious

---

[26] "Before the final visitation of God's judgments upon the earth there will be among the people of the Lord such a revival of primitive godliness as has not been witnessed since apostolic times. The Spirit and power of God will be poured out upon His children. ... The enemy of souls desires to hinder this work; and *before the time for such a movement shall come*, he will endeavor to prevent it by *introducing a counterfeit*. In those churches which he can bring under his deceptive power he will make it appear that God's special blessing is poured out; there will be manifest what is thought to be great religious interest. Multitudes will exult that God is working marvelously for them, when the work is that of another spirit" (White, *GC*, p. 464, emphasis added).

persecution in the end time will also be Jews—the true seed of Abraham, heirs of the everlasting covenant (see Gal. 3:26–29; Rom. 2:28, 29; Gen. 15; 17), those with God's 10 Commandment law written in their hearts (see Jer. 31:31–34; 2 Cor. 3:3).

Likewise, the end-time accusers will be spiritual Kasdim. Scripture appears to indicate that the Kasdim come from Kesed, son of Abraham's brother Nahor (see Gen. 22:22). The Kasdim were literally close cousins of Abraham, though not inheritors of the covenant promise. Therefore, in the end time, the counterpart to the true Jews referred to by Paul will be those who are, spiritually speaking, close cousins of the true Jews—they have had a knowledge of the truth as members of God's true church, but their hearts were never knit with His. They will seek to destroy their brethren who take hold of the covenant and become partakers of the divine nature (see 2 Peter 1:4).

The Hebrew worthies are brought before Nebuchadnezzar. He issues an ultimatum requiring their worship of his image, boldly adding, "Who is that god who will deliver you from my hands?" This reminds the reader of Pharaoh's impudent reply, when told by Moses that he must release the Hebrews to worship *Yahweh*: "Who is *Yahweh*, that I should hearken unto His voice to send Israel away? I do not know *Yahweh*; moreover, I will not send Israel away" (Exod. 5:2).

The 3 Jews assert that they will not worship the image that Nebuchadnezzar set up, regardless of their own security. They provide a beautiful illustration of those who "did not love their life, even unto death" (Rev. 12:11). In John 12:26, Jesus promises, "If anyone will serve Me, my Father will honor him." True to His word, God is about to wrest His faithful ones from the impotent hand of Nebuchadnezzar.

The Furnace: One Factor of Seven Hotter

Nebuchadnezzar is so incensed at the Hebrews' steadfast refusal to worship his golden image that "the image of his face was changed." In his rage, Nebuchadnezzar commands that the furnace be heated "1 factor of

7 more" than usual.[27] Further, the "image of gold" mentioned 7 times. In Daniel 2, the Revealer of secrets was mentioned 7 times. This key number will appear prominently in each chapter of Daniel 2–7.

The story of Daniel 1 suggested a test concerning the number 10 for those living in the end time. The "stone cut out without hands" in Daniel 2 points directly to the end-time judgment, the basis of which is the 10 Commandment law cut from the sapphire base of God's throne in the heavenly sanctuary. The most prominent feature of Daniel 3 is the "furnace," which is mentioned 10 times. In the last days, there will likewise be a death decree against those who adhere to the 10 Commandments, and refuse to worship the image of the beast (see Rev. 13:15).

Babylonian King's Strong Men Killed

Rather than praying to be delivered *from* the experience of the fiery furnace, the 3 Jews claimed the promise of Isaiah 43:2 that they would not be burned while walking *through* the fire. Christ honored their faith, which defied their senses and circumstances, and did indeed save them during their fiery trial. On the other hand, the king's soldiers who simply carried out their orders were killed by the same flames.

The Son of God Saves 3 Jews

Nebuchadnezzar expresses astonishment, for he sees not 3 men bound, but 4 men walking freely with no injury.[28] Nebuchadnezzar's remark that the fourth being in the furnace looks like the "Son of God" is a clear testimonial of the faithful life these young men had lived before this heathen

---

[27] The chiastic counterpart to "1 factor of 7" is the "1 stone" in Daniel 6:17. This linkage is explained in comments on Daniel 6.

[28] At the end of verse 23, the LXX adds that the Hebrews sing praises unto the Lord, while verse 24 adds that Nebuchadnezzar hears them singing. In between, it inserts a verse stating that Azariah stands, followed by his 66-verse prayer of praise.

king prior to this trial.[29] The Aramaic word for "God" is plural in form (just as in Hebrew), begging the question whether Nebuchadnezzar referred to "God" or "gods." This is clarified in verse 28, where he makes clear that God (singular) sent His Angel (the fourth being in the furnace).

Three Jews Investigated

In Daniel 1 the 4 faithful youths stood in review before the king who found them superior in wisdom. In Daniel 2, the 4 sets of Babylonians stood before the king who found them to be charlatans, and decreed death for them. In Daniel 3, the king sees 4 men walking in the fire; after he calls forth the faithful Jews, the 4 sets of Babylonians come to investigate. In each chapter, 4 people, or groups of people, come under royal review. We are reminded of Jesus' words: "[You will be] brought before kings and governors on account of my name. But for you it will turn into a testimony" (Luke 21:12, 13). The 4 sets of Babylonians learn that those who stand before the earthly king are those who are faithful unto death to the King of kings—the One who has power over fire.

From the moment the Hebrews are thrown into the furnace, Nebuchadnezzar's image is not mentioned again. The loud cry that heralded the call to worship in verse 4 has been trumped by the deafeningly quiet loud cry of the faithful lives of the 3 Hebrews. When Jesus says that "this gospel of the kingdom shall be proclaimed in all world for a testimony to all the nations, then the end will come" (Matt. 24:14), He refers principally to a proclamation through the lives of His people who perfectly reflect His character. Seeing that His people have been with Jesus, the world will be brought to the point of decision.

---

[29] "The Hebrew captives filling positions of trust in Babylon had in life and character represented before him the truth. When asked for a reason of their faith, they had given it without hesitation. Plainly and simply they had presented the principles of righteousness, thus teaching those around them of the God whom they worshiped. They had told of Christ, the Redeemer to come; and in the form of the fourth in the midst of the fire the king recognized the Son of God" (White, *PK*, p. 509).

Babylon's King Prohibits Speaking Against God

Nebuchadnezzar acknowledges the true God, but his death decree in verse 29 makes clear that his heart is not yet conformed to God's will. One cannot truly worship the living God (see Deut. 5:26; Rev. 7:2) and simultaneously proclaim a death decree against those who do not.

This attempt to honor God with forced worship illustrates why God condemns the union of church and state, as represented by the mingling of iron and clay in Daniel 2:42. No matter how well-intentioned, all attempts by the state to compel religious worship eventually wind up mandating death for dissenters. The tens of millions who lost their lives at the hands of an apostate church in the Dark Ages testify to this. God never forces worship; He woos us with the invitation, "Give me thine heart" (Prov. 23:26, KJV).[30]

SUMMARY: DANIEL 3

DANIEL 3: JESUS

Jesus is the Son of God, His Angel, who walks with the 3 faithful Jews in the fiery furnace.

DANIEL 3: THE STAND

It is stated 9 times that King Nebuchadnezzar "erected" (literally, "made stand") his image. In verse 3, it refers to everyone standing before the

---

[30] "God was pleased with the effort of the king to show Him reverence, and to make the royal confession of allegiance as widespread as was the Babylonian realm. It was right for the king to make public confession, and to seek to exalt the God of heaven above all other gods; but in endeavoring to force his subjects to make a similar confession of faith and to show similar reverence, Nebuchadnezzar was exceeding his right as a temporal sovereign. He had no more right, either civil or moral, to threaten men with death for not worshiping God, than he had to make the decree consigning to the flames all who refused to worship the golden image. God never compels the obedience of man. He leaves all free to choose whom they will serve" (White, *PK*, pp. 510, 511).

image, prior to the command to fall down and worship. Ironically, the only ones who *remain* standing after the command to fall down and worship are the very ones who *fall* into the furnace (see v. 23), but then walk with the Son of God. The great irony is that King Nebuchadnezzar then "stands" startled, calls forth those who stood, and makes a decree that no one speak against their God.

DANIEL 3: THE KING'S HAND

"Hand" appears twice in Daniel 3: In verse 15, when Nebuchadnezzar arrogantly asks, "Who is that god who will deliver you from my hands?" and in verse 17, when the 3 Jews respond that God will deliver them from the king's hand. The Babylonian king's hands represent his strength, while the Jews recognize God is their Deliverer who builds His kingdom *without* hands.

DANIEL 3: APPLICATION TO THE LAST DAYS

Babylon employed a "symphony of all kinds of music" to confuse the senses, leading everyone to worship falsely. The Christian is counseled to walk by faith, not by sight (i.e., one's senses). We are well-advised to avoid any music (even that which may be labelled Christian) that one cannot imagine Jesus and the angels of heaven singing or playing.

The end-time test concerns an investigation of our character, our fidelity to God's 10 Commandments. Those who are faithful will be reviewed not only by God, but by earthly kings and governors. The 3 Hebrews were thrown into the fiery furnace for their faithfulness to God, specifically their refusal to worship an image when commanded by the state. Likewise, God's end-time remnant will face a death decree for refusing to worship the image of the beast (see Rev. 13:15). Will we be faithful unto death like the 3 faithful Jews? If so, like them we may claim the promise of Isaiah 43:2. God will walk with us through the fiery trial, and deliver those who are faithful even unto death. In fact, He promises that the one who lives righteously will live forever *with* the consuming fire—Himself (see Isa. 33:14, 15; Heb. 12:29).

DANIEL 4: GOD'S HAND— HUMBLED 7 TIMES

Nebuchadnezzar: Humble King Praises God

4 ¹King Nebuchadnezzar unto all peoples, nations, and tongues who dwell in all the earth: may your peace abound. ²It seemed appropriate in my estimation to declare the signs and wonders which the Most High God has done for me. ³How great His signs! How mighty His wonders! His kingdom is an everlasting kingdom, His dominion is from generation to generation.

King Nebuchadnezzar Sees Dream, Calls Babylonian Advisors

⁴I, Nebuchadnezzar, was at ease in my house, flourishing in my palace. ⁵I saw a dream which frightened me; the imaginations upon my bed, the visions of my head, alarmed me. ⁶I issued a decree to bring in before me all the wise men of Babylon, that they might make known to me the interpretation of the dream. ⁷Then entered the magicians, astrologers, Kasdim, and diviners, and I recounted the dream before them, yet they did not make known its interpretation to me.

Daniel Comes

⁸Afterward Daniel came before me (whose name was Belteshazzar, according to the name of my god, and in whom was the spirit of the holy

gods), so I recounted the dream before him: ⁹"Belteshazzar, chief of the magicians, because I know the spirit of the holy gods is in you, and no secret baffles you: [Consider] the visions of[31] my dream which I saw, and declare its interpretation.

King Nebuchadnezzar Recounts Dream

¹⁰"The visions of my head upon my bed: I was watching, and behold, a tree in the midst of the earth. Its height was great. ¹¹The tree grew large and strong, its height reaching unto the heavens, and its visibility to the end of all the earth. ¹²Its foliage was beautiful, and its fruit abundant, with food in it for all. Underneath it the living creature of the field had shade, and in its boughs dwelt the birds of the heavens. All flesh fed from it.

¹³"I was watching in the visions of my head upon my bed, when behold, a watcher, a holy one, was descending from heaven, ¹⁴crying loudly. Thus he said: 'Fell the tree, lop off its branches, strip off its foliage and scatter its fruit![32] Let the living creature flee from beneath it, and the birds from its branches. ¹⁵However, leave the stock of its roots in the earth—with a band of iron and bronze—in the grass of the field. It shall be wet by the dew of the heavens, and with the living creature will its lot be among the herb of the earth. ¹⁶They shall change his heart from that of a man, the heart of a living creature will be given[33] to him, and 7 times will pass over him. ¹⁷This sentence is by decree of the watchers, this verdict by word of the holy ones,

---

[31] Aramaic "the visions of my dream which I saw, and its interpretation, tell." Theodotion's Greek reads, "Hear the vision of the dream which I saw, and its interpretation tell me." Theodotion recognized that Nebuchadezzar was not asking Daniel to recount his dream *and* its interpretation, for in Daniel 4:10–18, Nebuchadnezzar tells Daniel the dream, and in verses 19–27, Daniel provides only the interpretation. Theodotion appears to have understood that the verb *chazi* ("perceive") was implied before the noun *chezvey* ("visions of"), or perhaps the Aramaic manuscript from which he worked actually read *chazi chezvey* ("perceive the visions of"). The present translation allows Daniel 4:10–18 to inform us that the verb "consider" is needed prior to "the visions of my dream" to provide an understandable English translation.

[32] The commands in the first sentence of verse 14, the command of 15, and the command at the beginning of verse 16 are all masculine, plural.

[33] This verb is masculine, singular.

for this purpose: that those living may know that the Most High has rule over the kingdom of man, and to whomever He wishes, He gives it, and the lowliest of men He **appoints** over it.'

¹⁸"This dream I, King Nebuchadnezzar, have seen. Now you, Belteshazzar, declare its interpretation, for all of the wise men of my kingdom are not able to make known to me the interpretation. But you are able, for the spirit of the holy gods is in you."

Daniel Interprets Dream

¹⁹Then Daniel, whose name was Belteshazzar, was desolated about 1 hour; his thoughts troubled him. So the king said, "Belteshazzar, do not let the dream nor its interpretation trouble you." Belteshazzar replied, "My lord, if only the dream were for those who hate you, and its interpretation for your enemies!

²⁰"The tree which you saw, which grew large and strong, its height reaching unto the heavens, and its visibility to all the earth, ²¹whose foliage was beautiful, and its fruit abundant, with food in it for all, underneath which the living creature of the field dwells, and in whose branches dwell the birds of the heavens—²²it is you, your majesty, who have grown great and strong! Your greatness has grown great, and reaches unto the heavens, and your dominion to the end of the earth.

²³"Since the king saw a watcher, a holy one, descending from the heavens, saying 'Fell the tree and destroy it; however, leave the stock of its roots in the earth—with a band of iron and bronze—in the grass of the field. It shall be wet by the dew of the heavens, and with the living creature of the field will its lot be until 7 times pass over him,' ²⁴this is the interpretation, your majesty, it is the decree of the Most High, which has reached over[34] my lord the king: ²⁵They are going to drive you away from mankind, your dwelling place is to be with the living creature of the field, and they

---

[34] Or "come over" or "been passed against." This is the same Aramaic word used in Daniel 4:11, 20, and 22; just as Nebuchadnezzar's pride reached unto heaven, so God's judgment has reached over him.

will feed you herbage like oxen. They will make you wet by the dew of the heavens, and 7 times will pass over you until you know that the Most High has rule over the kingdom of man, and He gives it to whomever He wishes. ²⁶But since they said to leave the stock of the tree's roots, your kingdom will remain for you since you will know that the heavens have rule.

Daniel Counsels King Nebuchadnezzar

²⁷"Therefore, your majesty, may my counsel be acceptable to you: sever your sins via righteousness, and your deviant behaviors by showing favor to the afflicted, that there may be a lengthening of your prosperity."

Judgment: King Nebuchadnezzar Humbled

²⁸All the [foregoing] reached over³⁵ King Nebuchadnezzar. ²⁹At the end of 12 months, as he was walking upon the royal palace of Babylon, ³⁰the king said, "Is this not that great Babylon which I have built as a royal house by the might of my power, and for my majestic honor?"

³¹The utterance was still in the king's mouth [when] a voice from the heavens fell, "Regarding you, King Nebuchadnezzar, they say: 'The kingdom has departed from you. ³²They will drive you away from mankind. Your dwelling place is to be with the living creature of the field, they will feed you with herbage like oxen, and 7 times will pass over you until you know that the Most High has rule over the kingdom of man, and He gives it to whomever He wishes.'"

³³At that hour, the declaration was fulfilled concerning Nebuchadnezzar: he was driven away from mankind, he began eating herbage like oxen, and his body was made wet by the dew of the heavens, until his hair grew long like [that of] eagles, and his nails like [those of] birds.

³⁴At the end of the days I, Nebuchadnezzar, lifted up my eyes toward the heavens. My reason returned to me, I blessed the Most High, and

---

³⁵ See footnote 34.

Him who lives forever I praised and honored, for His dominion is an everlasting dominion, His kingdom is with generation after generation. ³⁵All those who dwell upon the earth are reckoned as nothing; He does according to His will with the army of the heavens and those who dwell upon the earth. There is no one who smacks[36] His hand, nor says to Him, "What have You done?"

³⁶At the appointed time, my reason returned to me, and for the honor of my kingdom, my majesty and splendor returned to me. My counselors and chief advisors sought me out. I was re-established over my kingdom, and extraordinary greatness was added unto me.

³⁷Now I, Nebuchadnezzar, am praising, exalting, and honoring the King of the heavens, because all of His works are truth and His paths judgment—because those who walk in pride He is able to bring low.

COMMENTARY: DANIEL 4

The chiastic peak of the Aramaic portion of Daniel is in chapters 4 and 5, which present a marked contrast; in Daniel 4, God's mighty humbling of Nebuchadnezzar results in his salvation, while Daniel 5 marks Belshazzar's willful pride, resulting in his death.

King Nebuchadnezzar: Humble Man Praises God

The greeting in verse 1 stands in contrast to the proclamation of the herald in 3:4. The same people groups are identified, but now instead of commanding false worship on pain of death, Nebuchadnezzar issues the testimony of his conversion to everyone. In fact, his greeting parallels the first angel's message of Revelation 14:6, which announces the end-time judgment message to "every nation, tribe, tongue, and people." Further,

---

[36] "Smacks" = Aramaic *macha'*—same word used for the stone which "struck" the image in Daniel 2:34–35.

the third angel's message of verses 9–12 culminates in the message of righteousness by faith: "Here is the endurance of the holy people: they keep God's commandments and Jesus' faith." Likewise, Daniel 4 details the judgment that befalls Nebuchadnezzar, resulting in his acceptance of God's righteousness and complete character transformation.

King Nebuchadnezzar Sees Dream, Calls Babylonian Advisors

As in Daniel 2, Nebuchadnezzar calls for his retinue of self-serving charlatans to explain the dream. This time, he does recount his dream for them, yet still they prove incapable. Why would Nebuchadnezzar retain such people in his service after their miserable performance in Daniel 2? The answer is simple: Not yet a converted man, his heart was still "deceitful above all things; it is incurable. Who can know it?" (Jer. 17:9). Hence, it is not surprising that he would continue to seek the counsel of wicked men.

Daniel Comes

God permits Nebuchadnezzar to inquire of his unfaithful counselors so that his servant Daniel may shine the brighter. Nebuchadnezzar states that he knows (from the experience of Daniel 2) that Daniel has within him the spirit of the holy gods. It should be noted that the original language permits one to translate Nebuchadnezzar's words as either "holy gods" or "holy God," context being the determining factor. It is clear that Nebuchadnezzar is unconverted at this point. His shock at seeing the Son of God at the close of Daniel 3 has faded by this time. Therefore, it seems he is referring to his "holy gods."

King Nebuchadnezzar Recounts Dream

The dream centers around a tree representing Nebuchadnezzar. The watcher gives orders to carry out the verdict rendered by the "watchers" and "holy ones" of verse 17. The work begins by cutting down the tree, limbing it, removing all leaves, and even scattering its fruit. Why such agricultural imagery? Scripture cannot be understood properly until one recognizes that it is saturated with agricultural imagery. In His parables, Jesus' most common reference is to agriculture.

In John 15:1–8, Jesus teaches that the farmer removes fruit from fruit-bearing branches so that they may bear more fruit. Since *all* of the fruit of the tree of Nebuchadnezzar's dream is purged, it must be that God intends Nebuchadnezzar to bear much more fruit. However, all of the branches are removed as well, preventing the production of fruit until they grow back. God recognizes that any fruit produced before time will be *bad*, hence its production must be halted. To prevent branches from growing back prematurely, the tree is cut down, leaving only its stock or trunk. This trunk is then bound with a band of iron and bronze, preventing its expansion.

Searching Scripture for the significance of iron and bronze, Leviticus 26:19 refers to the inability of heaven to provide rain as being like iron and the inability of the earth to produce food as being like bronze. In other words, heaven and earth were impervious to water and plant life, respectively. In Isaiah 45:2, *Yahweh* would enable Cyrus to conquer Babylon by breaking open the gates of bronze and bars of iron for him. This was to occur *after* Nebuchadnezzar's reign, so the iron and bronze imagery suggests that Nebuchadnezzar and his kingdom would remain impregnable during his 7 times[37] of mania.

Why must Nebuchadnezzar lose his mind for 7 times? We find the answer in Leviticus 26:18–20, addressed to those who refuse to listen to *Yahweh*, breaking covenant with Him by not observing His commandments. "Now if after this you will not hearken unto Me, I will increase your chastening sevenfold on account of your sins. I will break the exaltation of your might, I will make your heavens like iron and your land like bronze. Your strength will be used up in vain, your land will not put forth its

---

[37] A time is a year of 360 days.

produce, the tree of the land will not put forth its fruit." Nebuchadnezzar is described as a fruit tree in Daniel 4; he bears the fruit of pride, and heaven will stop this by withholding those sources that nurture such pride.

Now consider the testimony of Job 14:7–9: "There is hope for a tree, if it is cut down, that it will grow again, and its shoot not cease. Though its root grow old in the earth, and its stock die in the dust/dry ground, yet through the scent of water it will be caused to bud, and put forth branches like a plant." With no water for 7 times, surely Nebuchadnezzar's stock would die. There is hope for Nebuchadnezzar, though. Being cut down small and prevented from lateral expansion by the band, his roots might still grow *down* through the soil until, at the close of the 7 times, they would scent water, and his stock could once more bud and put forth branches. This strong root system enables his "tree" to withstand drought conditions, for it is not dependent on rain, but can rely on the waters deep within the earth. Nebuchadnezzar will no longer rely on his own strength, but having died to self, he will now drink deeply of the water of life.

The experience of the tree in Nebuchadnezzar's dream is applied to Nebuchadnezzar himself in verse 16, wherein his heart (likened to soil in Mark 4:4 and 15) is changed from that of a carnal man to that of a living creature. Why is Nebuchadnezzar's corrective period exactly 7 times?[38] According to Daniel 4:29, God gave Nebuchadnezzar 12 months' probation to test him. According to Genesis 7:11 and 24 and 8:4, a month contains 30 days, so 12 months is 360 days. According to Leviticus 26:18–20, those who continue to rebel against *Yahweh's* chastening will be chastened sevenfold more. Hence, Nebuchadnezzar's 12 months, or 1 time, of rebellion was to be corrected by a period sevenfold longer, which in his case equates to a period of 7 times. Of course, 7 is the number of God's perfection, so those who, like Nebuchadnezzar, endure the chastening become partakers of the divine nature, as promised in 2 Peter 1:4.

---

[38] Daniel 4:34 is clear that Nebuchadnezzar's kingdom was restored to him during his lifetime. Jehovah's Witnesses spiritualize away this plain reading, asserting that Nebuchadnezzar's kingdom was removed for 7 × 360 = 2,520 years, at the end of which God's spiritual kingdom was established in 1914 (see *What Does the Bible Really Teach?*, "1914—A Significant Year in Bible Prophecy," pp. 215–218).

Let it be clear: Leviticus 26 does *not* equate "sevenfold" with 7 periods of time, whether 7 years, or as some insist, 7 prophetic times which would be 2,520 years. "Sevenfold" refers to a judgment sevenfold greater, or more severe, as in Genesis 4:24. In the book of Daniel, God interrelates time and character, and that is why *in this particular case*, the sevenfold greater judgment of Daniel 4 *does* happen to correspond to a judgment 7 times longer in extent. Said another way, it is appropriate to recognize in Daniel 4 a *specific application* of Leviticus 26. However, it is *incorrect* to infer from Daniel 4 that the use of "sevenfold" in Leviticus 26 establishes a general rule that equates it with 7 years.

Daniel Interprets the Dream

Upon relating his dream to Daniel, whom "no secret baffles," Daniel "was desolated about 1 hour; his thoughts troubled him." His response indicates that this dream is a revelation of God's impending judgment. "Desolation" is used of judgment (see 9:2, 26), as is "1 hour" (see 4:33; 5:5; Rev. 14:7; 18:10, 17, 19).

In verses 20–22, Nebuchadnezzar may very well have swelled with pride, learning that this magnificent tree represented his own splendor, the very grandeur with which he is so pleased, but 12 months later, the hour judgment is visited upon him. However, beginning in verse 23, it becomes clear that the "greatness" of verses 20–22 was not so much a description of Nebuchadnezzar's kingdom as it was his *pride* in his kingdom. Pride indicates a heart that is "incurable" (see Jer. 17:9), so Nebuchadnezzar's tree cannot simply be cut down; it must be *destroyed*. God does not surgically repair our hearts. Incurably bad, they are fit only to die, and we must be born from above. In Psalm 51:10, David asks God to *create* a new heart for him. "Creating" is an activity exclusive to God, by which "those things which are seen do not come to exist out of those things which appear" (Heb. 11:3). Nebuchadnezzar's heart cannot be re-made; he is to be given an entirely new one.

Just as Nebuchadnezzar's pride swelled, reaching unto the heavens, so the decree of God reached *down* to Nebuchadnezzar. God's solution for Nebuchadnezzar is the same for us all: He brings us as low as necessary to see our wretchedness in comparison with Christ's perfection, that we will cry out as did Peter, "Lord, save me!" (Matt. 14:30). Solomon sums up Nebuchadnezzar's experience: "Before it is broken in pieces, man's heart is proud; before glory, [there must be] humility" (Prov. 18:12). God can save any one of us from ourselves as He did Nebuchadnezzar—if we are willing to meet Him on His terms.

Daniel reveals in verse 25 what awaits Nebuchadnezzar if he persists in his proud, rebellious course: He is to be reduced to the level of a brute beast. However, this is not retaliation on the part of God. In fact, it is not even punitive judgment. Rather, it is an object lesson. While Nebuchadnezzar is in the field with the beasts (literally, "living creatures"), God is changing his heart from that of a carnal man to that of a living creature. At one level, Nebuchadnezzar will learn to rely implicitly on God to provide food and shelter like the beast of the field does. At another, this points to the living creatures about God's throne in Revelation 4 and 5, which together illustrate the working out of the new-covenant experience (more on this later in this chapter).

Nebuchadnezzar is told that enough time will pass until he acknowledges God's supremacy—when he is brought to the point of full surrender. Simply put, God is telling him in advance that He will save him! While you and I may not have such a guarantee given us, we have Nebuchadnezzar's story on record as an assurance of salvation. In our case, we don't *need* a prophet to tell us that God will save us, for from this story, we know the conditions for salvation, and we see that what God promises, He fulfills.

Daniel Counsels King Nebuchadnezzar

In verse 27, we learn that God's judgment is conditional. If Nebuchadnezzar continues on his same path, he will experience God's heavy hand of judgment, calculated to bring about the needed reformation in his life. However, if he heeds Daniel's counsel to make a break from sin and partake of the righteousness that God longs to give him, there is no need for the threatened judgment. He is also counseled to show favor to the oppressed. Many Bibles render this "poor," suggesting that Nebuchadnezzar should become liberal to the less affluent. However, the primary sense of the word is "afflicted, oppressed, humbled," standing in marked contrast to Nebuchadnezzar's pride. Since he ignores Daniel's counsel, God is about to teach him compassion for those who are afflicted by granting 7 times worth of personal affliction and humbling. This humbling is the very process through which people go during the Day of Atonement (see Lev. 16:29–31; 23:27–32) and will be developed much more fully in Daniel 8–12. For now, recognize that Nebuchadnezzar's experience models the end-time Day of Atonement process for us.

Judgment: King Nebuchadnezzar Humbled

All of the predicted judgment came to pass on Nebuchadnezzar. Just as his pride reached *unto* the heavens, so heaven's judgment reached *down* to him. His pride has not yet been corrected, as indicated by his boast, "Is this not that great Babylon which I have built as a royal house by the might of my power, and for my majestic honor?" This boast flatly contradicts what Nebuchadnezzar had heard earlier: "The God of the heavens has given you a *kingdom*, *power*, *might*, and *honor*" (Dan. 2:37).

Four times in Daniel 4, Nebuchadnezzar's time of affliction was stated to be "7 times" (see vs. 16, 23, 25, 32). This is exactly 7 times longer than the 12 months of probation granted Nebuchadnezzar because *Yahweh* decrees that rebellion is followed by sevenfold greater chastening (see Lev. 26:18, 21, 24, 28). Hence, it is clear that the aim of Nebuchadnezzar's 7 times of affliction is to work out the new covenant in his life. Since Nebuchadnezzar was granted 12 months = 1 time in which to demonstrate true repentance (i.e., reformation) and failed to do so, he is now to be chastened for 7 times to eradicate his selfish character. Recalling that 7 is the number of God's perfection, we recognize that these 7 times are for developing the divine nature in Nebuchadnezzar (see 2 Peter 1:4).

Regarding Nebuchadnezzar's 12 months of probation, it is worth noting that his self-idolatry in Daniel 3 is referred to 12 times: 11 references to the image he made and 1 reference (see v. 19) to the image of his face. Hence, the 12 months of probation highlight heaven's primary concern with Nebuchadnezzar—his idolatrous obsession with his self-image.

An interesting detail is recorded in verse 33. During his mania, Nebuchadnezzar's hair and nails take on the semblance of an eagle. He is described as an eagle in Ezekiel 17:3 and 12, and Babylon (and by extension its king) is represented in Daniel 7:4 as a lion with eagle's wings that get plucked. This represents a humbling process according to Jeremiah 49:16: "'Though you make your nest as high as the eagle, from there will I bring you down', declares *Yahweh*." In harmony with Daniel 4, Daniel 7:4 states that the lion representing Nebuchadnezzar has his eagle-like glory plucked (no doubt when he lives as a humble ox), after which he is made to stand upon his feet like a man. God gives the king of Babylon a heart of righteousness!

At this point, we learn of the successful outcome of God's judgment in Nebuchadnezzar's life: "at the end of the days" comprising his 7 times, he no longer lifts himself, but his *eyes*, toward heaven, and his reason (literally "knowledge") returns. He now has that experiential knowledge of the living God, for lack of which "My people are cut off" (Hosea 4:6).

In contrast with verse 30, when Nebuchadnezzar directed all glory to his own accomplishment, now he blesses the Most High. He recognizes that those who dwell upon the earth are *nothing* in God's sight. One might understand this to mean that all people are worthless in God's sight, but this contradicts the fact that Jesus paid an infinite price to save all who will be saved. The correct understanding comes from the book of Revelation, which speaks of two classes of people: 1) those who dwell upon the earth, and 2) those who pitch their tents in heaven. The first group refers to those who are satisfied with their earthliness and make no efforts to conform to God's will; the latter group refers to those who live on earth while experiencing a foretaste of heaven because their heart is continually focused on God and the heavenly inheritance. At the close of Daniel 4, Nebuchadnezzar rejoices, recognizing that he is blessed "with all spiritual blessings in heavenly places in Christ" and God has "seated us together in heavenly places in Christ Jesus" (Eph. 1:3; 2:6).

The chapter concludes with the key to properly understanding God's work of judgment: "those who walk in pride he is able to bring low." This is a perfect understanding of God's judgment, which is not about getting revenge on His enemies, nor strictly punitive measures; it is about restoring the image of God in fallen humanity, making each of us as humble as is Jesus, who willingly left heaven to suffer and die on our behalf (see Phil. 2:5–11). In *Yahweh's* closing speech to Job, he summarizes His work of judgment thus:

> Job 40:8, 11, 14: Will you indeed frustrate My judgment? Will you declare Me guilty that you may be righteous? ... See every proud man and bring him low. ... Then I will acknowledge you, that your own right hand can save you.

To the question, "Who can bring a clean thing out of an unclean thing?" Job concluded there was "not one" (14:4). However, he was simply recognizing *man's* ability to purify himself; to make atonement with God. The Son of God that Nebuchadnezzar recognized in Daniel 3:25—the Son of man who enters upon the work of judgment in Daniel 7:9–14—can work in us "both to will and do concerning His good pleasure" (Phil. 2:13) that we may walk in the law of *Yahweh* as did Enoch and Noah (see Ps. 119:1; Gen. 5:22–24; 6:9).

SUMMARY: DANIEL 4

DANIEL 4: THE HOLY SPIRIT

Nebuchadnezzar is thoroughly converted at the end of Daniel 4, having experienced the fulfillment of God's everlasting covenant in his life.

From Ezekiel 36:26–27, we know that this corresponds to God putting his Spirit—the Holy Spirit—in the life of the believer. Three times (Dan. 4:8, 9, 18), Nebuchadnezzar remarked that "the spirit of the holy gods is in" Daniel. Though he probably meant "gods" rather "God," nevertheless, the Spirit of God—the Holy Spirit—was indeed in Daniel.

The Aramaic for "gods" in verses 8, 9, and 18 is plural, but depending on context, it may refer to "gods" or "God." This is true in Hebrew as well, where the singular and plural forms are both used of God, with no apparent significant difference in meaning. Interestingly, the references to a "watcher" and a "holy one" in verses 13 and 23 are singular, while "watchers" and "holy ones" in verse 17 are plural. The reference to the "spirit of the holy gods" (or "Spirit of the Holy God") in verses 8, 9, and 18 strongly hints that the "watcher" and the "holy one" of verses 13 and 23 is the Holy Spirit. As with "gods" or "God" in Aramaic and Hebrew, the plural of "watcher" and "holy one" in verse 17 need not indicate multiple beings, but more likely confirms that this is the Divine messenger. The Watcher comes down from heaven in verses 13 and 23, and a voice falls from heaven in verse 31, just as the Holy Spirit descended from heaven and the Father's voice came from heaven at Jesus' baptism (see Mark 1:10, 11).

Consider the following statements, noting especially the capitalization (original in these sources) of "Watcher," "Holy One," "Being," etc. (indicating Deity) and their equation with the Holy Spirit:

> In this Sanhedrin, assembled to plan the death of Christ, the Witness was present who heard the boastful words of Nebuchadnezzar, who witnessed the idolatrous feast of Belshazzar, who was present when Christ in Nazareth announced himself to be the Anointed One. This Witness was now impressing the rulers with the sinfulness of the work they were doing. Events in the life of Jesus rose up before them with a distinctness that alarmed them. ... The miracle just performed [the resurrection of Lazarus] appealed to their hearts, impressing them that Jesus was none other than the Son of God. ... Under the impression of the

Holy Spirit, the Pharisees could not banish from their minds the conviction that they were fighting against God. In their true significance, the Old Testament Scriptures regarding Christ flashed before their minds. (White, *YI*, May 18, 1899)

The holy Watcher from heaven is present at this season [the Lord's Supper] to make it one of soul searching, of conviction of sin, and of the blessed assurance of sins forgiven. Christ in the fullness of His grace is there to change the current of the thoughts that have been running in selfish channels. The Holy Spirit quickens the sensibilities of those who follow the example of their Lord. (White, *DA*, p. 650)

As the king gazed upon that lofty tree, he beheld "a Watcher," even "an Holy One,"—a divine Messenger, similar in appearance to the One who walked with the Hebrews in the fiery furnace. This heavenly Being approached the tree. (White, *YI*, November 1, 1904)

A Watcher, who was unrecognized, but whose presence was a power of condemnation, looked on this scene of profanation. Soon the unseen and uninvited Guest made his presence felt. At the moment when the sacrilegious revelry was at its height, a bloodless hand came forth, and wrote words of doom on the wall of the banqueting hall. Burning words followed the movements of the hand. "Mene, Mene, Tekel, Upharsin," was written in letters of flame. Few were the characters traced by that hand on the wall facing the king, but they showed that the power of God was there.

Belshazzar was afraid. His conscience was awakened. The fear and suspicion that always follow the course of the guilty seized him. When God makes men fear, they can not hide the intensity of their terror. (White, *YI*, May 19, 1898)

Could the curtain be rolled back before the youth who have never given their hearts to God, with others who are Christians in name, but who are unrenewed in heart and unsanctified in temper, they would see that God's eye is ever upon them, and they would feel as disturbed as did the king of Babylon. They would realize that in every place, at every hour in the day, there is a holy Watcher, who balances every account, whose eye takes in the whole situation, whether it is one of fidelity, or one of disloyalty and deception.

We are never alone. We have a Companion, whether we choose him or not. Remember, young men and young women, that wherever you are, whatever you are doing, God is there. To your every word and action you have a witness,—the holy, sin-hating God. (White, *YI*, May 26, 1898)

When Christ ascended on high, he sent his representative as a Comforter. This representative is by our side wherever we may be,—a watcher and a witness to all that is said and done,—standing ready to protect us from the assaults of the enemy if we will but place ourselves under his protection. But we must act our part, and then God will act his part. When we are brought into trial and affliction for his sake, the Comforter will stand by our side, bringing to our remembrance the words and teachings of Christ. (White, *YI*, August 20, 1896)

Prosperity and popularity had led [Nebuchadnezzar] to feel independent of God, and to use for his own glory the talent of reason that God had entrusted to him. Messages of warning were sent to him, but he heeded them not. The heavenly Watcher took cognizance of the king's spirit and actions, and in a moment stripped the proud boaster of all that his Creator had given him. (White, *YI*, March 28, 1905)

When Christ upon the cross cried out, "It is finished" (John 19:30), and the veil of the temple was rent in twain, the Holy Watcher declared that the Jewish people had rejected Him who was the antitype of all their types, the substance of all their shadows. (White, *DA*, p. 709)

DANIEL 4: THE STAND

The word for "stand" appears once, in verse 17, when the Watcher—the Holy One—the Holy Spirit states that God "appoints" the lowliest of people over the kingdom of humanity. Those of a humble spirit are the very ones God can entrust to be faithful rulers on earth. When Nebuchadnezzar became too proud, he was removed from the throne, but after 7 times, he was humbled to become the lowliest of mankind and reinstated as king.

DANIEL 4: GOD'S HAND

God's hand appears once, in verse 35, when Nebuchadnezzar states, "there is no one who smacks His hand," indicating that no one can impede the circumstances God sets in motion to win our hearts. Ironically, this points back to Daniel 2, in which the stone kingdom "strikes" (same word as "smacks") the image, and God's stone kingdom is set up without hands. In preparation for Daniel 5, bear in mind that God's strength manifests itself here in Daniel 4, not by coercion or human might, but rather by Nebuchadnezzar's willing submission to the leading of the Holy Spirit.

DANIEL 4: APPLICATION TO THE LAST DAYS

The end-time judgment occurs in the last days. From Daniel 4, we learn that God's judgment is about delivering His people from sin. He sends judgments upon us not as penalties, but to wake us up and steer us to put our complete dependence upon Him. If we do not respond, God increases His judgments sevenfold in an all-out effort to save us from our self-destructive ways.

DANIEL 4: GOD'S COVENANT, IMAGE WORSHIP, AND THE SABBATH

In Daniel 4, the phrase "7 times" appears four times (see vs. 16, 23, 25, 32). Similarly, in Leviticus 26, one finds the word "sevenfold" four times (see vs. 18, 21, 24, 28). While it is incorrect to conclude that Leviticus 26 refers to "7 times" (i.e., 7 years, or as some insist, 7 prophetic years = 2,520 literal years), the converse does hold. Daniel 4 does present a temporal realization of the "sevenfold greater" punishment of Leviticus 26:18–20 upon the world's most prominent king: a period of 7 literal years. In Leviticus 26:19, God's stated purpose is to "break your strong pride" by making "your heavens like iron and your earth like bronze"; in Daniel 4:22–23, God's judgment is to break Nebuchadnezzar's pride, which "reaches unto the heavens," and He describes Nebuchadnezzar as a stock of roots bound about with "iron and bronze."

Note how Leviticus 26 opens:

> Lev. 26:1, 2: You are not to make worthless things for yourselves. You are not to erect either carved image or [sacred] pillar for yourselves. You are not to set in your land a figured stone to bow down in worship before to it, for I am *Yahweh* your God. My Sabbaths you are to keep, and my sanctuary you are to reverence—I am *Yahweh*.

Verse 1 prohibits idolatrous images of any kind, while verse 2 commands the Sabbath, just as the remainder of Leviticus 26 juxtaposes God's blessings and curses. This presents image worship and the Sabbath as polar opposites. For reference, note what the 10 Commandments say concerning image worship and the Sabbath:

> Exod. 20:4–6: You will not make for yourself a carved image, nor the likeness of anything which is in the heavens above, in the earth beneath, or in the waters beneath the earth. You will not bow down to them, that you not be led to serve them, for I, *Yahweh* your God, am a jealous God, charging the iniquity of the fathers upon the sons unto the third and fourth generations of those who hate Me, but demonstrating a character of covenantal faithfulness to 1000's [of generations] of those who love Me— those who keep My commandments.

> Exod. 20:8–11: Remember the Sabbath day, to keep it holy. Six days you will labor and do all of your work, but the seventh day is the Sabbath of *Yahweh* your God. You will not do any work—you, your son, your daughter, your male servant, your female servant, your cattle, nor your sojourner who is within your gates—for in six days *Yahweh* made the heavens, the earth, the sea, and everything which is in them, then rested upon the seventh day. Therefore *Yahweh* blessed the Sabbath day, and made it holy.

Both refer to God's territory (heaven and earth) and employ His covenant name *Yahweh*. The one is negative ("You will not …"), the other positive ("Remember …"). These commandments are by far the longest. Why? Because they focus on worship—false worship and true worship. In essence, the entirety of Scripture revolves around whom we worship.

What has this to do with the book of Daniel? The recurring problem in the book of Daniel is image worship. The connection with Leviticus 26 here at the chiastic peak of the Aramaic portion of Daniel provides a subtle, yet strong, hint that God's solution to idolatrous worship is worshipping Him His way—keeping His Sabbath holy. This connection will become increasingly clear as we progress through Daniel.

The 10 Commandments as the basis of God's covenant with mankind is evident in Scripture:

> Exod. 34:28: He [*Yahweh*] wrote upon the tablets the words of the covenant—the 10 Words [the 10 Commandments].
>
> Deut. 4:13: [*Yahweh*] declared to you His covenant … the 10 Words. He wrote them upon 2 stone tablets.
>
> 1 Kings 8:9, 21: Nothing was in the ark, save the 2 stone tablets. … the ark, wherein is the covenant of *Yahweh*.

Lest anyone object that this was the *old* covenant, not the *new* covenant of grace, note that God Himself defines the new covenant as Him writing His law on our hearts (see Jer. 31:31–34; Ezek. 36:26, 27). In his letter to the Hebrews, Paul quotes twice from Jeremiah 31:31–34, underscoring the 10 Commandments as the basis of the new covenant (see 8:8–12; 10:16, 17). Loyalty to God is the ultimate expression of our love for Him: "If you love Me, keep My commandments" (John 14:15). While the 10 Commandments generally are the everlasting covenant, the Sabbath itself is the capstone and also called the everlasting covenant:

> Exod. 31:16–18: The sons of Israel shall guard the Sabbath, observing the Sabbath throughout their generations as an everlasting covenant between Me and the sons of Israel—it is an everlasting sign, for in 6 days *Yahweh* made the heavens and the earth, but on the seventh day, He ceased and took breath. He gave Moses, when He had finished speaking with him on Mount Sinai, the 2 tablets of the testimony, tablets of stone inscribed by the finger of God.

The prominent use of 7 in in each chapter of Daniel 2–7 buttresses this connection with the Sabbath. Seven times pass over Nebuchadnezzar; the faithful Hebrews risk death in the 7-times-hotter furnace for their faithfulness to the 10 Commandments; God is mentioned 7 times as the Revealer of the secrets of one's character. The Sabbath encompasses time, as the seventh day, and character, in its position at the apex of the 10 Commandments, the transcript of God's character.

"There is not anything new under the sun" (Eccles. 1:9). In the last days, Satan's ire is to be especially aroused against those in whom the everlasting covenant is fulfilled and who honor the 10 Commandments, particularly the seventh-day Sabbath. This will become increasingly clear as our study of Daniel progresses.

DANIEL 5: GOD'S HAND—WEIGHED 7 TIMES

Belshazzar: Proud King Praises False Gods

5 ¹King Belshazzar made a great feast for 1,000 of his chief advisors; before the 1,000 he was drinking wine. ²Belshazzar commanded—under the influence of the wine—to bring the gold and silver vessels which his father Nebuchadnezzar had brought forth from the temple[39] in Jerusalem so that the king, his chief advisors, his wives, and his concubines might drink from them. ³So they brought the gold vessels which they had brought forth from the temple, the house of God in Jerusalem. The king, his chief advisors, his wives, and his concubines drank from them; ⁴they drank wine, and they praised the gods of gold, silver, bronze, iron, wood, and stone.

King Belshazzar Sees Hand, Calls Babylonian Advisors

⁵At that hour, the fingers of a man's hand came forth, writing before the lampstand upon the plaster of the wall of the king's palace. The king saw the palm of the hand as it was writing. ⁶Then the splendor of the king's countenance changed, his thoughts alarmed him, the knots of his loins were loosened, and his knees were knocking one against another. ⁷The king began crying mightily to bring in the astrologers, the Kasdim, and

---

[39] Aramaic *heychal*, translated "temple" in Daniel 5:2–3 and "palace" in Daniel 4:4 and 29, 5:5, and 6:18.

the diviners. The king addressed the wise men of Babylon, "Any man who reads aloud this writing and declares to me its interpretation will be clothed with purple and a gold necklace upon his neck, and he will rule as third in the kingdom." ⁸Then all the king's wise men began coming in, but they were not able to read aloud the writing, nor make known its interpretation to the king. ⁹Then King Belshazzar began getting very alarmed, his splendor was changing upon him, and his chief advisors were stymied.

Daniel Brought

¹⁰Due to the clamorings of the king and his chief advisors, the queen entered the banquet house. The queen said, "Your majesty, live forever. Do not let your thoughts alarm you, nor let the splendor of your countenance be changed. ¹¹There is a man in your kingdom in whom is the Spirit of the Holy God; in the days of your father, illumination, insight, and wisdom—akin to the wisdom of God—was found in him. Your father King Nebuchadnezzar appointed him as chief of the magicians, astrologers, Kasdim, and diviners. Your father the king did so ¹²because an extraordinary spirit and knowledge, insight, interpreting of dreams, declaration of riddles, and untying of knots was found in this Daniel, whom the king assigned the name Belteshazzar. Now, let Daniel be called, and he will declare the interpretation."

¹³Then Daniel was brought before the king. The king addressed Daniel, "You are that Daniel from among the sons of the deportation of Judah whom my father the king brought from Judah? ¹⁴I have heard about you, that the Spirit of God is in you, that illumination, insight, and extraordinary wisdom are found in you. ¹⁵Now the wise men—the magicians—have been brought before me that they might read aloud this writing and make known to me its interpretation, yet they are not able to declare the interpretation of the matter. ¹⁶But I have heard about you, that you are able to make interpretations and untie knots. Now, if you are able to read aloud the writing and make known to me its interpretation, you will be clothed

in purple with a gold chain upon your neck, and you will rule as third in the kingdom."

Daniel Recounts King Nebuchadnezzar's Experience

¹⁷Then Daniel replied before the king, "Let your gifts be for yourself, and give your rewards to someone else. Nevertheless, I will read aloud the writing for the king, and make known its interpretation. ¹⁸Your majesty, the Most High God gave the kingdom, greatness, honor, and majesty to your father Nebuchadnezzar. ¹⁹Because of the greatness that he gave him, all peoples, nations, and tongues would tremble and fear before him. Whom he wished, he would execute; whom he wished, he would let live; whom he wished, he would exalt; and whom he wished, he would bring low. ²⁰But when his heart became lifted up, and his spirit grew strong to the point of presumption, he was deposed from the throne of his kingdom, and his honor they took from him. ²¹He was driven away from the sons of mankind, his heart became like that of the living creature, and his dwelling place was with the wild donkeys. They fed him herbage like oxen, and his body was wet by the dew of the heavens, until he came to know that the Most High God has rule over the kingdom of man, and whomever He wishes, He **appoints** over it.

Daniel Reproves King Belshazzar

²²"But you, his son Belshazzar, have not humbled your heart, though you knew all of this. ²³Rather, you have lifted yourself up against the Lord of the heavens, in that the vessels of His house they have brought before you, and you, your chief advisors, your wives, and your concubines have been drinking wine with them. You have praised the gods of silver, gold, bronze, iron, wood, and stone, which do not see, neither hear, nor know, but the God in whose hand is your breath, and whose are all of your paths, you have not honored. ²⁴Therefore the palm of the hand was sent from before Him, and this writing was inscribed.

Daniel Interprets Handwriting

²⁵"This is the writing that was inscribed: Mene Mene Teqel Upharsin. ²⁶This is the interpretation of the message: Mene—God has numbered your kingdom and finished it. ²⁷Teqel—you have been weighed in the balance scale and found deficient. ²⁸Peres—your kingdom has been divided and given to the Medes and Persians."

²⁹Then Belshazzar commanded, and they clothed Daniel in purple with a gold chain upon his neck, and they proclaimed that he should be third ruler in the kingdom.

Judgment: King Belshazzar Killed

³⁰During that very night, Belshazzar, king of the Kasdim was killed, ³¹and Darius the Mede received the kingdom, a son about 62 years old.

COMMENTARY: DANIEL 5

Belshazzar: Proud King Praises False Gods

The chapter opens with Belshazzar hosting an enormous feast "for 1,000 of his chief advisors." This enormous feast stands in marked contrast to Nebuchadnezzar's humility at the close of Daniel 4. Knowing how powerfully God worked in Nebuchadnezzar's life, Belshazzar's character should have reflected the divine image that much more closely. How great the enemy's power—and how frail mankind's steadfastness—if such testimonies of God's transforming power so soon lose their impact.

It is also worth noting that the king of Babylon is *drinking* right before the heavy hand of judgment comes down upon not only him, but also his kingdom. In Revelation 14:8 is given the message that spiritual Babylon of the last days has made all nations drunk with her wine, followed by the pronouncement in verse 10 that Babylon will in turn drink of God's wrath. Thus, Belshazzar's story typifies events at the close of earth's history, for in Daniel 5, God's wrath immediately follows the drinking of Babylon's wine. Belshazzar was without excuse for ignoring the history of Nebuchadnezzar, so the inhabitants of earth in the last days will be without excuse if they choose to drink the wine of end-time Babylon—the wine of papal Rome.

What comprises papal Babylon's wine? The story of Belshazzar associates drinking Babylon's wine with the defilement of the vessels of God's temple and worshipping false gods; in the end time, drinking Babylon's wine equates with accepting any of the papacy's false teachings concerning worship, God's temple (the heavenly sanctuary, especially the Holy of Holies), and clinging to any idol.

The text refers to Nebuchadnezzar as Belshazzar's father. Comparison with Jeremiah 27:6–7 helps us clearly understand what is meant by "father":

> Jer. 27:6, 7: Now have I given all these lands into the hand of Nebuchadnezzar, king of Babylon, My servant; moreover, the living creature of the field have I given him to serve him. All nations shall serve him, his son and his son's son, until the time of his land comes; then it will be that many nations and great kings will make *him* serve.

This prophecy of Jeremiah establishes that Nebuchadnezzar's *grandson* was to be on the throne when Babylon was subjugated to the Medes and Persians. History confirms that Nabonidus succeeded Nebuchadnezzar, and his son Belshazzar served as vicegerent in Nabonidus' absence.

It is worth considering *why* Daniel refers to Nebuchadnezzar as father, rather than grandfather as Jeremiah specified. God made mankind in his own image and likeness (see Gen. 1:26–28), but following mankind's fall, the only likeness Adam could now pass along to his posterity was the sin-tarnished likeness he took on when he transgressed (see 5:1–3). While Nebuchadnezzar did repent, and God molded his character so as to subdue the carnal nature, the fact remains that the only nature he could transmit to his posterity was the carnal nature he had inherited by birth and cultivated for so many years prior to his conversion. The transformation of character that comes with partaking of the divine nature (see 2 Peter 1:4) is entirely an *individual* matter that requires one to submit one's *own* will to God. Belshazzar was Nebuchadnezzar's son because he had forfeited the privilege of becoming a son of God (see 1 John 3:1).

Belshazzar deliberately calls for the vessels of God's temple to be desecrated in a pagan orgy dedicated to Babylon's false gods. To appreciate this desecration, recognize that the vessels in God's service represent His people (see Jeremiah 18:6) who are to be "filled unto all the fullness of God" (Eph. 3:19) and not "drunk with wine, in which is dissipation; rather, be filled by the Spirit" (5:18). God takes very seriously the desecration of anything associated with His temple. Nadab and Abihu intoxicated themselves, then proceeded to desecrate God's temple by using common fire in violation of His express command, for which God destroyed them (see Exod. 30:9; Lev. 10:1, 2). We are to expect the same for Belshazzar.

The observant reader will note the materials out of which the gods worshiped at this feast are fashioned. The gold, silver, bronze, and iron are identical to and in the same order as those comprising the metal image of Nebuchadnezzar's first dream (see Dan. 2:32, 33). The additional mention of wood and stone is a common way of referring to manmade idols in Scripture.[40] This last item of stone forms an ironic contrast with the stone that demolishes the image in Nebuchadnezzar's first dream. Babylon was built on an idolatrous foundation of image worship, whereas Jesus' kingdom is founded on the 10 Commandments cut from the sapphire pavement at the base of His throne in the heavenly sanctuary.

King Belshazzar Sees Hand, Calls Babylonian Advisors

Having detailed Belshazzar's transgression, verse 5 begins with the words "At that hour," followed by the mysterious writing on the wall. Without

---

[40] For example, see Deut. 4:28; 2 Kings 19:18; Isa. 37:19; Ezek. 20:32; Hab. 2:19.

reading the rest of the chapter, one can safely infer that what follows *must* be the pronouncement and execution of judgment, as the phrase "at that hour" finds an exact match in Daniel 4:33, when God pronounces and executes judgment upon Nebuchadnezzar. This is brought out forcibly by the observation that Belshazzar saw "the palm of the hand as it was writing." The only way to make out the palm of the hand as it was writing was for the hand to be see-through (i.e., the hand was deathly pale, drained of all life-giving blood).[41] The one writing on the wall is the same heavenly Watcher encountered in Daniel 4—the Holy Spirit.

God's judgments are perfectly suited to the cases He addresses. Nebuchadnezzar's army "brought forth" the sacred vessels from God's temple in Jerusalem, so the hand that writes on the wall "came forth" from God's heavenly temple in the New Jerusalem. Likewise, the mention of "plaster" (Aramaic *gir*) may seem an insignificant detail, but the lone use of its Hebrew counterpart in Isaiah 27:9 proves otherwise: "Therefore by this will Jacob's iniquity be atoned for, this is the entire fruitage of removing his sin: when he makes all of the altar stones like pulverized stones of *gir*, then Asherim and sun pillars will not arise." This text plainly associates *gir* with putting away false image worship, the recurring problem in Daniel 2–7. Hence, the handwriting on the wall prepares one for the *basis* of Belshazzar's judgment: his idolatry.

Observe that it is the fingers of the man's hand that write on the wall. This is highly important. During the third of the 10 plagues that befell Egypt, Pharaoh's magicians recognized that this judgment was "the finger of God" (Exod. 8:19). Again, it is "the finger of God" that writes the 10 Commandments, the basis of the end-time judgment (see Exod. 31:18; Eccles. 12:13–14). When the scribes and Pharisees brought a woman caught in adultery to Jesus, he stooped down and began writing their own transgressions of the law on the ground with His finger

---

[41] "When the revelry was at its height a bloodless hand came forth and traced upon the walls of the palace characters that gleamed like fire—words which, though unknown to the vast throng, were a portent of doom to the now conscience-stricken king and his guests" (White, *PK*, p. 524).

(see John 8:2–11). God counsels us to bind His commandments on our fingers (see Prov. 7:1–3). Scripture inseparably links God's 10 Commandments with our 10 fingers. Hence, the fingers of the mysterious hand are writing judgment upon Belshazzar for His transgression of God's law, specifically the first four commandments that deal with our relationship to God (observe that only one hand appears, and the thumb would not be used to trace letters).

Belshazzar is alarmed and immediately seeks for an interpretation. Not having learned from Nebuchadnezzar's experiences, he seeks not after God's prophet Daniel, but rather the worldly wisdom of Babylon. His call for the wise men and their inability to interpret the writing hearken back to the events following Nebuchadnezzar's dream in Daniel 4. This heightens all the more vividly the contrast in the final outcome of Nebuchadnezzar and Belshazzar's lives.

Daniel Brought

Belshazzar is pointed to the source of truth when the queen informs him that Daniel is capable of interpreting dreams. In contrast to the 6 different materials composing the false gods listed in verse 4, Daniel's God-given ability is described with 6 positive declarations in verse 12. Perhaps the richest irony is found in the last description, his "untying of knots," referring to his God-given ability to reveal answers to the most perplexing matters. The very same Aramaic phrase is used in verse 6, where it is said that "the knots of [Belshazzar's] loins were loosened." For every unrighteous act, God's judgment has a righteous parallel.

In verses 13–16, Belshazzar relates his dilemma to Daniel, promising him rich reward if he successfully interprets the writing. Once again, Daniel's experience in Babylon parallels that of Joseph in Egypt, for Pharaoh likewise gave Joseph his signet ring, fine Egyptian linen, and a gold chain, in addition to making him vicegerent (see Gen. 41:40–42). Daniel was promised to be third in the kingdom, history informing us that Belshazzar served as vicegerent in his father's absence.

Daniel Recounts King Nebuchadnezzar's Experience

Daniel responds to the king's request by refusing the king's gifts, expressing his willingness to relate the matter *without* reward. This hearkens back to Daniel 2:27–28, in which he gives credit to God for the miraculous ability to interpret dreams. This very humility is why God continues to honor Daniel with this supernatural gift.

Daniel reminds Belshazzar that judgment befell Nebuchadnezzar because, in his pride, he credited himself with the abundant success that God gave him after placing him upon the throne. By a word from God, he was deposed from the throne, and his honor was removed. Daniel informs Belshazzar that this was done just so that Nebuchadnezzar would come to realize that the Most High God has rule over all the affairs of humanity and alone decides who will rule as His representative.

Daniel Reproves King Belshazzar

The chilling note is struck in verse 22 with the words, "But you." Belshazzar was without excuse in his course of prideful rebellion, for he had the example of his grandfather from which to learn. Since Belshazzar did not acknowledge the God who holds his breath in His hand, God sent a hand devoid of life-giving blood to pronounce judgment on Belshazzar. Again, God's judgment perfectly matches the case.

No doubt, Belshazzar wished his golden Babylonian kingdom to continue (note that it was the gold vessels that were brought from the temple in verse 3). However, the attentive reader will note that Belshazzar called for both gold *and* silver vessels in verse 2, and the list of gods given in verse 23 differs from that in verse 4 in a key detail: Silver is now placed *ahead* of gold. In Daniel 2, we learned that gold represented Babylon, and silver its successor, Medo-Persia. In placing silver ahead of gold, Daniel provides a glaringly subtle hint as to the change in regime to take place momentarily.

Daniel Interprets Handwriting

Having established the inexcusability of Belshazzar's faulty character, Daniel proceeds to decipher the mysterious characters on the wall. The 4 words are pregnant with meaning, and Daniel summarizes their significance in verses 26–28. God has completed the process of numbering Belshazzar's kingdom. In Daniel 2, we learned that kings and kingdoms are used interchangeably, and what makes individuals unfit to serve is what causes kingdoms to fall.[42] Hence, while Belshazzar has been weighed on the balance scale and found deficient, his kingdom will suffer in consequence as well, being given over to the Medes and Persians.

What is meant by God weighing someone on a balance scale? From the following texts, it is apparent that God's work of judgment is to weigh each person's heart—one's *character*:

> Ps. 62:9, 12: Surely the sons of Adam are a vapor, the sons of man are a lie; they go up in the balance scale, together they are lighter than vapor. ... *Adonai*, character is Yours, for You will repay each man according to his work.
>
> Prov. 24:12: Does not He who weighs hearts discern it? ... Will He not repay each man according to his work?
>
> Eccles. 12:14: For every work God will bring into judgment, including every secret thing, whether good or evil.

With this understanding, we seek to understand the writing on the wall. "Mene" is the Aramaic equivalent of the unit of weight, the "mina." "Teqel" is the Aramaic equivalent for the well-known Hebrew weight, the sheqel. "Upharsin" means "and halves." Hence, the words on the wall tell us not only that God has weighed Belshazzar; they *quantify* God's measurement.

---

[42] "*Babylon*, shattered and broken at last, passed away because in prosperity *its rulers* had regarded themselves as independent of God, and had ascribed the glory of their kingdom to human achievement" (White, *PK*, pp. 501, 502, emphasis added).

It is critical to understand the balance scale God employs. A balance scale consists of a pair of pans hung from a balance beam centered on a post. In one pan is placed the standard of measurement, in the other pan the object being weighed against the standard. Hence, God's scale is not like today's bathroom scale, which reports the absolute weight of the object set upon it. Rather, the balance scale reports weight *relative* to God's standard of character.

Unlike pagan religions, Scripture does *not* teach that God weighs one's good deeds against one's bad deeds, the heavier side determining one's fate. He measures every person's character against the *same invariable standard*—His perfect holiness.

This means that we are each weighed against a standard that none of us in our own strength can possibly meet. A single sin in the life disqualifies us from meeting this standard of perfection, debarring us from heaven. However, this is where the good news comes in. Jesus provides us the way to meet His standard in *His* strength! The only way *any* of us can ever enter heaven is by choosing to yield our life to His control, allowing His atoning death to satisfy the penalty for our own corrupt past, and permitting the Holy Spirit to develop within each of us His perfectly holy life, one bearing good fruit as we abide in Him (see John 15:1–8).

To make sense of God's measuring process with Belshazzar, we need to quantify both God's standard of character *and* Belshazzar's shortfall. This requires that we add together the weights written on the wall. For reference, Table 2 lists the weights used in God's sanctuary, providing their values in terms of the well-known sheqel and the minimal unit of weight, the gerah:

Table 2: Relation of Sanctuary Weights One to Another

UNIT OF WEIGHT	WEIGHT IN TERMS OF SANCTUARY SHEQEL	WEIGHT IN TERMS OF SANCTUARY GERAH	SCRIPTURE
Gerah	1/20 sanctuary sheqel	1 gerah	Lev. 27:25
Beqa	1/2 sanctuary sheqel	10 gerahs	Exod. 38:26

(continued)

Table 2: Relation of Sanctuary Weights One to Another (*continued*)

UNIT OF WEIGHT	WEIGHT IN TERMS OF SANCTUARY SHEQEL	WEIGHT IN TERMS OF SANCTUARY GERAH	SCRIPTURE
Sheqel	1 sanctuary sheqel	20 gerahs	Lev. 27:25 (Exod. 30:13; Num. 3:47)
Mina	50 sheqels[43]	1,000 gerahs	1 Kings 10:17 (2 Chron. 9:16[44]; Ezek. 45:12[45])
Talent	3,000 sanctuary sheqels	60,000 gerahs	Exod. 38:25, 26

With this understanding, let us return to the pronouncement against Belshazzar. How do we determine God's standard of character *and* Belshazzar's shortfall? To answer this question, observe that the text does not explicitly state whether the final word "upharsin" (i.e., "and halves") refers to half a mina or half a sheqel. However, the word is plural ("halves," not "half"), which suggests that *both* meanings are to be considered. Taken

---

[43] For a time during and following the Babylonian captivity, the Jews adopted the Babylonian 60-sheqel mina. Prior to this, all agree that the mina was 50 sheqels. *The Jewish Encyclopedia of 1906* and TWOT affirm the pre-Babylonian 50-sheqel mina. ANLEX and LSJ assert that a mina is 1/60 of a talent, hence 50 sheqels. Marginal notes for Daniel 5:25 (NKJV, NASU) and Ezekiel 45:12 (ESV, NAB, NIV, NLT) agree, as does the table of "Weights and Monies" in *The New Strong's Exhaustive Concordance of the Bible.*

[44] Scripture omits a specific weight here, and the KJV supplies the word "shekels." This might lead one to erroneously conclude that the mina is 100 sheqels or 2,000 gerahs. However, Keil and Delitzsch note that the beqa (½ sheqel) had "acquired the name of *shekel* in the course of time, as the most widely-spread silver coin of the larger size" (*Keil & Delitzsch Commentary on the Old Testament*, entry on Ezekiel 45:12). If the beqa is understood here, the mina remains 50 sheqels.

[45] The LXX states, "50 sheqels the mina will be unto you," while the Hebrew states cryptically, "The sheqel will be 20 gerahs. 20 sheqels, 25 sheqels, 15 sheqels the mina will be to you." Does this add to 60 sheqels? God never changes (see Mal. 3:6; Heb. 13:8), so how could He alter the standard of character in His holy sanctuary by affirming the 60-sheqel Babylonian mina? The resolution, remarkably simple, is suggested by the balance scale in Ezekiel 45:10: in the left pan, place the suspect mina (of weight x) and the 20-sheqel weight; in the right pan, the 25 and 15-sheqel weights. The difference between pans is $x - 20$. Conduct another weighing: in the left pan, place the suspect mina and the 15-sheqel weight; in the right pan, the 25 and 20-sheqel weights. The difference between pans is now $x - 30$. These differences add to $2x - 50$, equal to 50 sheqels only when the suspect mina's weight $x = 20$ sheqels. Hence, the LXX and Hebrew harmonize perfectly. The mina at the time of the LXX was still 50 sheqels.

as half a mina, one arrives at the heavier value, God's standard of righteousness; taken as half a sheqel, one arrives at the lesser value, Belshazzar's weight. The difference between these gives us Belshazzar's shortfall.

To add the weights, they must be converted to a common unit. According to Leviticus 27:25, "each of your valuations will be according to the sheqel of the sanctuary, 20 gerahs to the sheqel." The gerah was the smallest unit of weight in the sanctuary system, suggestive of how perfectly God scrutinizes our lives. Using Table 2, we convert the writing on the wall into gerahs. The calculations are summarized in Table 3:

Table 3: God's Standard of Righteousness and Belshazzar's Shortfall

MEASURE	MENE	MENE	TEQEL	PERES	TOTAL
God's Standard	2,000 gerahs	2,000 gerahs	20 gerahs	½ mina = 500 gerahs	2,520 = 7 × 360 = 7 times of gerahs
Belshazzar's Character	2,000 gerahs	2,000 gerahs	20 gerahs	½ sheqel = 10 gerahs	2,030 gerahs
Belshazzar's Shortfall				½ mina − ½ sheqel = 490 gerahs	490 gerahs = 70 × 7 gerahs

These results reveal a most fascinating link between Daniel 4 and 5, which together form the chiastic peak of the Aramaic portion of the book. In both cases, judgment is meted out, and in both cases, God's standard is the same. In dealing out a judgment sevenfold greater than the 12 months during which his character was investigated, God perfected Nebuchadnezzar's character. In other words, this sevenfold judgment worked out to 7 biblical times, each time being a year of 360 days. In Daniel 5, God likewise compares Belshazzar's character against His standard of measurement, which is none other than His sevenfold judgment, equal to 7 times worth of gerahs, each time comprised of 360 gerahs.

God's handwriting in Daniel 5:25–28 reveals that in the judgment, He measures our character in relation to time via weights (specifically gerahs) associated with His sanctuary (in fact, this very work is the focus of Daniel 8–12). In judgment, God weighs our character against His perfect standard, which amounts to what we have done with that most precious gift of time. Have we idolized self or honored God? Consider the following observations concerning the parable of the talents found in Matthew 25:14–30:

> COL, p. 342: Our time belongs to God. Every moment is His, and we are under the most solemn obligation to improve it to His glory. Of no talent He has given will He require a more strict account than of our time.
>
> COL, p. 360: When the Lord takes account of His servants, the return from every talent will be scrutinized. The **work** done reveals the character of the worker.

We will meet with a period of 7 years once more in Daniel 9:27, detailing the final week of the prophetic 70 weeks, in the midst of which is Jesus' death at Calvary. Hence, not only is Belshazzar's rebellious life pitted against Nebuchadnezzar's humiliation; it is also contrasted with the prime example of self-humiliation, Jesus Himself (see Phil. 2:5–11).

Reference to Table 3 above shows another link with the 70 weeks of Daniel 9:24–27: Belshazzar's shortfall was measured at 490 gerahs, or 70 weeks' worth of gerahs. Our study of Daniel 9 will reveal that at the end of those 70 weeks, Jesus concluded His special work of judgment for the Jewish nation, having done everything possible to retain them as His covenant people. In rejecting their Messiah, they forfeited this special privilege (This does *not* mean the Jewish nation forfeited salvation, which is an *individual* work. Salvation remains open to all, Jew and non-Jew alike, who surrender fully to Jesus' purifying work in their lives). In coming short by 70 weeks' worth of gerahs in God's balance, Belshazzar forfeited God's forgiveness, thereby rejecting the atonement whereby he might secure entrance to heaven.

This understanding is brought out in Matthew 18:22, in which Jesus uses the expression "70 times 7" (identical to the Greek of Genesis 4:24) to mean that we should be willing to forgive others without measure (i.e., just as God demonstrated infinite forgiveness through the perfect sacrifice of Jesus at the cross). Similarly, Lamech boasts in Genesis 4:24 that his crime was so heinous as to be outside the bounds of God's mercy and forgiveness, and hence he was to be avenged "70 times 7." He so misunderstood God's character as to think He could not forgive him and change his heart, but that he must necessarily experience the wrath of God, unmingled with mercy.

Daniel's explanation in verses 26–28 makes clear that Belshazzar's *character* is judged. To better understand the relation of his character with *time* in the expression "Mene Mene Teqel Upharsin," consider the similar expression "time, [2] times,[46] and half a time" in Daniel 7:25. "Mene mene" matches the "[2] times," the single "teqel" matches with the single "time," and the "pharsin" (i.e., "halves") answers to the "half a time." To properly understand Daniel 4 and 5 is to recognize the difference in *character* developed by Nebuchadnezzar and Belshazzar over *time*.

Judgment: King Belshazzar Killed

Belshazzar is killed, then Darius the Mede receives the kingdom, being "about 62 years old." The number 62 appears only once more in the book of Daniel, namely Daniel 9:25–26, establishing yet another link between Daniel 5 and the 70 weeks of Daniel 9. The 70 prophetic weeks (490 years) are 7 times longer than the 70-year Babylonian captivity, fitting God's *modus operandi* of judging sevenfold greater when His rebellious people are slow to respond. Since the 70 prophetic weeks are broken down into 7 weeks, 62 weeks and 1 week, we should expect the 70 years to be broken down as 7 years, 62 years and 1 year.

Our study of Daniel 9 will show that the first 7 weeks of the 70 weeks mark a Jubilee period following the re-establishment of Jerusalem as a self-governing entity capable of rendering its own judgment. These are followed by 62 weeks, then the 70th week in which the Messiah is anointed

---

[46] Theologians of every religious persuasion understand "times" to mean 2 times, not an arbitrary number of times.

at the beginning, cut off in the midst, and the vision is sealed at the close of the week with a prophet's shed blood.

Are there indicators of a similar breakdown for the 70-year period? To begin, is there a significant event involving Jerusalem's self-autonomy for the first 7 years? Yes, indeed. Though Nebuchadnezzar bound King Jehoiakim in chains during his first siege of Jerusalem, he did not take him to Babylon, and Jehoiakim remained king until his death, at which point his son Jehoiachin reigned for 3 months and 10 days. This short reign extended until "the turn of the year," meaning the commencement of the new biblical year in the spring, marking the beginning of Nebuchadnezzar's first full year of reign. At this point, Nebuchadnezzar took Jehoiachin to Babylon and installed the final (puppet) king of Judah and Jerusalem, Zedekiah (see 2 Chron. 36:6–10). With her king appointed by an outsider, Jerusalem lost all self-government—our match with the first 7 weeks of Daniel 9:24–27. This occurred during "year 8 of his [Nebuchadnezzar's] reign" (2 Kings 24:12), 7 years after his first full year of reign began.

At this point, 63 years remain of the 70-year prophecy. Darius was said to be "about" 62 years old when he conquered Babylon. While the Bible does not tell us Darius' age exactly, there is a strong hint that he was born when the first 7 years were completed, hence his death would mark the end of the 62-year segment of the 70 years. Mark the following observation:

> Upon his [Darius'] death, within about two years of the fall of Babylon, Cyrus succeeded to the throne, and the beginning of his reign marked the completion of the seventy years since the first company of Hebrews had been taken by Nebuchadnezzar from their Judean home to Babylon. (White, *PK*, pp. 556, 557)

If the 70 years terminated the *moment* Cyrus ascended the throne, we have a conflict with our conclusion about Darius' age. However, the "beginning" of Cyrus' reign could certainly refer to his first year of reign. In this case, there is perfect harmony with the 70th week of Daniel 9:24–27, which details events at the beginning, middle, and end of the 70th week in relation to the Messiah. Note the parallels: Cyrus (called messiah in Isaiah 45:1) ascends the throne at the *start* of the 70th year. When the spring came (middle of the 70th year), marking the start of his first full year of reign, he issued the proclamation to rebuild *Yahweh's* house in Jerusalem (see 2 Chron. 36:22, 23; Ezra 1:1–4). In the seventh month (close of the 70th year), burnt offerings began to be offered once more (see Ezra 3:1–6).

SUMMARY: DANIEL 5

DANIEL 5: THE HOLY SPIRIT

The "Spirit of the Holy God" (clearly the Holy Spirit) is in Daniel. The judgment against Belshazzar is written by none other than the Holy Spirit who bears witness (see Rom. 8:16; 1 John 5:6).

DANIEL 5: THE STAND

In Daniel 5, the idea of standing is connected intimately with the presence of the Holy Spirit in one's life. The queen mother notes that Daniel was "appointed" (literally "made stand") to high office because of the extraordinary spirit found in him. Again, Daniel reminds Belshazzar that the Most High God "appoints" ("makes stand") whomever He wishes (compare with "the lowliest of men" in Daniel 4:17) over the kingdom of humanity. Hence, Nebuchadnezzar is restored to the throne as a humble man full of God's Spirit, while Belshazzar, devoid of God's Spirit, forfeits the throne by his pride.

DANIEL 5: GOD'S HAND

The hand that writes judgment against Belshazzar is linked with "the God in whose hand is your breath" (Dan. 5:23, 24), while Job 27:3 equates one's breath with the Spirit of God. Putting these texts together, we learn that God's Spirit is in His hand. In 2 Kings 3:15, after requesting a stringed instrument player, "the hand of *Yahweh*" came upon Elisha, and he began to prophesy (i.e., the Holy Spirit spoke through him). Similarly, the word of *Yahweh* was delivered by the hand of Haggai (see Hag. 1:1, 3; 2:1). In other words, it was inspired by the Holy Spirit. The following are very clear:

> Ezek. 3:14: The Spirit lifted me up, and took me away … the hand of *Yahweh* was strong upon me.
>
> Ezek. 8:3: He stretched forth the figure of a hand, and took me by a lock of my head; the Spirit lifted me up.
>
> Ezek. 37:1: The hand of *Yahweh* was upon me; he brought me forth by the Spirit and set me in the midst of the valley.

> It was not the hand of the priest that rent from top to bottom the gorgeous veil that divided the holy from the Most Holy Place. It was the hand of God. When Christ cried out, "It is finished," the Holy Watcher that was an unseen guest at Belshazzar's feast pronounced the Jewish nation to be a nation unchurched. The same hand that traced on the wall the characters that recorded Belshazzar's doom and the end of the Babylonian kingdom, rent the veil of the Temple from top to bottom. (White, *12MR*, p. 392)

> When Christ cried, "It is finished," God's unseen hand rent the strong fabric composing the veil of the Temple from top to bottom. … When the loud cry, "It is finished," came from the lips of Christ, the priests were officiating in the Temple. … the earth trembles and quakes, for the Lord Himself draws near. With a rending noise, the veil of the Temple is torn from top to bottom by an unseen hand, throwing open to the gaze of the multitude a place once filled with the presence of God. (White, *12MR*, pp. 409, 416)

DANIEL 5: RELATION OF SANCTUARY WEIGHTS TO TIME, CHARACTER, AND US

The phrase "Mene Mene Teqel Upharsin" employs sanctuary weights to express Belshazzar's character in relation to God's standard. From Exodus 30:11–16, we learn that 20 gerahs compose the sanctuary sheqel, and everyone 20 years old and older paid an atoning ransom of 10 gerahs. The 20 gerahs and 20-year age connect weight and accountability for those old enough to know good from evil (see Num. 14:29–31; Deut. 1:39) to everyone's need for atonement, since all have sinned and come short of the glory of God (see Rom. 3:23). According to 1 John 3:4, sin is lawlessness, the transgression of God's 10 Commandment law. Therefore, the atonement price was 10 gerahs. In God's economy, sanctuary weights connect time, age, and one's character in relation to the 10 Commandments.

From Daniel 4 and 5, we learn that God assesses our character by weighing it against His sevenfold judgment. For those of us living in the end-time judgment, it lies with us whether we yield to His corrective judgments or stubbornly hold to our greatest idol—self. If we harden our hearts like Belshazzar did, the end is death; if we yield like Nebuchadnezzar did, the humbling process may be trying, but the result glorious.

DANIEL 6: THE LIONS' HAND— THE PROHIBITION AND THE DEN

Medo-Persian King Appoints Daniel

6 ¹It was pleasing unto Darius that he **appoint** over the kingdom 120 satraps who would be throughout the kingdom, ²and above these, 3 chief officials, Daniel being 1 of them; these satraps would provide them an accounting that the king not be defrauded. ³So this Daniel became distinguished over the chief officials and satraps because an extraordinary spirit was in him, and the king was planning to **set** him over the entire kingdom.

State Prohibits True Worship

⁴Then the chief officials and satraps began seeking to find a pretext against Daniel pertaining to the kingdom, but they were not able to find either pretext nor corruption, for he was trustworthy; no negligence nor corruption was found against him. ⁵Then these men said, "We are not going to find any pretext against this Daniel, unless we find [it] against him in relation to the law of his God."

⁶So these chief officials and satraps came by collusion[47] to the king. They said thus to him: "King Darius, live forever. ⁷All of the chief officials

---

[47] Aramaic *ragash*, often translated "thronging" or "tumultuously." However, this word is best understood with reference to other explanatory Scriptures. The clearest is Psalm 2:1–2, which reads, "Why have the heathen *ragash*; why do the peoples meditate vanity? The kings of the earth station themselves; the rulers conspire together against *Yahweh* and His Messiah." The parallelism in these verses shows that *ragash* is synonymous with "conspire." Clearly, Darius' advisors would not persuade

of the kingdom, the prefects, satraps, counselors, and governors have consulted together to **establish** a royal **statute**, and enforce a prohibition for 30 days that whoever addresses a petition to any god or man except you, your majesty, be thrown into the lions' den. [8]Now, your majesty, **establish** the prohibition and sign the writing that it not be changed, according to the law of the Medes and Persians, which does not pass away." [9]Accordingly, King Darius signed the writing and prohibition.

Daniel Kneels Before God → Turned In

[10]Yet Daniel, when he knew that the writing had been signed, went up to his house—his windows being open in his upper room toward Jerusalem—and at 3 appointed times per day, he would kneel down upon his knees, praying and giving thanks before his God, just as he would do before this.

[11]Then these men went by collusion and found Daniel petitioning and imploring his God, [12]so they approached, addressing the king concerning the king's prohibition, "Did you not sign a prohibition for 30 days that any man who petitions any god or man except you, your majesty, would be thrown into the lions' den?" The king replied, "The statement is correct, according to the law of the Medes and Persians, which does not pass away."

[13]Then they replied to the king, "Daniel, who is among the sons of the Judean deportation, does not regard you, your majesty, nor the prohibition which you signed, but makes his petition 3 appointed times per day." [14]Then the king, when he heard the matter, was greatly displeased with himself, and set his mind upon delivering Daniel; until the going down of the sun, he was struggling to rescue him.

[15]Again, these men came by collusion before the king, saying to the king, "You do know, your majesty, that the law of the Medes and Persians is that any prohibition or **statute** that the king **establishes** is not to change."

---

him by coming in as a disorderly throng; rather, they would "come by collusion," hoping to achieve their aim by cloaking their motive.

The Den: One Stone is Sealed

¹⁶So the king gave command, and they brought Daniel and threw him into the lions' den. The king said to Daniel, "Your God, to whom you pay reverence continually—he will deliver you." ¹⁷So 1 stone was brought, set over the mouth of the den, and the king sealed it with his signet ring and the signet ring of his chief advisors, that nothing regarding Daniel might change. ¹⁸Then the king went to his palace and spent the night fasting, and did not have diversions brought in before him; his sleep fled from him.

The Angel of God Saves Daniel

¹⁹Then the king **arose** at the break of dawn, and in haste went to the lions' den. ²⁰As he approached the den, the king cried in an anguished voice to Daniel, "Daniel, servant of the living God: your God, whom you revere continually—was He able to deliver you from the lions?"

²¹Then Daniel spoke with the king, "Your majesty, live forever. ²²My God sent His Angel and shut the mouth of the lions. They have not injured me, for I was found pure before Him; further, I caused no injury before your majesty."

Daniel Investigated

²³Then the king was overjoyed concerning him, and commanded to bring Daniel up from the den. So Daniel was brought up from the den, and no injury was found upon him, because he trusted in his God.

Medo-Persian King's Conspirators Killed

²⁴Then the king commanded that they bring those men who had devoured Daniel's pieces, and they threw them, their sons, and their wives into the lions' den. They did not reach the bottom of the den before the lions dominated[48] them and broke all their bones in pieces.

---

[48] Aramaic *shalat*, identical to the word used in verse 26, referring to Darius' "dominion."

Medo-Persian King Commands Worship of True God

²⁵Then King Darius wrote unto all peoples, nations, and tongues who dwell in all the earth: "May your peace abound. ²⁶I issue a decree that throughout all the dominion of my kingdom, my subjects are to tremble and fear before the God of Daniel, for He is the living God, **enduring** forever; His kingdom is that which shall suffer no injury,⁴⁹ His dominion is unto the end. ²⁷He delivers and rescues, performing signs and wonders in the heavens and the earth, He who delivered Daniel from the hand of the lions."

²⁸So this Daniel prospered during the reign of Darius and the reign of Cyrus the Persian.

COMMENTARY: DANIEL 6

Medo-Persian King Appoints Daniel

This chapter opens with Darius setting up 120 satraps (provincial governors) and, over these, 3 officials to protect his revenue. The text specifically mentions that Daniel was 1 of these 3. He became distinguished over the chief officials and satraps, so Darius planned to set him over the entire kingdom. His "extraordinary spirit" ("the Spirit of the Holy God" in Daniel 5:11, 14) commended him to the king.

State Prohibits True Worship

The spirit that commended Daniel to the king had the opposite effect on the other officials. They grew envious of Daniel, so they sought to get rid of him. However, they could find no charge against him.

To conceal their design, Darius' cabinet appeals to his ego. What could better suit a monarch than for his subjects to treat him as a god?

---

⁴⁹ Aramaic *chabal*, translated "injured" and "injury" in verses 22 and 23.

Darius certifies their prohibition, providing the desired snare. Faithful to God, Daniel would certainly uphold the 10 Commandments, which begins, "Thou shalt have no other gods before me" (Exod. 20:3, KJV). As with Daniel 3, the story of Daniel 6 typifies what the faithful remnant may expect in the end time: Those who permit Jesus to make their character spotless will be persecuted on the basis of faithful worship in harmony with God's law. Our study of Daniel 6 will make clear which of the 10 Commandments will be especially targeted by earthly governments.

Flattered, King Darius signs the decree. The word for "signed" is the same as that which pertains to the irrevocable judgment "inscribed" in Daniel 5:24–25. In signing such a binding decree, Darius assumed a prerogative that belongs to the true Judge alone. The law of the Medes and Persians "does not pass away."[50] Such a statement is true *only* of God, for neither He nor His law changes (see Mal. 3:6; Heb. 13:8; Matt. 5:18).

Daniel Kneels Before God → Turned In

Daniel's character is immovable. When he learns of the consequence of remaining loyal to God, he goes to his house and not only continues to pray to God, but does so upon his knees and with windows open, that there be no question of his activity. This reminds one of the steadfastness of his companions in the fiery-furnace trial, when they remained standing as everyone around them fell upon their knees in false worship.

This parallel establishes the chiastic link between Daniel 3 and 6. In Daniel 3, the multitude is commanded to worship a graven image, while the faithful 3 refuse; in Daniel 6, the multitude are forbidden to worship the true God, yet Daniel continues to do so. These stories bring out both sides of fidelity—refusal to do wrong and unwavering commitment to do right. Seeking for the antitype to Daniel 3 and 6, one finds it in the activity

---

[50] This same irrevocable quality of Medo-Persian decrees occurs in the book of Esther, in which Haman beguiles the king into signing a decree to wipe out the Jewish people, charging that they don't observe the laws of the state (see 3:8–11).

of the apostate powers in Revelation 13, which establish decrees *requiring false image worship* and *forbidding true worship*—both violating explicit precepts of God's 10 Commandments.

As in Daniel 3, some of the king's advisors report Daniel's faithfulness, charging him with not "regarding" (Aramaic *sum*) the king's prohibition. From that moment until sunset, the king "set" (again, Aramaic *sum*) his mind upon delivering Daniel.

As in the story of Esther, the king is unable to reverse his death decree. The solution in Esther was to enact a new decree, permitting the Jews to defend themselves, thereby reversing the *consequence* of the original decree (see 8:8, 11; 9:1). Darius does not come up with a counter solution at this point, and the king's advisors are not slow to remind him that his decree is irreversible. However, as in the story of Esther, the false accusers of Daniel 6 will meet the very fate they thought to inflict upon Daniel.

The Den: One Stone is Sealed

Apparently helpless to rectify the situation, the king does recognize a great truth: Daniel's God will deliver him because he reveres Him continually. This unswerving allegiance gives Darius hope that his decree will come to naught. For us, this exemplifies Jesus' promise that when brought before rulers to answer for our faith, it will turn into a testimony in favor of the truth (see Luke 21:12–15).

The "prohibition" (Aramaic *'esar*) that Darius enacts appears 7 times in Daniel 6.[51] According to verses 8 and 9, this prohibition is established and unchangeable due to the king's signature and applies specifically to the realm of Medo-Persia over which Darius is king. From verse 17, we learn that the seal of the king's signet ring carries the same weight as does his signature, making his word unchangeable.

---

[51] Verses 7, 8, 9, 12 (2x), 13, and 15. The KJV translates these 7 instances of *'esar* as "decree." It also translates the Aramaic *tə'em* as "decree" in verse 26, but our concern is with the 7 instances of the Aramaic *'esar*.

Darius affirms a decision that is contrary to the 10 Commandment law of Daniel's God, and he does so by sealing it with a tripartite seal (name, territory, and title) on a stone. Our study of Daniel 2 revealed that the stone that hits the metal image alludes to the 10 Commandments that God etched in stone with his finger (see Exod. 31:18; Deut. 9:10), so it is expected that His truly unchangeable law likewise has a tripartite seal (name, territory, and title). His name (*Yahweh*) and territory (heaven and earth) appear twice in the 10 Commandments: in the commandment forbidding image worship and the commandment enjoining the keeping of the seventh-day Sabbath holy (see Exod. 20:4–6, 8–11). However, only the Sabbath commandment also includes the final element, God's title as "Maker."

In Daniel 3, Babylon clearly violated the commandment forbidding image worship. We have noted that the book of Daniel connects strongly with Leviticus 26, which opens with prohibitions against idolatry and the command to keep holy the Sabbath. As the chiastic counterpart to Daniel 3, it is not surprising then that Daniel 6 deals with the Sabbath.

"So 1 stone was brought ... and the king sealed it." The counterpart in Daniel 3:19 states that Nebuchadnezzar "gave orders to heat the furnace 1 factor of 7 hotter than it was [typically] seen to be heated." The intentional use of the number "1" establishes these verses as chiastic matches. It follows that "the king sealed it" matches with "factor of 7 hotter" (i.e., "seal" and "7" are equivalent). Darius' reference to God as "the living God" is highly significant as well. Revelation 7:2 refers to the end-time "seal of the living God," and in Acts 14:15, Paul connects "the living God" with the Sabbath by quoting from the fourth commandment: "turn from these vanities [idols] to the living God who made heaven, the earth, the sea and all things in them." Together, it becomes clear that God's seal is His seventh-day Sabbath.

Since sealing faulty Medo-Persian law made it unchangeable, it follows that God's seal—His seventh-day Sabbath—establishes the permanence of His unchangeable law. Further, God seals not only His law, but also His people in their foreheads (see Rev. 7:2–4). This means that

He causes His people to become perfect law-keepers and reflections of His character. This is precisely the fulfillment of the new-covenant experience, in which He writes His law in our minds (see Jer. 31:31–34), causing us to walk in His statutes and keep His judgments (see Ezek. 36:26, 27).

Most of the Christian world supposes that the Sabbath has been changed to Sunday. God's seal—the Sabbath—is at the heart of His 10 Commandment law, making His law unchangeable, so the Sabbath certainly cannot change. The change from Sabbath to Sunday is prophesied in Daniel 7. Our study of the next chapter will show how this came about and what it means for Christians living in the end time.

The Angel of God Saves Daniel

King Darius was bothered all night, so at the break of dawn, he hurries off to the den to learn Daniel's fate. Darius reaffirms Daniel's continual reverence for God, yet his faith is not as strong, as is evident in his assertion in verse 16, for now he asks whether God was able to deliver Daniel from the lions. As a further testimony of the character that God has developed in him, Daniel responds to the king with all the respect due a king. There is no hint of rebuke for permitting him to be thrown to the lions. God is so mighty that He can transform selfish creatures into beings that love their neighbors as themselves (see Lev. 19:18; Matt. 22:39). Daniel assures the king that God sent His angel to shut the lions' mouths.

In Daniel 3, the Son of God was the Angel who walked with the Hebrews in the fiery furnace. Since Daniel 3 and 6 are chiastic matches in the structure of Daniel 2–7, we deduce that the angel who rescues Daniel in chapter 6 is Jesus, the Angel of *Yahweh*, the Angel of the covenant (see Mal. 3:1).

Daniel Investigated

In his response to Darius, Daniel asserts that he was not injured by the lions because his character was pure. This determination and consequent deliverance involve an investigation and verdict, affirming God's role as supreme Judge. Like Daniel, we are all players in a cosmic trial in which God is investigating the record of our lives. For those who surrender and "follow the Lamb wherever He goes" (Rev. 14:4), He will develop a spotlessly pure character, with the promise of deliverance in the time of trouble (see Ps. 91).

Medo-Persian King's Conspirators Killed

The chapter now begins a sequence of contrasts. Whereas the king was "greatly displeased with himself" about being duped into requiring Daniel's death, now he is "overjoyed" at his deliverance. Those who sought Daniel's life are described as those "who had devoured Daniel's pieces," matching the description of the informants in Daniel 3:8 who sought the lives of his 3 friends. The wicked men, along with their sons and wives, are thrown into the lions' den, and the lions "dominate" them. By contrast, the fire has no "dominion" over the righteous in 3:27. In 4:22 and 28, Nebuchadnezzar's greatness "reaches unto the heavens," so God's judgment "reached over King Nebuchadnezzar" to humble him and save him from himself. By contrast, the wicked in Daniel 6, seeking supremacy at the expense of innocent blood, do not "reach the bottom of the den" before being destroyed.

This reversal of fortune under Medo-Persian rule appears again in the book of Esther. Wicked Haman seeks the lives of the Jews and is himself destroyed. The Jews triumph over those sent to destroy them. This corresponds to a principle of judgment found in Deuteronomy 19:15–21: If a witness brings charges against someone, then both involved in the controversy are to stand in judgment before *Yahweh* and His representatives. Investigation is performed, and if the charges are determined to be false by those who sit in judgment, then the penalty for the false charge falls upon the accuser. Thus, the evil is put away.

This is precisely what happens to the wicked who accuse Daniel, wicked Haman, and ultimately Satan, "the accuser of our brethren" (Rev. 12:10;

see also Zech. 3:1). Satan strives for us to receive the wages of sin, the second death in the lake of fire (see Rom. 6:23; Rev. 20:14). When it is demonstrated that he is a false accuser, God brings forth a fire from the midst of Satan that devours him, turning him to ashes, and so he ceases to be, having suffered the second death (see Ezek. 28:18, 19; Rev. 20:10).

Medo-Persian King Commands Worship of True God

As the chapter closes, King Darius writes, "unto all peoples, nations, and tongues who dwell in all the earth: 'May your peace abound.'" This matches word-for-word Nebuchadnezzar's opening address in Daniel 4:1, but Darius goes on to decree that his subjects are to "tremble and fear before the God of Daniel, for He is the living God ... He delivers and rescues." This demand for correct worship answers to Nebuchadnezzar's earlier decree in Daniel 3:28–29 that, on pain of death, people worship the true God because He "delivered" and "is able to rescue," establishing another chiastic link between Daniel 3 and 6.

Daniel 3 opens with a decree to worship falsely and closes with a decree forbidding dishonoring God. Daniel 6 opens with a decree forbidding true worship and closes with a decree commanding all to honor God. These cover all possibilities, legislating for and against true and false worship. They are all wrong, for each *forces* the conscience, not respecting religious liberty.

While Darius' description of God as "the living God" is accurate, and his objective may have been noble, we need to recognize that God created us as free beings and *woos* His wayward people to serve Him (see Hosea 2:14). Following the blow to the papacy that ushers in the end time, another kingdom arises answering to Medo-Persia (see Rev. 13:3, 11). Like its ancient predecessor, it calls for a laudable-sounding decree to worship the true God, yet its use of the strong arm of the law betrays it is as the false prophet of the beast power (see 19:20).

Darius' successor is called Cyrus the Persian. This shows that the 70th year of captivity has come, for 2 Chronicles 36:20 states that Persia, not Medo-Persia, was to rule following the 70 years. Called "messiah" in Isaiah 45:1, he is to proclaim release to the captives in Babylon (see Ezra 1:1–4).

SUMMARY: DANIEL 6

DANIEL 6: JESUS

The chiastic structure of Daniel 2–7 establishes that the angel who rescues Daniel in 6:22 is the same Angel who walked with the 3 Hebrews in the furnace—Jesus, the Son of God (see 3:25, 28).

DANIEL 6: THE STAND

The conspirators dupe Darius into "establishing" a "statute" (literally causing to "stand" a "standing" ordinance) prohibiting true worship, hoping to secure Daniel's demise. While the law of the Medes and Persians is not to pass away, in the end, the tables are turned. The conspirators are put to death, and Daniel is saved. Darius acknowledges the God of Daniel as the one "enduring" (literally "standing") forever. Only God's law and the kingdom of which it is the basis stand forever.

DANIEL 6: THE LIONS' HAND

Darius declares that God "delivered Daniel from the hand of the lions." In Daniel 3:15 and 17, Nebuchadnezzar's hand represented his earthly strength; so here, the lions' hand represents the strength of the unchanging Medo-Persian law. In both chapters, the earthly might of these monarchs was thwarted by the God who establishes His kingdom *without* hands. To be rescued from the hand of the lions is especially ironic, since God as Judge is represented as a Lion in Scripture (see Jer. 25:30; Hosea 11:10; Joel 3:16; Amos 1:2; Rev. 5:5). The Lion of the tribe of Judah reversed this unjust, earthly judgment!

DANIEL 6: APPLICATION TO THE LAST DAYS

God's people in the last days will have to disobey an earthly decree that forbids worship of the true God. The seal on the stone points to true worship based on the 10 Commandments written in stone, sealed by the fourth commandment, which enjoins keeping God's seventh-day Sabbath holy. Those sealed with the seal of the living God in the last days will keep the Sabbath, in spite of the state's decree forbidding it. The "den" in Daniel 6 is mentioned 10 times, just like the "furnace" of Daniel 3 is. The state's decree for honoring all of the 10 Commandments in the end time will be death. Like Daniel, the faithful remnant will be found pure before God, having caused no injury to the state. Likewise, the faithful remnant will stand with no injury, in spite of a death decree. And like the accusers in Daniel 6, the wicked who persecute the righteous remnant will themselves ultimately be destroyed.

DANIEL 7: THE HORN'S HAND—THE JUDGE AND HIS JUDGMENT

Introduction: Daniel Has a Dream

7 ¹In year 1 of Belshazzar, king of Babylon, Daniel saw a dream and visions of his head upon his bed; then he wrote out the dream, relating the chief points.

Daniel's Dream

²Daniel states, "I was watching in my vision during the night, and behold, the 4 winds of the heavens were breaking forth upon the great sea, ³and 4 great living creatures were coming up from the sea, each differing from the other.

⁴"The first was like a lion, with eagle's wings. As I was watching, its wings were plucked, it was lifted up from the earth, it was made to **stand** upon both feet like a man, and it was given a man's heart.

⁵"Then behold, another living creature, a second, resembling a bear. It was made to **stand** upon 1 side, and 3 ribs were in its mouth between its teeth, so they were telling it, '**Stand**! Devour much flesh.'

⁶"After this I was watching, and behold, another like a leopard which had 4 wings of a bird upon its back; the beast had 4 heads, and it was given dominion.

⁷"After this I was watching in the night visions, and behold, a fourth living creature—fearsome, terrible, and exceedingly strong. It had huge iron teeth. It was devouring and breaking in pieces, and with its feet it was trampling the remnant. It was different from every living creature which

preceded it, and it had 10 horns. **⁸**I was pondering the horns, when behold, another little horn came up among them, and 3 of the former horns were uprooted before it. Behold, there were eyes like the eyes of man in this horn, and a mouth speaking grandiose things.

Investigation: The End-time Judgment

⁹"I was watching until:

> Thrones were placed, and
> The Ancient of Days sat down.
> His garment was white as snow, the hair of His head like lamb's wool.
> His throne was fiery flames. Its wheels were burning fire.
> **¹⁰**A river of fire was flowing, emanating from before Him.
> Thousands upon thousands were serving Him, myriads upon myriads before Him were **standing.**
> The judgment sat, and
> The books were opened.

¹¹"I was watching, then, due to the voice of the grandiose words which the horn was speaking. I continued watching until the living creature was killed and its body was destroyed and consigned to the burning fire. **¹²**As for the rest of the living creatures, they took away their dominion, yet an extension of their lives was granted them until [the] appointed time and [for a fixed length of] time.[52]

---

[52] Aramaic "an appointed time [zəman] and a time ['iddan]." Up to this point, the Aramaic *zəman* has been translated "appointed time" so that the synonymous rendering "season" won't be confused with the agricultural seasons of spring, summer, fall, or winter. The Aramaic *'iddan* has been used in Daniel up to this point to signify a biblical time of 360 days or years, but in this case, a fixed time, though not necessarily 360 days or years, is in view, hence the bracketed words "for a fixed length of" qualifying "time." These 3 living creatures are permitted to live until the appointed time of destruction at the close of judgment; while the extensions of time granted each living creature are different, they all *terminate* together.

The Son of Man Receives His Kingdom

¹³"I was watching in the night visions, when behold, with the clouds of the heavens one like the Son of man was coming. He reached unto the Ancient of Days, and they brought Him before Him. ¹⁴To Him was given dominion, honor, and a kingdom; all peoples, nations, and tongues shall reverence Him. His dominion is an everlasting dominion which shall not pass away, His kingdom one which shall not be destroyed.

Daniel's Dream Interpreted

¹⁵"My spirit was distressed—I, Daniel—in the midst of its sheath; the visions of my head alarmed me. ¹⁶I approached 1 of those **standing**, and asked him the truth concerning all of this. He spoke to me and made known to me the interpretation of the matters: ¹⁷'These great living creatures, which are 4, are 4 kings which shall **arise** from the earth. ¹⁸But the holy people of the Most High shall receive the kingdom; they shall possess the kingdom forever, even forever and ever.'

¹⁹"Then I desired to ascertain the truth concerning the fourth living creature which differed from all of them. It was exceedingly fearsome: with its iron teeth and its bronze nails, it was devouring and breaking in pieces, and with its feet it was trampling the remnant.

²⁰"Further, [I desired to ascertain the truth] concerning the 10 horns upon its head, and the other which came up, before which 3 fell, that horn which had eyes and a mouth speaking grandiose things, whose appearance[53] surpassed that of its fellow [horns]. ²¹As I was watching, this horn was waging war with the holy people and prevailing against them ²²until:

> The Ancient of Days came,
>   then judgment was given in favor of the holy people of the Most High;
> The appointed time was reached,
>   then the holy people took possession of the kingdom.

---

[53] Same word translated "vision(s)" in verses 1, 2, 7, 13, and 15.

²³"So he said, 'The fourth living creature is the fourth kingdom which shall be upon the earth; it will differ from all the kingdoms; it will devour the entire earth, trample it, and break it in pieces. ²⁴The 10 horns out of this kingdom are 10 kings which will **arise**. Another [king][54] will **arise** after them: he will differ from the former [ones], and 3 kings he will bring low. ²⁵He will speak things against the Most High. He will wear out the holy people of the Most High. He will think to effect change of appointed times and law. They will be given into his hand until a time, times, and half a time [elapse].

²⁶"'But the judgment will sit, his dominion will be taken away to exterminate and destroy [it] unto the end, ²⁷while the kingdom, the dominion, and the greatness of the kingdoms under all the heavens, will be given to the people, the holy people of the Most High. His kingdom is an everlasting kingdom, and all dominions will reverence and hearken unto Him.'

Daniel Keeps Matter in His Heart

²⁸"Thus far is the end of the matter. As for me, Daniel, my thoughts greatly alarmed me and my splendor was changing upon me, but I kept the matter in my heart."

COMMENTARY: DANIEL 7

Introduction: Daniel Has a Dream

Daniel 7 opens as did Daniel 2, but this time it is Daniel who has a dream.

Daniel's Dream

Daniel's dream opens with the 4 winds of the heavens breaking forth upon the great sea. The great sea is identified in Numbers 34:6 as the western

---

[54] The adjective "another" is masculine, referring to king (masculine) rather than horn (feminine).

border of the Promised Land, which is the Mediterranean. Arising from Israel's western border, these 4 beasts are important in relation to God's people.

To appreciate the significance of this reference to the great sea, the following texts make plain the connection with the unconverted nations, as well as the wicked and sin itself:

> <u>Isa. 17:12, 13</u>: Alas, the roaring of many peoples, like the roaring of the seas they roar; the crashing of nations, like the crashing of mighty waters they crash. Nations like the crashing of great waters crash, but He rebukes him, and he flees far away; he is chased away like chaff of the mountains before the wind, like tumbleweed before a windstorm.
>
> <u>Isa. 57:20, 21</u>: "But the wicked are like the turbulent sea, which is not able to be stilled; its waters cast up mire and muddy clay. There is no peace," says my God, "for the wicked."
>
> <u>Isa. 60:5</u>: The abundance of the sea will turn itself over to you, the wealth of the nations will come to you.
>
> <u>Mic. 7:19</u>: Into the depths of the sea You will cast all of their sins.

Arising from this turbulent sea are "4 living creatures," commonly translated "beasts." However, the literal rendering permits one to see more readily that these are parodies of the 4 living creatures ("beasts," KJV) of the heavenly sanctuary (see Rev. 4:6). The angel explains in verse 17 that these creatures represent kings, and by extension, kingdoms (compare Dan. 2:38–40).

The first living creature is "made to stand upon both feet like a man" and "given a man's heart". Similarly, the second creature is "made to stand upon 1 side," while the third creature is "given dominion." The agent in each case is not specified, a common device in Scripture implying God as the agent. This harmonizes with Daniel 2:21, which states that God sets up and puts down kings.

The description of the first living creature represents Nebuchadnezzar and Babylon by comparison with the story of Daniel 4. The description as a lion with eagle's wings represents Nebuchadnezzar before his conversion, when it was said that his greatness had reached unto the heavens and his dominion to the end of the earth. Its wings being plucked corresponds to Nebuchadnezzar being humbled and made to eat grass along with the living creature of the field. The living creature being made to stand upon both feet corresponds to the restoration of Nebuchadnezzar's kingdom, sanity, and manhood at the end of the 7 times. The man's heart given to it represents Nebuchadnezzar's submission to the superiority of heaven when he is fully converted (see Ezek. 36:26, 27; Jer. 31:31–34).

The second living creature represents Babylon's conqueror, Medo-Persia. It was made to stand upon 1 side, for Persia proved superior in this 2-empire alliance. The 3 ribs in its mouth correspond to the 3 countries that it conquered in its rise to dominance: Lydia, Babylon, and Egypt.

The third living creature, the leopard, corresponds to Greece. Actually, prophecy points not to the small geographic area we refer to today as Greece, but the much broader area known anciently as Hellas. The 4 wings represent the incredible rapidity with which Alexander the Great completed his conquests (less than a decade, unmatched by any army of the day).

Before moving on to a discussion of the 4 heads, it is worth pausing to consider why a discussion of Greece is so important to a proper understanding of prophecy. As historian Will Durant observes, "Excepting machinery, there is hardly anything secular in our culture that does not come from Greece" (*SC2*, p. vii). Considering things from a prophetic vantage point, we might well drop the qualifier "secular," for Durant himself seems to recognize the impact of ancient Hellas on religious life:

> All the problems that disturb us today ... the perversions of conduct; the conflict of religion and science, and the weakening of the supernatural supports of morality ... all these agitated as if for our instruction, the brilliant and turbulent life of ancient

Hellas. There is nothing in Greek civilization that does not illuminate our own. (Durant, *SC2*, pp. vii, viii)

Durant also recognizes that the most lasting of her contributions is philosophy:

> Even her decline will be illustrious with the genius of Plato and Aristotle, Apelles and Praxiteles, Philip and Demosthenes, Diogenes and Alexander ... teaching the cult of the body and the intellect to the mystical Orient, reviving the glories of Egypt in Ptolemaic Alexandria ... formulating in Zeno and Epicurus the most lasting philosophies in history ... at last almost welcoming those conquering Romans through whom dying Greece would bequeath to Europe her sciences, her philosophies, and her arts as the living cultural basis of our modern world. (Durant, *SC2*, p. viii)

Having noted that ancient Greek thinking has permeated our lifestyle, indeed our very thinking, today, we now move on to a consideration of the 4 heads. Recall from Daniel 2:38 that the head of the image in Nebuchadnezzar's dream was Babylon's king. Further, verses 38–40 equate kings and kingdoms. Allowing the book of Daniel to interpret itself, we conclude that the 4 heads of the leopard are kings and kingdoms.

Some have speculated that the 4 generals Cassander, Lysimachus, Seleucus, and Ptolemy, who vied for control of Alexander the Great's empire following his death, are the 4 heads of the Grecian leopard. Did these 4 generals become 4 kings, and hence viable candidates for the 4 heads? Following Alexander's death in the year 323 BC, his empire was ruled by 5 individuals, namely Antipater, Lysimachus, Antigonus, Eumenes, and Ptolemy. By 311 BC, these had become Cassander, Lysimachus, Antigonus, Seleucus, and Ptolemy. By 301 BC, 22 years after Alexander's death, Antigonus was out, leaving the 4 generals familiar to historicist students of prophecy. Finally, when Seleucus killed Lysimachus in 281 BC, 42 years after Alexander's demise, the empire was reduced to 3 divisions: Macedonia, Egypt, and the Seleucid empire, which wound up losing all but Syria (see *SDABC4*, pp. 824, 825).

Following the turbulence of these initial 42 years, these 3 Hellenistic kingdoms became Roman provinces: Macedonia in 146 BC, when Roman general Metellus defeated Macedonian King Andriscus; Syria in 64 BC, when Pompey the Great defeated Armenian King Tigranes the Great and captured Syrian Antioch; and Egypt in 30 BC, when Octavian defeated Mark Antony and removed Cleopatra VII from the throne.[55] The division remained tripartite for the 135 years spanning from 281 BC to Macedonia's subjugation in 146 BC, representing 76% of the 177 years since Alexander's death in 323 BC (From that point on, only the 2 kingdoms of north and south, which feature in Daniel 11, remain.) To properly understand Daniel 7, Alexander's posthumous empire must be regarded as having 3 divisions, not 4.

This begs the question, How to account for the fourth head? At this point, we must jettison a key assumption that hinders efforts to determine the 4 heads. The prophecy does *not* indicate that all 4 heads arose from Alexander's empire. Does history confirm the existence of a significant Grecian entity that did *not* come under Alexander's dominion?

The answer is a resounding yes. In fact, this fourth kingdom is arguably the most important, by far, of the 4 heads allotted Greece. Before making the identification, a bit of terminology is in order. The word "Greece" does not appear in the Hebrew or Greek Scriptures. Rather, the Hebrew text refers to *Yavan* (*Javan* in the KJV). In English, this yields "Ionia" or its people "Ionians," referring to a region on the west coast of Asia Minor inclusive of islands on the west coast of Greece. The Septuagint translates *Yavan* as *Yovan* when referring to the name of the progenitor of the Greek peoples (see Gen. 10:2, 4; 1 Chron. 1:5, 7), and Hellas when referring

---

[55] "Macedonia (Roman province)," Wikipedia, https://1ref.us/yn (accessed January 22, 2020); "Roman Syria," Wikipedia, https://1ref.us/yo (accessed January 22, 2020); "Egypt (Roman province)," Wikipedia, https://1ref.us/yp (accessed January 22, 2020).

to the nation descended from him (see Isa. 66:19; Ezek. 27:13, 19). The words "Hellenic" and "Hellenistic" derive from the same root, making apparent the connection with Greece.

This work will use the word "Hellas" to refer to "all lands occupied, in antiquity, by peoples speaking Greek" (Durant, *SC2*, p. 67). Hence, Hellas is not limited to Alexander's empire geographically. The term is used of Greek-speakers pre-dating Alexander (died 323 BC) by centuries. Examples include Hesiod and Homer, who wrote circa 750 BC and 840 BC, respectively (Durant, *SC2*, p. 66).

Returning to our consideration of the fourth head of Greece, western Hellas did not come under Alexander's rule. Western Hellas includes areas of Italy (notably the Greek cities of southern Italy, dubbed Magna Graecia by the Romans), Sicily, southern Gaul and portions of Sardinia, Corsica, and western Spain. Greek civilization in Italy and Sicily was apparently at the same level as in Greece itself. In fact, the words "Greece" and "Hellas" have their origin in Italy. The Romans conquered the Greeks who lived near Italian cities like Naples, Venice, Ancona, and Magna Graecia and granted them Roman citizenship. "Biological assimilation followed. The Italian Greeks became Roman." The Italian expression *una faccia, una razza* ("one face, one race") is a saying used throughout Greece to assert that Italians and Greeks belong to the same race (see de Kock, *7 Heads and 10 Horns*, pp. 85, 86, 106).

Hence, Western Hellas, with its blending of Rome and Greece, is the fourth head of the Grecian leopard. What is the point of this focus on Greece? History confirms that Rome did not displace Greece in the prophetic lineup of kingdoms. Rather, the fourth beast—Rome—of Daniel 7:7–8 is permeated through and through with Grecian language, culture, and most importantly, its pagan philosophy, which has colored how western civilization thinks to the present day.

In our discussion of the image of Daniel 2, we noted that the bronze and iron in the upper and lower legs, respectively, pointed to the overlap of Greece and Rome. In Daniel 7:19, the iron teeth and bronze nails of the fourth beast once again point to its mixed Greco-Roman nature.

Likewise, the Roman sea beast of Revelation 13 has the body of a leopard, showing that it is overwhelmingly Grecian in its makeup.

No discussion of this nature would be complete without considering the effect of Greek philosophy upon Rome. The Greek Pythagoras, born around 570 or 580 BC, went to Crotona in the boot of Italy around 530 BC, establishing himself as a teacher. While his requirement of eating no flesh and recommending water might be commended for its health benefits for the body, his ideas on purifying the mind are more questionable. Such purification was done, not by thoughtful meditation on God's Word day and night (see Ps. 1:2), but by consideration of the sciences—geometry, arithmetic, astronomy, and music. Students were required for 5 years to observe "Pythagorean silence," apparently accepting instruction without question. Students were grouped into the *exoterici* and *esoterici*, the outer and inner circles, respectively. The *esoterici* were those permitted to garner the secret wisdom from Pythagoras himself. If this reminds one of initiation into the mysteries of heathen religions, in which one is a catechumen for a period of time before being initiated into the greater mysteries, that is because it is in fact the very same thing (Durant, *SC2*, p. 163).

Unlike the Egyptians before him, Pythagoras' math was not practical, but entirely abstract, and in fact, mystical, for the steps involved in geometric proofs served to "raise the student to a new platform ... from which he might view more widely the secret structure of the world." Pythagoras discerned that musical notes relate one to another by fixed ratios, from which he mystified astronomy by hypothesizing that planets in their orbit about earth (he took the earth as the center of the universe) produced tones that we never hear because we always hear them (Durant, *SC2*, p. 164).

From here, Pythagoras ventured into philosophy, apparently coining the term, a joining of 2 Greek words that together mean "love of wisdom." Since his math was already abstract, and he had spiritualized even this with his theory of unheard planetary music, he went the next step, proposing that all things interrelate via fixed ratios and sequences, and that the key factor in all things is *number*. To Pythagoras, "the only basic and lasting aspects of anything were the numerical relationships of its parts." Contrary to Scripture, "perhaps even the soul was *number*" (Durant, *SC2*, pp. 164, 165).

For Pythagoras, the soul consisted of 3 parts: feeling and intuition (which animals also possess), as well as a supposedly *immortal* quality unique to mankind: reason. At death, the soul was purified in Hades, then returned to earth in a new body. This process ended when the goal of a completely virtuous life was attained. Durant notes that "we catch again a glimpse of the trade in ideas that bound sixth-century Greece, Africa, and Asia when we reflect that this idea of metempsychosis was at one and the same time capturing the imagination of India, of the Orphic cult in Greece, and of a philosophical school in Italy" (Durant, *SC2*, p. 165).

The so-called transmigration of souls is what we today call reincarnation, and the attainment of the virtuous life is what Hindus call *nirvana*. Indeed, the link between Indian Hinduism and Greek philosophy is very real. More than this, the observant reader will recognize that the notion of purging the soul in Hades is what Roman Catholicism teaches, an evidence of the Greek philosophical base of its beliefs.

According to Genesis 2:7, God breathed breath into the body, and Adam became a living soul. Hence, the soul is a tangible reality (the body) with life in it, not an abstract concept like *number*. Oddly and sadly enough, most Christians believe that the soul *is* some nebulous entity, entirely spiritual and separate from the "lesser" body. As our brief consideration of Greek philosophy should make clear, this misunderstanding is nothing but the importation of pagan Greek philosophy into Christianity, permitting it to supplant the truths of Scripture.

Pythagoras' influence is incalculable. His society survived for 3 centuries throughout Greece, and most importantly, Plato was in every way influenced by him. Durant states that "at every turn he takes from him—in his scorn of democracy, his yearning for a communistic aristocracy of philosopher-rulers, his conception of virtue as harmony, his theories of the nature and destiny of the soul, his love of geometry, and his addiction to the mysticism of number" (Durant, *SC2*, p. 166).

In 510 BC, Xenophanes came to Elea and founded the Eleatic school. Living for a century, he spent 67 of those years wandering the land of Hellas (southern Italy). He held to a pseudo-monotheistic paganism, asserting that there was one god (over both people *and gods*, though) who did not resemble mortals in form or mind (contra Genesis 1:26, which asserts that we *are* in God's image and likeness). Xenophanes asserted that this god ruled everything by his mind, making him abstract and divorced from everyday human experience. Xenophanes held that this god was the universe (pantheism), and that under all the chaos and variety of forms, is an unchanging unity, which is the true reality of God. His disciple, Parmenides of Elea, picked up from his master, proceeding to the idealistic philosophy that shaped Plato and his followers (Durant, *SC2*, p. 168).

Plato is well known for his theory of forms. Simply put, the world around us is not the real thing, but merely a copy of the true. The true world is one of unchanging forms or ideas. There is a stark demarcation between the world of sensory perception that we experience and the "real" world of ideas somewhere "out there." What has this to do with anything? Very much. This pagan Greek philosophic notion was accepted by the Roman Catholic Church and, with some modification, is accepted by the majority of Christians today. While the Bible states that it is our *sins* that have separated us from our God (see Isa. 59:2), the Christianized version of Plato's erroneous philosophy is that there is an unbridgeable gap between God's sphere and humanity's sphere (what theologians call "dualism") due to the hypothesized *timelessness* of God, while mankind is supposedly confined *within* time.

Ironically, the very first chapter of the Bible (Genesis 1:1–2:3) delineates what God did *within* time over a period of 6 days, culminating in His setting apart and blessing the seventh-day Sabbath. The timelessness of the Christianized version of Plato's philosophy paves the way for disposing of the true Sabbath, the importance of which will become increasingly apparent as our study of the books of Daniel and Revelation continues. Hence, it is not surprising that Greece (Hellas) figures prominently in the 4 living creatures of Daniel 7 (see also 8, 11; Rev. 13).

Having considered secular history, let us turn to Christian sources that note the influence of Hellas on Rome:

> The ideas of Pythagoras, apparently under Orphic and earlier Indo-European influence, were similar to those that would later be taught by Plato, Philo Judaeus, the Neoplatonists, and the Gnostics. Italy therefore seems to be where Greek dualism first established itself prominently. ... Dualism, as fostered by the Greeks and their predecessors, was a key component in the ancient Mediterranean apostasy. Here we note that its Hellenic cradle, rocked by Pythagoras and his disciples, was southern Italy. (de Kock, *7 Heads and 10 Horns*, pp. 117, 118)

> Strangely enough, Rome itself under the emperors was essentially a Greek city, with Greek as its second language. The first sermons preached at Rome were in Greek; for the mass of the poorer population, among whom Christianity took root, were predominantly Greek speaking. Paul wrote to the Roman church in Greek, as did Clement, and various others that followed. The apologies to the Roman emperors were phrased in Greek. (Froom, *PFF*, vol. 1, p. 254)

In fact, de Kock notes that until the early fourth century, Greek was the language of the church (*7 Heads and 10 Horns*, p. 124). This harmonizes with the remarkably simple observation that the language of the New Testament (and the Septuagint two centuries before Christ) is Greek. One might have expected the language of the New Testament to be Latin, since Rome was the superpower in John's day, but the Greek influence on Rome affected even its language.

Before continuing on with our study of Daniel 7, one may wonder how else Greece (Hellas) relates to the message of Daniel. Philo was a Jewish professor enamored of the Greek philosophers, particularly Plato. Since Greek mythology is entirely polytheistic (with the gods exhibiting the worst traits of fallen, sinful humanity's nature), it is incredible that Philo saw the pagan philosophy of the Greeks in the Torah of Moses, and he conjectured that they had in some way drawn from Moses (de Kock, *The Use and Abuse of Prophecy*, p. 15).

Philo used the allegorical interpretation of Scripture, which permits one to see just about anything one wishes in the plainest statements of Scripture. This allegorizing method was also favored by Clement, himself well-versed in pagan literature, and his student, Origen, the most prominent of allegorical expositors. Origen passed his ideas on to his protégé, Eusebius, author of the *History of the Church from Christ to Constantine*. However conscientious Eusebius may have been in his research, his work is marred by his presuppositions in favor of the Church of which he was a member:

> This view is a reconstruction for ideological purposes. Eusebius represented the wing of the Church which had captured the main centres of power, had established a firm tradition of monarchical bishops, and had recently allied itself with the Roman state. He wanted to show that the Church he represented had always constituted the mainstream of Christianity, both in organization and faith. The truth is very different. (Johnson, *A History of Christianity*, p. 43)

He was particularly fond of Constantine, who had shown himself favorable to the Roman Catholic Church. Eusebius claimed that Constantine fulfilled Revelation 12 by casting down the dragon of paganism, the New Jerusalem of Revelation 21 was the church established by Constantine, and the millennium was already in progress under Constantine (Froom, *PFF*, vol. 1, pp. 385–387). This false line of prophetic interpretation extended for centuries in Catholic interpretation.

The next major figure in prophetic interpretation is Augustine (AD 354–430), bishop of Hippo in North Africa. His work *The City of God* remains highly influential to this day. Froom summarizes his prophetic understanding:

> The imperial Catholic Church is the stone shattering all earthly kingdoms, until it fills the entire earth. The Old Testament prophecies are claimed for the new ecclesiastical empire. He assents to the four standard empires of Daniel, but makes Antichrist come, nevertheless, at the end of the thousand years. Thus the union of church and state becomes a caricature of the millennial kingdom before its time. A new era in prophetic interpretation is thus introduced; this specious Augustinian theory of the millennium, spiritualized into a present politico-religious fact, fastens itself upon the church for about thirteen long centuries. ... Augustine expects Antichrist to reign three years and a half. (Froom, *PFF*, vol. 1, pp. 479, 486)

The assertion of a 3.5-year reign of antichrist following the millennium is similar to the teaching of futurism that antichrist will reign for 3.5 years following the second coming. The connection is not imaginary. Futurism traces back to Spanish Jesuit Francisco Ribera (1537–1591). Contrary to what some Protestants may assume, this Jesuit teaching was not entirely original with Ribera, but represented a modification of the teachings of Origen, Eusebius, and Augustine (de Kock, *The Use and Abuse of Prophecy*, p. 25). Many evangelicals today are ardently dispensationalist (a variation on Roman Catholic futurism, and popular in the fictitious *Left Behind* novels of Tim LaHaye and Jerry Jenkins) in their prophetic understanding. They would raise an eyebrow at the charge that they have adopted Roman Catholic teaching.

We have seen that pagan Greek thought has influenced modern culture nearly universally, and with respect to theology, it has brought in a false concept of dualism (the supposed timelessness of God forming an insurmountable barrier between Himself and mankind), paved the way for doing away with the Sabbath, and led to false interpretations of prophecy.

The vision transitions in verse 7 to the fourth living creature, which receives Daniel's greatest attention. This creature is not described in terms of other known creatures as were the first 3 kingdoms, for it is said to be different from those. Our study of Daniel 2 revealed the fourth kingdom to be Rome, which began as a metal (iron) kingdom like its predecessors, but in later years became a blend of iron and clay (i.e., a union of church and state). Here in Daniel 7, it has 10 horns, which are explained as 10 kings in verse 24.

The fact that it is described as so totally vicious is significant. In verse 5, Medo-Persia is commanded to "devour much flesh," and Isaiah 13:18 describes the Medes as dashing Babylon's young men to pieces, having no compassion on infants or children. Rome goes further, "devouring and breaking in pieces, and with its feet it was trampling the remnant." With this description, God emphasizes the tyranny that arises from the union of church and state. Ironically, Jesus' stone kingdom will "break in pieces" the preceding kingdoms, including Rome (see Dan. 2:44). While the fourth living creature is ultimately consigned to the fire and destroyed, the stone kingdom stands forever.

Daniel begins to puzzle over this beast, pondering the 10 horns, when he notices another little horn coming up among the 10. The 10 horns correspond to "the Germanic peoples who took over the Western Roman Empire, and later became European nations that still exist" (de Kock, *Christ and Antichrist*, p. 250). These 10 Germanic people groups are typically enumerated as Ostrogoths, Visigoths, Franks, Vandals, Suevi, Alamanni, Saxons, Heruli, Lombards and Burgundians. Just as Medo-Persia eliminated 3 contenders (the 3 ribs in the bear's mouth) on its rise to supremacy, so the little horn uprooted 3 of these 10 kingdoms during its ascendancy.

It is evident that these 3 horns are *not* 3 kingdoms that Rome conquered during the days of its Republic or the subsequent Caesars, for the little horn arises *after* the 10 horns, which are themselves the result of the fragmentation of the Western Roman Empire into 10 kingdoms. Hence, the task is to figure out what power is represented by the little horn and the 3 horns it uproots.

The 10 Horns[56]

Our study of Daniel 2 showed that pagan Rome was succeeded by a blend of church and state, which history plainly records as papal Rome. However, this succession was not immediate. Rather, the Western Roman Empire fragmented into 10 Germanic kingdoms over the course of roughly a century. Until AD 376, various Germanic peoples immigrated to the Western Roman Empire or were in fact brought in *by* the Romans. Following the Huns' invasion of the Visigoths (approximately AD 376), the Huns marched toward the Danube, marking the border of the Roman Empire. The displaced Visigoths pled with Rome for assistance, which was granted. Some of the Visigoths paid for the land granted them. In other cases, wealthy Roman senators (from whom the majority of popes came) had their own land confiscated to help the Visigoths. Hence, tensions grew between Rome and the incoming Germanic people.

From this time onward, incoming Germanic peoples were no longer well-behaved immigrants. There began to flow in a mass of refugees whose desperation did not always equate with good behavior. The key date to mark the beginning of the dismantling of the Western Roman Empire is August 9, 378. On that date, the Ostrogoths dealt a crushing blow to the Roman army at Adrianople. Fully two-thirds of the Roman army forces were killed. The fragmentation of the empire was complete in AD 476, when the Western emperor was removed and a German was made king over Italy.

Moving back a bit in history, Constantine was made emperor of the Roman Empire in AD 306. He saw the benefit to be accrued by procuring

---

[56] The historical material in this section draws freely from de Kock, *Christ and Antichrist*, ch. 20, "The Ten Horns," pp. 250–268.

the favor of the Roman Church, and thus combined the religion of Scripture with paganism, particularly Mithraism and its attendant sun worship. He passed the first national Sunday law on March 7, 321, became sole ruler of West and East in 324, and dedicated Constantinople May 11, 330.

The Christianity of the Visigoths and other Gothic peoples pre-dated the Mithraic corruption that Constantine embraced and encouraged. The Visigoths invaded Cappadocia around AD 250, and while enslaved, the Cappadocians shared their faith with them. The result was the Germanic Church. The Visigoths are usually characterized as Arian (those who hold to the heresy that Christ is a created being), but as de Kock points out, the major problem with this is that Arius began actively promoting his deviant belief 50 years *after* the introduction of Cappadocian Christianity. In other words, Germanic Christianity was already well-established *prior* to Arius, and hence, grounds are lacking for charging them with any such heresy.

While the charge of Arianism is at best doubtful, it *is* highly likely that they were Sabbath-keepers (see Hardinge, *Jesus is My Judge*, pp. 145, 146).[57] As will be shown later in this commentary, Sunday is the very mark of Roman Catholic authority, so any group holding to the seventh-day Sabbath necessarily finds itself at odds with the authority of the Roman Catholic Church. While all 10 horns were Germanic and hence Sabbath-keepers, only those who would not concede to Rome's demand for Sunday worship were to be wiped out. The others remained.

Before examining the horns to find out which bowed the knee to Rome and which chose to remain faithful to Scripture, it is worth noting that the fourth living creature of Daniel 7 deals with Western, not Eastern, Rome. The Roman Empire did encompass both, but it was the Western Empire that was fragmented into 10 pieces. The Eastern Empire succumbed much later to Moslem aggression, its capital, Constantinople, finally falling May 29, 1453. The history of the Eastern Empire is dealt with under the fifth and sixth trumpets of Revelation 9.

---

[57] See also Wilkinson, *Truth Triumphant*, pp. 143, 144, quoting Apollinaris, *Epistolae*, lib. 1, epistola 2, found in Migne, *Patrologia Latina*, vol. 58, p. 448.

The Little Horn[58]

We now consider the little horn, which we have already asserted to be papal Rome. A popular belief among some segments of Christianity is that the little horn is in fact the Greco-Macedonian king of Syria, Antiochus IV Epiphanes. While many Protestants today believe this, they do not realize that its popularity owes largely to the work of Luis de Alcazar (1554–1613), a Jesuit during the Counter Reformation, the period in which the Roman Catholic Church attempted to point the accusing finger away from the papacy as antichrist.

Alcazar is responsible for promulgating the prophetic school of preterism, though he did not originate it. Three centuries prior, Rabbi Hayyim Galipapa (died AD 1380) promulgated the idea (Froom, *PFF*, vol. 2, p. 214). Toward the end of the first century AD, Josephus mentioned this theory as well (Josephus, *Complete Works of Flavius Josephus: Antiquities of the Jews*, bk. 10, ch. 11).

There are some serious flaws with the Antiochus Epiphanes identification. For one thing, he reigned approximately two centuries before Christ, while Christ in Matthew 24 speaks of the abomination of desolation as yet *future*, which was fulfilled when Rome destroyed Jerusalem in AD 70. Further, antichrist was to reign for 3.5 times, or 1,260 days, while Antiochus reigned from Chislev 15, 168 BC until Chislev 25, 165 BC, some six months short of the prophetic requirement. In Revelation 12:14, John refers to the 3.5 times during which the woman was to be protected in the wilderness. Since he wrote at the close of the first century AD, and the very first verse states that the material in Revelation deals with the *future*, Antiochus is again ruled out.

Another prophetic approach very popular among evangelicals and dispensationalists is futurism, also Roman Catholic in origin. Anglican priest Cardinal Henry E. Manning converted to Catholicism and became head of the Roman Catholic Church in England. In lectures given in 1861

---

[58] The historical material in this section draws freely from de Kock, *Christ and Antichrist*, ch. 21, "Another Horn," pp. 269–286.

entitled "The Present Crisis of the Holy See, tested by Prophecy," Manning states that one of its basic tenets—that antichrist would be a Jew—appeared in ancient Catholic writers such as "St. Irenaeus, St. Jerome, and" many others, after which he adds "Ribera repeats the same opinion, and adds that Aretas, St. Bede, Haymo, St. Anselm, and Rupert affirm that for this reason the tribe of Dan is not numbered among those that are sealed in the Apocalypse" (Strachey, *Eminent Victorians*, pp. 114, 115).

The Ribera to whom Manning refers is Spanish Jesuit Francisco Ribera (1537–1591), who, like Alcazar, aimed to deflect attention away from the papacy during the Counter Reformation. He denied the Protestant view that the antichrist was the Catholic Church, asserting that the antichrist was in fact one man who would rebuild the temple in Jerusalem, abolish Christianity, and be received by literal Jews, all in a period of 1,260 literal days.

A huge problem with futurism is the introduction of a gap into the 70 weeks of Daniel 9:24–27, with the initial 69 weeks already fulfilled, and the final week detached and relegated to the end of earth's history. Our analysis of Daniel 9 will show that nothing in the text of Daniel warrants such a division of the prophecy.

Futurism, upon which Protestant dispensationalism is based, has as its specific aim deflecting the accusing finger of biblical prophecy away from the papacy as antichrist. How did Protestants come to accept Roman Catholic teaching? It began with Anglican Samuel R. Maitland (1792–1866), who in 1826 published *An Enquiry into the Grounds on Which the Prophetic Period of Daniel and St. John Has Been Supposed to Consist of 1260 Years*. It opposed the year-day principle so long understood by prophetic expositors, which of course does away with 1,260 years of papal rule during the Dark Ages, stained with the blood of millions of martyrs.

While Donnellan lecturer at Trinity College in Dublin, Ireland, Maitland's student James H. Todd (1805–1869) lectured against the Protestant Reformers' Historical School view that the pope was antichrist. John Henry Newman (1801–1890) took up Maitland's and Todd's views.

He wrote "The Protestant Idea of Antichrist" 5 years before joining the Roman Catholic Church. Newman is quoted as follows:

> The question really lies, be it observed, between those two alternatives, either the Church of Rome is the house of God or the house of Satan; there is no middle ground between them. The question is, whether, as he [Todd] maintains, its fulfilment is yet to come, or whether it has taken place in the person of the Bishop of Rome, as Protestants have very commonly supposed. (John Henry Newman, quoted in Froom, *PFF*, vol. 3, p. 667)

Newman asserts incorrectly that the Historical School originated from "three heretical bodies" between the 11th and 16th centuries (the Albigenses, Waldenses, and the Spiritual Franciscans, the last being a Roman Catholic group), and was then propagated by the Hussites, Lutherans, Calvinists, and English Reformers (Froom, *PFF*, vol. 3, pp. 667, 668). The truth is that the Historical School goes back to the likes of Hippolytus (170–235) and Tertullian (circa 155–240).

The 3 Uprooted Horns[59]

We now consider what history has to say about 3 of the 10 Germanic kingdoms that proved a threat to the papacy. Note that in all 3 cases, the perceived threat to the papacy was met with *military* strength, provided by the emperor in Constantinople (i.e., the emperor of the *Eastern* Roman Empire).

First, we consider the Heruli. Odoacer was given charge of a group of Heruli in the armies under the *magister militum* ("master of soldiers") Orestes. In this capacity, he assisted Orestes in deposing (Western) Emperor Julius Nepos in AD 475. In return, the soldiers desired the third

---

[59] This section's historical material draws freely from de Kock, *Christ and Antichrist*, ch. 22, "Uprooting Three," pp. 287–308.

part of Italy, which Orestes denied. The result was that Odoacer was made king (his capital was not in Rome, but rather Ravenna in northeastern Italy, which served as the capital of the Western Roman Empire from 402 to 476), and Orestes was murdered August 28, 476. In terms of rule by western emperors, the Western Empire came to an end.

Odoacer had first entered Italy among Heruls. The papacy frowned upon Odoacer, charging him with Arianism. They liked him less when he sent Basilius to the papal election convened to replace the recently deceased Simplicius (died 483). Basilius demanded that the election, begun without him present, begin anew. Odoacer involved himself in the politics of the Illyrian provinces, leading Eastern Emperor Zeno, a "friend of the pope" (Smith, *Daniel and the Revelation*, p. 132), to determine to do away with him. Zeno accomplished his aim through Theodoric, an Ostrogoth, by promising him land for his fellow Ostrogoths. In 493, Theodoric had Odoacer murdered.

Hence, the first of the 3 horns (the Heruli in Italy) was uprooted with the help of an Eastern Emperor (Zeno) who was friendly to the papacy. Their story does not end in 493, though, for the Heruli outside Italy lived another 15 years before being decimated by King Tato and the Lombards in 508. This latter date proves important in dealing with the relation of the 1,260 and 1,290 days of Daniel 12:11.

The next horn to be considered is the kingdom of the Vandals. We take up their history as Boniface, Rome's supreme commander in Africa, is seeking more power in the west by warring against the western emperor, as well as control of Africa in a campaign against the Goths. Boniface settled upon procuring help from Gunderic, king of the Vandals with a promise of land for the Vandals. Gunderic died in 428, and his half-brother Genseric was elevated to king of the Vandals. He moved his people, as well as some Alans, to North Africa using ships provided by Boniface. To Boniface's dismay, Genseric began taking North Africa for himself. He set up his kingdom in Carthage, making Germanic Christianity the state religion.

Genseric is known as incredibly fierce, yet a few remarks from history are in order. While the Vandals are often characterized as barbarians, the truth is that they held the North African Catholics in contempt for their immoral lifestyle. Hodgkin describes it thus:

> Houses of ill-fame swarming in each street and square, and haunted by men of the highest rank, and what should have been venerable age; chastity outside the ranks of the clergy a thing unknown and unbelieved, and by no means universal within that enclosure; the darker vices, the sins of Sodom and Gomorrah, practised, avowed, gloried in ... Into this City of Sin marched the Vandal army, one might almost say, when one reads the history of their doings, the army of the Puritans. With all their cruelty and all their greed they kept themselves unspotted by the licentiousness of the splendid city. They banished the men who were earning their living by ministering to the vilest lusts. They rooted out prostitution with a wise yet not a cruel hand. In short, Carthage, under the rule of the Vandals, was a city transformed, barbarous but moral. (Hodgkin, *Italy and Her Invaders*, vol. 1, pt. 2, pp. 931, 932)

For all his violent warfare, Genseric could not be said to be viler than his Catholic opponents. Genseric could not be conquered, so he died peacefully in Carthage January 25, 477 at age 88.

Moving ahead a few decades, we meet up with Justinian, who succeeded to the throne of the Eastern Roman Empire in Constantinople in AD 527. He not only wanted to re-unite the Roman Empire, but also establish Catholicism throughout the Empire. Note what Froom says:

> In the fullest and most unequivocal form Justinian recognized, maintained, and established by imperial authority the bishop of Rome as the chief of the whole ecclesiastical body of the empire. ... And for the purpose of preserving the unity of the apostolic see, Justinian states that he has exerted himself to unite all the priests of the Eastern church and subject them to the bishop of Rome, and that he does not permit anything pertaining to the

state of the church to be unknown 'to Your Holiness,' 'because you are the Head of all the holy churches.' He was, of course, already the actual head in the West. Justinian concludes by declaring the doctrine held by the bishop of Rome to be the standard of the faith and the source of unity to all the Christian world. (Froom, *PFF*, vol. 1, pp. 511, 512)

While the pope was to be regarded as head of all the churches, the emperor held himself higher still. This decree of Justinian was established in early AD 533. In this same year, he sent his general Belisarius to fight the Vandals in North Africa. By March of the following year, Belisarius had conquered the Vandal kingdom. While there was rebellion for 10 more years on the part of the conquered Vandals who did not welcome this religious interference, the fact is that in AD 534, the Vandals no longer were an independent people. To the papacy's satisfaction, the extinction of the Vandals coincided with the end of Germanic Christianity in North Africa.

We now consider the last of the 3 uprooted horns, the Ostrogoths. The Byzantines began a double push against them in AD 535, with an army coming by land via Dalmatia and another army under Belisarius coming by sea. The latter captured Sicily, then moved on to Italy, capturing Naples and Rome.

Belisarius captured Rome on December 10, 536, but Ostrogoth forces gathered in Ravenna to face Belisarius at Rome, with the result being that he and his army were put under siege in Rome from March 2, 537 to March 12, 538. This was indeed dire, for Belisarius's forces were a mere 5,000, while the Ostrogoths were 150,000. Belisarius managed to send a courier to Constantinople with request for reinforcements. The requested reinforcements were dispatched immediately. At the same time, the Ostrogoths had cut the aqueducts to Rome, which had the unfortunate effect of creating malarial conditions among their own ranks. Together, these conditions led to defeat for the Ostrogoths.

On March 12, 538, Ostrogothic king and general Vitiges withdrew the Roman siege, and the tide was turned. The Ostrogothic stronghold of Ravenna surrendered in AD 539, and Vitiges abandoned the Germanic faith in favor of Catholicism. "The emperor [Justinian] received with honourable courtesy both Vitiges and his more noble consort; and as the king of the Goths conformed to the Athanasian faith, he obtained, with a rich inheritance of land in Asia, the rank of senator and patrician" (Gibbon, *The History of the Decline and Fall of the Roman Empire*, vol. 4, p. 271). This "conversion" carried with it the understandable result that Germanic Christianity was squelched, and all of its churches were turned over to the Catholic Church.

Some further Ostrogoth events followed, notably the resistance begun in AD 541 under Totila. He determined to raze Rome, but Belisarius retook Rome in AD 547, and in 552, Narses, a general from Constantinople, defeated Totila and brought to an end all remaining resistance. That said, "great conflicts do not always end abruptly, yet their outcome is often determined by a crucial battle" (de Kock, *Christ and Antichrist*, p. 304). For the Ostrogoths, that crucial moment occurred when Vitiges withdrew the siege of Rome in AD 538, marking both the uprooting of the third and final horn and the point at which Germanic resistance to the papacy was assuredly doomed. This made it possible for Justinian's decree of 5 years previous to go into effect, namely, the pope could now assume to be "head of all the holy churches."

Historical Conclusions from Daniel 7:7–8[60]

As we conclude this survey of European history, it is well to review a few key points. To begin, the fourth living creature is not to be confounded with Rome solely. The body of the beast represents Rome, going back to its early, pre-papal days. In the animal kingdom, horns form on an animal as it ages, so as Rome developed over the centuries, eventually becoming imperial Rome under the Caesars, the 10 horns formed once the Western Empire began to dissolve. These 10 horns are not Rome at all, but rather 10 Germanic kingdoms of Western Europe. Over the centuries, these kingdoms

---

[60] The material in this section draws freely from de Kock, *7 Heads and 10 Horns*, pp. 89–99.

interacted with the little horn (Rome in its later papal phase). This answers to the lower legs of iron and feet of iron mixed with clay in Daniel 2.

While many learned as school children that the Roman Empire broke up in AD 476, it is more correct to say that the process of dissolution *began* at that date for the *Western* Roman Empire. Further, AD 476 should not be looked at as the end of pagan Rome, leading to papal Rome. In a sense, pagan Rome has *never* ended, for we will soon review numerous evidences that papal Rome is an incredible conglomeration of paganism with Christianity. Hence, of more interest than the end of pagan Rome is the end of the *Greco-Roman* empire. This can be best understood as occurring in the days of Constantine, the man who established the syncretism of pagan Mithraism and Christianity as the official religion of the empire. In the interest of assigning a date, one might choose AD 313, the year of Constantine's Edict of Milan, or AD 330, the year in which the seat of the empire moved east to Constantinople. As argued in remarks on Daniel 11, the latter date seems more appropriate.

It is to be noted that every emperor to follow Constantine, except Julian the Apostate (who reigned as sole Augustus from November 6, 355 to June 26, 363), was a professing Christian. Further, Christendom refers not to Christianity as a whole, as popular usage might suggest, but to areas of the world where Christianity is the *official, state-imposed* religion. Hence, we need not apply the designation "Christendom" to a time period following the breakup of Western Rome in AD 476, or to the removal of the last of the 3 horns in AD 538. Rather, we can quite correctly apply the term to the days of Constantine's rule onward, encompassing the second Roman Empire and the subsequent states of Europe.

One must also be careful not to confuse Christendom with the Holy Roman Empire. While Christendom refers to Constantine's reign to our time, the Holy Roman Empire refers to the relationship of church and state beginning on Christmas, AD 800 with the crowning of Charlemagne as Augustus Caesar.

Finally, it is well to remember that the fourth living creature of Daniel 7:7–8 does not mark an abrupt end to the preceding third living creature. As Daniel 7:12 makes clear, the living creatures continued for a time, even after their dominion was removed; that is, they lived on via the absorption of their principles by the fourth living creature, which is Rome and the various successor European states. What principles might these be? Babylon certainly contributed polytheism and astrology, Medo-Persia contributed elements of the worship of Mithras, and Greece contributed its philosophy of dualism.

A final element that they all contributed was sun worship. This is evident in Babylon, home of Etemenanki, a ziggurat dedicated to Marduk, whose name seems to come from *amar-Utu*, meaning "bull calf of the sun god."[61] Nebuchadnezzar "determined to raise the head of Etemenanki to rival the heavens" (i.e., to rebuild Etemenanki, which is generally supposed to be the biblical tower of Babel).[62] As mentioned earlier, Medo-Persia contributed the worship of Mithras. Note the connection with sun worship, as well as its spread to Rome:

> In Indo-Iranian tradition, Mithra is associated with (the divinity of) the sun … The name Mithra was adopted by the Greeks and Romans as *Mithras*, chief figure in the mystery religion of Mithraism. At first identified with the Sun-god Helios by the Greeks, the syncretic Mithra-Helios was transformed into the figure Mithras during the 2nd century BC, probably at Pergamon. This new cult was taken to Rome around the 1st century BC and was dispersed throughout the Roman Empire. ("Mitra", Wikipedia, https://1ref.us/yq [accessed January 22, 2020])

The text of verse 8 says that the little horn, the papacy, has "eyes like the eyes of man." It is helpful to compare this with the first reference to eyes in Scripture, Genesis 3:5–7. Here, Eve's eye perceives that the fruit of

---

[61] "Etemenanki," Wikipedia, https://1ref.us/yr (accessed January 22, 2020); "Marduk," Wikipedia, https://1ref.us/ys (accessed January 22, 2020).

[62] *Eerdmans Dictionary of the Bible*, articles "Babylon," p. 139, "Marduk," p. 856, "Nebuchadnezzar," p. 953.

the tree of the knowledge of good and evil is good for imparting a [seemingly] desirable wisdom. Afterward, Adam and Eve's eyes are opened, and they know their condition without God.

Jesus observes that "the eye is the lamp of the body. Accordingly, if your eye is single-minded, your entire body will be enlightened; but if your eye is evil, your entire body will be dark. So if the light in you is darkness, that darkness is indeed great" (Matt. 6:22, 23). In context, Jesus contrasts a single-minded focus on serving God with one that seeks the world's gain.

Perhaps most relevant to understanding the "eyes of man" is Psalm 19:7–8, which states that "the Torah of *Yahweh* is perfect, leading a person to repent … the commandment of *Yahweh* is pure, enlightening the eyes." Hence, the little horn's eyes show it to be unrepentant, willfully disregarding God's law. Indeed, Daniel 7:25 states that the little horn thinks to change God's appointed times and law. God wants His people to conform to His law, counseling them in Revelation 3:18 to procure eye salve that they might see their true condition.

The little horn is also said to speak "grandiose things." This is explained by the complementary statement in Revelation 13:6, where the beast speaks blasphemy against God, His name, His tent (the heavenly sanctuary), and those who pitch their tents in heaven (those who dwell spiritually in heavenly places while still alive on earth). The little horn power, the papacy, is utterly at war with God and those who stand for the truth. It is Satan's agent *par excellence*.

The little horn comes up among the existing 10 horns and, as we will see in our study of Daniel 8, institutes its own false worship system, diametrically opposed to Jesus' system of worship established in His heavenly tent, the sanctuary.

Investigation: The End-time Judgment

The focus now shifts to the opening of the final judgment, described poetically in a chiasm, the indentation in the translation indicating matching points: The thrones of judgment are placed, and the books are opened;

the Ancient of Days sits, the judgment itself is seated; the Ancient of Days is spotlessly white, as are the countless beings who are to stand before Him and serve Him (see Rev. 15:6); the chiastic center is God's fiery throne of judgment and the fiery river emanating from it. Only those who are themselves spotlessly pure can dwell in the presence of the devouring fire (see Isa. 33:14–17), which is God Himself (see Deut. 4:24; Heb. 12:29). The stories of Nebuchadnezzar and Belshazzar at the chiastic center of Daniel 2–7 highlighted God's judgment of our character. Thus, Daniel 7:9–10 points to the final judgment in relation to God's glory—His character.

The thrones and the act of sitting point unmistakably to the commencement of God's work of end-time judgment. Perhaps no passage of Scripture is clearer on this point than Psalm 9 is:

> Ps. 9:4, 7, 8, 16, 19: For You execute my judgment, even my vindication; You sit upon the throne as the righteous Judge. ... *Yahweh* will sit unto the age; He has established His throne for judgment. ... He will judge the world with righteousness; He will vindicate the peoples with uprightness. ... *Yahweh* is known by the judgment He executes. ... Arise, *Yahweh*, let not man prevail; let the nations be judged before You.

One might well ask whether the beings standing before God in verse 10 are people whose life records have come up in judgment, or whether they are God's angels. Those who surround God's throne, numbering myriads of myriads, are angels (see Rev. 5:11). Hence, those in Daniel 7:10 are angels.

Daniel's attention is again brought back to the fourth living creature and the little horn. How fitting that the fourth living creature is to be destroyed by burning fire, since God describes Himself as a consuming fire for the enemies of His people (see Deut. 9:3), and only those who are righteous can dwell with the everlasting burnings (see Isa. 33:14, 15).

However, Daniel is also shown that while there is to be a succession of kingdoms, they are not each destroyed at the time of their removal.

Rather, they live on "until [the] appointed time and [for a fixed length of] time." Recall that the sea beast of Revelation 13:2 (papal Rome) is described as a composite of the 3 preceding kingdoms: the Grecian leopard, Medo-Persian bear, and Babylonian lion. As noted earlier in this chapter, the papacy absorbed Babylonian polytheism and astrology, Persian Mithraic worship, and Greek philosophy (particularly dualism). It is in this manner that the living creatures live on.

When is the appointed time of their demise? We learn the answer by matching Daniel 7:11–12 up with the chiastic counterpart in Daniel 2:34–35: The iron and clay (the fourth living creature) and the previous metals (the 3 previous living creatures) are "broken in pieces as 1 [unit]" (i.e., simultaneously, when the stone strikes the feet of iron and clay). Hence, the papal beast and prior living creatures are destroyed simultaneously at Christ's second coming (see Rev. 19:20), marking the close of the pre-advent judgment.

The Son of Man Receives His Kingdom

Beginning with verse 13, Daniel's attention is once more brought back to the commencement of the end-time investigative judgment. Having just witnessed the overthrow of the final persecutor of God's people, Daniel sees the Son of man come to the Ancient of Days, who sat down at the judgment in verses 9 and 10. Hence, the Son of man (Jesus) is understood to participate in the end-time judgment which culminates in the overthrow of this persecutor. Jesus explains, "the Father judges no one, but has delegated all judgment to the Son," granting "authority to him to conduct judgment, because he is the Son of man" (John 5:22, 27).

The fact that he "reached unto" the Ancient of Days further signifies judgment, for this same word was used to describe Nebuchadnezzar's pride "reaching" unto heaven (see Dan. 4:22, 24, 28), which brought upon him heaven's judgment. Again, in Daniel 6:24, the bodies of the wicked men and their families did not "reach" the bottom of the lions' den before the lions destroyed them. Likewise, in Daniel 7:22, Daniel learns of a time being "reached" when the holy people possess God's kingdom, coincident with their vindication at the close of the pre-advent judgment.

According to verse 14, the judgment at which Jesus arrives results in His reception of an everlasting kingdom, hearkening back to Daniel 2:44, in which the stone hits the metal statue upon the feet, demolishing the preceding kingdoms, filling the earth with God's glory, and standing forever. Jesus' kingdom will "not pass away," built as it is on His law that does not pass away. It is ironic that the little horn attempts to establish its government by military coercion via the 10 horns, while the strength of God's kingdom rests on an infinitely stronger foundation—willing submission to the unalterable 10 Commandments.

The language of verse 14 is very similar to that of Daniel 4:36, referring to the restoration of the kingdom to Nebuchadnezzar after his heart was humbled. Of course, the kingdom given to Jesus is composed of such humble people (see Matt. 5:3, 5), He Himself being the supreme example of humility (see Phil. 2:5–11).

Daniel's Dream Interpreted

At this point, the record of Daniel's vision concludes. In describing his perplexity in verse 15, he affirms one of the great Bible truths, namely, that his being is comprised of a spirit within his body. This is precisely the truth that is taught for the first time in Genesis 2:7: "Then *Yahweh* God fashioned the man with dust of the ground, and breathed into his nostrils the breath of life, so that the man became a living being." Job equates the "breath of life" with the "spirit of God": "All the while my breath is in me, and the spirit of God is in my nose" (Job 27:3).

While many people, even a great many Christians, hold to the ancient pagan belief that each person is composed of a body, a spirit, and a soul, the Bible plainly teaches that the soul, which is literally translated as "living being", is not separate from the body and spirit, but rather is the *composite* of body and spirit. While we are alive, it is God's breath, His spirit, that keeps us alive. When we die, "then shall the dust return to the ground as it was, and the spirit will return to God who gave it" (Eccles. 12:7)—the reversal of humanity's creation in Genesis 2:7.

Many Christians believe that at death, fellow believers go immediately into God's presence as a bodiless soul praising His name. To such, it may come as a surprise to learn that Scripture teaches that "the dead do not praise Yah[weh], neither those who descend into silence [the grave]" and "his spirit departs, he returns to the ground; in that day his thoughts perish" (Ps. 115:17; 146:4). To be sure, there is coming a day when the righteous dead *will* be with God, praising Him all the day long as one hymn says, but this occurs at Jesus' second coming, when all believers meet Him *at the same time*: "For the Lord Himself, with a shout, with the Archangel's voice, with the trumpet of God, will descend from heaven, and the dead in Christ will rise first, then we who have been left alive will be snatched up along with them in the clouds to meet the Lord in the air; thus shall we always be with the Lord" (1 Thess. 4:16, 17).

It may seem strange that a teaching like this appears in the middle of a chapter detailing much of European history and the final judgment. However, this is very fitting, for it will be recalled that the third and fourth living creatures represent Hellas and the Greco-Roman conglomeration, respectively. Among other things, ancient Hellas foisted upon the world the false, philosophical notion of dualism, an aspect of which is the sharp distinction between the material and the spiritual. It is only fitting that in this chapter, detailing the horrible work of these living creatures, that the chief error contributed by Hellas is flatly contradicted and corrected.

Bothered as he is, Daniel approaches one of the angels and solicits understanding. The angel confirms that the 4 living creatures are indeed kingdoms, and though they have their day to wreak havoc, God's people in the end receive Jesus' kingdom. According to verse 18, that kingdom will stand unchallenged for eternity.

Daniel presses for more information, specifically concerning the fourth living creature. He desires to know the truth of the 10 horns and the little horn that comes up later. Again, the angel provides the requested interpretation. He confirms that the fourth living creature is the fourth kingdom, which our study has revealed is the Greco-Roman Empire. Comparison with Daniel 2:40 shows that it not only breaks in pieces with iron (Roman) teeth, but it uses its bronze (Grecian) nails (false philosophies, including dualism) to stomp the end-time remnant which holds to solidly biblical beliefs. In other words, the most dangerous weapon wielded against the end-time faithful remnant is *not* physical force, but *wrong thinking*.

Rome will bring down or humble (verse 24) 3 kings on its rise to power, much like Nebuchadnezzar brought down many prior to his own humbling (see Dan. 5:19). Since it is for God to humble those who need humbling, Rome's assumption of God's prerogative hints at its demise.

The iron teeth and bronze nails of the Greco-Roman beast are reminiscent of the band of iron and bronze when Nebuchadnezzar was humbled (see Dan. 4:23), ultimately tracing back to Leviticus 26:19, where God's humbling judgments are described in terms of His power over nature: Iron heavens (no rain) and bronze earth (no crops). However, God humbles by withholding blessings that otherwise would make us fruitful, while the Greco-Roman beast, particularly in its papal phase, humbles by destructive *force*.

The religious nature of the little horn is confirmed by the "grandiose words" it speaks, which the angel clarifies are words against the Most High, God Himself. As will become clear in Daniel 8, the little horn goes so far as to claim to be God Himself (cf. 2 Thess. 2:4), following in the steps of the archenemy, Lucifer, who sought God's place, but whose end is utter annihilation (see Isa. 14:13, 14; Ezek. 28:17–19).

Daniel watches as the conflict rages between the little horn and the holy people. While the little horn's use of force seems to give it the advantage, verses 21 and 22 reveal that the end-time judgment is God's means of delivering His faithful remnant. It occurs at an appointed time, meaning that no matter how the little horn may fight, deliverance is certain. The little horn will be overthrown, and the holy people will possess the kingdom that can never be overturned.

The angel explains that this fourth living creature is different from the prior kingdoms. It is a composite of the prior 3 kingdoms; it continues for a vastly longer stretch of time than the others did (until the end of the world); and it morphs into a distinctly religious power (the little horn) that co-exists with various civil powers (the 10 horns).

The angel draws attention to the 10 horns, specifying that they are 10 kings, which we have shown represent the 10 Germanic fragments into which the Western Roman Empire split. The angel also notes that they rise up. It is evident that they arise in their *own* strength *against* God, for they certainly don't stand in the end-time judgment, but are destroyed when Christ sets up His kingdom.

The little horn also arises in its own strength in opposition to God, not being able to stand in the end-time judgment. We have detailed how, by cooperating with imperial power, the little horn brings down 3 of the 10 horns that hold to their Germanic Church roots, refusing to submit to the papacy. The apostate religious nature of this little horn is brought out with the charge that "he will speak things against the Most High," meaning that he will assume prerogatives that belong to God alone. In the case of the papacy, it is straightforward to show that it claims the ability to forgive people's sins, which belongs to God alone, and more than this, the popes claim to be God Himself! Along with warring against God's people, and claiming the ability to change God's law, the apostate nature of Roman Catholicism is evident.

As to forgiving people's sins, the well-known practice of going to a confessional, enumerating sins since one's last visit, and seeking absolution from one addressed as "Father" is plainly contrary to Scripture. In Matthew 23:9, Jesus forbids us to address fellow human beings as "Father" (in the sense of standing in the place of God, not as a male parent), and it is blasphemy to claim the divine prerogative of forgiving another's sins (see Luke 5:21) with the words *ego te absolvo a peccatis tuis in nomine Patris, et Filii, et Spiritus Sancti* ("I absolve you from your sins in the name of the Father, and of the Son, and of the Holy Spirit").[63] Notice what the current catechism of the Catholic Church teaches, though:

---

[63] "Absolution," Wikipedia, https://1ref.us/yt (accessed January 22, 2020).

> Since Christ entrusted to his apostles the ministry of reconciliation, bishops who are their successors, and priests, the bishops' collaborators, continue to exercise this ministry. Indeed, bishops and priests, by virtue of the sacrament of Holy Orders, have the power to forgive all sins "in the name of the Father, and of the Son, and of the Holy Spirit." (*Catechism of the Catholic Church*, 2nd ed., 1461)

> "The whole power of the sacrament of Penance consists in restoring us to God's grace and joining us with him in an intimate friendship." [*Roman Catechism*, II, V, 18] Reconciliation with God is thus the purpose and effect of this sacrament. ... Indeed the sacrament of Reconciliation with God brings about a true "spiritual resurrection," restoration of the dignity and blessings of the life of the children of God. (*Catechism of the Catholic Church*, 2nd ed., 1468)

As to claiming to be God, evidences abound. As just mentioned, claiming the title of "Father" is in itself such a claim. Bolder and more direct is the claim that the pope is "as it were God on earth, sole sovereign of the faithful of Christ, chief king of kings, having plenitude of power, to whom has been entrusted by the omnipotent God direction not only of the earthly but also of the heavenly kingdom" (Ferraris, *Prompta Bibliotheca*, Vol. 6, article "Papa," p. 18). Again, Pope Leo XIII asserted, "We hold upon this earth the place of God Almighty" (Pope Leo XIII, *The Great Encyclical Letters of Pope Leo XIII*, "The Reunion of Christendom," p. 304). More recently, the late Pope John Paul II declared:

> Have no fear when people call me the "Vicar of Christ," when they say to me "Holy Father," or "Your Holiness," or use titles similar to these, which seem even inimical to the Gospel. Christ himself declared: "Call no one on earth your father; you have but one Father in heaven. Do not be called 'Master'; you have but one master, the Messiah." (Mt 23:9–10). These expressions,

nevertheless, have evolved out of a long tradition, becoming part of common usage. One must not be afraid of these words either. (Pope John Paul II, *Crossing the Threshold of Hope*, p. 6)

As to wearing out the holy people of the Most High, history provides ample testimony:

> It has been calculated that the popes of Rome have, directly or indirectly, slain on account of their faith, fifty millions of martyrs; fifty millions of men and women who refused to be parties to Romish idolatries, who held to the Bible as the word of God. (Guinness, *The Approaching End of the Age*, p. 212)

> What a long roll of bloody persecutions is her record! The extirpation of the Albigenses, the massacre of the Waldenses, the martyrdoms of the Lollards, the slaughter of the Bohemians, the burning of Huss, Jerome, Savonarola, Frith, Tyndale, Ridley, Hooper, Cranmer, Latimer, and thousands of others as godly and faithful as they, have been her acts; the demoniacal cruelties of the Inquisition were invented by her mind, and inflicted by her hand—that Inquisition which was for centuries the mighty instrument of her warfare against devoted men and women whose crime was only this, that they *"kept the commandments of God and the faith of Jesus."* The ferocious cruelties of the Duke of Alva in the Netherlands, the bloody martyrdoms of Queen Mary's reign; the extinction by fire and sword of the Reformation in Spain and Italy, in Portugal and Poland; the Massacre of St. Bartholomew; the long and cruel persecutions of the Huguenots, and all the infamies and barbarities of the Edict of Nantes, which flung its refugees on every shore of Europe, were perpetrated by Papal Rome.
>
> Her victims have been innumerable. In Spain alone Llorente reckons as the sufferers of the Inquisition, 31,912 burnt alive,

and 291,450 so-called penitents forced into submission "by water, weights, fire, pulleys, and screws," and "all the apparatus by which the sinews could be strained without cracking, and the bones bruised without breaking, and the body racked exquisitely without giving up the ghost." A million perished in the massacre of the Albigenses. In the thirty years which followed the first institution of the Jesuits nine hundred thousand faithful Christians were slain. Thirty-six thousand were dispatched by the common executioner in the Netherlands, at the direction of the Duke of Alva, who boasted of the deed. Fifty thousand Flemings and Germans were hanged, burnt, or buried alive under Charles V. And when we have added to this the Thirty Years' War in Germany, and the long agony of other and repeated massacres of Protestants in England, Ireland, Scotland, France, Spain, Italy and the Netherlands, we have to remember that for all this, "no word of censure ever issued from the Vatican, except in the brief interval when statesmen and soldiers grew weary of bloodshed and looked for means to admit the heretics to grace." (Guinness, *Key to the Apocalypse*, pp. 91–94)

Further, Daniel 7:25 prophesies that the little horn will arrogate to itself the prerogative of changing appointed times and law. The angel has informed Daniel that the little horn's attack is against God, so it is evident that the appointed times and law that the little horn thinks to change are those that belong to God. Of course, the ultimate expression of God's law is none other than His immutable 10 Commandments, recorded in Exodus 20:1–17 and Deuteronomy 5:6–21. Note this bold assertion: "The Pope can modify divine law, since his power is not of man but of God, and he acts as vicegerent of God upon earth with most ample power of binding and loosing his sheep" (Ferraris, *Prompta Bibliotheca*, Vol. 6, article "Papa," p. 19).

Has the papacy altered God's 10 Commandment law? In the *Catechism of the Catholic Church*, just prior to "SECTION TWO: THE TEN

COMMANDMENTS," there is a two-page spread with the 10 Commandments from Exodus 20:2–17, Deuteronomy 5:6–21, and the traditional catechetical formula placed side-by-side. In the formula, the second commandment forbidding image worship (idolatry) is removed entirely. Further, the longest of the 10 Commandments, the fourth, commanding worship on the seventh-day Sabbath, is reduced to a mere 7 words, "Remember to keep holy the LORD'S Day," without specifying which day of the week this is. Finally, to retain a total of ten, the tenth commandment forbidding coveting has been cut into two pieces, re-arranged and abridged as "You shall not covet your neighbor's wife" and "You shall not covet your neighbor's goods" (*Catechism of the Catholic Church*, 2nd ed., pp. 496, 497).

Consider the following astonishing remarks from an older catechism:

> Q. *What is the Third Commandment?*
> A. The Third Commandment is: Remember that thou keep holy the Sabbath day.
>
> Q. *Which is the Sabbath day?*
> A. Saturday is the Sabbath day.
>
> Q. Why do we observe Sunday instead of Saturday?
> A. We observe Sunday instead of Saturday because the Catholic Church transferred the solemnity from Saturday to Sunday.
>
> Q. *By what authority did the Church substitute Sunday for Saturday?*
> A. The Church substituted Sunday for Saturday by the plenitude of that divine power which Jesus Christ bestowed upon her. (Geiermann, *The Convert's Catechism of Catholic Doctrine*, pp. 50, 51)

Consider the following bold assertions from Catholic professor Johann Meyer, better known as Dr. Eck, in his famous contest with Martin Luther:

> Scripture teaches: "Remember the Sabbath day, to keep it holy; six days you will labor and do all your work, but the seventh is the Sabbath of the Lord your God," etc. But the Church has

> changed the Sabbath into the Lord's [day] by its own authority—for which you have no Scripture. (Eck, *Enchiridion*, fols. 4v, 5r)

> The Sabbath is many times by God commanded; neither in the Gospels nor in Paul is it declared that the Sabbath has ceased; however, the Church has instituted the Lord's day by the traditions of the Apostles—without Scripture. (Eck, *Enchiridion*, fol. 42v)

One of the boldest admissions concerning the change of Sabbath to Sunday is from the *Catholic Mirror*, the weekly organ of Cardinal Gibbons. A series of four consecutive editorials in September 1893 was published as "The Christian Sabbath: The Genuine Offspring of the Union of the Holy Spirit and the Catholic Church His Spouse. The Claims of Protestantism to Any Part Therein Proved to Be Groundless, Self-contradictory and Suicidal." The first editorial poses three questions:

> 1st. Which day of the week does the Bible enjoin to be kept holy?
>
> 2d. Has the New Testament modified by precept or practice the original command?
>
> 3d. Have Protestants, since the sixteenth century, obeyed the command of God by keeping "holy" the day enjoined by their infallible guide and teacher, the Bible? and if not, why not? ("The Christian Sabbath," *Catholic Mirror*, September 2, 1893)

The following week's editorial is a Bible study furnishing all pertinent Bible evidence proving the sacredness of the seventh-day Sabbath throughout Scripture, focusing especially on the New Testament. It concludes with these words: "Hence the conclusion is inevitable; viz., that of those who follow the Bible as their guide, the Israelites and Seventh-day Adventists have the exclusive weight of evidence on their side, whilst the Biblical Protestant has not a word in self-defense for his substitution of Sunday for Saturday." ("The Christian Sabbath," *Catholic Mirror*, September 9, 1893)

The third editorial takes up the subject of Sunday sacredness in the New Testament, examining the handful of references to be found. With regard to Acts 2:1, in which the Christians were assembled on Pentecost, we find these words: "Who but the Biblical Christian, driven to the wall for a pretext to excuse his sacrilegious desecration of the Sabbath, always kept by Christ and His apostles, would have resorted to the Jewish festival of Pentecost for his act of rebellion against his God and his teacher, the Bible?" The editorial concludes that the writer has "disposed of every text to be found in the New Testament referring to the Sabbath (Saturday), and to the first day of the week (Sunday); and having shown conclusively from these texts, that, so far, not a shadow of pretext can be found in the Sacred Volume for the Biblical substitution of Sunday for Saturday." ("The Christian Sabbath," *Catholic Mirror*, September 16, 1893)

The final editorial in its rather lengthy conclusion provides the following challenge:

> What Protestant can, after perusing these articles, with a clear conscience, continue to disobey the command of God, enjoining *Saturday to be kept*, which command his teacher, the Bible, from Genesis to Revelation, records as the will of God? ... The Protestant world at its birth found the Christian Sabbath too strongly intrenched [sic] to run counter to its existence; it was therefore placed under the necessity of acquiescing in the arrangement, thus implying the Church's right to change the day, for over three hundred years. The Christian Sabbath is therefore *to this day*, the acknowledged offspring of the Catholic Church as a spouse of the Holy Ghost, without a word of remonstrance from the Protestant world. ("The Christian Sabbath," *Catholic Mirror*, September 23, 1893)

Hence, the Roman Catholic Church, which the Bible charges with the crime of tampering with His unchangeable law, most boldly admits to doing so. Of course, Roman Catholicism does not assert to go by the Bible alone, the rallying cry of Protestants, but rather, the Bible and tradition, and where Church tradition is at odds with Scripture, tradition triumphs.

We have noted that Leviticus 26, which discusses God's covenant, begins by focusing on the two commandments that deal most directly with worship—false image worship and true Sabbath worship—followed by an admonition to honor His sanctuary. Idolatry has been the key problem throughout Daniel 2–7, and our study of this section of the book has revealed God's remedy: the Sabbath (interestingly enough, the focus of Daniel 8–12 is God's heavenly sanctuary). Is it mere chance that, in tampering with the 10 Commandments, the papacy has wrought the greatest change in those dealing with image worship and the Sabbath? Indeed, within God's 10 Commandment law are the appointed times that are the focus of the little horn's wrath: God's weekly seventh-day Sabbaths, which from the foundation of the world He blessed and set apart as holy time (see Gen. 2:1–3).

While the little horn usurps the prerogatives of God, humbles other kings, eliminates the prohibition against idolatry, and attempts to do away with His seventh-day Sabbath, the angel asserts that its oppression of God's holy people is constrained to a time, times, and half a time. Recalling that a biblical time is 360 days, the 3.5 times granted to the papacy work out to 1,260 prophetic days, or 1,260 literal years.

Where is this historical period located in history? Recall from remarks on verses 7 and 8 that the year AD 538 marked the year of the uprooting of the third horn and hence the point at which Germanic resistance to the papacy was assuredly doomed. At that point, Justinian's decree of 5 years previous could go into effect, (i.e., the pope could now assume to be "head of all the holy churches"). Marching ahead 1,260 years, we arrive at 1798, when French emperor Napoleon's general Berthier entered Rome, demanding the resignation of Pope Pius VI on February 10. This not being granted, Berthier forcibly took the pope captive on February 20. While Pius VI died August 29, 1799, the succession of popes has continued, and the papacy has been regaining temporal authority, particularly under John Paul II (1978–2005) and his successors, Benedict XVI and Francis. Papal Rome's crushing blow in 1798 only *appeared* mortal (see Rev. 13:3). Though Vatican City is the smallest independent state in the world, it is the only *religious* body to be a state and has ambassadors from all over the world.

In spite of the little horn's blasphemy, the angel affirms that God's end-time judgment puts an utter end to the little horn's blasphemous reign, God's holy people are given the kingdom, and all will revere and obey Him (see Isa. 45:23; Phil. 2:10, 11).

Daniel Keeps the Matter in His Heart

The vision so disturbs Daniel that his thoughts "greatly alarmed" him, and his "splendor was changing," employing the very same words used of Belshazzar's terrified reaction (see Dan 5:6) when the mysterious hand wrote out his own judgment on the wall. The chapter concludes with the words, "but I kept the matter in my heart." In Daniel 2 and 4, Nebuchadnezzar was so bothered by his dreams that he sought counsel from his advisors to no avail. By contrast, Daniel seeks *no* counsel from another person. Herein is a most valuable lesson for us all: When dealing with the great strains of marital infidelity, financial reverses, or health challenges, we are to take our problems to God in prayer, not to a pastor, counselor, close friends, or family members. Though common practice with many, such practice has no sanction whatever in the Scriptures.[64]

SUMMARY: DANIEL 7

DANIEL 7: JESUS

Jesus is the Son of man who comes to the Ancient of Days at the commencement of the end-time judgment. His is the only kingdom built on a foundation to last for eternity—the 10 Commandments.

---

[64] "When perplexities arise, and difficulties confront you, look not for help to humanity. Trust all with God. The practice of telling our difficulties to others only makes us weak, and brings no strength to them. It lays upon them the burden of our spiritual infirmities, which they cannot relieve. We seek the strength of erring, finite man, when we might have the strength of the unerring, infinite God. You need not go to the ends of the earth for wisdom, for God is near" (White, *COL*, p. 146).

DANIEL 7: THE STAND

In verse 4, the judgment that resulted in Nebuchadnezzar's conversion leads him to "stand" on both feet with a man's heart. In verse 5, Medo-Persia is God's agent of judgment. Being caused to stand on 1 side refers to the eventual dominance of Persia in the relationship, and under King Cyrus, Persia was used of God to liberate his people from the 70-year Babylonian captivity. In verses 10 and 16, the angels stand before God's throne during the end-time judgment. By contrast, in verses 17 and 24, the earthly kingdoms attempt to stand in their own strength, but ironically, when the judgment *sits*, the horn's dominion is taken away, and the kingdom is given to the saints of the Most High.

DANIEL 7: THE HORN'S HAND

The little horn, the papacy, attempts to set up an earthly kingdom upon the same false earthly principle as did the preceding kingdoms (represented by the beasts in chapter 7): Might makes right. This is brought out forcibly in verse 25, in which those who are true to God's law and refuse to go along with the papacy's attempts to change His appointed times and law are given into his hand for 1,260 years. History bears ample testimony that the papacy's hand is responsible for the slaughter of tens of millions of faithful Christians. This reveals the spirit of the dragon, Satan himself.

Contrast this with God's stone kingdom from chapter 2, cut out of heavenly Mount Zion "without hands" during the end-time judgment. This means that it is not established by force, but by His Holy Spirit leading His people to the point of full surrender, convicting them of the claims of His immutable law.

DANIEL 7: APPLICATION TO THE LAST DAYS

The papacy's reign was for 1,260 literal years, terminating in 1798 with the (apparently) mortal wound inflicted on it. This event marked the beginning of the end time of earth's history, during which period the end-time judgment would begin. The date marking the commencement of the end-time judgment is presented in Daniel 8. For now, we assert without proof that we are living in that very time. This hour—the judgment hour—is the most sober of earth's history, for once God's end-time judgment of our characters closes, nothing remains but for Jesus to come to claim those who have proven faithful and slay by the breath of His lips those who have persisted in rebellion (see Isa. 11:4; 2 Thess. 2:8).

Though incredibly bothered by his dream and the explanation given by the angel, Daniel kept the matter in his heart, setting an example for all of us, no matter our troubles. May those of us living in the end time trust all to God as did Daniel, and like him, develop a character that earns the approbation of heaven.

DANIEL, PART 2: THE KEY POINTS

DANIEL 2–7: JESUS AND THE HOLY SPIRIT

Table 4 summarizes the role of Jesus and the Holy Spirit in Daniel 2–7:

Table 4: Jesus and the Holy Spirit in Daniel 2–7

REFERENCE	JESUS AND HOLY SPIRIT IN DANIEL 2–7
Dan. 2:28–30 Dan 2:34, 35, 44, 45	Jesus is the Revealer of secrets, both in the future and our hearts. Jesus is King of the stone kingdom.
Dan. 3:25, 28	Jesus is the Son of God, the Angel (of the covenant), who walks with the faithful 3 in the fiery furnace.
Dan. 4:8, 9, 18 Dan. 4:34–37 Dan. 4: 13, 17, 23, 31	The "spirit of the holy gods," i.e., the Holy Spirit, is in Daniel. Nebuchadnezzar given new heart = filled with the Holy Spirit. "Watcher(s)" and "holy one(s)" (plural → divinity) descend from heaven, and a voice falls from heaven in judgment. The "watcher" is the Holy Spirit.
Dan. 5:11–14 Dan. 5:23, 24	The "spirit of the holy gods," i.e., the Holy Spirit, is in Daniel. Hand that writes judgment linked with "God in whose hand is your breath" = "Spirit of God" (Job 27:3). Therefore, it is the Holy Spirit who writes on the wall.
Dan. 6:22	Jesus is the Angel who shuts the mouths of the lions.
Dan. 7:13, 14	Jesus is the Son of man, the end-time Judge (deliverer).

DANIEL 2–7: THE STAND

Standing in the end-time judgment pervades Daniel 2–7 and is brought out vividly in the contrast between Nebuchadnezzar, who was humbled 7 times, and proud Belshazzar, who was weighed against God's sevenfold judgment. God causes the lowliest of people to stand over the kingdom of humanity.

DANIEL 2–7: THE HAND

God's kingdom is established without hands in Daniel 2 (i.e., without force or human might). The Babylonian king's hand, the Medo-Persian lions' hand, and the papacy's hand (see Daniel 3:15–17, 6:27, and 7:25, respectively) showed how these earthly kingdoms sought supremacy by human might—and failed miserably. God's hand cannot be stopped by human devising (see 4:35), and the Holy Spirit manifests Himself in Daniel 5 as God's hand writing judgment against Belshazzar, who has forever hardened his heart. The spirit of Satan prompts us to rely on the hand of mankind. Those who rely on God's hand reveal His Spirit.

DANIEL 2–7: CHIASTIC STRUCTURE

Table 5 provides a simple structure for Daniel 2–7. Table 6, Table 7, and Table 8 provide greater detail:

Table 5: Simplified Chiastic Structure of Daniel 2–7

CHAPTER	EVENT		CHAPTER
4	Judgment for 7 times: Nebuchadnezzar humbled.	Sevenfold Judgment: Belshazzar destroyed.	5
3	Command to bow down to golden image.	Prohibition against true worship.	6
	Those who don't bow down are cast into fiery furnace.	Those who don't comply are cast into den of lions.	
	Son of God/Angel delivers from furnace.	Angel/Son of God delivers from den of lions.	
2	Nebuchadnezzar investigates and God reveals secret.	Ancient of Days investigates and Jesus reveals secret.	7
	Stone kingdom cut out without hands.	Judgment sits.	
	Stone kingdom arrives at second coming.	God's people given kingdom at second coming.	

Table 6: Panel Structure of Daniel 2 and 7

DANIEL 2	PANEL PARALLELS		DANIEL 7
	INTRODUCTION: KING HAS A DREAM	**INTRODUCTION: DANIEL HAS A DREAM**	
2:1–3	Year 2 of Nebuchadnezzar: King has dreams.	Year 1 of King Belshazzar: Daniel sees dream and visions.	7:1
	INVESTIGATION: THE KING SEEKS TO KNOW HIS DREAM	**INVESTIGATION: THE END TIME JUDGMENT**	
2:4b–11	Nebuchadnezzar sits upon throne (implied in his role as king/judge). Counsellors **standing before king** (cf. v. 2) are investigated.	Ancient of Days sits upon throne. Angels **stand before him**, judgment sits, books opened.	7:9, 10
2:12, 13	Wise men to be destroyed, about to be killed.	Fourth living creature killed, body destroyed.	7:11
2:14–23	Daniel requests set time from king. Prays not to be destroyed with the rest.	Extension of lives granted to rest of living creatures until set time.	7:12
2:24, 25	"Bring me before the king. I will declare the interpretation."	Son of man brought before Ancient of Days for judgment.	7:13
	KING'S DREAM	**DANIEL'S DREAM**	
2:28–30	"Your dream and the visions of your head upon your bed."	"Daniel saw a dream and visions of his head upon his bed."	7:1
2:31	"Your majesty was watching, and behold, 1 great image."	"I was watching ... and behold, ... the great sea."	7:2
2:32	Head of fine gold	Lion w/ eagle's wings	7:4
2:32	Chest and arms of silver	Bear standing on 1 side	7:5
2:32	Belly and thighs of bronze	Leopard w/ 4 wings and 4 heads	7:6
2:33	Calves of iron	Fourth living creature: huge iron teeth	7:7
	Feet	Its feet trample the remnant	
	Partly iron and partly clay	Little horn (clay) comes up among 10 horns (iron).	

(continued)

Table 6: Panel Structure of Daniel 2 and 7 (*continued*)

DANIEL 2	PANEL PARALLELS		DANIEL 7
2:34	A stone which had been cut out without hands	Ancient of Days sat down. Judgment sits.	7:9, 10
2:34, 35	Stone strikes image upon feet. Iron, clay, and prior metals broken as 1.	Fourth creature and prior creatures destroyed at second coming.	7:11, 12
2:35	Stone becomes great mountain, fills earth.	Son of man given everlasting kingdom, all revere Him.	7:14
	KING'S DREAM INTERPRETED	**DANIEL'S DREAM INTERPRETED**	
2:36	"This was the dream; now its interpretation we will tell before the king."	He made known the interpretation of the matters [the dream].	7:16
2:36–40	Nebuchadnezzar = first king. Three kingdoms **arise** after him.	Great living creatures = four kings which **arise** from earth.	7:17
2:40	Fourth kingdom strong as iron; breaks in pieces and crushes like iron.	Fourth creature: iron teeth, bronze nails, devours, breaks in pieces.	7:19, 23
2:41–43	Feet and toes of iron and clay → kingdom becomes divided.	Ten horns on fourth creature's head; other [little] horn comes up.	7:20, 21
2:44a	"In the days of those kings," i.e., kings over divisions of fourth kingdom.	Ten horns out of this kingdom = ten kings which arise. Another king arises after them.	7:24, 25
2:44, 45	God establishes kingdom never to be destroyed.	The judgment will sit.	7:22, 26, 27
	God's kingdom breaks in pieces, ends all these kingdoms.	Little horn dominion taken away to destroy it unto the end.	
	God's kingdom not left to other people.	God's kingdom given to holy people of the Most High.	
	Kingdom **stands** forever.	God's kingdom is everlasting.	
	Stone cut out of mount w/out hands breaks in pieces other kingdoms.	All dominions reverence and hearken unto Him.	

(*continued*)

Table 6: Panel Structure of Daniel 2 and 7 (*continued*)

DANIEL 2	PANEL PARALLELS		DANIEL 7
	THE SECRET OF KING'S HEART REVEALED	DANIEL KEEPS MATTER IN HIS HEART	
2:46–49	Daniel able to reveal the secret [of king's heart, cf. v. 30]	Daniel keeps matter in heart	7:28

Table 7: Panel Structure of Daniel 3 and 6

DANIEL 3	PANEL PARALLELS		DANIEL 6
3:1–3	Babylon's king erects image	Medo-Persian king appoints Daniel	6:1–3
3:4–7	State mandates false worship	State prohibits true worship	6:4–9
3:8–18	Three Jews don't bow to image → turned in	Daniel kneels before God → turned in	6:10–15
3:19–21	A: Furnace heated **1 factor** of 7 hotter	B': Daniel cast into den	6:16–18
	B: Three Jews cast into furnace	A': **1 stone** to **seal** den	
3:22–27	A: Babylonian king's strong men killed	B_1': The Angel of God saves Daniel	6:19–24
	B_1: The Son of God (His Angel) saves 3 Jews	B_2': Daniel investigated	
	B_2: Three Jews investigated	A': Medo-Persian king's conspirators killed	
3:28–30	Babylon's king prohibits speaking against God	Medo-Persian king commands worship of true God	6:28

Table 8: Panel Structure of Daniel 4 and 5

DANIEL 4	PANEL PARALLELS		DANIEL 5
4:1–3	Nebuchadnezzar: humble king praises God	Belshazzar: proud king praises false gods	5:1–4
4:4–7	King sees dream, calls Babylonian advisors	King sees hand, calls Babylonian advisors	5:5–9
4:8, 9	A: Daniel comes	B': Queen mother asserts Spirit of Holy God is in Daniel	5:10–16
	B: King asserts spirit of holy gods is in Daniel	A': Daniel brought	

(*continued*)

Table 8: Panel Structure of Daniel 4 and 5 (*continued*)

DANIEL 4	PANEL PARALLELS		DANIEL 5
4:10–18	King recounts dream	Daniel recounts Nebuchadnezzar's experience	5:17–21
4:19–26	A: Daniel interprets dream	B': Daniel reproves king	5:22–24
4:27	B: Daniel counsels king	A': Daniel interprets handwriting	5:25–29
4:28–37	King vainly attempts to continue kingdom	King vainly attempts to preserve position	5:30, 31
	That hour, declaration fulfilled	That night, writing fulfilled	
	Seven times judgment commence → king humbled	Sevenfold judgment completed → king killed	
	Nebuchadnezzar re-established over kingdom	Darius the Mede receives kingdom	

Numbers in Daniel 2–7

Table 9: The Number Seven in Daniel 2–7

REFERENCE	USE OF THE NUMBER 7
Dan. 2:19, 22, 28, 29, 30, 47 (2x)	Secret(s) "revealed" 7 times. God is the Revealer of secrets.
Dan. 2:21	God alone alters the "appointed times." In Daniel 7, "appointed times" → seventh-day Sabbath.
Dan. 3:1, 5, 7, 10, 12, 14, 18	"Image of gold" occurs 7 times.
Dan. 3:5, 6, 7, 10, 11, 15, 23	"Fall" occurs 7 times: "fall down and make obeisance" (6 times) + "fell" into furnace (once).
Dan. 3:19	Furnace heated 7 times hotter.
Dan. 4:16, 23, 25, 32	The "7 times" pass over Nebuchadnezzar.
Dan. 5:7, 8, 15–17, 24, 25	*Kətab* ("writing") occurs 7 times.
Dan. 5:25–28	Belshazzar weighed against "7 times" of gerahs.
Dan. 5:25–28	Belshazzar falls short of God's standard of judgment by 7 times 70 gerahs.

(*continued*)

Table 9: The Number Seven in Daniel 2–7 (*continued*)

REFERENCE	USE OF THE NUMBER 7
Dan. 5:8, 15–17, 21–23	*Yada'* ("know," "make known") occurs 7 times.
Dan. 5:7 (2x), 8, 12, 15–17	*Qara'* ("read aloud," "crying," "be called") occurs 7 times.
Dan. 6:7, 8, 9, 12 (2x), 13, 15	*'esar* ("prohibition") of true worship occurs 7 times.
Dan. 6:4, 7 (2x), 11, 12, 13 (2x)	"Petition" occurs 7 times: five times as *bə'a'* (verb "petition") and twice as *ba'û* (noun "petition").
Dan. 6:17	Stone sealed, just as seventh-day Sabbath seals God's law in stone.
Dan. 7:4–8	Total of 7 heads on the four living creatures ("beasts").
Dan. 7:25	Rome attempts to change "appointed times" = seventh-day Sabbath; Rome to reign for half of 7 times.
Dan. 2:44; 3:25; 4:23; 6:22, 23, 26; 7:14	*Chabal* ("destroy") is used 7 times in Daniel 2–7. Appears in each chapter except Daniel 5.

Table 10: The Numbers Four, Seven, and Ten in Daniel 2–7, Sorted by Chapter with Chiastic Matches Indicated

CHP	#	SIGNIFICANCE	SIGNIFICANCE	#	CHP
4	4	Phrase "7 times" occurs 4 times.	"Hand" that writes judgment occurs 4 times.	4	5
	7	The "7 times" pass over Nebuchadnezzar.	"Writing" (*kətab*) occurs 7 times. Mene Mene Teqel Upharsin = 7 times.	7	
3	4	Four faithful to God's law walk through fire unscathed. Four Babylonian groups investigate fire's lack of dominion.	"Law" occurs 4 times. *Chabal* ("injured, injury, destroyed") occurs 4 times.	4	6
	7	"Image of gold" occurs 7 times. "Fall" occurs 7 times. "Heat the furnace 1 factor of 7" hotter.	"Prohibition" occurs 7 times. "Petition" occurs 7 times. "So 1 stone … sealed" (Sabbath seals God's law in stone.)	7	

(*continued*)

Table 10: The Numbers Four, Seven, and Ten in Daniel 2–7, Sorted by Chapter with Chiastic Matches Indicated (*continued*)

CHP	#	SIGNIFICANCE	SIGNIFICANCE	#	CHP
	10	"Furnace" mentioned 10 times.	"Den" mentioned 10 times.	10	
2	4	Four sets of officials stand before Babylon's king.	Four living creatures. Babylon's lion stands.	4	7
		[Four sets of] wise men to be destroyed and killed.	Fourth living creature killed, body destroyed.		
	7	God "reveals" secrets 7 times.	Total of 7 heads on four living creatures. Little horn changes "appointed times" = seventh-day Sabbath.	7	
	10	Aramaic "saw" occurs 8 times. Hebrew "dreamed" twice. (Hebrew "dreamed" = Aramaic "saw" (see Dan. 7:1)).	Daniel "saw" 10 times.	10	
		Feet of image have 10 toes.	Fourth living creature has 10 horns.		
		Stone kingdom founded on the 10 Commandments.	Fourth kingdom's strength is the 10 horns.		

Table 11: Other Key Numbers in Daniel 2–7, Sorted by Number

NUMBER	REFERENCE	SIGNIFICANCE
6	Dan. 3:1	Width of image in cubits.
12	Dan. 3:1–19	"Image" appears 12 times. Last instance of "image" refers to Nebuchadnezzar's face.
	Dan. 4:12	Nebuchadnezzar granted "12 months" for his character to be investigated.
60	Dan. 3:1	Height of image in cubits.
62	Dan. 5:31	Darius' approximate age when he ascends throne. Compare 62 weeks (Dan. 9:25, 26).
360	Dan. 3:1	Area of Nebuchadnezzar's image in square cubits (60 cubits high by 6 cubits wide).

(*continued*)

Table 11: Other Key Numbers in Daniel 2–7, Sorted by Number (*continued*)

NUMBER	REFERENCE	SIGNIFICANCE
	Dan. 4:16, 23, 25, 32	The 7 times (360 days each) pass over Nebuchadnezzar.
	Dan. 5:25–28	Belshazzar's sevenfold judgment consists of 7 times (360 gerahs each).
490	Dan. 5:25–28	How far short Belshazzar came (in gerahs) of God's holy standard.

3:
GOD'S ATONEMENT—
SEVENTY TIMES SEVEN

DANIEL 8 AND 9: GOD'S HAND—DELIVERANCE BY MESSIAH'S ATONING SACRIFICE

Introduction: Daniel by the Stream Ulai

8 ¹In year 3 of the reign of King Belshazzar, a vision appeared unto me—me, Daniel—after [the vision that] appeared to me at the beginning.

The Vision: Christ's Sanctuary

²I looked into the vision, and while I was looking, then I was in Shushan the citadel, which is in Elam the province. I looked into the vision, and I was by the stream Ulai.
³Then I lifted my eyes, looked, and behold: One ram **standing** before the stream. He had 2 horns, and both horns were high, yet the 1 was higher than the second, and the higher [horn] was coming up afterward. ⁴I saw the ram butting seaward, northward, and southward. No living creatures could **stand** before him, nor was there any to rescue from his hand. He did according to his will, and grew great.
⁵As I was contemplating, behold, a male goat of the goats was coming from the sunset over the surface of all the earth, without even touching the earth. The male goat [had] a conspicuous horn between his eyes. ⁶He came unto the ram possessing the 2 horns, which I saw **standing** before the stream, and ran toward him in his strong fury. ⁷I saw him reaching close beside the ram; embittered against him, he struck the ram and shattered his 2 horns. There was no strength in the ram to **stand** before him.

Then he cast him to the ground and trampled him. There was nobody to rescue the ram from his hand. **⁸**So the male goat of the goats grew very great, yet when he was mighty, the great[fem] horn[fem] was shattered[fem].[65]

There came up[fem] 4[fem] conspicuous[fem] [horns[fem]] in its[fem] place toward the 4[fem] winds[fem] of the heavens[masc]. **⁹**From number 1[fem][66] of them[masc], 1[fem] horn[fem] from insignificance[fem] emerged[masc]. It exalted[fem] itself unto prominence[masc] toward the south, the sunrise, and the beauty. **¹⁰**It exalted[fem] itself against the host of the heavens. It caused[fem] some of the host to fall to earth; some of the stars it trampled[fem]. **¹¹**Even unto the Ruler[masc] of the host it exalted[masc] itself. From Him[masc] it lifted[masc] out the continual ministration[67]; the foundation of His[masc] sanctuary was cast down. **¹²**Because of rebellion, it was given[fem] a host against the continual ministration. It cast[fem] truth to the ground; it did[fem] so, and thrived[fem].

Question and Answer: Jesus and Gabriel by the Ulai

¹³Then I heard 1 holy being speaking; 1 holy being said to the Palmoni who was speaking, "Until what point does the vision concerning the continual ministration and the desolating rebellion extend, to give over both sanctuary and host to be trampled?"

¹⁴Then He said to me, "Until 2,300 evening-mornings [elapse]—then the sanctuary will be restored to its righteous condition."

Daniel Stands: The Vision Explained

¹⁵Then while I—I, Daniel—was watching the vision and seeking understanding, behold, one **standing** before me with the appearance of a man.

---

[65] Subscripts "[fem]" and "[masc]" in verses 8–12 indicate the grammatical gender of the corresponding Hebrew words.

[66] Literally, "the 1," signifying the first. Daniel often prefers cardinal numbers (1, 2, 3, etc.) to ordinals (first, second, third, etc.).

[67] The marginal reading in the Hebrew text renders this passively: "From Him, the continual ministration was lifted out."

¹⁶Then I heard a man's voice from the midst of the Ulai; he called out and said, "Gabriel, make this particular one understand the appearance." ¹⁷So he came alongside **where I stood**; when he came, I was terrified, and fell upon my face. He said to me, "Understand, son of man, that the vision pertains to the end time."

¹⁸As he was speaking with me, I was unconscious upon my face toward the ground, so he touched me, **enabling me to stand** where I **had been standing**. ¹⁹Then he said, "Behold, I am letting you know what will occur in the latter part of the outrage, for at an appointed time is the end.

²⁰"The ram which you saw possessing the 2 horns: the kings of Media and Persia. ²¹The male goat, the buck: the king of Hellas. The great horn which is between his eyes: he is the first king. ²²Being shattered, the 4 [horns] which **stood** in its place are 4 kingdoms which **stand up** from a people group—though not with his strength.

²³"In the final part of their kingdom, as the rebels develop their character fully, there will **stand up** a king, goat-faced,⁶⁸ one who understands dark sayings. ²⁴Mighty will be his strength—but not by reason of his own strength. He will corrupt wonderfully. He will thrive, and do so. He will corrupt those who are mighty, even the people of the greater [i.e., heavenly] sanctuary.⁶⁹ ²⁵By his cunning insight, he will also cause deception to

---

⁶⁸ The Hebrew words *'az* ("strong") and *'ez* ("female goat") share identical consonants, differing only in their initial vowel. The Masoretes added vowel pointings to the Hebrew text in approximately AD 900. Thus, while the Masoretic vowel pointing suggests the Roman king is "strong of countenance," note the evidence in favor of "goat-faced": Hellas is represented by goat imagery in Daniel 8:5–8; the goat is a symbol of strength outside the Bible (see comment by Alexander the Great's soldiers in this chapter); the word "buck" refers to "goat-demons" (see Lev. 17:7 and 2 Chron. 11:15). Prophecy shows that Hellas and Rome are inextricably intertwined, so Rome's description in verse 23 as "goat-faced" is a perfect play on words.

⁶⁹ Often translated "holy people." However, the way to state this in Hebrew is *'am-qodesh*, in which both *'am* ("people") and *qodesh* ("holy") are singular (see Isa. 62:12; 63:18; Dan 12:7). In Daniel 8:24, however, the phrase is *'am-qedoshim*, in which *qedoshim* is plural, not agreeing with *'am*, which is singular. The plural *qedoshim* can refer to the "holy places" that comprise the sanctuary, or it can be used in a comparative sense, meaning "the place which is holier than" that with which it is being compared. This occurs in Hebrews 9:8, in which the "holy places" (the heavenly sanctuary) are greater than the "first tent" (the earthly sanctuary). Similarly, in verse 23, Christ's sacrifice is referred to as "better sacrifices [plural] than these," the plural designating the *superiority* of His single sacrifice in

thrive by his hand. In his heart he will exalt self. Through a sense of peace he will corrupt many. Even against the Ruler of rulers he will **stand**—yet without hand, he will be shattered.

²⁶"Now, the appearance portion of the evening and the morning which was mentioned is truth, but you are to shut up the vision, for it pertains to many days [hence]."

Daniel Does Not Understand, Pleads with *Adonai*

²⁷So I, Daniel, was overcome, and made sick for days. Then I arose and did the king's work. I was left desolate by the appearance, and there was no one to give understanding.

9 ¹In year 1 of Darius the son of Ahasuerus, of the seed of the Medes, who was made king over the realm of the Kasdim—²in year 1 of his reign, I, Daniel, understood among the scrolls the number of years which was, per the word of *Yahweh* to Jeremiah the prophet, to be fulfilled in relation to the ruins of Jerusalem: 70 years.

We Have Broken Your Covenant

³Then I set my face toward *Adonai* God to seek Him by prayer and petitions, with fasting, sackcloth, and ashes. ⁴So I prayed to *Yahweh* my God. I confessed, saying, "Please, *Adonai*—the great God who is to be feared, keeping the covenant and [maintaining] godly character toward those who love Him, those who keep His commandments—⁵we have sinned, acted deviantly, done wickedly, and rebelled in turning aside from Your commandments and from Your judgments. ⁶Further, we have not hearkened unto Your servants the prophets, who have spoken in Your name to our kings, our rulers, our fathers, and to all the people of

---

comparison with the animal sacrifices of the earthly sanctuary system. Since Daniel 8 points to Jesus' work in the heavenly sanctuary, the best reading is "people of the greater [i.e., heavenly] sanctuary."

the land. ⁷To you, *Adonai*, belongs righteousness, but unto us belongs shamefacedness as at this day—to the men of Judah, to those who dwell in Jerusalem and to all Israel, those near and those far away in all the lands where You have banished them due to their infidelity by which they have acted unfaithfully toward You. ⁸*Yahweh*, to us belongs shamefacedness—to our kings, to our rulers, and to our fathers—for we have sinned against You.

The Curse and Sevenfold Oath

⁹"To *Adonai* our God belong plentiful compassion and forgiveness,[70] for we have rebelled against Him. ¹⁰Neither have we hearkened to the voice of *Yahweh* our God, to walk in His laws, which He set before us by the hand of His servants the prophets. ¹¹Indeed, all of Israel have transgressed Your Torah, turning aside, not hearkening to Your voice; therefore, the curse (i.e., the sevenfold oath which is written in the Torah of Moses, the servant of God) has been poured out on us, for we have sinned against Him. ¹²Now He has established His words which He spoke against us and against our judges who judged us, by bringing upon us great evil which has not been done under all the heavens as it has been done in Jerusalem.

¹³"As it is written in the Torah of Moses, all this evil has come upon us, yet we have not entreated the face of *Yahweh* our God, that we might turn from our deviant behavior and become wise by Your truth. ¹⁴So *Yahweh* kept watch concerning this evil, and brought it upon us, for righteous is *Yahweh* our God concerning all His works which He does—yet we have not hearkened to His voice. ¹⁵Now, *Adonai* our God, who brought out Your people from the land of Egypt by a mighty hand, and made Yourself a name as it is day—we have sinned, we have done wickedly.

---

[70] Hebrew "compassions and forgivenesses," the plural signifying how extensive God's compassion and forgiveness is.

God's Sanctuary

¹⁶"*Adonai*, in harmony with all Your righteous attributes, please turn away Your anger and Your wrath from Your city Jerusalem, the mountain of Your sanctuary,⁷¹ because for our sins and the deviant acts of our fathers, Jerusalem—Your people—are a reproach to all those around us. ¹⁷Therefore, hearken, our God, to the prayer of Your servant and to His petitions; cause Your face to shine upon Your desolated sanctuary for the sake of *Adonai*. ¹⁸Incline, my God, Your ear and hearken, open Your eyes and observe our desolations, and the city which is called by Your name; for not on account of our righteous attributes do we lay our petitions before you, but on account of the numerous instances of Your compassion.

¹⁹"*Adonai*, hearken! *Adonai*, forgive! *Adonai*, give heed and act! Do not delay—for Your sake, my God—for by Your name are Your city and Your people called."

Gabriel's Timeline Explains Early Part of Vision

²⁰While I was speaking and praying, confessing my sin and the sin of my people Israel, laying my petition before *Yahweh* my God concerning the holy mountain of my God—²¹while I was speaking in prayer, the man Gabriel whom I had seen in the vision at the beginning, having been sent forth in flight, reached me about the time of the evening grain offering. ²²He gave understanding. He spoke with me and said, "Daniel, now I have come to make you wise with understanding. ²³At the start of your petitions a decree went forth, and I came to declare it, for you are of high esteem. Therefore, understand the matter—understand the appearance:

> ²⁴"Seventy weeks have been cut off concerning Your people, concerning Your holy city,⁷² to:

---

⁷¹ Or, "of Your holiness." God's "sanctuary" is literally His "holy" place. God's sanctuary is on Mount Zion (see Ps. 20:2).

⁷² Or, "city of your sanctuary."

Finish the rebellion, seal up sins,[73] make atonement for deviant behavior,

Bring in everlasting righteousness, seal up vision and prophet, and anoint the Holy of Holies.

25a "Know and understand: from the going forth of the decree to bring back [to its former condition] and to build Jerusalem until Messiah the Agent there are to be 7 weeks, then 62 weeks.

25b "It will return [to its former condition] and be built—public square and site of judgment decree—though in pressing times.

26a "After the 62 weeks, Messiah will be cut off—He will have no one.

26b "The people of the coming agent will ruin both the city and the sanctuary. The end thereof[74] will be with the flood. Until the end of war, there is a decree of desolations.

27a "He will confirm [the] covenant with the multitudes 1 week. In the middle of the week, He will cause sacrifice and grain offering to cease.

27b "However, upon the wing of detestable idols is one who will make desolate, even until the consummation. Then that which is decreed is to be poured out upon the one who makes desolate."

---

[73] The marginal reading in the Hebrew is "finish up" = "put an end to sins." However, Theodotion's Greek text reads "seal up," suggesting that the Hebrew text he used (centuries older than the Masoretic text we use today) also read "seal up."

[74] Literally, "his end," signifying either the end of the "sanctuary" (grammatically masculine), or the end that the agent himself brings upon the city and sanctuary. Either way, Jerusalem's destruction was to be like a flood.

COMMENTARY: DANIEL 8 AND 9

Introduction: Daniel by the Stream Ulai

Daniel receives his vision in year 3 of Belshazzar's reign, hence after the vision of Daniel 7 (year 1 of Belshazzar), yet before the demise of Belshazzar recorded in Daniel 5. This timing provides a subtle hint of judgment, for Daniel 1 likewise opened with judgment upon Jerusalem in year 3 of Jehoiakim. In fact, all the imagery in Daniel 8 directs our attention to the Day of Atonement, the day of judgment.

In Daniel 7, we saw contrasting sides of judgment. Verse 22 spoke of judgment in *favor* of the holy people, and verse 26 spoke of judgment *against* the little horn's dominion. Likewise, Daniel 8 deals with judgment for and against the same entities.

The Vision: Christ's Sanctuary

Daniel mentions that his vision occurs at the stream of Ulai. While there was such a stream or canal in Shushan (Susa, 230 miles east of Babylon[75]), why is it mentioned? After all, God wants us to focus our energies on the grand biblical theme of judgment, not get bogged down in geographical minutiae.

For a proper understanding of the Hebrew *'ulai*, any standard lexicon (or even Strong's Concordance) proves helpful. Only in Daniel 8:2 and 16 is the word a proper noun referring to the canal of Ulai; everywhere else, *'ulai* is an adverb meaning "perhaps," "suppose," etc. Letting the Bible explain itself, the significance of this canal name is determined by its usage as an adverb elsewhere in Scripture.

---

[75] In notes on Daniel 8:2, the NET states that it was "apparently a sizable artificial canal in Susa," while *SDABC4* asserts that it is "identified with the Ulai of the cuneiform tablets, and the Eulaeus of the classical Greek authors. The river passed Susa in a southerly and southeasterly direction and entered the river Karun."

The initial use of *'ulai* is in Genesis 16:2, in which Sarai suggests to Abram that they implement God's covenant promise with him (the seed of Genesis 15) in *their own strength*: "'*Yahweh* has restrained me from bearing. Please, go in unto my maidservant—*'ulai* ["perhaps"] I will be built up [i.e., have a household of children] by her.' So Abram listened to the voice of Sarai." God's covenant has already figured prominently in the book of Daniel, particularly as Daniel 4 and 5 relate to Leviticus 26. We are to rely on God's promises *alone* to fulfill His covenant, without resort to *any* human devising.

Next, *'ulai* occurs in Genesis 18:24 and 28–32, where Abraham intercedes with *Yahweh* on behalf of wicked Sodom. Each verse is of the form, "'*Ulai* ["suppose"] there are 50 righteous people in the midst of the city—will You indeed sweep it away, and not bear with the place on account of the 50 who are righteous, those inside it?" Hence, *'ulai* is connected with Abraham in the context of intercession prior to *Yahweh's* investigation of Sodom and subsequent execution of judgment (see vs. 18:20, 21; 19:24, 25).

In Daniel 8:9, we find a fascinating confirmation of the connection between Abraham's intercession for Sodom and the "horn from insignificance." The word for 'insignificance' is *tsa'ir*, answering to the town to which Lot fled before Sodom was destroyed. "Is it not insignificant [*mits'ar*]? ... Therefore the name of the city was called insignificant [*tso'ar*]" (Gen. 19:20, 22).

We should also note that the word translated "stream" in Daniel 8:2 is the Hebrew word *'uval*, which is a variant spelling of *yuval* (see BDB, s.v. *'uval*), the word familiar to Bible students as "Jubilee." *Yuval* refers properly to a ram, and by association, its horn, which was blown on the Day of Atonement marking a Jubilee year (see Lev. 25:10). In other words, the *'uval* ("stream") of Daniel 8:2 hints that the vision ties in with the Jubilee release of Leviticus 25. While Daniel 8 focuses on the Day of Atonement, Daniel 9 will tie the Jubilee release to the soul cleansing on the Day of Atonement.

The vision opens with a ram standing before the stream of Ulai. The ram butts seaward (west), north, and south, hence it comes from the sunrise (east). In verse 20, Gabriel states that this ram refers to the kings of Media and Persia, and Bible maps confirm Medo-Persia is to the *east* of Babylonia. In Isaiah 45:1, Cyrus (founder of Medo-Persia and conqueror of Babylonia) is called *Yahweh's* messiah, for his decree was to free the Judean captives. Cyrus typifies Jesus as Messiah, who will also come from the sunrise (see Matt. 24:27).

Why the symbolism of the ram? Table 12 provides the most pertinent references:

Table 12: Scriptural Significance of Ram

SCRIPTURE	SIGNIFICANCE OF RAM
Gen. 15:9, 10	Offered when *Yahweh* cut the everlasting covenant with Abram.
Gen. 22:13	*Yahweh* provides a ram as a substitute burnt offering for Isaac.
Lev. 9:2, 4, 18–24	Used to inaugurate earthly sanctuary.
Lev. 16:3, 5	Used as burnt offering on the Day of Atonement.

What Table 12 indicates is vital to a proper understanding of Daniel 8. The ram is associated with the *fulfillment of God's everlasting covenant via his work of atonement*. God used a ram when he initiated the everlasting covenant with Abram. Later, in providing a ram for Abraham when He asked him to sacrifice his own son Isaac, the substitutionary phase of God's atonement was typified, for Jesus was later sent to be the atoning sacrifice on Calvary as our substitute. The opening words of Daniel 8:3—"I lifted my eyes, looked, and behold, 1 ram"—point back to Genesis 22:13, in which "Abraham lifted his eyes, looked, and behold, a ram" (in fact, the marginal Hebrew reading is "one ram") ensnared in the thicket by its horns. Similarly, in Daniel 8:7, the very horns that the ram uses to force his will prove to be his downfall and are smashed.

The rams used at the inauguration of the earthly sanctuary and during the Day of Atonement ritual each typified the second phase of God's atonement. As the remainder of Daniel 8–12 makes clear, Jesus is now completing the work of judgment during the Day of Atonement by applying His atoning blood in the heavenly sanctuary to perfect our characters. When that is complete, He will return to bring His children home.

Note this key difference between the ram and God: The ram uses *force* to become great, as no one he seeks to conquer can be delivered from his hand[76]; God conquers "without hand," i.e., without the use of force—He respects religious liberty. In verse 25, Rome will be shattered "without hand."

The reader is introduced to a male goat of the goats in verses 5–8. This goat moves above the ground from the sunset (west), in opposition to the ram, which came from the sunrise (east). This indicates the western power that overthrew Medo-Persia, i.e., Hellas (Greece), as Gabriel confirms in verse 21. Recall that the ram in many ways mirrors Jesus as our Deliverer, so this suggests that the male goat represents the archenemy, Satan. In fact, the book of Genesis associates the male goat's eastward movement with rebellion, as Table 13 makes clear:

Table 13: Eastward Movement and Rebellion Against God in Genesis

SCRIPTURE	SIGNIFICANCE OF EASTWARD MOVEMENT
Gen. 3:24	After their sin, Adam and Eve leave the Garden of Eden on the east side.
Gen. 4:16	After committing murder, Cain moves to Nod on the east of Eden.
Gen. 11:2	Those who founded Babel (Babylon) move eastward.[77]
Gen. 13:11, 12	After selfishly choosing the best land, Lot moves east toward Sodom.
Gen. 25:6	Abraham sent his concubines' sons—those according to flesh, not God's promise (see Gal. 4:23)—east.
Gen. 29:1	After securing Isaac's blessing by fleshly means, Jacob moved east.

---

[76] "Hand" and "power" are often synonymous in Scripture (see Gen. 32:11; Exod. 3:8; 23:31; 32:11).

[77] Some translations indicate the founders moved *from* the east, whereas others (e.g., ASV, CEB, ERV, GWN, JPS 1917, LEE, NASU, NET, NIV, NJB, NLT) correctly recognize "toward the east" or "eastward" in the underlying Hebrew. The Hebrew "eastward" of Genesis 11:2 is *identical* to that of Genesis 2:8; 3:24; 12:8; 13:11, all of which clearly indicate "eastward" or "east of". The founders of Babel, representatives of rebellion *par excellence*, moved eastward.

Hence, the western origin of the male goat points to the western Greeks of Hellas. Its eastward movement indicates it is the agent of Satan and highlights its rebellious nature.

To appreciate the symbolism of the male goat of the goats, we need to see how the phrase is used elsewhere in Scripture. Outside of Daniel 8:5 and 8, this exact phrase is used only in 2 Chronicles 29:21, in which 7 male goats of the goats were offered following King Hezekiah's cleansing of the temple. In verse 29, these 7 male goats of the goats are called bucks. Gabriel, too, identifies the male goat of the goats as a buck in Daniel 8:21. Why does Gabriel make this connection for us? The answer is found in 2 Chronicles 29:24: "the priests slaughtered them, and made a sin offering with their blood on the altar to *make atonement for all Israel*" (emphasis supplied).

Like the ram, the goat imagery of Daniel 8 points back to God's earthly temple (a ram for inauguration, a buck for atonement following cleansing). The connection with atonement is even clearer in Leviticus 16, in which 2 bucks of the goats were used on the Day of Atonement. One was presented to *Yahweh*, the other to *Azazel*. *Azazel* is a combination of two Hebrew words, *'az* ("goat") and *'azal* ("go away"), hence "the goat that goes away," a name for the chief goat-demon, Satan. *Yahweh's* goat was killed, and its blood was used to make atonement for the sanctuary. This illustrates how Jesus died on our behalf and uses His blood to make atonement in the heavenly sanctuary. On the other hand, *Azazel's* goat does *not* make atonement. Rather, the sins of the people were transferred from the sanctuary and placed on its head, and then it was let go in the wilderness. This illustrates what happens when Jesus has completed atonement for the heavenly sanctuary. All records of sin are placed upon the head of Satan, and then he is left in the wilderness of a desolated earth prior to his destruction (see Rev. 20, 21).

Scripture often associates the goat with the devil. Jesus refers to the wicked at his return as goats (see Matt. 25:33, 41), and goat-demons in heathen worship are called "bucks" (see Lev. 17:7; 2 Chron. 11:15).

A summary of the key verses explaining "male goat of the goats" and "buck" is found in Table 14:

Table 14: Scriptural Significance of "Male Goat of the Goats" and "Buck"

SCRIPTURE	SIGNIFICANCE OF BUCK
2 Chron. 29:21	Seven male goats of the goats offered after temple is cleansed under Hezekiah.
2 Chron. 29:23, 24	"Male goats of the goats" and "buck" synonymous. Used to make atonement for all Israel.
Lev. 16:5, 8–22	Two bucks of the goats used on the Day of Atonement: • One buck for *Yahweh*, one buck for *Azazel*. • Buck for *Yahweh* killed. Buck's blood atones for sanctuary. • Buck for *Azazel*: sins placed on back, led into wilderness.
Lev. 17:7; 2 Chron. 11:15	"Bucks" used to refer to heathen goat-demons.

A goat to represent Greece is very appropriate, for the goat was quite common on Macedonian coins minted from the 500–146 BC time period (see photographs of plaster casts of such coins in Froom, *PFF*, vol. 1, pp. 130, 131). When Alexander the Great saw the immense army of Persian king Darius III, he feared that defeat at this point would nullify his victories thus far. Plutarch records his soldiers buoying his spirits with these words: "Be of good cheer, Sire, and do not fear the great numbers of the enemy; for they will not be able to stand the very smell of goat that clings to us."[78] For such a statement to have any meaning, the goat was a clearly an apt symbol of Grecian might!

Nobody can rescue from the goat's hand, as evidenced by his defeat of the ram. He is described as furious and embittered and grows, not merely *great* like the ram, but *very* great. Alexander's forces were far fewer in number than those he opposed. Ancient historian Arrian of Nicomedia (considered Alexander's most reliable historian) estimates his forces

---

[78] Plutarch, "L 245 Plutarch Moralia III Kings Commanders Romans Spartans," The Internet Archive, https://1ref.us/yu (accessed January 22, 2020).

at 40,000 infantry and 7,000 cavalry. At the battle of Issus (November, 333 BC), he met the Persian army, a force of 600,000 men. Using cavalry for attack and infantry for defense, Persian King Darius III fled. On October 1, 331 BC, the decisive victory was gained against the Achaemenid Empire of Persia at Gaugamela near Arbela. Alexander's slim forces made up for this by their rapid, unpredictable rushes against the enemy. Darius III fled, and his generals assassinated him for his cowardice. That winter (early 330 BC), Alexander seized Persepolis, capital of the Achaemenid Empire. He raided the city, his soldiers stole, raped, and killed, and later he had the city burned to the ground. Alexander did indeed strike the ram, shatter its 2 horns, cast it to the ground, and trample it! He enjoyed a series of conquests throughout central Asia and eastward into India (see Durant, *SC2*, pp. 542–547).

Alexander died in June of 323 BC, just shy of his 33rd birthday in July. Historians Plutarch and Diodorus agree that he imbibed a large quantity of alcohol approximately 2 weeks before his death,[79] demonstrating an ironic lack of *self*-control for one who brought the world to its knees.

For the better part of his life, Alexander was quite temperate. He counseled that "the greatest need after our victories is to avoid the vices and weaknesses of those whom we have conquered." Refusing rich foods, he was abstemious in diet and, until the last part of his life, drink (Durant, *SC2*, p. 539). What led Alexander to drink at the close of his life? Among other things, he decided to be treated as a god (perhaps as a political maneuver to secure unity in his empire), which his army officers did not like. He executed Philotas (who conspired to kill him) and Philotas's father, the general Parmenio (whom Philotas implicated while being tortured), only worsening relations with the army. Alexander grew increasingly suspicious, seeking solace with alcohol (see Durant, *SC2*, pp. 549, 550).

In remarks on Daniel 7, it was shown that the 4 heads of the leopard correspond to the western Greeks of Italy and Sicily, along with the

---

[79] "Alexander the Great," Wikipedia, https://1ref.us/yv (accessed January 22, 2020).

threefold division of Alexander's empire following his death. Likewise, the 4 horns of the Grecian goat represent the same fourfold makeup.

The chapter transitions to the next world power, Rome, by continuing the use of horn imagery. We have seen that the thighs of bronze and calves of iron in the legs of the metal image of Daniel 2 point to the blend of Hellas (Greece) and Rome. Likewise, the iron teeth and bronze nails on the fourth beast of Daniel 7 indicate its Greco-Roman nature. In Daniel 8:9, the Roman horn from insignificance growing up among the horns of the Grecian goat again points to the same Greco-Roman blend.

This next world power is described as a horn from insignificance. This description might lead one to suppose that the horn is not particularly noteworthy. However, the word "insignificance" simply points to its (seemingly) insignificant *origin*. Jesus, the most significant personage in history, came from humble Nazareth. As a counterfeit of Jesus, this horn shares an insignificant origin as well.

The horn from "insignificance" points the reader back to the story of Lot and his deliverance from Sodom. When directed to flee unto the mountain that he be not swept away in the conflagration about to befall the cities of the area, Lot countered that such an escape might itself lead to his destruction. He proposed fleeing to "an insignificant" city, and then queried, "is it not an insignificant one?" (Gen 19:20). The name of the city was Zoar, and the Hebrew words for "insignificant one" and "insignificance" are inflections of this Hebrew name.

Lot was under the delusion that, though the cities of the plain would be overthrown for their sinfulness, this city's small size indicated a much smaller threat than that of Sodom. However, after his arrival, "Lot went up from Zoar ... for he was afraid to dwell in Zoar, so he dwelt in a cave" (Gen. 19:30). Despite its small size, he recognized the same wicked influences that destroyed his family in Sodom; thus it is with the horn from insignificance. Its unassuming origin is no indicator of its great wickedness at full maturity.

We are now prepared to investigate the horn from insignificance in verses 9–12. We begin with its origin, of which verse 9 states that it emerges "from the 1$_{[fem]}$ of them$_{[masc]}$," which gets smoothed out in English as "from the first$_{[fem]}$ of them$_{[masc]}$" or "from number 1$_{[fem]}$ of them$_{[masc]}$." What does this mean? The gender markers[80] included in the translation help answer this question by permitting us to compare this statement with the explanatory statement in verse 8. Following Alexander's death, 4 horns$_{[fem]}$ came up "toward the 4$_{[fem]}$ winds$_{[fem]}$ of the heavens$_{[masc]}$." In other words, each of the 4 horns$_{[fem]}$ was associated with a particular wind$_{[fem]}$ (compass direction) of the heavens. This enables us to equate "number 1$_{[fem]}$ of them$_{[masc]}$" with the first horn and its associated compass direction of the heavens (i.e., the western Greeks of Italy and Sicily).

As we consider verse 9, it is natural to ask why the horn from insignificance "emerged" (grammatically masculine verb), yet also "grew" (grammatically feminine verb). Is this gender change significant? It is, and the answer is found in verses 22 and 23, in which Gabriel identifies the preceding 4 horns as kingdoms (feminine), but the horn from insignificance as a king (masculine). In other words, what emerges from the first western horn (the western Greeks) and ultimately becomes prominent is a kingly power, but in its early stages, it is particularly the *kingdom*, not the *king*, that is of note. History records that Rome's earliest centuries were characterized by strife between the wealthy elite and small landowners, as well as incessant warfare with the Italian groups of Etruscans, Latins, Volsci and Aequi. These lesser disputes kept it off the stage of historical greatness. It wasn't until the Punic Wars of 264–146 BC and Macedonian Wars of 212–168 BC that Rome began to establish itself as a significant presence in the Mediterranean.[81]

Growing great toward the south (Egypt), sunrise (east), and beauty (Israel) finds historical fulfillment. Rome protected Egypt when the Senate ordered Antiochus Epiphanes in 168 BC to withdraw his army and leave Egypt, and by 30 BC, Rome had reduced Egypt to a province. Rome

---

[80] Many languages assign every noun a grammatical gender. For instance, in Spanish, *el libro* ("book") is masculine (note the article *el* and the *o* ending), whereas *la revista* ("magazine") is feminine (note the article *la* and the *a* ending).

[81] "Rome," Wikipedia, https://1ref.us/yw (accessed January 22, 2020).

subjugated Syria in the east in 65 BC and made it a province, and Judea became a province in 63 BC, following the league 98 years prior in 161 BC (see *SDABC4*, comments on Daniel 8:9). Of particular interest is *why* Judea entered into league with Rome. The answer is that the kingdom of Hellas had imposed a grievous yoke upon them, "reducing Israel to slavery" (1 Macc. 8:18). Rome was only too delighted with this request, and in an incredible twist of irony, produced a "letter which they wrote in reply upon bronze tablets and sent unto Jerusalem to be by them there as a record of peace and alliance" (1 Macc. 8:22). We have noted several instances where Scripture associates bronze with Hellas, and further, how Rome is inextricably bound up with Hellas. Now history corroborates both these points. Nevertheless, since Rome had conquered Macedonia (part of Hellas) in 168 BC, just 7 years prior (Smith, *Daniel and the Revelation*, p. 153), the Jews no doubt concluded Rome would be their best ally in removing the Grecian yoke. They were happy that Rome had already written to Demetrius, threatening retaliation if they received further complaint from the Jews regarding him (see 1 Macc. 8:31, 32). The Jews had forgotten Isaiah 8:12, which expressly forbade such alliances with heathen nations. Thus, in less than a century, Obadiah 7 was realized all too clearly: "Unto the border have all the men of your covenant sent you; they have deceived you, they have overcome you, the men of your peace."

Comparison with Psalm 75 shows that these compass directions have a spiritual significance as well. This passage also refers to 3 compass directions and horns. God will cut off those of the wicked, while exalting those of the righteous. The psalm warns against exalting one's own horn (greatness) or seeking exaltation from the issuance (east), sunset/evening (west), or the wilderness (south), for God is the Judge. According to Isaiah 14:13, it is in the farthest parts of the north that God sits enthroned as Judge.

As already established, the horn from insignificance comes from the west, whence one should not seek exaltation. True exaltation is associated with God as Judge (see Ps. 75:7), while Lucifer sought to exalt himself to God's position in the north (see Isa. 14:13). The one direction toward which the horn does not yet grow is the north, so Daniel 8:9 provides a hint that the horn is Satan's earthly agent through which he works (unsuccessfully) to secure his ultimate aim: displacing God as supreme Judge. The "he" of Daniel 8:9 refers to the emperors and popes that have ruled Rome, and ultimately Satan, who has employed them as his puppets.[82]

In verse 10, the description of the horn and its activities is entirely feminine. As noted earlier, this means the focus is not on the king, but the kingdom. It exalts itself against the host of the heavens, so we need to understand what the host of the heavens is. First, the "host" is the word God uses to refer to His people as an army when he led them forth out of Egypt (see Exod. 6:26; 7:4; 12:17, 41, 51). Why does the text refer to God's people as "of the heavens"? In Genesis 15:5, *Yahweh* instructs Abram to "Look now unto the heavens. Count the stars, if you are able to count them. ... So will your seed be." The starry hosts of the heavens are a figure for those who take fast hold of the Abrahamic (everlasting) covenant. They are those who, while still living upon the earth, are dwelling in heavenly places (see Rev. 12:12).

Evidently, this horn kingdom is not simply imperial Rome of the Caesars, but rather its religious successor, papal Rome. The Roman papacy was to exalt itself against God's people, those faithful to His covenant. The papacy, guided by Satan himself, managed to cause "some of the host to fall to earth." Does this refer to their martyrdom, or apostasy? Comparison with Revelation 12:4 shows that Satan drew a third of the stars of heaven to the earth with his tail, meaning he caused their disaffection, or apostasy, from God by his lies (the tail represents a lying prophet in Isaiah 9:15). Likewise, in Luke 10:18, Jesus says he saw Satan fall like lightning from heaven, referring to his rejection from God's favor. Thus, when Satan's papal system causes "some of the host to fall to earth," it means

---

[82] The dragon of Revelation 12 also represents both Satan and the rulers of Rome: "The dragon is said to be Satan (Revelation 12:9); he it was that moved upon Herod to put the Saviour to death. But the chief agent of Satan in making war upon Christ and His people during the first centuries of the Christian Era was the Roman Empire, in which paganism was the prevailing religion. Thus while the dragon, primarily, represents Satan, it is, in a secondary sense, a symbol of pagan Rome" (White, *GC*, p. 438).

that they fall from their steadfastness, and thus tragically, from God's favor. Those "stars" that the papacy did not succeed in getting to apostatize, it trampled, referring to the excruciating tortures inflicted upon those who dissented from her doctrines. Such an understanding of the host of heaven and their trampling harmonizes with history, for indeed, the Roman Catholic Church persecuted tens of millions of God's faithful people throughout the 1,260 years, the centuries of papal rule during the Dark Ages.[83]

In verse 11, the horn power is once again described using masculine language. What does this tell us? Whereas the previous verse presented a conflict between Satan's church (the papal system) and God's church (termed the "host of the heavens"), the current verse presents a conflict between Satan (the true ruler of the papal system) and the Ruler of the host. According to Joshua 5:15, the Ruler of the host is Jesus Himself, for He accepts Joshua's worship; mere angels refuse worship (see Rev. 19:10; 22:9).

To better appreciate the relationship between Satan's false church and Satan himself, first note that God has a bride in Scripture—His church of faithful followers.[84] Satan has a counterfeit of everything true, so he has a counterfeit church through whom he works as well. The following verses illustrate the *correct* relationship between Jesus and His true church:

> Jer. 23:5, 6: "Behold, days are coming," declares *Yahweh*, "When I will raise up unto David a righteous shoot. Then a king shall reign, and He will act wisely and execute judgment and

---

[83] For brief synopses of the Roman Catholic Church's systematic torture of the Waldenses who dissented from her doctrines, the reader is referred to Wylie, *The History of Protestantism: Protestantism in the Waldensian Valleys*, especially chapters 5 ("Persecutions and Martyrdoms") and 9 ("Extinction of Waldenses in Calabria"). In light of Wylie's statement in chapter 5, paragraph 16 that "to depict the revolting and infamous details would be to narrate what no reader could peruse. We shall only quote part of the brief summary of Muston," what he *does* go on to relate is so astonishingly gruesome that one can only shudder at the events he chose to exclude.

[84] For example, see Rev. 12:1; 19:7, 8; 21:9; Jer. 6:2; Matt. 25:1–13; Prov. 31:10–31.

righteousness in the earth. In His days, Judah shall be saved and Israel will abide in security. This is His name by which He will be called: *Yahweh* our righteousness."

<u>Jer. 33:15, 16</u>: In those days and at that time, I will cause to shoot up unto David a shoot of righteousness. He will execute judgment and righteousness in the earth. In those days Judah will be saved, and Jerusalem will dwell in security. This is what He will call her: *Yahweh* our righteousness.

These verses are very similar, but Jeremiah 23:5–6 describe *Jesus* as *Yahweh our righteousness*, whereas Jeremiah 33:15–16 describe Jesus' faithful *followers* as *Yahweh our righteousness* (i.e., they have His character).

Returning to Daniel 8:11, we expect to understand that Satan's church has his character as well. His character is evil, but it is helpful to home in on his chief attribute, the desire to be *supreme*:

<u>Isa. 14:13–15</u>: You have said in your heart, "I will ascend the heavens; above the stars of God I will elevate my throne. I will sit on the mount of assembly, in the farthest reaches of the north. I will ascend above the high places of the dark cloud—I will make myself like the Most High!" Yet unto the grave you will be brought down, unto the farthest reaches of the pit.

<u>Ezek. 28:17–19</u>: Your heart swelled because of your beauty, you corrupted your wisdom on account of your splendor. I will cast you upon the earth, before kings I will place you that they may look upon you. Due to the multitude of your deviant acts, by the wickedness of your trafficking, you polluted your sanctuaries. I will bring forth a fire from your midst, it will consume you, and I will turn you into ashes upon the earth before the eyes of all who look upon you. All who know you among the peoples will be left desolate concerning you. You have been a terror, but you will cease to be forevermore.

Ever since Satan's rebellion in heaven, described in the foregoing verses, he has endeavored to secure to himself the position he covets above all—Jesus' rightful position as supreme Judge on the mount of assembly, the heavenly Mount Zion. Recall that Jesus' designation as Ruler pictures him as One whose word carries the final authority of Judge (see Exod. 2:14; 18:21–26). In Daniel 8:11, Satan seeks to usurp this office of Jesus through his false church on earth.

The horn lifts out, or removes, the "continual ministry" from "Him," i.e., Jesus. What is this "continual ministry"? The context of Daniel 8 so far guides us to the answer. First, the *'uval* ("stream") in verse 2 is a variation on *yuval*, the Hebrew word for Jubilee, which occurred on the Day of Atonement (see Lev. 25:9). Second, the ram and male goat point to the sanctuary and Day of Atonement. Third, Jesus' designation as Ruler points to him as Supreme Judge. These ideas meet on the Day of Atonement, on which the high priest, the one who wears the breastplate of judgment throughout the year (see Exod. 28:15–30), serves as judge. Thus, the "continual ministry" must relate to the sanctuary, specifically Jesus' role as High Priest and Judge during the end-time Day of Atonement.

To establish this clearly, we need to search the Scriptures for the Hebrew word *tamid* ("continual ministry"). Table 15 summarizes its 104 occurrences in Scripture:

Table 15: Use of Hebrew *tamid* in Scripture

PART OF SPEECH	ENGLISH TRANSLATION	TOTAL COUNT	SUMMARY OF USE
Adverb	"continually"	71	One hundred percent of thirteen occurrences in Exodus and Leviticus deal with the sanctuary: • Exod. 25:30: Bread of Presence on table continually. • Lev. 24:8: Aaron (high priest) to set bread of Presence in order each Sabbath continually.

(continued)

DANIEL 8 AND 9: GOD'S HAND—DELIVERANCE BY MESSIAH'S ATONING SACRIFICE

Table 15: Use of Hebrew *tamid* in Scripture (*continued*)

PART OF SPEECH	ENGLISH TRANSLATION	TOTAL COUNT	SUMMARY OF USE
			• Exod. 27:20: Menorah lamp to be lit up continually. • Lev. 24:2–4: Aaron (high priest) to tend menorah lamps continually. • Exod. 28:29, 30: Aaron (high priest) to bear names on breastplate of judgment continually. • Exod. 28:38: Aaron (high priest) to wear "Holiness to *Yahweh*" on forehead continually. • Exod. 29:38, 42: 2 lambs offered each day continually. • Exod. 30:8: Incense burn continually on altar of incense. • Lev. 6:13: Fire burn continually on altar of sacrifice.
			Seven more occurrences outside Exodus and Leviticus deal with the sanctuary: • 1 Chron. 16:37: Priests minister before ark continually. • Burnt/grain offerings offered continually. 1 Chron. 16:40; 23:31; 2 Chron. 24:14; Ps. 50:8; Ezek. 46:14, 15.
Noun	"the continual ministration"	24	One hundred percent of occurrences outside the book of Daniel deal with the sanctuary: • Num. 4:7: Continual bread on table of Presence. • Rest refer to continual grain/burnt/drink offerings: Num. 4:16; 28:10, 15, 23, 24, 31; 29:6, 11, 16, 19, 22, 25, 28, 31, 34, 38; Neh. 10:33 (twice).
			All 5 occurrences of "the continual ministration" within the book of Daniel follow: • Dan. 8:11: Horn lifts out the continual ministration from Jesus. • Dan. 8:12: Horn given host against the continual ministration.

(*continued*)

Table 15: Use of Hebrew *tamid* in Scripture (*continued*)

PART OF SPEECH	ENGLISH TRANSLATION	TOTAL COUNT	SUMMARY OF USE
			• Dan. 8:13: The vision concerning the continual ministration. • Dan. 11:31: Arms take away the continual ministration and establish the detestable idol that desolates. • Dan. 12:11: The continual ministration taken away to establish the detestable idolatry that desolates.
Adjective	"continual"	9	• Lev. 6:20: Continual grain offering on the day the high priest is anointed. • Five uses for continual bread of Presence and grain/burnt offerings: Num. 28:3, 6; 2 Chron. 5:4; Ezra 3:5; Ezek. 46:15. • Three uses unrelated to sanctuary: 2 Kings 25:30; Prov. 15:15; Jer. 52:34.

The data in Table 15 reveals that "the continual ministration" as a noun outside the book of Daniel *always* concerns God's sanctuary. Likewise, every instance of "the continual ministration" in the books of Exodus and Leviticus deals with the sanctuary. More specifically, several of these uses deal specifically with the high priest: setting the bread of the Presence in order each Sabbath; tending the menorah lamps continually; bearing the names of Israel's sons on the breastplate of judgment continually; wearing "Holiness to *Yahweh*" on his forehead continually; a continual grain offering on the day of the high priest's installation.

From this, we conclude that "the continual ministration" in Daniel refers to Christ's work as High Priest in the heavenly sanctuary. With that said, what does it mean that the horn from insignificance lifts this continual ministration out from Christ? To answer, we investigate the Hebrew word *rum*, translated "lifted out." The precise inflection used in Daniel 8:11 appears only in Leviticus 4:10 and Exodus 29:27. We begin by examining Leviticus 4:8–10, and the passage to which it refers, Leviticus 3:3–5:

> Lev. 4:8–10: All the fat of the young bull of the sin offering he will lift out [*rum*] from it: the fat covering the innards (as well as the fat which is upon the innards), both kidneys (along with the fat which is upon them which is by the loins), and the lobe over the liver by the kidneys he will remove [*sur*], just as it is lifted out [*rum*] of the sacrificial ox of the peace/well-being offerings. The priest will make them smoke upon the altar of burnt offering.
>
> Lev. 3:3–5: Then he shall present from the sacrifice of the peace/well-being offerings a fire offering unto *Yahweh*: the fat covering the innards (as well as all the fat which is upon the innards), both kidneys (along with the fat which is upon them which is by the loins), and the lobe over the liver by the kidneys he will remove [*sur*]. Then Aaron's sons will make it smoke upon the altar (upon the burnt offering which is upon the wood upon the fire)—a fire offering, a soothing odor for *Yahweh*.

Comparison of these nearly identical passages shows that "lifting out" fatty tissue in Leviticus 4:10 is equivalent to "removing" the same fatty tissue in Leviticus 3:4. To get the full significance of "lifted out" in Daniel 8:11, we investigate Exodus 29:27:

> Exod. 29:27: You will consecrate the breast of the wave offering and the lower leg of the excised offering [noun based on the verb *rum*]—which was waved and which was lifted away [*rum*]—from the ram of the installation, from that pertaining to Aaron and from that pertaining to his sons.

In Exodus 29:27, we see again the lifting away of a special offering, the lower leg of the ram used to install Aaron as high priest. In Daniel 8:11, when Satan seeks to remove the continual ministration from Jesus, it has nothing to do with the solemn service of installing Jesus as High Priest. Rather, the horn from insignificance casts down the foundation of Jesus' sanctuary. While Satan cannot actually remove Jesus as High Priest, he can effectively nullify His work by removing from the minds of Christians everywhere any knowledge of His work as High Priest in the heavenly sanctuary.

Connecting the pieces of Daniel 8 together, we see that just as Satan worked through the Grecian male goat to cast the Medo-Persian ram to the ground, so through Rome he cast down the continual ministration, the foundation of the sanctuary, removing the lower leg of the ram (see Exod. 29:27), as it were. When we recall that the lower legs of the image in Daniel 2 represented Rome, we discern that the papacy's removal of Jesus' continual ministration was achieved by Satan simultaneously installing the papacy as his counterfeit high priest on the earth. This also helps us better understand why the horn in Daniel 8:9–12 is sometimes referred to in the feminine (viewing Roman Catholicism as a church) and sometimes in the masculine (focusing on Satan working through his false high priest, the papacy). It also sheds light on Revelation 17:4–5, which pictures the papacy as a whore (feminine), dressed as a transvestite counterfeit of the high priest (masculine) of Exodus 28.

Why is Satan so intent on doing away with the heavenly sanctuary? Consider the following:

> Exod. 15:17: You will bring them in, You will plant them in the mountain of Your inheritance; a foundation for Your dwelling You have made, *Yahweh*; a sanctuary, *Adonai*, Your hands have established.
>
> Exod. 25:8: Let them make Me a sanctuary, that I may dwell among them.
>
> Ezek. 37:26–28: I will cut a covenant of peace with them; it will be an everlasting covenant with them. I will establish them, multiply them and set My sanctuary among them forever. My dwelling will be over them; I will be their God, and they will be My people. The Gentiles will know that I, *Yahweh*, make Israel holy when My sanctuary is among them forever.

The sanctuary is God's means of dwelling among His people, and Satan knows this. In Ezekiel 37:26–28, God promises to set His sanctuary among His people in whom is fulfilled the new-covenant experience. This experience is the writing of God's law in our hearts and minds (see Jer. 31:31–34; Heb. 8:8–12); His 10 Commandments are kept in the ark of the covenant in the Holy of Holies of the sanctuary (see 1 Kings 8:9; Heb. 9:3–5). If Satan can shut us away from God's heavenly sanctuary, he effectively prevents Jesus from writing His law in our hearts. This gives a whole new appreciation for Jesus' words: "Abide in me, and I in you. Just as the vine is not able to bear fruit of itself, except it abide in the vine, so neither can you, except you abide in me" (John 15:4). Referring to the dwelling place of the Holy Spirit, Paul calls our physical bodies the "temple" (see 1 Cor. 3:16, 17; 6:19, 20), establishing a link between God's people and His sanctuary.

Before moving on, let us revisit Table 15. "The continual ministration" of Daniel 8:11 directs our attention to the various activities of the sanctuary, including its various offerings, even the grain offering that commenced with the anointing of the high priest in Leviticus 6:20. This is contra almost every English translation of Daniel 8:11, including the KJV, which renders it "the daily *sacrifice*." Nevertheless, this translation is erroneous.[85]

Why focus on the grain offering? It serves as an ongoing reminder of the harvest, and in Matthew 13:39, Jesus states that "the harvest is the end of the age." What "age" does He mean? "The harvest is the end of probationary time" (White, *COL*, p. 72), at which point the cases of all have been decided forever, for weal or woe. Then it is that Jesus "immediately sends forth the sickle, for the harvest stands ready" (Mark 4:29).

Of course, Satan, in his false earthly sanctuary, has a counterfeit of the continual grain offering:

> The Eucharist is thus a sacrifice because it *re-presents* (makes present) the sacrifice of the cross, because it is its *memorial*

---

[85] "The word 'sacrifice' was supplied by man's wisdom, and does not belong to the text" (White, *RH*, November 1, 1850).

and because it *applies* its fruit ... The sacrifice of Christ and the sacrifice of the Eucharist are *one single sacrifice*: "The victim is one and the same: the same now offers through the ministry of priests, who then offered himself on the cross; only the manner of offering is different." "And since in this divine sacrifice which is celebrated in the Mass, the same Christ who offered himself once in a bloody manner on the altar of the cross is contained and offered in an unbloody manner ... this sacrifice is truly propitiatory." (*Catechism of the Catholic Church*, 2nd ed., 1366 and 1367, all emphases exactly as they appear in the catechism)

Notice how different the catechism is from Scripture, which states that by the will of God the Father "we are made holy through the offering of the body of Jesus the Messiah once for all" (Heb. 10:10). The Roman Catholic mass establishes among its adherents a false hope that continual participation in the daily mass essentially keeps their salvation current by renewing the death of Christ. The biblical truth is that Christ died a perfect atoning death *once*, and "the God of peace who brought up from the dead the great Shepherd of the sheep via the blood of the everlasting covenant, our Lord Jesus—may He fit you in every good deed to do His will, doing in you that which is well-pleasing before Him though Jesus Christ, unto whom be the glory forever and ever" (Heb. 13:20, 21).

In verse 12, emphasis again moves from Satan to the Roman Catholic Church. She was given a "host," meaning an army of those who follow and adhere to her teachings. This is incontestably true, for today, her adherents number approximately 1.313 billion people,[86] or approximately 17.4% of the United Nations mid-year, estimated world population for 2017 (last updated January 2019) of 7.550 billion people.[87] In light of remarks on verse 11 concerning the wafer and the mass, note that "host" is the very word

---

[86] "Presentation of the Pontifical Yearbook 2019 and the Annuarium Statisticum Ecclesiae 2017, 06.03.2019," Holy See Press Office, https://1ref.us/yx (accessed January 22, 2020).

[87] "Population and Vital Statistics Report," United Nations Department of Economic and Social Affairs Statistics Division, https://1ref.us/yy (accessed January 22, 2020).

Catholicism uses to refer to the wafer broken and offered in an "unbloody manner" to the hosts attending the mass. Indeed, this wafer "host" is against Jesus' continual ministration in the heavenly sanctuary, though most Roman Catholics don't know that this practice denies Christ and His free salvation.

The horn "cast truth to the ground; it did so, and thrived." In altering God's 10 Commandments by doing away with the second commandment, prohibiting idolatry, and redefining the fourth commandment so as to exalt the day of the sun rather than God's holy Sabbath, and by instituting a counterfeit of God's heavenly sanctuary here on earth, she has indeed cast truth to the ground. Further, *all* rituals of the Roman Catholic system counterfeit some aspect of Christ's true work or are contrary to His explicit directions: confessing one's sins to a priest, rather than to Christ alone (see 1 Tim. 2:5); repeating the rosary or prayers such as the "Our Father," "Hail Mary," "Apostles' Creed," or "Act of Contrition" (see Matt. 6:7); kneeling in prayer before pictures at stations of the cross (see Exod. 20:4–6); offering votive prayers and praying to Mary and the saints (see Matt. 6:6–9; 1 Tim. 2:5)[88]; baptism by sprinkling (see John 3:23; Acts 8:36–39); employing fermented (alcoholic) wine to represent Jesus' pure blood (see Prov. 23:29–35; Isa. 65:8); etc. Each and every one of these unbiblical practices comes straight from paganism, with nothing but the thinnest veneer of Christianity for a covering, to make it more palatable to those who would reject more overt paganism.

The papacy persecuted God's true people throughout the 1,260 years, and to outward appearances, she thrived. At the end of that time, she received a (nearly) mortal wound (see Rev. 13:3). However, she revived and is increasing her influence every day. Nevertheless, her sinful course is marked, and her end certain:

> Eccles. 8:11–13 (KJV): Because sentence against an evil work is not executed speedily, therefore the heart of the sons of men is

---

[88] We are to pray to the Father through His Son Jesus. Besides, Mary and the saints are dead, so they cannot hear prayer (see Eccles. 9:5; Ps. 115:17; 146:4).

fully set in them to do evil. Though a sinner do evil an hundred times, and his days be prolonged, yet surely I know that it shall be well with them that fear God, which fear before him: But it shall not be well with the wicked, neither shall he prolong his days, which are as a shadow; because he feareth not before God.

Question and Answer: Jesus and Gabriel by the Ulai

At this point, a holy being notes that the vision concerns the continual ministration and the desolating nature of Satan's rebellion. The phrase "desolating rebellion" refers to Satan's rebellion against the Most High. With the inauguration of his own, false, earthly sanctuary, with the papacy serving as a false high priest, Satan seeks to effectively remove Christ's work as High Priest in the heavenly sanctuary. By removing Jesus' sanctifying influence from people's lives, he leaves them desolate.

The length of time allotted for the trampling, 2,300 evening-mornings, is astonishing. Since Genesis 1:5 informs us that an evening and a morning comprise a complete day, and a day stands for a literal year in symbolic prophecy (see Num. 14:34; Ezek. 4:6), this prophecy covers a period of 2,300 years. At this point, we know only the *extent* of the 2,300 years. In Daniel 9, Gabriel provides the information necessary to determine the beginning of this incredibly long prophetic period.

The question is addressed to one called the *Palmoni*. It is most often translated as "a certain one," based on the assumed contraction of 2 Hebrew words, *pəloni tsalmoni* (see BDB, s.v. *pəloni*). Militating against this hypothesis is the observation that these words *always* appear in Scripture as two distinct words; there is *no* instance of the contraction of these two words. The more natural understanding is to view the word as the union of the verb *pala'* ("to be wonderful") and *manah* ("to count, to number"), hence "Wonderful Numberer." This accords well with the subsequent numerical decree of "2,300 evening-mornings" in verse 14, the prior numbering of Belshazzar's kingdom in Daniel 5, and the extensive use of numbers throughout the book of Daniel. Further, it stands in clear contrast with the king of verse 24 who "corrupts wonderfully." This Wonderful Numberer is Jesus, the Ruler of the host, for in verse 16, He commands Gabriel to explain the vision to Daniel.

The heavenly sanctuary, though trampled by the horn from insignificance, will be restored to its righteous condition. What is meant by "righteous condition" is evident from the reference to "evening-mornings," rather than "days." This wording hearkens back to Genesis 1, for the account of each day of creation week ends with the formula "there was evening, and there was morning" (see Gen 1:5, 8, 13, 19, 23, 31). Just as everything was perfect at creation, the promise of Daniel 8:14 is that the heavenly sanctuary will be restored to spotless perfection.

How could the sanctuary possibly be polluted, since it is in heaven? In Daniel 7, we learned of the record books comprising the judgment. Since the end-time judgment takes place in God's sanctuary, the very *records of sin* are contaminants that must be blotted out before the sanctuary is restored to perfection. Even in the earthly sanctuary, the high priest made atonement for both the sanctuary *and* the people on the Day of Atonement (see Lev. 16:20, 30). This is good news indeed! When the heavenly *sanctuary* is fully purged of the sins of God's professed people, the *people themselves* stand on earth—*in this life*—without a single stain of sin upon their record; they reflect Christ fully, no longer yielding to the strong pull of sin upon their carnal nature. They have become "partakers of the divine nature, having escaped the corruption that is in the world through lust" (2 Peter 1:4, KJV).

Daniel Stands: The Vision Explained

Daniel actively seeks to understand the vision. This illustrates Christ's teaching in Matthew 7:7: We are to seek that we may find. We are promised that we will find Him when we seek Him with our whole heart (see Jer. 29:10–14). Following Daniel's example, let us look closely at verses 15–17, noting the chiastic arrangement so as to discern the main point:

> v. 15: I, Daniel, was watching the vision
>> v. 15: Seeking understanding
>>> v. 15: One **standing** before me
>>>> v. 15: With the appearance
>>>>> v. 15: Of a man [Hebrew *gever*].
>>>>>> v. 16: I heard a man's [Hebrew *'adam*] voice from the midst of the Ulai,
>>>>> v. 16: "Gabriel ["God is my *gever*"], make this particular one understand"
>>>>> v. 16: "the appearance [early portion of 2,300 evening-mornings]."
>>>> v. 17: He came alongside **where I stood**
>>> v. 17: "Understand"
>> v. 17: "Son of man, the vision pertains to the end time."

The chiastic peak of these verses is the voice that Daniel hears from the midst of the Ulai. This may not seem to mean much on the surface, but the fact that Jesus' voice is designated a man's voice (literally, "voice of *'adam*") shows how fully He identifies with His poor, fallen creatures. In verse 17, Gabriel addresses Daniel as "son of man." This implies a couple of things:

1. While always fully God, Jesus became a true son of Adam. "Therefore, He ought in all things to become identified with His brothers, so that He could become a merciful—and faithful—High Priest in the things pertaining to God, in order to make atonement for the sins of the people." "For we do not have a High Priest who is unable to sympathize with our weaknesses, but one who was tried in all points in like manner—*without sin!* Therefore, let us come with confidence to the throne of grace, that we may receive mercy, and find grace for timely help" (Heb. 2:17; 4:15, 16).
2. Daniel has the high privilege of being considered a son of Jesus, the last Adam (see 1 Cor. 15:22, 45).

The voice that Daniel hears comes "from the midst of the Ulai." As discussed in remarks on verse 2, this points to the covenant with Abram. Hence, the voice Daniel hears from the midst of the Ulai is God's assurance that His covenant still stands. Though Daniel is troubled, a proper understanding of the vision—particularly that portion Jesus designates "the appearance"—is designed to inspire hope.

In verse 18, Daniel is enabled to stand just prior to learning what will occur in "the latter part of the outrage, for at an appointed time is the end." This seemingly incidental mention of standing is instructive for God's people in the last days. On the one hand, His "people are destroyed for lack of knowledge" (Hosea 4:6). Conversely, a proper understanding of Jesus' work as High Priest during the end-time judgment bolsters our faith in God's promise to enable us to stand when all earthly support will fail us.

Gabriel refers to an "outrage." This outrage refers to the horn's rebellious attempt to take Jesus' place as Judge and High Priest and its ruthless slaughter of millions of Christians who steadfastly refused such papal arrogance. However, this outrage is to be followed by the end-time judgment, during which Jesus cleanses the heavenly sanctuary, vindicating Himself and those who (apparently) died in vain.

Gabriel assures Daniel that "at an appointed time is the end." We learned that the end time began with the conclusion of the "time, times, and half a time" of Daniel 7:25, namely the year 1798. In Daniel 9, Gabriel will provide additional information to establish the beginning of the 2,300 evening-mornings and hence the *conclusion* of the 2,300 evening-mornings when the end-time judgment commences.

Gabriel explains the ram's horns as the kings of Media and Persia. Since the Persians emerged as dominant, the ram was a particularly fit symbol, for the ram was a "common emblem" for the Persians (de Kock, *7 Heads and 10 Horns*, p. 127).

Gabriel's explanation of the male goat is very succinct. It is a representation of the king of Hellas, and the great horn is that greatest of Grecian kings, Alexander the Great. Why does Gabriel highlight this first king of

Greece? It is of note that Alexander was the product of pagan Greek philosophy, being the pupil up to age 16 of Aristotle, himself the pupil of Plato, who was in turn taught of Socrates. Greek philosophy offers a godless worldview, entirely dependent on mankind's faulty reasoning. Thus, Alexander's kingdom and the 3 kingdoms into which it divided following his demise share the same Greek philosophical mold that originated with the fourth head of the leopard in Daniel 7—the western Greeks of Hellas.

The 4 kingdoms are from the *goy*, a Hebrew word that *can* mean "nation" or "Gentiles," though its root meaning is simply "people." Many have assumed that the "nation" of Alexander is here meant, leading to the erroneous identification of the 4 horns with Alexander's 4 leading generals. Since history testifies that the 4 horns are the 3 posthumous divisions of Alexander's empire in conjunction with the western Greeks of Hellas, *goy* in this context refers to a "people group," those with a common ethnic origin.

Gabriel refers to "the final period of their kingdom," meaning the point at which the horn from insignificance emerges from the first of the 4 horns, the western Greeks. This horn is "strong of countenance," or better, "goat-faced" (see footnote 68). For Rome to be "goat-faced" means that it is not an entirely new power, but rather an outgrowth of Hellas, in harmony with the historical record.[89]

"The king" is synonymous with the horn from insignificance, through whom Satan works his deceptions. What "dark sayings" does he understand? The words of the wise are dark sayings (see Prov. 1:6). Wisdom, understanding, and the parable are synonymous with dark sayings (see Ps. 49:3, 4). God takes delight in being the Revealer of secrets of Daniel 2, while Satan does his best to obscure the plan of salvation through the false teachings developed in Greek philosophy (e.g., immortality of the soul), carried over into pagan Rome, and ultimately mixed with a veneer of Christianity in the false Roman papal system.

---

[89] Major Greco-Roman linkages: 1) The bronze thighs (Hellas) and iron calves (Rome) of the Daniel 2 image; 2) the iron teeth (Rome) and bronze nails (Hellas) of the fourth beast in Daniel 7:19; 3) the little horn emerges from "number 1 of them" (Daniel 8:9), referring to both the first horn and its associated direction, i.e., the western Greeks; 4) the goat-faced papal king of Daniel 8:23.

This horn from insignificance that arises is said to have mighty strength, yet it is not his own strength. The implication is that there is another power, that of Satan himself, which gives the horn from insignificance its great strength. Satan gave pagan Rome strength, just as later the dragon (Satan working through pagan Rome) was to give the beast (papal Rome) its power, seat, and great authority (see Rev. 13:2).

Satan, through Rome, will "corrupt wonderfully," a clear contrast with the "Wonderful Numberer" of Daniel 8:13. The horn from insignificance corrupts wonderfully by leading "even the people of the greater [i.e., heavenly] sanctuary" to sin, thereby corrupting the heavenly sanctuary with the record of their sins and downfall. This is a most solemn warning for all. Let none entertain the idea that "I am saved" or "I have been saved," for this is misleading. Whenever we take our eyes off Jesus, we are liable to fall.[90]

Many translations state that the horn will "destroy [Hebrew *shachat*] wonderfully." Pagan Rome did put to death the "Wonderful Numberer" at Calvary, and during the Dark Ages, papal Rome did put to death an astonishing number of dissenters (estimates range from 50 to 100 million). Interestingly, *shachat* encompasses the ideas of "corruption" *and* "destruction," as in Genesis 6:11–13: "The earth was corrupt (*shachat*) before God; the earth was filled with violence. God saw the earth, and behold, it was corrupt (*shachat*), for all flesh had corrupted (*shachat*) its way upon the earth. So God said to Noah, 'The end of all flesh has come before up Me, for the earth is full of violence because of them. Behold, I am about to destroy (*shachat*) the earth.'" In fact, the root idea of *shachat* is corruption. The Israelites corrupted themselves in the golden calf episode, and the people were warned against corrupting themselves by

---

[90] "Never can we safely put confidence in self or feel, this side of heaven, that we are secure against temptation. Those who accept the Saviour, however sincere their conversion, should never be taught to say or to feel that they are saved. This is misleading. Every one should be taught to cherish hope and faith; but even when we give ourselves to Christ and know that He accepts us, we are not beyond the reach of temptation. ...

... Those who accept Christ, and in their first confidence say, I am saved, are in danger of trusting to themselves. ... Our only safety is in constant distrust of self, and dependence on Christ" (White, *COL*, p. 155).

making another graven image (see Exod. 32:7; Deut. 4:16). Thus, here in Daniel 8:24, Rome is corrupt at its very core, so it will "corrupt wonderfully," leading to destruction for many.

How does the horn corrupt many with a "sense of peace?" This refers back to the Jews' league with pagan Rome in 161 BC, when they sought protection from their enemies, culminating in Judea's subjugation as a Roman province in 63 BC (see comments on verses 9–12). With the sad history of the Jews' subjugation and the warning of Obadiah 7 against such pagan alliances before us, let us take heed not to enter into any alliance with *papal* Rome in our day. As Satan's special tool, Rome never changes.

The true aim of Satan is given at the end of Daniel 8:25: "Even against the Ruler of rulers he will stand." This was fulfilled at the cross: "Rome, finally, in the person of one of its governors, stood up against the Prince of princes, by giving sentence of death against Jesus Christ" (Smith, *Daniel and the Revelation*, p. 182). Satan attempted to prevent Jesus from rising from the dead (see Matt. 27:63–66) so that He would forever forfeit His seat as Judge, and the devil could then claim it. Later, through papal Rome, Satan would exalt himself against the Ruler of the host (compare verses 10–12), trying to undermine Jesus' work in the heavenly sanctuary. In the end, though, Rome will be shattered "without hand." This points back to Daniel 2:34 and 45, in which Jesus' stone kingdom is to cut out of the mountain without hands, and at the second coming, following the close of the end-time judgment, this stone breaks in pieces all false kingdoms, of which this horn in its papal phase is the supreme development.

The appearance portion (i.e., the first portion)[91] of the 2,300 evening-mornings of verse 14 is left unexplained. Gabriel will provide the explanation of this part of the vision at the close of Daniel 9.

---

[91] The present author is indebted to Michael Oxentenko (*The Two Distinct Visions of khazon and mar'eh in Daniel 8 and the Relationship of the 2300 Evenings and Mornings of Daniel 8:14 to the Seventy Weeks of Daniel 9:24–27*) for this understanding of the *mar'eh* ("appearance," often translated "vision") as referring to only the first portion of the 2,300 evening-mornings, rather than the entirety of the 2,300 evening-mornings. The present author became aware of Oxentenko's findings in

Daniel Does Not Understand, Pleads with *Adonai*

Daniel concludes by mentioning that no one could give him understanding. Gabriel has told Daniel to shut up the vision, for it pertains to the future. For an understanding of the mysterious "appearance" (the first portion of the 2,300 evening-mornings), Daniel must await Gabriel's explanation in chapter 9, followed by an encounter with the "appearance" of Jesus Himself in chapter 10. For now, though, the sense of desolation Daniel experiences hints at the significance of the mysterious "appearance." Jesus would be desolated as the weight of the sins of the world rolled upon Him in Gethsemane, culminating in His death at Calvary when the first portion of the 2,300 evening-mornings neared its close. The latter portion of the vision will be explained in Daniel 11 and 12.

As chapter 9 opens, Daniel is searching the Scriptures to determine how long Jerusalem was to remain in ruins—would it extend another 2,300 years? His search of Jeremiah leads him to conclude that the Babylonian captivity is to be 70 years. "These nations will serve the king of Babylon 70 years. Then, 70 years being fulfilled, I will punish the king of Babylon and that nation." "Upon completion of 70 years at Babylon I will visit you ... to cause you to return to this place [Jerusalem]" (Jer. 25:11, 12; 29:10). Clearly the 2,300 years refers to something *other* than the Babylonian captivity.

The Jews went into captivity because they refused to follow God's direction to have the land keep Sabbath every seventh year (see 2 Chron. 36:21; Lev. 25:1–7). The land had no Sabbath rest for 70 Sabbatical years covering a 490-year period, so God gave it 70 years of rest while the Jews were in captivity. As Gabriel explains in Daniel 9:24, the Jews were to be given *another* 490 years to determine if they had learned their lesson.[92] We have the Jews' experience on record, so there will be no additional probationary periods granted to those of us in the judgment hour. Either we

---

reviewing portions of Richard Davidson's yet-unpublished work, *A Song for the Sanctuary*, specifically pages 64–70 of chapter 22 ("The Sanctuary in Daniel 9: Christ, the Cross, and Chronology").

[92] "As the time approached for the close of the seventy years' captivity ... [Daniel] saw that the time was at hand when God would give His chosen people another trial" (White, *SL*, p. 46).

honor God faithfully in all matters, and He seals us for eternity, or probation closes, and we will have our place in the lake of fire (see Rev. 14:1–5; 20:11–15).

We Have Broken Your Covenant

Daniel remains in perplexity concerning the 2,300 years, so he does what anyone should do when troubled: he goes to God in prayer. An examination of Daniel's prayer in verses 3–19 reveals that he employs the title *Adonai* 10 times when addressing God. The only other use of *Adonai* in the book is Daniel 1:2, in which *Adonai* gave the king of Judah and part of the sanctuary vessels into Nebuchadnezzar's hand as an act of judgment. Daniel's tenfold use of *Adonai* has another link with chapter 1: The 10-day trial of Daniel and his companions, after which they were found to be 10 hands wiser.

The connection of *Adonai* in Daniel 1 with judgment (corrective for Jerusalem, favorable for Daniel and his companions) leads to the conclusion that *Adonai* is the One who administers judgment on faithful and unfaithful alike. This accords with Genesis 18:22–32, in which Abraham calls *Yahweh* "Judge of all the earth," then pleads with *Adonai* to be merciful in his judgment of Sodom and spare it if fewer than 50 righteous people be found, pleading on down to a minimum of 10 righteous people. Going back further, the initial use of *Adonai* is found in Genesis 15:2 and 8, in which Abram twice addresses God as *Adonai Yahweh*, who in turn promises both numerous seed and an inheritance of the land of the covenant. Since "the words of the covenant" are the 10 Commandments (see Exod. 34:28; Deut. 4:13; 1 Kings 8:9, 21), which are in turn the basis of judgment (see Eccles. 12:13, 14), *Adonai* is the Judge of all matters pertaining to His covenant.

Daniel recognizes that the 70 years have come as a *judgment* on God's people for their unfaithfulness to His *covenant*. Discerning, albeit dimly, that the 2,300 years likewise connect with judgment, Daniel pleads with God as *Adonai*, the covenant-keeping Judge.

Daniel addresses his prayer in verse 4 to *Yahweh*, the covenant name of God. Opening his prayer in relation to the covenant, Daniel goes on to remind God that He keeps covenant with those who obey His commandments, then confesses that he and his people have sinned, departing from His commandments and judgments. In Exodus 24:12, God identifies the law He wrote in tables of stone as "commandments" and details their life application in the judgments of chapters 21–23. Therefore, when Daniel refers to commandments and judgments in 9:5, it is clear that he has in mind the 10 Commandments. Since the 10 Commandments are the words of the covenant, the people's disobedience means they have not kept covenant with God.

Another remarkable observation is in order. In verse 5, Daniel includes *himself* among those of Judah who have rebelled against God. Scripture does not record any of Daniel's transgressions, so in voluntarily placing himself in this light, Daniel typifies Jesus, who, though He knew no sin (i.e., never committed sin), nevertheless was *made* sin for us (see 2 Cor. 5:21).

Daniel notes in verse 6 that God's people have ignored the prophets He sent. "Believe his prophets, so shall ye prosper" (2 Chron. 20:20, KJV). Their Babylonian captivity was the natural result of this willful ignorance. Their captivity stands as a solemn reminder of *our* need to still heed God's prophets today.[93]

The Curse and Sevenfold Oath

Daniel acknowledges that the condition of his people is not undeserved. Indeed, they have brought "the curse (i.e., the sevenfold oath which is written in the Torah of Moses)" upon themselves. One may wonder what is meant by "the sevenfold oath." The Hebrew word *shava* is usually

---

[93] "Satan's purpose is, through his devices, to make of none effect the testimonies of the Spirit of God. If he can lead the minds of the people of God to see things in a perverted light, they will lose confidence in the messages God sends through His servants; then he can the more readily deceive, and not be detected" (White, *12MR*, p. 201).

translated as simply "he swore" or "he made an oath," but the consonants comprising the word are identical to those for the number "7." Hence, in Hebrew thinking, when one makes an oath or cuts a covenant, one demonstrates its binding nature by "sevening" oneself before God. This traces back to Genesis 21:27–33, in which Abraham cuts a covenant with Abimelech, giving him 7 ewe lambs as a witness that a certain well was his. The site is thereby named Beersheba, meaning "well of the 7," the "7" referring to both the 7 ewe lambs and the oath of which they are a witness.

With a better understanding as to what "oath" means in Hebrew thinking, one is now prepared to identify the "sevenfold oath" that is designated a curse in the Torah of Moses. Since Daniel mentions in verse 2 that he has been examining the prophetic scrolls and determined from Jeremiah's writings (see Jer. 25:11, 12; 29:10) that 70 years are to come upon Jerusalem in consequence of not letting the land rest every seventh year, we do well to inquire whether those passages in Jeremiah in turn reference passages from the Torah of Moses that contain "the curse" (i.e., the sevenfold oath).

In fact, one finds God's command to let the land rest every seventh year in Leviticus 25:3–4. In 26:33–35 is recorded the judgment upon failing to let the land rest every seventh year: "You I will scatter among the nations, and I will unsheathe a sword after you. Your land will become a desolation, and your cities will become a waste. Then the land will discharge its Sabbaths all the days of its desolation, while you are in the land of your enemies. Then the land will keep Sabbath and discharge its Sabbaths. All the days of its desolation, it will keep Sabbath, because it did not keep Sabbath during your Sabbaths [i.e., your sabbatical years] when you dwelt upon it." Additionally, verses 14–35 contain 4 sevenfold oaths that apply if God's people refuse to be corrected by Him. Let us compare Daniel 9:13 (in which Daniel recognizes that God's judgments are for the purpose of turning people away from rebellion) with the sevenfold oaths of Leviticus 26:

> <u>Lev. 26:18</u>: If for all of these things you will not hearken unto me, I will increase your chastening sevenfold for your sins.

Lev. 26:21: If you walk in opposition to me, and are not willing to hearken unto me, I will increase your affliction sevenfold according to your sins.

Lev. 26:23, 24: If by these you will not be corrected by me, but walk in opposition to me, then I likewise will walk in opposition to you, I will strike you—indeed, I will—sevenfold according to your sins.

Lev. 26:27, 28: If for this you will not hearken unto me, but walk in opposition to me, then I will walk in wrathful opposition to you, I will chasten you—indeed, I will—sevenfold according to your sins.

Daniel notes in verse 13 that he and his people have not "entreated the face of *Yahweh* our God." In Genesis 19:13, the cry against the land of Sodom is so great "before the face of *Yahweh*" that His angels are sent to destroy it. Daniel recognizes that if rebellion persists, Jerusalem's fate will be no different. On the other hand, if God's people seek Him in repentance, the blessing of grace and peace associated with the face of *Yahweh* in the priestly benediction of Numbers 6:24–27 (often used at the close of church services today) may also be theirs.

Daniel's reference to bringing people out of the land of Egypt by a mighty hand hearkens back to the experience of Moses, who in Exodus 32:9–11 pleads that *Yahweh* spare His people, for He brought them "out of the land of Egypt with great strength and by a mighty hand." The same language appears in the Sabbath commandment of Deuteronomy 5:15. Hence, the mighty hand is associated with deliverance and hearkens back to the command to keep the seventh-day Sabbath, the violation of which brought about the Babylonian captivity in Daniel's day. In Exodus 7:4, *Yahweh* tells Moses that He will "bring forth My hosts, My people—the sons of Israel—from the land of Egypt by great judgments." Hence, God's "mighty hand" executes "great judgments." Thus, here in Daniel 9:15, Daniel pleads with "*Adonai* our God" as Deliverer and Judge.

God's Sanctuary

Daniel reminds *Adonai* that His desolated city Jerusalem is identical with the "mountain of Your sanctuary." He charges the people with this desolation, acknowledging that it is their sins that are the root cause. In their efforts to conform to the world, they have become "a reproach to all those around us." This is a solemn warning to us today. We are to reform, not conform. Let us not deceive ourselves into thinking that we will have more influence with the world by becoming more like the world. This is a sad and fatal mistake. If we would have a true and saving influence, let us live out our profession, show our faith by our righteous works, and make the distinction great between the Christian and the world. Then a holy influence will be shed upon all, and all will take knowledge of the fact that we have been with Jesus.

Daniel calls for God's face to shine upon His sanctuary. According to Exodus 25:8, His plan has always been to dwell with His people in His sanctuary. In John 15:4, Jesus takes this a step further: God's plan is to dwell *in* His people. The "mountain of Your sanctuary" points back to Exodus 15:17, which equates *Yahweh's* sanctuary with the "mountain of Your inheritance." Further, Psalm 33:12 says, "blessed is the nation whose God is *Yahweh*, the people He has chosen for His inheritance." Finally, Psalm 74:2 merges these ideas, equating God's people with Mount Zion. Hence, the mountain of God's inheritance is Mount Zion, which in turn points to the people of His inheritance, His covenant people, those who now dwell upon heavenly Mount Zion by faith and will ultimately dwell there forever.

In verses 18 and 19, Daniel places supreme emphasis upon God's name and compassion. Having already referred 7 times to *Yahweh* in verses 2–14, he concludes his prayer by thrice invoking the name of *Adonai* to hearken, forgive, and act without delay. He recognizes *Adonai* as the Judge, the one ultimately responsible for fulfilling His covenant in His people.

Gabriel's Timeline Explains Early Part of Vision

Verses 20–23 form a bridge between Daniel's prayer and Gabriel's response. In verse 20, Daniel refers to the "holy mountain of my God" (or "mountain of the sanctuary of my God") identified in verse 16 as God's people, Jerusalem. One is reminded of the stone in Daniel 2:35, which strikes the image of Nebuchadnezzar's dream and then becomes a great mountain, filling the earth. This mountain represented God's kingdom, based on His eternal 10 Commandment law. Hence, in spite of their current sinfulness and rebellion, Daniel clings to God's promise to develop a people who comprise this law-abiding kingdom.

God promised Abram seed, even when he was "dead" sexually, calling the things that are not as though they were (see Rom. 4:17). We would do well to imitate Daniel whenever things look hopeless for God's people; pray earnestly for the development of sanctified Christian character in both ourselves and His people, recalling God's promise to fulfill His covenant to have a surrendered, obedient people.

In verse 21, Gabriel arrives. He states that he was sent right away in answer to Daniel's prayer, as he is once again in Daniel 10:12. We can take heart that God immediately dispatches angels who wing their way to strengthen those who are surrendered to Him and earnestly desire to understand and please Him.

Of no minor importance is the observation that Gabriel arrives about the time of the evening grain offering. It was also about the time of the evening *burnt* offering, for Numbers 28:3–8 prescribes burnt *and* grain offerings each morning and evening. We will say more about the connection of the sacrificial burnt offering and grain offering in remarks on verse 27. For now, Gabriel's arrival underscores the prophecy of the Messiah's death prophesied in verses 24–27, toward which all burnt offerings pointed. Today, dispensationalists, the Protestant offspring of Roman Catholic futurism, hold that the one cut off in verse 26 is not Christ, but antichrist, though this contradicts the plain reading of the text, which states that "Messiah will be cut off." Recalling that Jesus died at the ninth hour (see Luke 23:44–46), the time of the evening sacrifice, Gabriel's arrival at precisely this time dispels any doubt as to whether it is Jesus who is cut off in verse 26.

At the end of verse 23, Gabriel indicates that verses 24–27 give understanding of the "appearance." These verses detail a 70-week prophecy culminating in Jesus' sacrifice on Calvary in AD 31, hence the "appearance" refers specifically to the *first* portion of the 2,300 evening-mornings of Daniel 8:14.

Daniel 9:24–27 provides Gabriel's explanation of the "appearance" that he was commanded to provide the prophet in 8:16. Gabriel introduces a new prophetic period, the 70 weeks. Since there were 70 neglected Sabbatical years during the 490 years prior to Nebuchadnezzar's initial conquest of Jerusalem in 605 BC, God appointed 70 years of Babylonian captivity during which the land would lie fallow. Afterward, *another* 70 weeks' worth of years would be given His people as a trial (see footnote 92). Would they come up "unto a perfect man, unto the measure of the stature of the fulness of Christ" (Eph. 4:13, KJV)?

The number 490, marked as 70 times 7, appears twice more in Scripture. When asked by Peter if one should forgive his brother 7 times, "Jesus saith unto him, I say not unto thee, Until seven times: but, Until seventy times seven" (Matt. 18:22, KJV). The Greek of Matthew 18:22 is identical to that of Genesis 4:24 (LXX), indicating that Jesus' use of "70 times 7" has the same basic meaning. In Genesis 4:24, Lamech boasts of the judgment awaiting him, since he killed a man knowing God's judgment upon Cain's murder of Abel: "Since vengeance has been exacted sevenfold from Cain, then from Lamech [it is to be exacted] 70 times 7."

Comparing Daniel 9:24 with Matthew 18:22 and Genesis 4:24, we learn that 1) God is longsuffering and continues to forgive sin, provided Israel comes to Him in repentance, and 2) if Israel persists in rebellion, in light of God's prior judgments, then her sin will be punished "70 times 7"—that is, to the utmost.

God appointed this probationary period of 490 years in order to fully reproduce His character in His hitherto highly rebellious people. This is evident from Gabriel's statements that "70 weeks have been cut off … to finish the rebellion." The history of Israel and Judah as recorded in Scripture is one of continued rebellion: Their murmurings immediately following deliverance from Egypt (see Exod. 15:24); their failure to eradicate the heathen occupants of Canaan after crossing the Jordan (see Josh. 18:3); dissatisfaction with the judges God appointed, culminating in their request for a king, so as to be like the heathen nations (see 1 Sam. 8:5); and ultimately, their increasing rebellion under the kings until the Babylonian captivity (see Dan. 1:1, 2).

Gabriel presents 6 goals of the 70 weeks. The first 3 deal with rebellion, sins, and deviant behavior. *All* sin is to be finished, sealed up and atoned for, God's goal being to eradicate sin from His people. The final 3 goals deal with the flip side, replacing sin with a righteous character. The death of Messiah was to bring in (i.e., make available) everlasting righteousness. Anointing the Holy of Holies refers to inaugurating the heavenly sanctuary and Jesus as High Priest for His post-resurrection ministry (compare Exod. 40:9–15). Finally, the 70-weeks vision was to conclude when a prophet was "sealed up," referring to the death of a particular prophet, namely, Stephen in Acts 7.[94]

Stephen's death occurred 3.5 years following Christ's death. He charged the leaders of Israel with the death of Jesus and hence, rejection of God's covenant. In consequence, the time of probation for Israel closed. This close of probation for the Jewish nation is recorded in Acts 7:54–60, in which Stephen looks into heaven and sees the Son of man standing at the right hand of God, following which those present at the council seek to stone him. They recognized his use of "Son of man" from Daniel 7:9–14 to refer to Jesus as divine Judge and His act of standing to indicate their probation had closed and final judgment was to be administered (see Ps. 7:6; Dan. 12:1). At this point, the gospel began to go to the Gentiles (see Acts 8:1–5).

Of course, the foregoing refers to the Jewish nation as a whole, *not individual Jews*. Any person, Jew or Gentile, is free to heed Christ's

---

[94] This is explained well in Davidson, *A Song for the Sanctuary*, ch. 22, pp. 53–57.

invitation, "Turn to me, that you may be saved, all ends of the earth." "Come unto me, all who labor and are burdened, and I will give you rest" (Isa. 45:22; Matt. 11:28).

Since the Jewish people as a whole (not necessarily individual Jews) did not take hold of God's covenant, did God fail? No. Rather it was the people's own perverse will that refused to yield. These 490 years had been "cut off" from the totality of the 2,300 years to give a special opportunity for the Jewish people to repent. Since Jesus' work did not result in the reproduction of His character among His people, such work was to await the conclusion of the 2,300 evening-mornings prophesied in Daniel 8:14. At that point, the heavenly sanctuary was to be "restored to its righteous condition."

Let us not be overwhelmed at the prospect of character perfection, but eternally grateful. Remember that *we* do not perfect our character, otherwise our position would be hopeless (our hearts are "incurably bad" according to Jeremiah 17:9). Rather, *Yahweh* promises to fill us with the Holy Spirit, thereby *causing* us to walk in His statutes (see Ezek. 36:27); He *causes* us to ride on the high places of the earth (see Isa. 58:14).

At this point, Gabriel provides details that would occur during the 490-year period. He begins by providing a crucial detail to locate *when* this 490-year period and, coincident with it, the 2,300 years of Daniel 8:14 commence. The key event is the going forth of the decree to bring Jerusalem back to its former condition.

What is this decree, and when did it go forth?[95] A survey of the book of Ezra records events following the Babylonian captivity, including the release of the Jews and several decrees relative to the rebuilding of Jerusalem. To help, following is a synopsis of each decree recorded in Ezra:

> Ezra 1:1–4: Cyrus commands that God's people in his realm (i.e., the Jewish Babylonian captives) return to build God's house at Jerusalem. It states that this occurs in year 1 of Cyrus *to fulfill*

---

[95] In commenting on Daniel 9:25a, the present work draws freely from Davidson, *A Song for the Sanctuary*, ch. 22, pp. 33–39.

the prophecy in Jeremiah 25:11–12 and 29:10 (i.e., this decree marks the end of the prophesied 70 years' captivity). It says nothing about rebuilding Jerusalem per Daniel 9:25. Further, the decree was issued around 537 BC, so were this the decree specified by Gabriel, it would necessitate that Christ's death in the middle of the 70th week (a lapse of 486.5 years) occur around 50 BC. Clearly, this is *not* the prophesied decree.

Ezra 4:17–22: Following Cyrus and his successor Cambyses, the false Smerdis (called Artaxerxes in Ezra 4:7[96]) reigned for a short time in 522 BC. He orders that the city *cease* being built until he should indicate otherwise. Clearly this counter-decree is *not* the one prophesied.

Ezra 6:3–12: Darius I issues a detailed decree in year 2 of his reign to rebuild God's house, as the work decreed under Cyrus had been disrupted and ultimately discontinued (see Ezra 4:4, 5, 24). It specifies that firm foundations be laid and that temple articles taken by Nebuchadnezzar during his siege be returned. Remarkably, the cost is to be at *his* expense from tax revenue, and everything for sacrifice is to be provided as well. Anyone altering the decree is to be put to death. Note that the decree refers only to building the *temple* in Jerusalem, not the area of Jerusalem's public square where judgment is issued. This cannot be the decree of which Gabriel speaks in Daniel 9:25.

Ezra 7:12–26: Artaxerxes issues a decree. Several directions are given: 1) All who are willing may return to Jerusalem; 2) silver and gold is sent with the returnees to purchase bulls, rams, and lambs, along with their grain and drink offerings, as an offering on the altar; 3) articles of service in the house of God are to be

---

[96] "During the reign of Cambyses the work on the temple progressed slowly. And during the reign of the false Smerdis (called Artaxerxes in Ezra 4:7) the Samaritans induced the unscrupulous impostor to issue a decree forbidding the Jews to rebuild their temple and city" (White, *PK*, pp. 572, 573).

returned, and anything else needed is to be paid for with funds from the king's treasury; 4) Artaxerxes' treasurers beyond the River are to provide whatever Ezra says is needed; 5) those who serve in God's house are to be free of taxation; 6) those who know the laws of God are to be appointed to judge the people and teach those who do *not* know the laws of God. This decree was written in the seventh year of his reign (verse 8), which was from the fall of 458 BC to the fall of 457 BC in modern reckoning. This is the decree of Daniel 9:25 to restore and build Jerusalem, specifically its ability to judge.

Having identified the correct decree, we need to determine what marks its "going forth." It is tempting to assume that this coincides with Artaxerxes' pronouncement, sometime before Ezra's departure from Babylon on day 1 of the first month (see Ezra 7:9), which was April 26, 457 BC (see Davidson, *A Song for the Sanctuary*, p. 31). However, the going forth of a decree need not be limited to its *issuance*. In fact, the word for "issuing" Artaxerxes' decree in Ezra 7:21 is *sim*, while "going forth" in Daniel 9:25 is *motsa'*. It is better to understand "going forth" as "going into effect". For Artaxerxes' decree to "go into effect," each of its various directives must commence.

The first criterion was satisfied when Ezra and the returnees arrived at Jerusalem on day 1 of the fifth month (Ezra 7:9), which was August 22, 457 BC (see Davidson, *A Song for the Sanctuary*, p. 35). In Ezra 8:33, we read that on the fourth day of the fifth month (August 25) is documented the weighing and recording of the silver, gold, and articles. In verse 34, this offering is described, albeit without an accompanying date, satisfying the second and third criteria of Artaxerxes' decree. Coincident with this offering, the king's directions for the treasurers beyond the River are given them (verse 36), satisfying the fourth and fifth criteria.

This leaves us with the sixth criterion, namely, the appointment of judges who may judge and teach, as well as determining the date of the offering. We know from Ezra 10:9 that a meeting was convened on day 20 of the ninth month, which was January 6, 456 BC (see Davidson, *A Song for the Sanctuary*, p. 36). This meeting was to rebuke the people for their sin, not to implement Artaxerxes' decree. Further, it took place in the public square, implying that it had *already been restored to service* (Daniel 9:25 prophesied this must take place). Hence, the offering and appointment of judges occurred between August 25, 457 BC and January 6, 456 BC.

How do we narrow things down to a precise date? There is a big hint in the animals prescribed in Artaxerxes' decree: bulls, rams, and lambs. When we consider Numbers 28 and 29, which detail the offerings for each of the sacred dates of the Hebrew calendar, it is observed that there are 3 such annual dates in the fall: The Feast of Trumpets, the Day of Atonement, and the Feast of Booths. Right away, we can rule out the Feast of Booths, for this 8-day feast required 13 bulls and 14 lambs on just the first day, more than was obtained per Artaxerxes' decree. The Feast of Trumpets and Day of Atonement each required 1 bull, 1 ram, 7 lambs, associated grain offerings, 1 buck of the goats for a sin offering, and the regular burnt offering with grain and drink offerings. In Ezra 8:35, the returning captives offer 12 bulls for all Israel, 96 rams, 77 (or "70 times 7," as explained in the next paragraph) lambs, and 12 male goats.

The animals offered match perfectly with those prescribed for the Feast of Trumpets and the Day of Atonement. The fact that the bulls, rams, and male goats are multiples of 12 of what was required on those days is explained by Ezra 8:35 itself: These offerings were for *all* of Israel (i.e., each of the 12 tribes was represented). The 77 (or quite possibly "70 times 7"[97]) lambs seem to correspond best with the 70 weeks of Daniel 9:25 (a week is 7 days, and the Hebrew word for "week" is simply the number "7"). Observe that the feasts called for "1 buck of the goats" each, while Ezra records that 12 "male goats" were offered. This switch in wording may seem insignificant, but it is exactly what we saw earlier: Daniel

---

[97] We saw earlier that the Hebrew expression for the number 77 (literally "70 and 7") is also how one renders "70 times 7" or 490, as in Matthew 18:22 (cf. Gen. 4:24). Hence, the 77 lambs very likely are to be understood as 70 times 7, or 490, lambs.

8:5 and 8 referred to a "male goat," while verse 21 identified the "male goat" as a "buck." Since we established that everything in Daniel 8 points to the Day of Atonement, this switch from "buck" in Numbers 29:11 to "male goat" in Ezra 8:35 is yet another evidence hinting very strongly that Artaxerxes' decree went into effect on the Day of Atonement (the tenth day of the seventh month in 457 BC).

To finish off our argument in favor of the Day of Atonement, we recall from Daniel 8:2 that the prophet received his vision by the *'uval*, which we noted was a variant spelling of *yuval*, or "Jubilee." Incredibly, the year 458-457 BC was a Sabbatical year, and further, the fall of 457 BC marked the beginning of a Jubilee year (see Davidson, *A Song for the Sanctuary*, p. 32). In Leviticus 25:13, it states that "in this Jubilee year, each of you will return to his possession." This is in fact *precisely* what happened when Ezra and those with him returned to Jerusalem. How supremely fitting it is that God arranged for the return of His people at the start of the Jubilee. Only the Wonderful Numberer of Daniel 8 could architect such precise timing as this! Not only this, but recall that the 70 weeks of Daniel 9:24–27 represent the initial part of the 2,300 evening-mornings of Daniel 8:14. Since the 70 weeks went into effect on the Day of Atonement in 457 BC, we conclude that the 2,300 evening-mornings began on the Day of Atonement, and likewise terminated 2,300 years later on the Day of Atonement in AD 1844. The 2,300 evening-mornings began with the restoration of earthly Jerusalem as a place of judgment; they close as heavenly Jerusalem's locale for judgment, the sanctuary, begins its process of cleansing or restoration.

Having established the start date for the 70 weeks, Gabriel notes that there is to be 7 weeks, then 62 weeks, a total of 69 weeks (483 years) until the Messiah. What does this mean? Starting from the Day of Atonement (tenth day of the seventh month) in the fall of 457 BC, 483 years brings one to the fall of AD 27. The prophecy is not speaking of when Jesus was to enter the world, but rather when He was to become Messiah, meaning "anointed one." Just as David was anointed with oil when selected by *Yahweh* as king, and the Spirit of *Yahweh* came upon him at that time (see

1 Sam. 16:1, 13), so Jesus as the antitypical David was anointed with the Holy Spirit at His baptism, sealing Him for His ministry (see Matt. 3:16; John 6:27; Eph. 1:13).

The text refers to Jesus not only as Messiah, but as the Agent, a designation that merits attention. The Hebrew *nagid* refers to a person of the highest authority. It is first used in 1 Samuel 9:16 of Saul as earthly ruler over God's people, later of David in 2 Samuel 6:21, and again in 2 Chronicles 35:8 to refer to the earthly rulers of God's house (i.e., chief priests). These usages typify Messiah the Agent of Daniel 9:25 and the Agent of the covenant in 11:22—Jesus Christ, Ruler of *Yahweh's* host and High Priest (see Josh. 5:15; Heb. 3:1).

Saul and David each served as God's agent and were *anointed* when consecrated to office. As such, they well typify Jesus as Messiah and Agent of the covenant. Satan has a counterfeit for every truth, so in Ezekiel 28, we learn that the king of Tyre, Satan himself (see verses 11–19), at one point had the earthly king of Tyre as his agent (see v. 2). Similarly, Satan's agent appears in Daniel 9:26.

Jerusalem was to be rebuilt with a special emphasis on "public square and site of judgment decree." What does this mean?[98] The public square is where public proclamations were made and military officers received instruction (see 2 Chron. 29:4; 32:6). The public square is located by the city gate in 2 Chronicles 32:6, where elders met to make decisions, as in Ruth 4:11. The "site of judgment decree" is the Hebrew term *charuts*, with the root meaning of "cut." While it takes on this literal meaning in Leviticus 22:22, elsewhere it takes on the sense of acting decisively (see 2 Sam. 5:24) or making a decision (see Isaiah 10:22–23, in which *Yahweh* makes an irrevocable decree concerning the fate of Assyria).[99] Perhaps the clearest of all texts is Joel 3:11–17, in which *Yahweh* gathers all nations at the climax of earth's history to the "valley of decision" where He sits

---

[98] For greater detail, the reader is referred to Owusu-Antwi's dissertation, *The Chronology of Daniel 9:24–27*, pp. 149–161, wherein he refers to "square and decision-making."

[99] To "decide" or "make a decision" refers to settling a matter by rendering judgment. The Latin root *decidere* means to "cut."

to "judge" them and, as the Lion of the tribe of Judah, "roars" forth His verdict. Hence, Daniel 9:25 indicates that Jerusalem, the earthly model of heavenly Jerusalem and Mount Zion, will have authority to govern itself and render its own judgments *restored*. This harmonizes with the overall theme of judgment in the book of Daniel.

Gabriel now gets to the heart of his message—the cutting off of the Messiah after a period of 62 weeks. Recall from Daniel 5:31 that Darius the Mede took over Babylon when he was about 62 years old, followed shortly thereafter by Cyrus, the messiah who would free God's people from their 70 years of captivity. "The forces of the enemy were held in check all the days of Cyrus, who reigned for seven years" (White, *RH*, December 5, 1907). Thus, after 62 weeks, Jesus the Messiah would confirm the covenant, delivering His people during the final week of 7 years. We begin to see that the history recorded in Daniel, including the time periods involved, typifies very precisely events in the life and work of Jesus.

At His crucifixion, it seemed to Jesus' human nature as though He were eternally forsaken of His Father (see Ps. 22:1, 2; Matt. 27:46). It appeared so to onlookers as well (see Isa. 53:4), for *Yahweh* was "pleased to crush Him" (Isa. 53:10). However, when Daniel 9:26 says, "Messiah will be cut off," does it simply mean Jesus would die?

The first use of the Hebrew word translated here as "cut off" is Genesis 9:11, where God says that He will establish His covenant, the everlasting covenant, with Noah and his seed after him so that never again will all flesh be "cut off" by a flood. The next use is in 15:6, where *Yahweh* "cuts" His covenant, the everlasting covenant, with Abram. He signifies this by passing through the pieces of sacrificed animals, indicating that He himself would die to ensure the promises of the covenant, namely numerous seed and the Promised Land (see Gen. 15:9, 10, 17, 18). On the flip side, Genesis 17:14 indicates that the one who breaks God's covenant by not being circumcised—circumcision of the flesh symbolizing the truth of a circumcised *heart*, a heart not rebellious toward God (see Deut. 10:16; 30:6; Jer. 4:4; Rom. 2:29)—will be cut off—that is, not partake of the reward of the everlasting covenant, but taste everlasting death.

These references from Genesis 15 and 17 are especially powerful in light of the book of Hebrews. In Hebrews 7:22, we read that "Jesus has become Guarantor [or, the "Guarantee" itself] of a better covenant." This "better" covenant, also called the new covenant, was better in that it was based on *His* promise, not Israel's promise, to keep it (see Heb. 8:6–13). Further, Hebrews 6:17 states, "In this matter, God wanting to demonstrate more convincingly to the heirs of the promise the irrevocability of His resolve, mediated [or, "pledged"] surety with an oath." In combination with Hebrews 7:22 above, we conclude that God interposed *Himself* with an oath, pledging His very existence to fulfill the covenant and its necessary death requirement. This is confirmed in Hebrews 9:15–17, which clarifies that a covenant is the same as a will. Just as a will requires the death of the testator for it to take effect, so God's covenant requires the death of the one making the covenant—in this case, God Himself in the person of His Son, Jesus. "For God so loved the world, that he gave his only begotten Son, that whosoever believeth in him should not perish, but have everlasting life" (John 3:16, KJV).

Contrary as it is to the simple reading of the text, some maintain that Daniel 9:26a refers to the work of antichrist, not Christ. Apart from the foregoing observations that necessitate the Messiah's death to fulfill God's everlasting covenant, the phrase "He will have no one" serves to dispel any confusion on the matter. Note the following texts:

> Ps. 22:11: Do not be far from me, for distress is near—for *'eyn 'ozer* ["there is no one to help"].
>
> Dan. 9:26a: After the 62 weeks, Messiah will be cut off—*'eyn lo* ["He will have no one"].
>
> Dan. 11:45: Yet he will come to his end—*'eyn 'ozer lo* ["he has no one helper"].

The close similarities of these texts make plain that it is Jesus' death spoken of in Daniel 9:26a, hearkening back to Psalm 22:11 (the entirety of Psalm 22 details the Messiah's death), while Daniel 11:45 prophesies that the papacy will ultimately come to its end, with nobody to resurrect it to eternal life.

The second half of verse 26 switches from a discussion of Messiah following the 62 weeks to a discussion of Satan's agent in relation to Jerusalem and its sanctuary. To understand this verse, it is helpful to consider Jesus' remarks in Matthew 24, Mark 13, and Luke 21 concerning the impending destruction of Jerusalem in AD 70. In Matthew 24:2, Jesus states that not one stone of the temple would be left in place, and in verse 15, He states that "the abomination of desolation, spoken of by Daniel the prophet" is the indicator that destruction is nigh. This desolating abomination appears right here in Daniel 9:26–27. What is the "abomination of desolation?" In Mark 13:14, Jesus states that the abomination of desolation would stand where it ought not to stand. Matthew 23:38 records Jesus as saying that "your house is left unto you desolate." In Luke 21:20, Jesus refers to Jerusalem surrounded by armies. Both Mark and Luke record Jesus as saying that those in Judea are then to flee to the mountains.

Putting these Gospel accounts together, it is clear that the abomination of desolation refers to the idolatrous standards placed by the Roman armies in the holy area surrounding the city of Jerusalem.[100]

---

[100] "Jesus declared to the listening disciples the judgments that were to fall upon apostate Israel, and especially the retributive vengeance that would come upon them for their rejection and crucifixion of the Messiah. ... And the Saviour warned His followers: 'When ye therefore shall see the abomination of desolation, spoken of by Daniel the prophet, stand in the holy place, (whoso readeth, let him understand:) then let them which be in Judea flee into the mountains.' Matthew 24:15, 16; Luke 21:20, 21. When the idolatrous standards of the Romans should be set up in the holy ground, which extended some furlongs outside the city walls, then the followers of Christ were to find safety in flight. ...

... Not one Christian perished in the destruction of Jerusalem. Christ had given His disciples warning, and all who believed His words watched for the promised sign. 'When ye shall see Jerusalem compassed with armies,' said Jesus, 'then know that the desolation thereof is nigh. Then let them which are in Judea flee to the mountains; and let them which are in the midst of it depart out.' Luke 21:20, 21. After the Romans under Cestius had surrounded the city, they unexpectedly abandoned the siege when everything seemed favorable for an immediate attack. The besieged, despairing of successful resistance, were on the point of surrender, when the Roman general withdrew his forces without the least apparent reason. ... Upon the retreat of Cestius, the Jews, sallying from Jerusalem, pursued after his retiring army; and while both forces were thus fully engaged, the Christians had an

Understanding "wing of detestable idols" to refer to the "extremity of detestable idols,"[101] we understand that these idolatrous standards were placed throughout the extremity of the holy area around Jerusalem. Following the initial siege of the city in AD 66, General Cestius retreated for a short while, permitting those who recognized the sign to flee. The Roman army returned under Titus in AD 70, brought the temple to the ground, and slaughtered those who remained. Therefore, Titus is the agent of verse 26.

Beyond this, Titus typifies the end-time apostate power, the Roman papacy. Just as Titus brought destruction like a flood as his army overwhelmed Jerusalem in AD 70, so the Roman papacy in Daniel 11:40 will "overflow" (same root as "flood" in 9:26). Why the flood imagery? The explanation is found in Isaiah 8:1–10, particularly verses 7 and 8:

> Isa. 8:7, 8: *Adonai* is about to bring up against them [the rebellious people of Israel] the mighty and abundant waters of the [Euphrates] River: the king of Assyria and all of his glory. He will go up over all of his channels and overflow all his banks. Then he will pass on through Judah, flood and pass over. Unto the neck he will reach.

In this passage, the king of Assyria is described as the Euphrates River in flood stage, overthrowing the coalition between Syria and the northern kingdom of Israel. Tiglath-Pileser defeated the Syrian capital of Damascus in 732 BC, and his son Shalmaneser V opposed the last king of northern Israel, Hoshea (see 2 Kings 17:3), with the northern kingdom falling in 722 BC[102] Later, Assyria came against Judah.

---

opportunity to leave the city. ... Without delay they fled to a place of safety—the city of Pella, in the land of Perea, beyond Jordan" (White, *GC*, pp. 25–31).

[101] "Wing" often signifies "end" or "extremity." See, for example, Numbers 15:38 and Ruth 3:9 ("extremity" of the garment).

[102] See, for example, *Andrews Study Bible*, comments on 2 Kings 17:3 and Isaiah 8:4.

While the 70-weeks prophecy closed in the fall of AD 34 with the stoning of Stephen, the destruction of Jerusalem occurred afterward, in AD 70. Likewise, the "consummation" and "that which is decreed is poured out upon the one who makes desolate" refer to the ultimate decimation of Rome at Jesus' second coming. This blending of events during the 70 weeks with those afterward, even reaching to the end of the world, should not be surprising. In fact, in Matthew 24:3, Jesus' disciples asked when these things would be (AD 70), and what would mark the sign of His coming and the end of the age (the end of the world at Jesus' second coming). In His explanation (see Matt. 24; Mark 13; Luke 21), Jesus conflates these two events, while clearly drawing from Daniel 9:24–27.[103]

In establishing the prophetic fulfillment of verses 26 and 27b, we passed over the first part of verse 27. We return there to finish our study of Daniel 9. To properly understand this verse, we need to discern who it is that confirms the covenant. Many today suppose it is the antichrist, equating this individual with the evil agent of verse 26. This may seem to be what the grammar suggests to an English reader, but it is contrary to the structure and sense of Daniel 9:24–27 as a whole.

To understand things properly, note that the translation presented in this book splits up each of verses 25–27 as 25a and 25b, etc.[104] Observe that the *second* half of each verse refers to the city and uses the word for "decree." Verse 25b refers to the restoration of Jerusalem, especially the area where judgment decrees are rendered, during pressing

---

[103] "As they were gathered about the Saviour upon the Mount of Olives, they asked: 'When shall these things be? and what shall be the sign of Thy coming, and of the end of the world?' Verse 3.

The future was mercifully veiled from the disciples. Had they at that time fully comprehend the two awful facts—the Redeemer's sufferings and death, and the destruction of their city and temple—they would have been overwhelmed with horror. Christ presented before them an outline of the prominent events to take place before the close of time. His words were not then fully understood; but their meaning was to be unfolded as His people should need the instruction therein given. The prophecy which He uttered was twofold in its meaning; while foreshadowing the destruction of Jerusalem, it prefigured also the terrors of the last great day" (White, *GC*, p. 25).

[104] This analysis largely follows Davidson, *A Song for the Sanctuary*, ch. 22, pp. 14–60 and Doukhan, *Secrets of Daniel*, pp. 145–156.

times. Verse 26b refers to the Roman agent and his people who desolate Jerusalem, as well as a decree of desolations. Verse 27b refers to the desolator, his utter devastation of the city (notice, though, that the city is not explicitly mentioned, but rather implied by comparison with verse 26b), and the ironic decree that pours desolation upon *him* in the eschatological end of all things.

By contrast, the *first* half of each verse refers to time periods and Messiah. In verse 25a, 7 weeks and 62 weeks precede the appearance of Messiah the Agent. In verse 26a, Messiah is cut off after the 62 weeks. In verse 27a, "He" will confirm the covenant for "1 week," causing the sacrifice and grain offering to cease in the middle of this 70th week. Just as the city is not explicitly mentioned in verse 27b, but implied by comparison with verse 26b, so here in verse 27a, Messiah is not explicitly mentioned, but implied by comparison with verse 26a. The one who confirms the covenant in verse 27a is none other than the "Agent of the covenant" in Daniel 11:22. If we move ahead 69.5 prophetic weeks, or 486.5 years, from the fall of 457 BC, we get to the spring of AD 31, when Jesus died for our sins. This did in fact fulfill the death requirement of the covenant/will with Abram in Genesis 15, where it was promised that Messiah would die on our behalf.

The text says that Messiah's death causes the sacrifices and grain offerings of the ceremonial system to "cease," literally "keep Sabbath." This suggests a strong link between Christ's death on Calvary and the Sabbath. In fact, comparison of the 10 Commandments recorded in Exodus 20 and Deuteronomy 5 reveals that the Sabbath is to be kept by God's people for 2 reasons: As our Maker and Redeemer from the bondage of sin, God is worthy of worship. More than simply putting an end to the ceremonial system forever, Christ's death ensures deliverance from our bondage to sin, and He promises to enable us to keep the law, the violation of which necessitated His death in the first place. Jesus' death thereby establishes the Sabbath, the seal of God's law, as a permanent memorial of His death and deliverance.

While Jesus' death *ended* the ceremonial system of the *earthly priesthood*, it simultaneously served to *establish* His role as *heavenly High Priest*.

In Leviticus 9:4, sacrifice and grain offering are required for inaugurating the earthly priesthood. Speaking of Jesus' self-sacrifice at Calvary, Paul says in Hebrews 9:23, "it was a necessity that the patterns of things in the heavens be cleansed by these [sacrifices of the earthly sanctuary], but the heavenly realities themselves by better sacrifices [the plural indicating the supremacy of Jesus' sacrifice] than these." According to John 20:17, when Jesus rose from the dead, He had not yet ascended to the Father, but was to do so before appearing to the rest of the disciples. He had to present Himself before the Father following His resurrection, for according to Leviticus 23:11–13, on the day after the Sabbath following the Feast of Unleavened Bread, not only a lamb, but also a first-fruits barley offering, were to be offered to *Yahweh*. According to Leviticus 23:15–21, 50 days would be counted, and then the priest would present a first-fruits offering of the wheat harvest as well. According to Matthew 27:52–53, there were some who slept in the grave who were raised with Jesus, and according to Ephesians 4:8, these were taken to heaven with Him 40 days later, and 10 days after that (a total of 50 days), Jesus was inaugurated as heavenly High Priest at Pentecost, and the gift of the Spirit was poured out (see Acts 2:1–4).

Hence, while Jesus' atoning sacrifice was perfect, it does not represent the *totality* of His work of atonement. That is, as heavenly High Priest, He must also *apply* His shed blood to the lives of believers in order to make it effective for us. He has been doing that since His ascension in AD 31, removing sin from the lives of His followers so that they may die with the assurance of sins cleansed. Now, in the antitypical Day of Atonement, He takes this to its conclusion. For those who surrender fully, He is removing sin *entirely* from their lives so that they may be translated at His second coming, having never tasted death.

Thus closes Gabriel's explanation of the "appearance," the first portion of the 2,300 evening-mornings. In Daniel 10–12, Daniel glimpses the "appearance" of Jesus, and further detail is given regarding the *close* of the 2,300 evening-mornings and the end-time judgment that precedes Jesus' second coming.

SUMMARY: DANIEL 8 AND 9

DANIEL 8 AND 9: JESUS

Jesus is the Ruler of the host (see Dan. 8:11) against whom Satan, through the papacy, exalted himself, attempting to do away with Christ's ministration in the heavenly sanctuary. Jesus is also *Palmoni*—the Wonderful Numberer—of Daniel 8:13, who promises that the heavenly sanctuary will start being cleansed at the end of the 2,300 evening-mornings. In the days of Christ, Rome stood up against the Ruler of rulers when he was put to death on the cross (see v. 25). In chapter 9, Daniel prays to *Adonai*, a title for God as Judge. Since God has committed all judgment to the Son (see John 5:22, 27), *Adonai* is Jesus. In the 70-weeks prophecy of Daniel 9:24–27, Jesus is the Messiah who is cut off in the middle of the final week.

DANIEL 8 AND 9: THE STAND

The Medo-Persian ram stands during its period of dominance (see Dan 8:3–7). It cannot stand when the stronger Grecian goat comes. In verse 22, the Grecian goat's 4 horns stand in their own strength. In verses 23–25, goat-faced Rome stands up against the Ruler of rulers, but not in its own strength (rather, by the devil's strength). Rome is shattered without hand (i.e., by the stone of Daniel 2) when Jesus comes.

In Daniel 8:15–18, Daniel's reaction to the message of the heavenly sanctuary is to fall upon his face unconscious. Gabriel comes along and touches him, enabling him to stand. Daniel's experience models our own. The sanctuary message reveals our infinite need, and when we lose all confidence in our own strength, God provides us His own strength to enable us to stand.

DANIEL 8 AND 9: GOD'S HAND

In verses 4 and 7, the earthly strength of the Medo-Persian ram and Grecian goat is such that no one is able to "rescue from his hand." Likewise, in verse 25, the might of Rome is described as causing "deception to thrive by his hand." Ironically, Rome is to be shattered "without hand" (i.e., by Jesus' stone kingdom of Daniel 2). In Daniel 9:10, Daniel affirms that God set forth His laws before His people "by the hand of His servants the prophets" (i.e., by His Holy Spirit inspiring the prophets with the message of truth). Finally, in verse 15, Daniel reiterates that God delivered His people from Egypt "by a mighty hand"—by the triumph of divine wisdom and truth over human might.

DANIEL 8 AND 9: JUBILEE AND DAY OF ATONEMENT

The Jubilee is hinted at in Daniel 8 with reference to the "stream" Ulai. The Hebrew word for "stream" is *'uval*, a variation of *yuval*, which refers to a ram and, by association, its horn, blown on the Day of Atonement marking a Jubilee year. The ram of Daniel 8:3–7 aligns with this Jubilee imagery. Finally, the "going forth of the decree" to restore Jerusalem (Dan. 9:25) occurred on the Day of Atonement in 457 BC, coincident with the Jubilee year. The 70 weeks, or 490 years, represent 10 Jubilee cycles, hence their close on the Day of Atonement in a Jubilee year was meant to be a great deliverance, but in a tragic irony, it marked the close of probation for the Jewish nation as a whole in consequence of the leaders' hardheartedness. The great Jubilee of the ages must await Jesus' return at the second coming.

The Day of Atonement theme is prominent in Daniel 8–12. It is implied in the foregoing references to the Jubilee. Beyond that, the ram and goat imagery of Daniel 8 points to Leviticus 16, in which the annual Day of Atonement ritual is outlined. This prepares the reader for Messiah's death as the great atoning sacrifice in Daniel 9:26–27 (see also Lev. 16:9), as well as the antitypical Day of Atonement at the end of the 2,300 evening-mornings introduced in Daniel 8:14 and elaborated upon in chapters 10–12, during which the Messiah applies His blood during the end-time judgment (see also Lev. 16:15–19).

DANIEL 10–12: RAISED HANDS—MESSIAH APPLIES ATONEMENT IN JUDGMENT

Introduction: Daniel by the Great River Chiddeqel

10 ¹In year 3 of Cyrus, king of Persia, a matter was revealed to Daniel who was called by the name Belteshazzar: the truth of the matter and [the associated] great host.[105] He understood the matter—he had understanding of the appearance.[106] ²During those days, I, Daniel, was mourning 3 weeks of days. ³Highly desirable[107] food I did not eat, neither flesh nor wine entered my mouth, nor did I anoint myself at all until 3 weeks of days were fulfilled.

The Appearance: Jesus as High Priest of the Sanctuary

⁴Now, on day 24 of the first month, while I was by the side of the great river, i.e., the Chiddeqel, ⁵I lifted my eyes, looked, and behold: One Man clothed in linen, His loins girded with fine gold of Ufaz. ⁶His body[108] was

---

[105] *Tsaba'* is sometimes translated "war," which suits the conflict between Jesus and Satan (and their respective hosts of angels) in Daniel 10–12. However, the clear connection with Daniel 8:10–13 (the only other place in the book of Daniel where this word appears, and where it means "host"), favors translating *tsaba'* as "host" for internal consistency.

[106] See Daniel 9:23, in which Daniel is told to "understand the matter—understand the appearance."

[107] Same word translated "high esteem" in Daniel 9:23, 10:11 and 19, 11:38 and 43.

[108] *Geviyyah* usually signifies "corpse" (see Judges 14:8, 9; 1 Sam. 31:10, 12; Ps. 110:6; Nah. 3:3), or those near death (see Gen. 47:18; Neh. 9:37). However, it is *also* used of the 4 *living* creatures

like a beryl, His face like the appearance of lightning, His eyes like torches of fire, His arms and the location of His feet like the sight of burnished bronze, and the sound[109] of His words like the voice of a multitude.

Daniel Stands: The Vision Explained

⁷Then I, Daniel, saw the appearance by myself, while the men who were with me did not see the appearance; rather, a great trembling fell upon them, and they fled away in order to hide. ⁸So I was left alone, and I saw this great appearance: no strength was left in me, my splendor was turned against me into corruption, and I retained no strength.

⁹Then I heard the sound of His words; as I heard the sound of His words, I was unconscious upon my face, and my face was toward the ground.

¹⁰Then, behold, a hand touched me, assisting me up upon my knees and the palms of my hands. ¹¹And he said to me, "Daniel, man of high esteem, understand the matters of which I am about to speak to you. **Stand** upon **the place where you were standing**, for now I have been sent to you." When he had spoken this word with me, I **stood** trembling.

¹²Then he said to me, "Do not fear, Daniel, for from the first day you set your heart to understand and to humble yourself before your God, your words were heard, and I have come in response to your words. ¹³However, the ruler of the kingdom of Persia **was standing** in opposition to me 21 days. Then behold, Michael, [number] 1 of the foremost rulers, came to help me, for I had remained there beside the kings of Persia. ¹⁴So I have come to make you understand what will confront your people in the last days, for there is still a [part of the] vision pertinent to those days."

¹⁵When he had spoken with me according to these words, I put my face to the ground, and was left speechless. ¹⁶Then behold, one with

---

about *Yahweh's* throne in Ezekiel 1:11 and 23. Both meanings fit here: the description of *Yahweh* in Ezekiel 1:27–28 matches that of Jesus here in Daniel 10:5–6; Jesus also died to satisfy the terms of the covenant. Jesus appears in the same form to John in Revelation 1:18, where He mentions that He *was* dead, but is now *alive*.

[109] Hebrew *qol*, translated "voice" later in this verse.

the likeness of the sons of man touched my lips, so I opened my mouth and spoke, saying to the one **standing** opposite me, "My lord, due to the appearance, my pangs of anguish have overwhelmed me, and I have retained no strength. ¹⁷How will the servant of this lord of mine be able to speak with this lord of mine? As for me at the moment, no strength **stands** inside me, no breath remains in me."

¹⁸Once again, one with the appearance of man touched me, thereby strengthening me. ¹⁹He said, "Do not fear, man of high esteem—peace be unto you. Be strong, be strong!" While he was speaking with me, I gained strength. Then I said, "Let my lord speak, for you have strengthened me."

²⁰Then he said, "Do you know why I have come to you? Presently I must return to fight against the ruler of Persia. I am about to go forth, and behold, the ruler of Hellas is coming. ²¹Nevertheless, I will inform you of what is inscribed in the document of truth. There is not 1 to provide strength with me[110] against these[111] except Michael, your[112] Ruler.

Before the Rise of Rome

Persia Until Xerxes I

11 ¹"Yet I, in year 1 of Darius the Mede, had taken my **stand** to strengthen him and to serve as his protection. ²Now I will tell you the truth. Behold, there are still 3 kings who will **stand** for Persia, then the fourth will amass greater wealth than all. According to the strength he has by his wealth, he will stir up all with [i.e., "against"] the kingdom of Hellas.

Alexander (Greece): Does According to His Own Will

³"Then a mighty king will **stand** who will rule over a great dominion and do according to his own will. ⁴Yet when he has **stood**, his kingdom will be

---

[110] Michael came to help/strengthen Gabriel as Gabriel sought to strengthen Darius (cf. Dan. 10:13; 11:1).

[111] "These" refers to the ruler of Persia and the ruler of Hellas.

[112] "Your" is plural, indicating that Michael is Ruler of all of Daniel's people, not Daniel alone.

shattered and divided unto the 4 winds of the heavens—but not unto his posterity, and not according to his dominion over which he ruled, for his kingdom will be uprooted and [divided] unto others besides these.

⁵"Then the king of the south will be strong, yet from among his rulers, one will grow strong against him and rule over a dominion greater than his dominion.

Failed Marriage: Daughter of King of the South and King of the North

⁶"Toward the end of years they will unite, and the daughter of the king of the south will come to the king of the north in order to make equitable terms. However, she will not retain strength of arm; likewise, he will not **stand**, nor his arm. She will be given over, as will those who brought her, he who fathered her and he who strengthened her in those times.

South Prevails Against North

⁷"But from a shoot of her roots, one will **stand** in his place. He will come against the army, then come into the stronghold of the king of the north, deal with them, and prevail. ⁸Further, their gods (along with their molded images and esteemed implements of silver and gold) he will bring into captivity in Egypt. He will **stand** more years than the king of the north. ⁹Thus the king of the south will enter the kingdom, then he will return to his own land.

South versus North Again

¹⁰"But his sons will ready themselves and gather a multitude of great armies; then he will surely come, sweep over flood-like, and pass over. Then he will return and they will ready themselves against his stronghold.[113] ¹¹The king of the south will be embittered, and go forth to wage

---

[113] Following the Hebrew consonantal text, in agreement with YLT, ESV, NET, and NAB. The Hebrew Bible also provides a marginal reading—"he will ready himself against his stronghold"—followed by many English translations, including the KJV.

war with him, with the king of the north; he also will **muster** a great multitude, yet the multitude will be given into his hand. ¹²But when he bears away the multitude, his heart will be lifted up; though he will cause tens of thousands to fall, yet he will not be strong. ¹³Indeed, the king of the north will return and **muster** a multitude greater than the former. At the end of these times (which are years), he will surely come with a great army and abundant provisions.

Rome's Entrance in Prophecy Until Jesus' Atoning Sacrifice Completed

Jews Seek Protection, League with Rome

¹⁴"Now during these times, many will **stand** against the king of the south; further, the sons of those who tear down your people will lift themselves up, in order to **establish** the vision—but they will be overcome.

¹⁵"The king of the north will come, pour out [earth for] a siege mound, and take a most fortified city; the arms of the south will not **stand**, even the choicest of his people—there will be no strength to **stand**.

Rome: Does According to His Own Will

¹⁶"But he that comes to [i.e., "against"] him will do according to his own will, and none will **stand** before him. He will **stand** in the beautiful land, and all of it will be in his hand.

Failed Affair: Daughter of Women and Rome

¹⁷"He will set his face to enter by power his entire kingdom, upright people with him, and so he will do. The daughter of women he will give to him, to corrupt her. She will not **stand**, nor will she be for him. ¹⁸Then he will turn his face to the islands, and he will capture many. However, a commander will make his haughty conduct toward him cease; instead, he will turn his haughty conduct back upon himself. ¹⁹Then he shall turn his

face back toward the strongholds of his own land, but he will be overcome, fall, and not be found.

The Atoning Sacrifice: The Agent of the Covenant Shattered

[20]"There shall **stand** in his place one who causes an exactor of tribute[114] to pass through the splendor of the kingdom, yet in a few days he will be shattered, though not in anger nor in battle. [21]In his place shall **stand** one who is despised; indeed, they will not accord him royal majesty. He will enter in peaceably, and seize the kingdom with smooth [words]. [22]The arms of the flood will be swept away flood-like from before him; they will be shattered—as well as the Agent of the covenant.

Rome's Entrance in Prophecy Until Jesus' Atoning Judgment Completed

Pagan Greco-Rome Dominates Until Time of Constantine

[23]"Upon uniting with him, he will deal treacherously. He will increase in strength among a small nation. [24]Peaceably, and into the fattest provinces, he will enter. He will do that which his fathers and his fathers' fathers did not do: he will distribute pillage, plunder, and property to them, while against [their] fortifications he will devise his stratagems—for a time.

Rome Versus King of the South

[25]"He will stir up his strength and heart against the king of the south with a great army. Likewise, the king of the south will rouse himself for battle with a great army, exceedingly large, but he will not **stand**, for they will devise stratagems against him. [26]Those who eat his delicacies will shatter him; his army will sweep over flood-like, and many pierced through will fall.

---

[114]The Hebrew expression emphasizes the economic "squeeze" put on the people by a tax collector (see Deut. 15:2, 3).

Pretended Union: Rome and King of the South

²⁷"Concerning both of these kings, their heart is set upon wickedness, and at 1 table they will speak deception, yet it will not prosper, for the end is still at the appointed time. ²⁸He will return to his land with great property; his heart set against the holy covenant, he will take action and return to his land.

From Eastern Roman Empire to Papacy

²⁹"At the appointed time, he will return and enter the south, but it will not be as the former, nor as the latter. ³⁰There will come unto him ships of Kittim; he will become unnerved, return, and be outraged against the holy covenant; he will take action, return, and identify with those who desert the holy covenant. ³¹Arms on his behalf will **stand** and pollute the sanctuary, the stronghold. They will take away the continual ministration and establish the detestable idol that desolates.

The Papacy's 1,260 Years

³²"Those who act wickedly regarding the covenant, he will defile with smooth [words], but the people who know their God will be strong and take action. ³³Those who are wise among the people will cause the multitudes to understand, though they be overcome by sword, by flame, by captivity, and by pillage [many] days. ³⁴While they are being overcome, they will be helped with a little help, though many will join with them with smooth [words]. ³⁵Some of those who are wise will be overcome in order to refine those among them—to purify and make white—until the end time, for it is still for an appointed time.

³⁶"The king will do according to his own will: he will raise himself up, exalting himself above every god; against the God of gods he will speak wonderful things; he will thrive until the outrage is concluded—for that which has been decreed must be done. ³⁷Concerning the God

of his fathers, he will give no consideration; concerning the desire[115] of women and concerning every god he will give no consideration, for above every [god] he will exalt himself. **38**In his place, he will give glory to a god of strongholds; unto a god whom his fathers did not know he will give glory with gold, with silver, with precious stone, and with articles of high esteem. **39**Thus he will do concerning fortifications of strongholds with a foreign god. Whom he acknowledges, he will increase in glory, grant them rule over many, and the land he will divide for a price.

Kings of South and North Unite Against God's People

40"In the end time, the king of the south will engage in butting with Him; the king of the north will come against Him[116] like a whirlwind with chariotry, horsemen, and many ships. He[117] will enter lands, sweep over flood-like, and pass over. **41**He will enter the beautiful land, and many will be overcome, yet these will be delivered out of his hand: Edom, Moab, and the foremost of the sons of Ammon. **42**He shall stretch forth his hand against the lands, but the land of Egypt will not serve as an escape. **43**He will rule over the secret stores of gold and silver, and over all the articles of high esteem of Egypt, and the Libyans and Ethiopians will be at his steps. **44**Then reports will alarm him from the sunrise and from the north, so he will go forth in a great rage to exterminate, devoting many to annihilation. **45**He will pitch the tents of his ephod[118] between the seas, in lieu of the beautiful mountain of the sanctuary,[119] yet he will come to his end—he has no helper.

---

[115] Translated "desirable" in Daniel 10:3, "esteemed" in 11:8, and "of high esteem" in 9:23, 10:11 and 19, 11:38 and 43.

[116] Each "Him" in verse 40 refers to the "God of gods" and "god of his fathers" in verses 36–39. In other words, the king of the south butts against God, and the king of the north comes against God. In Revelation 13, the 2-horned dragon/ram beast unites with the papacy in the final war against God.

[117] "He" = the king of the north. All references to "he," "his," and "him" in verses 41–45 refer to the king of the north.

[118] See commentary for why "his ephod" is preferable to the traditional "his palace."

[119] Or "beautiful holy mountain." See commentary for why "beautiful mountain of the sanctuary" is preferable.

The End of the Controversy

12 ¹"Now, at that time, Michael shall **stand**, the great Ruler who **stands** [guard] over the sons of your people; then will be a time of distress such as has not been since becoming a nation until that time. At that time, your people will be delivered, everyone who is found written in the scroll. ²Then many of those sleeping in the dusty ground will awaken—some to everlasting life, others to reproaches, to everlasting abhorrence. ³The wise will blaze forth, like the brilliance of the firmament; those instrumental in leading many to become righteous as the stars forevermore.

⁴"Now you, Daniel, shut up the words and seal the scroll until the end time. Many will go to and fro, and knowledge will increase."

Question and Answer: Jesus and Gabriel by the Nile

⁵Then I, Daniel, looked and, behold, 2 others **standing**, 1 on this side of the Nile, and 1 on that side of the Nile. ⁶And he said to the Man clothed in linen who was upon the waters of the Nile, "Until what point [until one finally reaches] the end of these wonders?" ⁷I heard the Man clothed in linen who was upon the waters of the Nile: He raised His right hand and His left hand to the heavens, and He made a sevenfold oath by Him who lives forever, "It is to be for an appointed time, [2] appointed times, and a half; after completely dashing to pieces the hand of the holy people,¹²⁰ all of these [wonders] will finish."

Daniel Does Not Understand, Questions "My Lord"

⁸I heard, yet I did not understand, so I said, "My lord, what is the end result of these [wonders]?"

---

¹²⁰ Or "hand of the people of the sanctuary."

Gabriel's Timeline Explains Latter Part of Vision

⁹He said, "Go, Daniel, for these words are shut up and sealed until the end time. ¹⁰Many shall be purified, whitened, and refined. The wicked ones will act wickedly; none of the wicked ones will understand, though the wise will understand.

¹¹"From the time the continual ministration is taken away in order to establish the detestable idolatry that desolates, there are to be 1,290 days.

¹²"Blessed is he who waits and arrives at the 1,335 days.

¹³"But you, go on to the end. You will rest, yet you will **stand** according to your lot at the end of the days."

COMMENTARY: DANIEL 10–12

Introduction: Daniel by the Great River Chiddeqel

In verse 1, we are informed that Daniel "understood the matter—he had understanding of the appearance." This refers to Gabriel's explanation at the end of Daniel 9, for in verse 23, he told Daniel to "understand the matter—understand the appearance" that had troubled him at the end of chapter 8. Gabriel's explanation at the close of Daniel 9 informs us that the "matter" and the "appearance" culminate in Christ's sacrifice on Calvary, occurring at the close of the appearance (i.e., the close of the first 70 prophetic weeks, or 490 years, of the 2,300 evening-mornings in the spring of AD 31).

It is clear from Daniel 10:2–3 that *something* still troubles Daniel. Verse 1 tells us that what is revealed to him in chapters 10–12 is "the truth of the matter and [the associated] great host," yet Gabriel already explained the matter (i.e., the appearance) at the close of Daniel 9. We infer that greater light is now to be shed upon the appearance, showing its relation to the great host that battles against Jesus and His sanctuary (see 8:10–13). Gabriel states in Daniel 10:14 that he has come to give understanding of what will happen to Daniel's people "in the last days." From this, we infer that his troubled thoughts don't concern the 2,300-evening-morning prophecy of Daniel 8:14 in its entirety (after all, Gabriel explained the first 490 years of this period at the close of Daniel 9). Instead, they must focus largely on what will happen to his people at the *close* of the 2,300 evening-mornings. This period of 8:14 introduced Daniel to Christ's work of cleansing the heavenly sanctuary during the end-time judgment (from the autumn of 1844 onward). This cleansing work of judgment is to take on far greater significance as the High Priest, Jesus the Messiah, appears before Daniel in 10:5–6.

The phrase "3 weeks of days" in verses 2 and 3 may seem a curious way to report time, but it clearly distinguishes these 3 weeks (21 *days*) from the 70 prophetic weeks (490 *years*) of Daniel 9:24–27.

The Appearance: Jesus as High Priest of the Sanctuary

Recall that Daniel 1 opened with a 10-day trial. At the close of this trial, the steadfastness of Daniel and his companions to God's 10 Commandment law resulted in them being judged 10 hands above all. Now on the tenth day from the commencement of the Feast of Unleavened Bread,[121] the day on which Christ would die centuries later for our unfaithfulness to God's law,[122] Daniel glimpses One dressed in high priestly, Day of Atonement linen (see Lev. 16:4).

---

[121] The Feast of Unleavened Bread began the day after Passover (14th day of the first month), running 7 days from the 15th through the 21st (see Lev. 23:6–8). Counting inclusively from the 15th, the tenth day is the 24th day of the first month.

[122] This may come as a surprise to many, as it is natural to assume that as our Passover (see 1 Cor. 5:7), Jesus died *on* the Passover. However, it is instructive to note the order of events surrounding the original Passover as the Israelites prepared to leave Egypt: the typical Passover lamb was chosen on the 10th day of the first month (see Exod. 12:3); slaughtered the evening of the 14th (see v. 6; Lev. 23:5); eaten after the sun had set, marking the transition from the 14th to the 15th (see Exod. 12:8; Lev. 23:6); after the Passover meal was eaten on the 15th, the death of the firstborn—even the firstborn of the king—occurred at midnight (see Exod. 12:12, 29).

By comparison, Jesus arrived in Bethany six days before Passover so as to spend the Sabbath at Bethany. "He, the antitypical Lamb, by a voluntary act set Himself apart as an oblation" (White, *DA*, p. 571), making His triumphal entry on Sunday the 10th (see John 12:12). His disciples killed the

This parallels John's opening vision of Jesus in Revelation 1:12–17. Is Daniel likewise beholding Jesus in chapter 10? Consider the opening words of verse 5: "I lifted my eyes, looked, and behold: One Man." Comparison with the following passages settles the matter: In Genesis 18:2, Abraham "lifted his eyes, looked, and behold, 3 men," one of whom is identified as *Yahweh* and "Judge of all the earth" (see Gen. 18:22, 25); again, in 22:13, "Abraham lifted his eyes, looked, and behold, a [some manuscripts "one"] ram" when he was about to offer up Isaac, the promised seed. Having manifested faith mature enough to believe that God would raise his son from the dead (see Heb. 11:19), God provided a ram as a substitute. Clearly, this typified Jesus' sacrifice and resurrection centuries later.

These twin concepts—the substitutionary nature of Jesus' atoning sacrifice and His role as "Judge of all the earth"—are at the heart of Daniel 8–12. In 8:3, Daniel "lifted my eyes, looked, and behold: One ram." Not only was the ram a representation of Medo-Persia, as stated in verse 20, but Cyrus the Persian was also a messiah, the deliverer of God's people from Babylonian captivity. In this respect, Cyrus typified the true Messiah, Jesus, our Substitute and Deliverer from the power of sin. The transition from the earthly priesthood and sanctuary to the heavenly sanctuary and

---

Passover lamb on Thursday the 14th (see Mark 14:12), and that evening (i.e., after sunset, marking the beginning of the 15th), Jesus ate the Passover with His disciples (see Mark 14:17). "On the day the Passover was eaten He was to be sacrificed" (White, *DA*, p. 642), for not only was He the true paschal lamb, but as the Firstborn of the King, He must die on the same day as the typical firstborn during the tenth of the Egyptian plagues (see Exod. 12:12, 29). Though He finally expired Friday afternoon, recall that in Gethsemane He decided that "He will become the propitiation of a race that has willed to sin. His prayer now breathes only submission: 'If this cup may not pass away from Me, except I drink it, Thy will be done.' Having made the decision, He fell dying to the ground" (White, *DA*, p. 693). His decision to be sacrificed was finalized in Gethsemane at midnight on the 15th, so true to type, Jesus began to die at that point, and would have expired right then and there, had not the angel come from heaven to strengthen Him as He sweat great drops of blood (see Luke 22:43, 44).

Thus, Jesus' death and burial on Friday afternoon fell on the 15th, or the first day of Unleavened Bread, the day *following* Passover. The interested reader is encouraged to study the exodus narrative closely; Treiyer, *The Apocalyptic Times of the Sanctuary*, pp. 49–50 is also helpful.

priesthood was prophesied in Daniel 9:24–27, so in 10:5, the emphasis shifts from Jesus as our substitutionary sacrifice to "Judge of all the earth."

Jesus' description in Daniel 10:5–6 depicts Him dressed in linen, the garb specified for Israel's high priest on the Day of Atonement (see Lev. 16:4). What does this tell us? Recall that Daniel 8 introduced the end-time judgment with its attendant cleansing of the heavenly sanctuary. Upon Gabriel's return to explain the appearance (the early portion of the 2,300 evening-mornings), Daniel 9:24–27 focused on Jesus' atoning death. During the Day of Atonement, the high priest of ancient Israel would apply the blood from *Yahweh's* goat to cleanse the earthly sanctuary. Thus, Daniel 10 introduces Jesus as the heavenly High Priest who will cleanse the heavenly sanctuary with His own shed blood during the end-time Day of Atonement at the close of the 2,300 evenings-mornings.

Jesus' loins are girded with fine gold of Ufaz. The phrase "loins girded" points back to the initial Passover meal, for the Israelites were directed to eat the Passover lamb with their "loins girded" (Exod. 12:11) after they had slaughtered their lamb and applied its blood to their doorpost. As High Priest, Jesus applies the blood of His atoning sacrifice to the heavenly sanctuary, with a corresponding removal of sin from our character here.

What does "fine gold" signify? Fine gold is not as precious as wisdom is, and to trust therein is iniquity, meriting negative judgment (see Job 28:16, 19; 31:24, 28). On the other hand, one who reproves wisely is like an ornament of fine gold upon the willing ear (see Prov. 25:12). Again, Isaiah 13:9 and 12 say that *Yahweh* will make mankind more precious than the fine gold of Ophir in His day. Putting these together, Jesus exercises perfect wisdom in the exercise of judgment, orchestrating events to perfect His character within us and thereby complete the covenant experience.

What about "Ufaz"? The only other instance of this word is in Jeremiah 10:9, which identifies Ufaz as the source of gold (not the "fine gold" of Daniel 10:5) used in making idols. These worthless idols are contrasted in verse 10 with "*Yahweh*, the true God ... the living God and eternal King.

Due to His wrath, the earth will quake." Note the contrast: Unbelievers seek *common* gold from Ufaz for selfish, idolatrous purposes; on the other hand, the heavenly Judge girds himself with *fine* gold from Ufaz, for only with perfect wisdom can He deliver from sin those who are willing, and with unerring accuracy identify those who persist in rebellion to become subjects of His unmingled wrath.

His body is described as a beryl. This identifies Jesus as the High Priest, for beryl is the tenth of 12 stones upon the high priest's breastplate of judgment (see Exod. 28:20). It identifies Him as the One who dies to fulfill the everlasting covenant/will, for *gevviyah* literally means "corpse." It points to Jesus as the One entitled to occupy the throne as Judge, for the bodies of the cherubs about the throne are likewise called *gevviyah*, and the wheels by the cherubs look like beryl (see Ezek. 1:16; 10:9). The throne itself is for judgment (see Ps. 9:4, 7; 89:14). Hence, Daniel 10 pictures Jesus as the One who is to die to fulfill the everlasting covenant, qualifying Him to sit as High Priest and Judge on the throne.

Jesus' face has the "appearance" of lightning. "Appearance" is the very word used in Daniel 8 to refer to the *early* portion (i.e., the 70 weeks of Daniel 9:24–27) of the 2,300 evening-mornings, which *end* with the pre-advent judgment. Hence, the use of "appearance" in 10:6 links Jesus' *sacrifice* at the end of the 70 weeks with the *application* of His cleansing blood during the judgment at the end of the 2,300 evening-mornings. More than this, Jesus' face looks specifically like lightning, taking one back to the initial occurrence of lightning in Scripture, when the Israelites were summoned to Mt. Sinai for the giving of the 10 Commandments (see Exod. 19:16; 20:18), the basis of all judgment (see Eccles. 12:13, 14). God tells Israel that if they hearken to His voice and keep His covenant (the 10 Commandments; see Exod. 34:28; Deut. 4:13; 1 Kings 8:9, 21), they will be His possession above all peoples of the earth (see Exod. 19:5). That Jesus' face is like the appearance of lightning indicates that the cleansing of the heavenly sanctuary corresponds to the fulfillment of God's covenant, the writing of His law in the hearts of believers here on earth.

What about the description of His eyes as "torches of fire?" This phrase first appears in Genesis 15:17, in which a torch of fire passed between the pieces when God cut the covenant with Abram. Note how the book of Hebrews explains the significance of this act of passing between the pieces:

> Heb. 6:17: To demonstrate ... the irrevocability of His resolve, mediated [or, "pledged"] surety with an oath.
>
> Heb. 7:22: Accordingly, Jesus has become Guarantor [or, the "Guarantee" itself] of a better covenant.
>
> Heb. 9:15–17: For this reason He is the Mediator of a new covenant, that, a death having occurred for redemption of the deviations in relation to the first covenant, those who have been called might receive the promise of everlasting inheritance. For where there is a covenant/will, it is necessary that the death of the will maker be brought forward. For a will is legally binding at death, since it has absolutely no strength while the will maker lives.[123]

When *Yahweh* cut the covenant with Abram in Genesis 15:17–21, He was making a will. This implies that *Yahweh* was promising Abram that He would die in the person of Jesus, so that the details of His will and testament (the promised land) could one day be a reality to the inheritors of the promise. The eyes like torches of fire here in Daniel 10:6 indicate that Jesus is the One who was to die to satisfy the covenant terms. This explains why Jesus' body is called a *geviyyah* ("corpse") in verse 5.

Jesus' arms and feet are described as "like the sight of burnished bronze," matching the 4 cherubs surrounding *Yahweh's* throne (see Ezek. 1:7; 10:14, 15). According to Exodus 25:18, there were 2 cherubs attached

---

[123] The words "covenant" and "will" are translations of the same Greek word *diatheke*.

to the atonement lid ("mercy seat," KJV) of the ark of the covenant. In Daniel 4, God fulfilled His covenant with Nebuchadnezzar by passing him through experiences that correspond to the 4 faces of the cherubs (i.e., man, lion, ox, and eagle). Further, while heaven is associated with iron, the earth is associated with bronze (see Lev. 26:19). Hence, this aspect of Jesus' appearance points again to His covenant, specifically His role as the Mediator who reaches down from heaven and stands upon the earth (see 1 Tim. 2:5; Rev. 10:1).

Jesus' words are "like the voice of a multitude." "Multitude" is first used in God's covenant promise to make Abram the "father of a multitude of nations" (Gen. 17:4, 5). Just prior to the second coming, Revelation 19:6–8 speaks of the voice of a "great multitude," rejoicing that God's people are fully ready to meet Jesus at His return. Again, the "voice of a multitude" of rain occurs right after Elijah's showdown with the prophets of Baal at Mount Carmel and shortly before a dark rain cloud is seen (see 1 Kings 18:41–45). The great rain that follows typifies the outpouring of the Holy Spirit in latter-rain proportion upon those people in whom God's covenant is fulfilled just prior to Jesus' return on a cloud (see Joel 2:28–32; Rev. 14:14; 19:11–21).[124] Finally, there is a "voice of a multitude" when *Yahweh* gathers His army for the destruction of Babylon (see Isa. 13:4). Thus, Jesus' words in Daniel 10:6 point forward to the return of Jesus for those people in whom is fulfilled His covenant, as well as the final downfall of all who have sided with the end-time Babylonian apostasy, the papacy (see Rev. 17:5).

Table 16 below summarizes the significance of the symbols in verses 5 and 6:

---

[124] "Soon there appears in the east a small black cloud, about half the size of a man's hand. It is the cloud which surrounds the Saviour and which seems in the distance to be shrouded in darkness. The people of God know this to be the sign of the Son of man. In solemn silence they gaze upon it as it draws nearer the earth, becoming lighter and more glorious, until it is a great white cloud, its base a glory like consuming fire, and above it the rainbow of the covenant. Jesus rides forth as a mighty conqueror" (White, *GC*, pp. 640, 641).

Table 16: Symbolism of Jesus' Description in Daniel 10:5–6

PHRASE	REFERENCE	SIGNIFICANCE
"I lifted my eyes, looked, and behold: One Man"	Gen. 18:2, 22, 25	This Man is *Yahweh*, Judge of all the earth.
"clothed in linen"	Lev. 16:4	This Man is the High Priest dressed for the Day of Atonement.
"loins girded"	Exod. 12:11	This Man leads people out of Egypt and is prepared to die following Passover.
"with fine gold"	Job 28:16, 19; 31:24, 28; Prov. 25:12; Isa. 13:9, 12	This Man is wise enough to serve as Judge and perfect humanity's character.
"of Ufaz"	Jer. 10:9, 10	This Man is *Yahweh*, the living God.
"His body [corpse] like a beryl"	Exod. 28:20	This Man is High Priest (beryl = tenth stone on breastplate of judgment).
	Judges 14:8; Rev. 1:18; Heb 6:17; 7:22; 9:15–17	This Man (corpse) dies to fulfill His everlasting covenant.
	Ezek. 1:16; 10:9	This Man is qualified to sit on throne (cherubs about throne by beryl-like wheels are "corpses").
"His face like the appearance"	Dan. 8:26, 27; 9:23	This Man dies at close of "appearance" (seventy weeks); applies His blood during judgment.
"of lightning"	Exod. 19:16; 20:18	This Man gave the 10 Commandments and judges all people by that law.
"His eyes like torches of fire"	Gen. 15:17	This Man cut the covenant with Abram, and dies to fulfill that covenant.
"His arms ... feet like ... burnished bronze"	Ezek. 1:7; Exod. 25:18; Lev. 26:19; 1 Tim. 2:5; Rev 10:1	This Man is Mediator of the covenant, reaching down from heaven, standing upon earth.
"His words like the voice of a multitude."	Gen. 17:4, 5	This Man is the one who gathers the multitude in whom His covenant is fulfilled.
	Isa. 13:4	This Man is *Yahweh* who gathers His army to destroy end-time Babylon.

Daniel Stands: The Vision Explained

Daniel's experience parallels that of Ezekiel at the beginning of his book. While standing by water (see Ezek. 1:3), Ezekiel sees "appearances of God" (see v. 1) that are glorious (see vs. 26–28), causing him to fall upon his face as he hears a voice speaking (see v. 28). Daniel says he has no strength, and "my splendor was turned against me into corruption," mirroring the experience of John, who falls to the ground as though dead. He is touched and told not to fear (see Rev. 1:13–17), just as Gabriel touches Daniel and tells him, "Do not fear." Each of these prophets was overwhelmed by an appearance of Jesus focused on the Day of Atonement.

While Daniel is overwhelmed at the appearance of Jesus, an angel (Gabriel; compare Dan. 8:16; 9:21–23) is sent once more. He places his hand upon the trembling Daniel, setting him upon his knees and the palms of his hands. Gabriel reassures him that he is a "man of high esteem," and Daniel finds himself able to stand. As Paul says, "When I am weak, then I am strong," (2 Cor. 12:10).

To fully appreciate this scene, we must recognize that the book of Daniel consistently uses "hand" in reference to God's judgment. A lone hand writes out the sentence against Belshazzar (see Dan. 5:5); the horn from insignificance is shattered without hand (see 8:25); the establishment of Jesus' kingdom via the end-time judgment is represented as a stone cut out of the mountain without hands (see 2:34, 45). Now Gabriel extends his hand, hinting at God's saving judgment, as when He brought Israel out of Egypt by a strong hand (see Ps. 136:11, 12).

Daniel's experience of pleading for wisdom, seeing Jesus as supreme Judge, and finally being enabled to stand—though trembling—models the experience of those people who are to have the privilege of standing in the end-time judgment while they are *alive*, their characters perfectly reflecting that of Jesus.

Upon standing, Gabriel informs Daniel that his prayer was heard from the moment he began to humble himself, 21 days prior. What an encouragement! Though there may be a delay, as in Daniel's case, we are to persevere. As long as we are walking according to God's commandments and praying in harmony with His will, we can be certain God is accomplishing the answer (see 1 John 5:14, 15; Prov. 28:9).

Gabriel notes that he was sent when Daniel began to "humble" himself, just as God's people are to do on the Day of Atonement (see Lev. 23:27). In harmony with Daniel's vision of Jesus as High Priest in Day of Atonement attire, this mention of "humble" hints that the message of Daniel 10–12 relates to the end-time judgment. Like Daniel, we are to humble ourselves and persevere if we are to receive divine aid to stand in the final judgment.

Gabriel explains his delay in arrival: The ruler of Persia withstood him 21 days. At that point, Michael steps in, freeing Gabriel to come to Daniel. Many translations refer to Michael as "1 of" the chief princes, rather than "number 1" or "first." However, we have seen that the book of Daniel consistently employs the Hebrew and Aramaic words for "1" in the sense of "first," as in "first year" (see 1:21; 7:1; 9:1; 11:1). Further, Jesus is designated the highest Ruler (see 8:25), and we have learned that a ruler can serve as judge (see Exod. 2:14; 18:21, 22). It is Michael who stands for God's people when probation closes, indicating identity with Jesus, "[number] 1 of the foremost rulers," the one to whom the Father commits all judgment (see John 5:22, 27).

If Jesus is the foremost Ruler, then it stands to reason that the ruler of Persia with whom Gabriel had to contend is not Cyrus, whom Scripture consistently identifies as the king of Persia,[125] but Satan himself. Other passages support this conclusion. In Ezekiel 28:2, a prophecy is directed against the earthly agent of Tyre, Ithobaal III, but verses 12–19 redirect attention to the king of Tyre, with abundant evidence that this is Satan. Again, Isaiah 14:4 prophecies against the earthly king of Babylon, but verse 12 shifts attention to Lucifer, the name for Satan before his fall. This distinction between earthly and spiritual holds for God and His people as well. When Israel became a monarchy, God used Saul as an earthly agent,

---

[125] See 2 Chron. 36:22, 23; Ezra 1:1, 2, 7, 8; 3:7; 4:3, 5; 5:13, 14, 17; 6:3, 14; Dan 1:21; 10:1.

while God Himself was king (see 1 Sam. 9:16; 12:12). Likewise, Satan was the true ruler of Persia.

What verse 13 reveals is a great controversy, hidden to human eyes, between Christ and Satan for the loyalty of every person. If Jesus can win the hearts of men like Nebuchadnezzar and Cyrus,[126] the latter issuing the initial decree to release the Jews from Babylonian captivity, there is certainly hope for the rest of us!

Gabriel informs Daniel that he is about to relate the part of the vision of Daniel 8 that relates to the last days. Back in 8:15, Daniel had been seeking the meaning of the vision he saw, while in verse 16, Jesus commanded Gabriel to explain only the appearance (the beginning portion of the 2,300 evening-mornings). Gabriel noted in verse 17 that the vision pertained to the end time, and now he has come to explain the *latter* end of that vision, specifically the end-time judgment.

Daniel is again overcome, and someone "with the likeness of the sons of man" touches his lips. Let us compare this with Isaiah 6. After Isaiah sees *Adonai* sitting on a throne, high and lifted up, a seraph touches his lips. Here in Daniel 10, Daniel sees an appearance of Jesus, after which one having "the likeness of the sons of man" is sent to him, and then his lips are touched. By comparison with Daniel 8:16–17, we conclude that this being is once again Gabriel. Since Daniel 8–12 is concerned with the Day of Atonement, during which time God restores His likeness in fallen humanity, we observe that Jesus and Gabriel condescend to come down to our level (son of man), that we may in the last days be restored to God's likeness via the message entrusted to Daniel.

Daniel's remark that "no breath remains in me" pictures him as Adam before God breathed the breath of life into him (i.e., dead; see Gen. 2:7). The interaction between Gabriel and Daniel in verses 18 and 19 mirrors that between the angel and Jesus in Luke 22:43, when the angel

---

[126] "The king of Persia was controlled by the highest of all evil angels. He refused, as did Pharaoh, to obey the word of the Lord. Gabriel declared, He withstood me twenty-one days by his representations against the Jews. But Michael came to his help, and then he remained with the kings of Persia, holding the powers in check, giving right counsel against evil counsel" (White, *11MR*, p. 99).

strengthens Jesus as He sweats great drops of blood while in mortal agony in Gethsemane. In fact, Theodotion's Greek translation of Daniel 10:18–19 employs the same Greek word for "strengthen" as used in Luke 22:43. Just as Gabriel strengthens Daniel to stand, so the message that he gives to Daniel is designed to strengthen us to stand during the judgment hour.

Gabriel notes that no one strengthens him except Michael, the Ruler of Daniel and his people. Gabriel's name means "Strong man of God" (or perhaps "God is my strong Man"), so if no one strengthens Gabriel but Michael, it follows that Michael is God Himself (i.e., Jesus). Likewise, Revelation 13 and 14, as well as the close of Daniel 11, make clear that in the end, there will be no one to strengthen God's faithful remnant except Jesus. To stand in the end-time judgment, we must learn to rely exclusively on Jesus, as does even the angel Gabriel.

Before the Rise of Rome

Persia Until Xerxes I[127]

To make sense of the prophetic outline beginning in Daniel 11:2, we need to know where Daniel is in the stream of time as the chapter opens. The section begins in 10:1, which states that the current ruler is King Cyrus of Persia. The 3 rulers following King Cyrus are universally agreed to be Cyrus's son Cambyses (530–522 BC), the false Smerdis (522 BC, pseudonymously called Artaxerxes in Ezra 4:7[128]) and Darius I (522–486 BC) Following these, Xerxes I (the Ahasuerus of the book of Esther) reigned

---

[127] Information for Daniel 11:2–15 is drawn freely from Smith, *Daniel and the Revelation* (classic Seventh-day Adventist work on prophecy), *SDABC4*, and *Andrews Study Bible* (more recent Seventh-day Adventist scholarly productions), as well as NET (non-Adventist study Bible that confirms the standard Seventh-day Adventist identifications made in Daniel 11:2–15). Analysis of verses 16–35 continues to draw freely from these same sources except for NET, for it adheres to the popular but erroneous belief that Antiochus Epiphanes, not Rome, is the focus of these verses.

[128] "During the reign of Cambyses the work on the temple progressed slowly. And during the reign of the false Smerdis (called Artaxerxes in Ezra 4:7) the Samaritans induced the unscrupulous impostor to issue a decree forbidding the Jews to rebuild their temple and city" (White, *PK*, pp. 572, 573).

from 486–465 BC. He was indeed noted for his immense wealth, as well as launching an enormous, failed invasion of Greece (the ancient Greek historian Herodotus puts the force in the order of 1,000,000 men[129]).

Alexander (Greece): Does According to His Own Will

Other Persian kings followed Xerxes I, including the Artaxerxes of Ezra, whose provision made possible the going forth of the decree that marked the beginning of the 70 weeks (see Dan. 9:25) and the 2,300 evening-mornings of Daniel 8:14. However, the prophecy of Daniel 11 jumps from 465 BC to the Greek empire following the death of Alexander the Great in 323 BC. It is true that Alexander's kingdom was not continued by his own posterity, but what is of greater interest is that it was also not to be "according to his dominion over which he ruled, for his kingdom will be uprooted and [divided] unto others besides these."

Taken by itself, the word "dominion" can be understood as either "authority" or the "territory" itself over which authority is exercised. Some versions opt for "authority,"[130] but how does one determine for sure which is correct? Using only linguistic skills, one cannot make the determination. Any sound interpretation of prophecy is rooted in the historicist method of interpretation, which seeks historical fulfillment of prophecy. As discussed in our study of Daniel 8, the 4 heads of Hellas included the western Greeks of Italy and Sicily, which were never part of Alexander's empire. Hence, history authoritatively confirms that Alexander's kingdom divided "not according to [the territory of] his dominion over which he ruled, for his kingdom will be uprooted and [divided] unto others [other territories] besides these."

Seleucus I Nicator was a general for Ptolemy I Soter of Egypt. Seleucus assumed control of Babylon, but was driven out later by Antigonus,

---

[129] "Xerxes I," Wikipedia, https://1ref.us/yz (accessed January 22, 2020).

[130] For example, EBR reads, "nor according to his own authority which he wielded." See also RSV, NET, CJB, and NJPS.

fleeing to Egypt. Ptolemy (died 285 BC) helped him regain Babylon. Seleucus lived until 281 BC. The Ptolemaic empire remained, but the Seleucid was greater.

This part of Daniel 11 focuses on powers designated the kings of the south and the north. This contrasts with Daniel 8, in which the conflict was between the ram from the east and the goat from the west. Out of that east-west conflict arose the 4 horns of Hellas, and from the horn representing the western Greeks of Italy and Sicily arose the horn from insignificance, Rome.

Here in Daniel 11, the 4 horns appear in verse 4 as Alexander's kingdom is "shattered and divided unto the 4 winds of the heavens." Why are not all 4 of them given prominence in Daniel 11? Recall that of the 4 divisions, only 3 arose from Alexander's territory. The Macedonian area was initially under Cassander and his successors, but these were overcome by Lysimachus, hence Greece and Macedon came under his dominion, being annexed to Thrace. However, Lysimachus was in turn overcome by Seleucus, with the result that Macedon and Thrace were annexed to Syria. The absorption of this Macedonian horn means it is *included* in any reference to the king of the north.

What about the fourth non-Alexandrine region of Western Italy and Sicily? As the source of Rome, it most assuredly plays a prominent role in the closing portion of the book of Daniel. Rome comes onto the prophetic stage in verse 14 and plays a prominent role up through the close of chapter 11.

Failed Marriage: Daughter of King of the South and King of the North

In verse 6 is introduced a political alliance between Ptolemy Philadelphus (king of the south) and Antiochus Theos (king of the north) by marriage of their offspring. These formed a peace treaty, whereby Antiochus put away his wife Laodice and her 2 sons, married Ptolemy's daughter Berenice, and received a large dowry. Much to the chagrin of Berenice, Antiochus brought *back* Laodice and her sons. Dissatisfied with this arrangement,

Laodice poisoned Antiochus, Berenice, and her baby boy; thus was fulfilled the prophecy that "she will not retain strength of arm; likewise, he will not stand, nor his arm." The throne then went to Laodice's eldest son, Seleucus Callinicus.

It is worth noting that the peace treaty between north and south proved unsuccessful, hearkening back to earlier episodes in Israelite history in which the marriage union was weakened by a woman of Egypt. In a botched attempt to fulfill God's covenant in their own carnal strength and way, Abram hearkened to his wife Sarai and took her Egyptian maidservant, Hagar (see Gen. 16:2; 17:15–21). In spite of God's explicit counsel against marrying heathen idolaters (see Deut. 17:17), Solomon took the daughter of Pharaoh, king of Egypt (king of the south in Solomon's day). Many more such inappropriate marriages followed, with Egyptian idolatry weakening Solomon's kingdom, and his character reflecting that of Satan until his repentance in advanced age.[131]

South Prevails Against North

The roots of Berenice are the parent stock from which she was born, hence "a shoot of her roots" refers to a sibling, in this case her brother Ptolemy Euergetes, who came to the throne in 246 BC. Outraged at the murder of his sister Berenice, Ptolemy gathered an army to go to Syria to attack the

---

[131] "In seeking to strengthen his relations with the powerful kingdom lying to the southward of Israel, Solomon ventured upon forbidden ground. Satan knew the results that would attend obedience; and ... he sought to bring in influences that would insidiously undermine Solomon's loyalty to principle and cause him to separate from God. ... 'Solomon made affinity with Pharaoh king of Egypt, and took Pharaoh's daughter, and brought her into the City of David.' ...

... But in forming an alliance with a heathen nation, and sealing the compact by marriage with an idolatrous princess, Solomon rashly disregarded the wise provision that God had made for maintaining the purity of His people. ...

... So gradual was Solomon's apostasy that before he was aware of it, he had wandered far from God. Almost imperceptibly he began to trust less and less in divine guidance and blessing, and to put confidence in his own strength. Little by little he withheld from God that unswerving obedience which was to make Israel a peculiar people, and he conformed more and more closely to the customs of the surrounding nations" (White, *PK*, pp. 53–55).

murderess Laodice and her son Seleucus II Callinicus (king of the north). He indeed prevailed against them, conquering not only Syria but also the land toward Babylon. Called back to Egypt by reports of uprising, he took immense wealth and 2,500 images of the gods with him. In consequence of Egypt's devotion to idolatry, he earned the moniker Euergetes, meaning "benefactor." As prophesied in verse 8, Ptolemy then left his rival alone and stood as king longer. He died in 221 BC, 2 years after Seleucus Callinicus died from a fall from his horse.

South Versus North Again

In response to Ptolemy III's invasion, Seleucus II Callinicus led an expedition in 242 BC, but had to return home in defeat. The prophecy then records that his sons waged war upon Egypt. The older of his 2 sons, Seleucus III Soter ("Saviour"), lived up to his more common designation, Seleucus Ceraunus, for like a quick "thunderbolt," his reign was but a short 3 years before being assassinated by his own army officers in 223 BC. His brother, Antiochus III the Great, was named king in 222 BC, reclaiming Seleucia and Syria. He bested Egyptian general Nicolas in battle and considered invading Egypt. This is he who was to "surely come, sweep over flood-like, and pass over."

Ptolemy IV Philopator (son of Ptolemy III Euergetes) was "embittered" against Antiochus III the Great who initiated a campaign to regain Palestine from Ptolemy. They met at the Battle of Raphia, with Polybius reporting that Antiochus mustered a "great multitude" of 62,000 infantry, 6,000 cavalry, and 102 elephants, while Ptolemy had under him 70,000 infantry, 5,000 cavalry, and 73 elephants. Polybius reports the Seleucid casualties at approximately 10,000 soldiers, with another 4,000 Seleucid soldiers taken prisoner,[132] answering to the prophecy of verse 11.

Observe that verse 11 describes the king of the south as "embittered," and the multitude of the king of the north was to be "given into his hand."

---

[132] Barnes, *Notes on the Old Testament*, comments on Daniel 11:11.

This description matches Daniel 8:7, in which the conflict is between east and west. Both conflicts portray in miniature the great controversy between Christ and Satan. Similar to Daniel 11:11, observe that no one could deliver the ram from the east (representing Jesus, Cyrus was God's messiah) from the "hand" of the "embittered" goat from the west (representing Satan).

While the Battle of Raphia put the northern part of the realm under his control, verse 12 prophesied that Ptolemy's heart would be "lifted up," and he would "not be strong." History records that he gave himself up to a dissolute life rather than taking seriously the sober realities of running a kingdom. As for causing "tens of thousands to fall," Ptolemy visited Jerusalem and desired to enter the Holy of Holies, which he was forbidden to do. Infuriated, he retaliated, persecuting the Jews in Alexandria, Egypt. Whether one accepts Eusebius' figure (40,000 Jews killed) or Jerome's estimate (60,000 killed), history confirms that Ptolemy did "cause tens of thousands to fall." Such treatment of the Jews, who had been permitted as much privilege as any other citizens since Alexander's day, further ensured that "he [Ptolemy] will not be strong."

Ptolemy Philopator died ingloriously, indulging his base passions. His son Ptolemy V Epiphanes succeeded his father. Being a boy only 5 years old, Antiochus seized the opportunity to try once again to take Egypt, mustering "a multitude greater than the former" when he had gone against Ptolemy IV Philopator. However, the easy victory anticipated by Antiochus was thwarted by the unwelcome interloper introduced in verse 14—Rome.

Rome's Entrance in Prophecy Until Jesus' Atoning Sacrifice Completed

Jews Seek Protection, League with Rome

Antiochus III leagued with Philip of Macedon to secure and divide the territory of the new Ptolemy. "Many will stand against the king of the south." Indeed, there was intrigue in the Ptolemaic court itself. Sosibius and the prime minister Agathocles had Ptolemy IV Philopator's sister and wife Arsinoe III murdered; later, Agathocles (brother of Ptolemy IV's mistress Agathoclea) was killed by the Alexandrian mob.[133]

With the Ptolemaic kingdom facing self-destruction (corrupt advisors took charge of the boy king one after another), as well as outside persecution, emissaries were sent forth to seek help. While pleas with Antiochus to respect the peace treaty he signed with Ptolemy IV in 217 BC proved ineffectual, a hitherto obscure power proved willing to aid the Ptolemaic cause—Rome.

While Rome's aid was welcome for the king of the south, verse 14 identifies this power by its future relation to God's people: "those who tear down your people." Scripture identifies Rome as the supreme persecutor of God's people. Rome's appearance at this point of the vision is the very quality that will "establish the vision," hearkening back to Gabriel's assertion that "there is still a [part of the] vision pertinent to those days" (Dan. 10:14).

"They will be overcome" can refer to Antiochus III and Philip of Macedon, who were thwarted by Rome in their attempt to conquer the Ptolemaic empire. Ultimately, though, this points ahead to the end of Rome itself at the end of days, despite its apparent strength through many centuries of persecution.

In verse 15, attention is refocused on the king of the north, Antiochus III Epiphanes, who met in battle with Scopas, a general in the service of the Ptolemies. Scopas was from Ætolia, brought in by Ptolemy's guardian Aristomenes to ward off Philip and Antiochus. Antiochus wished to reclaim Palestine and Cœle-Syria, so Scopas opposed him. Scopas met with defeat, then fled to Sidon, where he was besieged. More Egyptian generals ("the choicest of his people") were sent forth, but their assistance was not able to break the siege against Sidon, for it was prophesied that "there will be no strength to stand" against the king of the north. Scopas eventually surrendered, thereby saving his life, with the successful siege of Sidon answering to the taking of "a most fortified city."

---

[133] Smith, *Daniel and the Revelation*, p. 230. See also "Agathocles of Egypt," Wikipedia, https://1ref.us/z0 (accessed January 22, 2020).

Numerous Bible texts equate Egypt's strength with its horses and chariots (see Exod. 14:9, 23; Deut. 11:4; 20:1), so it is only natural in Daniel 11:15 that Egypt, sensing her vulnerability, hires outside military help to defend herself. However, Scripture plainly warns, "Put not your trust in princes, nor in the son of man, in whom there is no help" (Ps. 146:3, KJV). "Woe to them that go down to Egypt for help; and stay on horses, and trust in chariots, because they are many; and in horsemen, because they are very strong; but they look not unto the Holy One of Israel, neither seek the LORD!" (Isa. 31:1, KJV). It is little wonder that Egypt met with defeat.

Rome: Does According to His Own Will

The prophetic outline now moves to the time when Rome, in its rapidly increasing strength, prevails over the Seleucid Empire. Roman general Pompey arrived in Syria in 64 BC, removing Antiochus XIII Asiaticus from office and turning Syria into a Roman province. Not only this, but the prophecy states that Rome would "stand in the beautiful land," a reference to Judea (see Ezek. 20:6, 15; Jer. 3:19). This occurred in 63 BC when Pompey intervened in the conflict between Hyrcanus II (a Pharisee) and Aristobulus (a Sadducee) for the position of high priest in Judea. After a 3-month siege of Jerusalem, the temple was taken, and 12,000 Jews were killed. Though the Jews had entered into an alliance with Rome a century earlier (see comments on Daniel 8:9–12 for the history of the Jewish league with Rome in 161 BC), Judea was now conquered and reduced to a Roman province.

The prophecy says that "none will stand before him." This hearkens back to Daniel 8:7, in which the Medo-Persian ram could not stand before the Alexandrine goat. Once again, Rome shares the characteristics of Greece. Further, the reference to Judea as "the beautiful land" hearkens back to Daniel 8:9, in which Rome, under the symbol of the horn from insignificance, was said to grow great toward the "beauty" (short for "beautiful land").

Failed Affair: Daughter of Women and Rome

Having conquered the Seleucid Empire (the king of the north), Rome now set its sights on Egypt, the seat of the Ptolemaic Empire (the king of the south). Ptolemy XII Auletes died in 51 BC, leaving the throne to his children, Ptolemy XIII and Cleopatra VII, approximately 10 and 18 years of age, respectively. These children were put under the care of Rome, with the general Pompey selected as their guardian.

Pompey and Julius Caesar were at odds with each other. Defeated at the Battle of Pharsalus, Pompey fled to Egypt, where he was killed at Ptolemy's direction. Caesar then assumed guardianship of Ptolemy and Cleopatra. Adding to the turmoil, Cleopatra was coming into her own as queen, while Ptolemy sought supremacy as king. Not wishing to lose her position, Cleopatra employed her feminine wiles to advantage with Caesar. Rumor spread that Caesar planned to grant Cleopatra sole, not joint, power. The upshot was naval war between Egypt and Rome. Caesar burned the Egyptian fleet, which, due to its proximity to buildings in the city, resulted in the burning of the famous Alexandrian library. Answering to the "upright people" of verse 17, Antipater, along with 3,000 Jews, supported Caesar in his conquest.

At the Battle of the Nile in 47 BC, Ptolemy was drowned. Hence, Egypt was brought under the dominion of Caesar and his mistress Cleopatra. Again, answering to the prophecy, Cleopatra did not "stand" [for Caesar], nor would "she be for him," eventually taking up with Antony against Rome. Cleopatra's alliance with Caesar reminds one of verse 6, in which the daughter of the king of the south (Ptolemy Philadelphus's daughter Berenice) is married to the king of the north, Antiochus Theos. Both cases demonstrate that such politically motivated alliances, corrupting the purity of marriage, are doomed to failure.

Before going on, note a key difference between Rome and Jesus: Rome "set his face to enter" Egypt by force of arms; Jesus "set his face to go toward Jerusalem" (Luke 9:51) to conquer sin by His death.

In verse 18, it is prophesied that Caesar would capture many islands. This was fulfilled during his campaign against Pharnaces in the Cimmerian

Bosporus. This is the time when he made his famous boast, "I came, I saw, I conquered!" Following this, Caesar returned to Rome, where he was made dictator. At this point, it is foretold that he would "stumble, fall and not be found." Unlike Enoch, who "walked with God; and he was not, for God took him" and "was not found, for before his translation he had this testimony, that he pleased God" (Gen. 5:24; Heb. 11:5), Caesar's life did *not* please God. Rather than "walking" with God right into heaven at the close of his life, Caesar stumbled and fell. He was not found because he was struck down under divine judgment.

Concerning the "commander" (Hebrew *qatsin*) of verse 18, there seems to be a deliberate ambiguity. On the one hand, Caesar had had a falling out with his general Pompey, who was ultimately killed by Ptolemy XIII. Ironically, Caesar was murdered at the foot of a statue of Pompey. Hence, Caesar's "haughty conduct" toward Pompey did indeed cease and return upon himself. On the other hand, *qatsin* is used in Micah 3:1 and 9 of those who are expected to know judgment. A number of similar designations have been used of God in the book of Daniel. Jesus is called the Ruler (Judge and High Priest), as well as Messiah the Agent, so ultimately, it would seem that He causes Caesar's haughty conduct toward Pompey to cease and turn back on Caesar himself.

Caesar's interest in capturing the islands provides a significant contrast with Jesus. As a servant of Satan, Caesar sought to conquer the islands by force. By contrast, *Yahweh* will send His messengers to the Gentiles of the remote islands to declare His glory (see Isa. 66:19). Likewise, there is coming a time when people will worship *Yahweh* from every place, even the islands of the Gentiles (see Zeph. 2:11). Hence, God does not seek to dominate the islands, but rather to *win the hearts* of the Gentiles of those islands, that He might fit them for heaven.

The Atoning Sacrifice: The Agent of the Covenant Shattered

Next on the prophetic horizon was Octavius, whose great-uncle on his mother's side was Julius Caesar. Following his death in 44 BC, examination of Julius Caesar's will revealed that Octavius was both adopted son and heir. Along with Marcus Lepidus and Marc Antony, a triumvirate (a threefold political alliance) was formed on November 26, 43 BC to dispatch those who assassinated Julius Caesar. This being accomplished at Philippi, the leaders divvied up the Roman Republic, each ruling as dictator over his area. As might be expected, the rulers' ambitions conflicted, and following the exile of Marcus Lepidus and the death of Antony after defeat at the Battle of Actium in 31 BC, Octavius referred to himself as *Princeps Civitatis* ("Principal Citizen"). Under his rule, Rome entered its Empire phase, and the senate named him Augustus ("Great One").

His rule began the period known as the *Pax Romana* ("Roman Peace"), suggestive of "the splendor of the kingdom." Of course, the rule of Solomon (whose name signifies "peace") centuries earlier had already established the cost of such peace: oppressive taxation via conscripted labor and grinding taxes (see 1 Kings 5:13–16; 9:15). Augustus' reign renovated much of Rome and introduced many elements of civilization, including a system of roads, an army, and civil services, including police, fire fighting, and courier. All of these benefits necessitated heavy taxation, so Augustus issued a decree for all to be enrolled for the purpose of compiling an official tax list (see Luke 2:1–3).

For all the "splendor of his kingdom," Augustus nevertheless was to be "shattered" (die) in AD 14, albeit under more auspicious circumstances than that of his predecessor Julius Caesar. The use of "shattered" provides yet another ironic parallel with the life of Jesus, whose own death in verse 22 is described as Him being "shattered." Ultimately, "without hand, he [Rome at the zenith of its papal power in the last days] will be shattered" (Dan. 8:25; 2:34, 45).

The prophecy now transitions to Augustus' successor. Augustus intended for his son-in-law Agrippa (husband to Augustus' daughter, Julia) to succeed him, but he died prematurely in 12 BC. He then took interest in his adopted sons, Gaius and Lucius Caesar (born to his third wife Livia in a former marriage), yet Lucius died in AD 2, and Gaius died in AD 4. Following Gaius' death, Tiberius (also son of Livia by a former marriage) was summoned to Rome (quite reluctantly, apparently) and officially adopted by Augustus and placed in a number of influential positions calculated to seat him as emperor following Augustus' death in AD 14. He came to power without dispute ("peaceably"), following a number of military victories as general. He was to take the kingdom "by smooth words," likely referring to his affected decline of his father's position at the multiple solicitations of the senate.

Not only did Augustus Caesar indicate a dislike for his adopted son Tiberius, but standard histories of the Caesars indicate that Tiberius' life was characterized by considerable vice (immoral sexual behavior, drunkenness, questionable deaths of potential rivals), making him a reproach in the eyes of many.

The prophecy describes the evil over which Tiberius held sway as a "flood," and though he held power for a while, eventually, "the arms of the flood" (his support) would be "swept away flood-like from before him" and be "shattered." This ironic turn of events is reminiscent of Daniel 8:7–8, in which Alexander the Great first "shatters" the 2 horns of the Medo-Persian empire before he himself is "shattered." It also points forward to the time when Rome (ultimately in its papal phase) will be "shattered" (v. 25).

We will defer comment on the flood imagery of verse 22 until we get to verses 40–45 and discuss the end-time king of the north, which "sweeps over flood-like and passes over." At this point, we observe simply that Rome, in verse 22, typifies the king of the north in verse 40, both of whom are described as floods that come to an end. Thankfully, *Yahweh* promises that such rivers will not overflow His people (see Isa. 43:2).

The great irony in verse 22 is that Jesus was to suffer the same fate as these wicked Romans did, being "shattered" at Calvary. How could such a thing be? Jesus was shattered not as the natural consequence of a self-centered life, but because He willingly paid the price for our rebellion. Recall Paul's words: "For he hath made him to be sin for us, who knew no sin; that we might be made the righteousness of God in him" (2 Cor. 5:21, KJV). If wicked rulers of Rome warranted such death, how could the Son of man suffer any less, having taken not only their sins, but everyone else's as well, upon Himself?

Rome's Entrance in Prophecy Until Jesus' Atoning Judgment Completed

Pagan Greco-Rome Dominates Until Time of Constantine

In verse 14, the specter of Rome reared its ugly head, and in verse 16, the Jews entered into an alliance with Rome in 161 BC, contrary to God's express prohibition of such covenants (see Exod. 23:32; Deut. 7:2; Judges 2:2) and with full knowledge of the biblical record of prior leagues (see Josh. 9). The death of Jesus in verse 22 spotlights how disastrous this union with Rome was.

We are now reminded in verse 23 that "upon uniting with him, he will deal treacherously," pointing out that evil did not simply follow many years afterward, but rather, treachery was in effect from the beginning of the alliance. The prophecy returns to the formation of this alliance in 161 BC, and Daniel 11:23–12:1 traces the events down to the victory of Christ and His faithful remnant over the end-time papal apostasy, culminating in the second coming.

In 1 Maccabees 8 is recorded how Judas Maccabeus heard that the Romans were willing to befriend those who came to them. In verses 17–20, the Jews, being persecuted by the Syrians, sent Eupolemos and Jason to address the senate and request an alliance, which was entered into in 161 BC. However expedient such an alliance may have seemed at the time, God's people are to shun such alliances, fear only *Yahweh* of hosts, and make *Him* their sanctuary (see Isa. 8:12–14). Rome would work against the Jews' best interests, increasing in strength from a small nation (the horn from insignificance of Daniel 8).

While outwardly appearing to seek the best interests of those with whom Rome enters into alliance, verse 24 makes clear that any apparent generosity in distributing plunder to these annexed provinces is for the purpose of removing them as threats to its rise to power. Previously, nations gained territory and wealth by conquering opponents and subjugating them. Rome entered upon a new policy. Kings would voluntarily relinquish their kingdoms to the control of Rome. Those living in such jurisdictions still enjoyed the use of their property and, of course, the comfort of knowing that Rome, in exchange for these large acquisitions, promised to protect these territories should outside threats emerge.

This policy would continue "for a time." While not the same Hebrew word *mo'ed* used in the expression "time, times, and half a time" (Dan. 12:7), *'et* in verse 24 does signify a very precise time (as it does in 9:21). In this case, it has a very definite beginning marked by the events of verse 25—the showdown between Augustus Caesar and Antony for complete control of the Roman Republic at the Battle of Actium. Remarkably, it also happens to correspond to a prophetic "time" of 360 years.

Rome Versus King of the South

Antony had allied himself with Cleopatra VII (the same who had been involved with Julius Caesar), thereby coming to power in Egypt, hence the reference to him as "king of the south" in verse 25. His "great army, exceedingly large" numbered 125,000 soldiers and a fleet of 500 ships, while Augustus came against him with 80,000 soldiers and half as many ships. Prophecy foretold that Antony would "not stand": he lost the battle to Augustus by foolishly following the cowardly retreat of Cleopatra, who had no experience in war.

A biblical "time" is 360 literal years. Since the "time" of verse 24 commenced with the Battle of Actium on September 2, 31 BC, it follows that this period would conclude 360 years later in AD 330. In response to those who may question whether the "time" (Hebrew *'et*) of verse 24 should be understood as prophetic time (usually the Hebrew *mo'ed*), secular historian Will Durant makes a most intriguing observation concerning the demise of Greek civilization. Having traced Greek history down to the dissolution of the Achaean League in 146 BC following the capture of its citadel, Corinth, by Mummius, Durant writes, "Greek civilization was not dead; it had yet several centuries of life before it; and when it died it bequeathed itself in an incomparable legacy to the nations of Europe and the Near East." For the phrase "when it died," Durant supplies a footnote stating, "We may arbitrarily date this at A.D. 325, when Constantine founded Constantinople, and Christian Byzantine civilization began to replace the 'pagan' Greek culture in the eastern Mediterranean" (*SC2*, p. 667).

This disagrees not at all with our conclusion. Durant recognizes the importance of the founding of Constantinople (AD 325), whereas prophecy focuses attention on the dedication of the city in AD 330,[134] for then power moved from Rome (seat of the Western Roman Empire) to Constantinople (seat of the Eastern Roman Empire). Historicist de Kock agrees, noting that pagan Rome (equated with the Greco-Roman Empire) "ended with the Edict of Milan in 313, just after Constantine's conversion, or when he founded New Rome (Constantinople) in 330 as an explicitly Christian city" (de Kock, *7 Heads and 10 Horns*, p. 93). Understanding Daniel 11:24–25 to foretell the demise of pagan Rome, we assert that prophecy points to AD 330, a biblical "time" after the Battle of Actium.

In verse 26 is summarized the end of Antony's quest for power. Reminiscent of the "delicacies" provided for those whom Nebuchadnezzar was grooming for positions of influence in Daniel 1:5–16, "those who eat his delicacies" refers to those in the service of Antony. In what way did they "shatter him"? Some of Antony's Egyptian forces surrendered to Augustus, while others switched allegiance, as did those in Libya. Realizing his military powerlessness and believing (mistakenly) that Cleopatra had committed suicide, Antony took his own life. The mass exodus from Antony's service to that of Augustus helps us understand the statement that his "army will sweep over flood-like." Augustus' greatly increased forces enabled his signal victory on September 2, 31 BC at Actium. As noted in the comments on verse 22, prophecy routinely describes Rome as a

---

[134] "Constantine the Great", Wikipedia, https://1ref.us/z1 (accessed January 22, 2020).

flood, and the flood-like imagery is particularly apt for the naval battle in verse 26.

Pretended Union: Rome and King of the South

Our attention is refocused on what preceded the battle of Actium. Following Lepidus' banishment from the Second Triumvirate (the confederation of Augustus, Antony, and Lepidus that divvied up the empire among them), both Augustus and Antony desired supreme control, rather than power limited to their respective provinces. The description of them as "at 1 table they will speak deception" is highly ironic. Sharing the same table evidences harmony, but these 2 kings' false friendship became manifest in the open conflict, resulting in Antony's death and Augustus' emergence as sole dictator and emperor.

"It will not prosper, for the end is still at the appointed time." In context, the "end" refers to the end of the "time" of verse 24, i.e., AD 330, when Constantinople replaced Rome as the seat of power, long after the conflict between Antony and Augustus concluded. However, these references hint that the historical events of verses 25–28 typify events during the "appointed time" (the end time beginning in 1798), specifically those events designated "the end," referring to the end-time judgment from the fall of 1844 until the second coming (see Dan. 8:19; 11:35; 12:13).

We read in verse 28 that "he will return to his own land with great property." In consequence of his defeat of Antony, Augustus came into possession of tremendous Egyptian wealth, which he highlighted with a 3-day triumphal celebration.

Having conquered Egypt, the next biblically significant Roman conquest was that of Jerusalem. The historical event in view is determined by the wording, "his heart set against the holy covenant." This points back to verse 22, when the Jewish authorities used Rome to crucify the Agent of the covenant in AD 31. In rejecting Jesus, they rejected the covenant itself. In our study of Daniel, we have examined Leviticus 26, the chapter of covenant blessings and curses. In the final section detailing curses, verse

29 prophesies that parents would eat the bodies of their own children. This was fulfilled when Titus besieged Jerusalem, leading to famine conditions. In verse 31, it was foretold that cities and sanctuaries were to be desolated. Cities that rejected Christ (Galilee, Chorazin, Bethsaida, and Capernaum) were taken. Also, while Titus wanted the Jerusalem temple spared, his soldiers grew enraged at the Jews and burned the temple to the ground. In verse 33, *Yahweh* promised He would draw out a sword after the inhabitants. In fact, 1.1 million Jews died in the siege, and another 97,000 were taken prisoner (Josephus, *Complete Works of Flavius Josephus: Wars of the Jews*, bk. 6, ch. 9, par. 3, p. 587).

The Jews, by their impenitent rejection of God's covenant, brought destruction upon themselves. Nevertheless, Rome was the agent used to carry out God's judgments upon those who broke covenant. Hence, Rome is spoken of as having "his heart set against the holy covenant." As prophesied, Titus returned to Rome in AD 71, becoming emperor following his father's death in AD 79.

From Eastern Roman Empire to Papacy

The text moves forward to "the appointed time," previously identified as the end of the 360-year "time" of verse 24. Constantine decided to move the seat of the empire from Rome to Byzantium. On May 11, 330, the city was founded as Constantinople. To be sure, a move from Rome to Byzantium is due east, not south, as indicated in verse 29. However, the prophecy merely states that once the appointed time has been reached—marked by the establishment of "New Rome" in Constantinople—Rome would venture south.

History confirms this southward march. Our historical survey in Daniel 7 revealed the trouble that the Germanic peoples caused the papacy. North of Rome, in Ravenna, Odoacer the Herul and Theodoric the Ostrogoth presented a challenge to papal supremacy, while another group posed a challenge to the south of Rome, specifically in North Africa. At this point, note that the text states that this southern challenge "will not be as the former, nor as the latter." The "former" challenges with the south were all in geographic Egypt, and the "latter" challenge is with end-time Egypt in verses 40–43 (to be identified in the comments on those verses, but distinct from geographic Egypt). The challenge in verses 29–31 is with Carthage, which is at the northern tip of modern-day Tunisia, northwest of Libya and due east of the northeast tip of Algeria.

What was this Carthaginian challenge? At this point, attention is drawn to the "ships of Kittim," a reference to the islands of the Mediterranean. Genseric the Vandal had moved his people from this Mediterranean area to Carthage. This mighty naval conqueror established Germanic Christianity in Carthage. It is Genseric's naval warfare and its devastating effect upon Rome (see comments on Daniel 7) that is referred to by the phrase "ships of Kittim."

As for being "outraged against the holy covenant," we turn to the Eastern emperor, Justinian I. Apart from any religious motivation, Justinian had political reason to link up with the Roman papacy:

> [In A.D. 533,] he was already planning to send Belisarius, his famous general, to subject the Vandals in North Africa. After this, he meant to overthrow the Ostrogothic regime in Italy. But for his plans to succeed, the emperor also needed the cooperation of the senatorial class, which was centered in Rome. Under both the republic and the subsequent empire, they administered Italy and still wielded great influence. With their vast estates and influence, they were a power to be reckoned with. They had long since allied themselves with the papacy. It was therefore impossible for the emperor to secure the support of those senators without involving the pope. (de Kock, *666*, vol. 1, p. 194)

Justinian decided to elevate the pope to the position of head of all the churches by incorporating the decision into the Civil Code. The 131st Novella states, "Hence, in accordance with the provisions of these Councils, we order that the Most Holy Pope of ancient Rome shall hold the first rank of all the Pontiffs, but the Most Blessed Archbishop of Constantinople, or New Rome, shall occupy the second place after the Holy Apostolic See of ancient Rome, which shall take precedence over all other sees" (Froom, *PFF*, vol. 1, p. 513, citing Scott's translation of Novella 131 of Justinian, 9th collection, title 6, chap. 2).

Justinian informed Pope John II of his decision via a letter sent by 2 Eastern prelates. It begins, "To your Holiness, because it [Your Holiness] is head of all the holy churches" (Froom, *PFF*, vol. 1, p. 511). In the letter, he states that he has exerted himself to unite all the priests of the Eastern church in subjection to the bishop of Rome.

As de Kock notes, "Justinian's decision to recognize the pope as the head of all the churches was naturally subject to the unspoken proviso that the emperor occupied a still higher place. He meant ecclesiastical precedence, not dominion of a temporal nature; for he himself remained the *vicarius Christi*. Like all Byzantine emperors, both before and after him, he was the real head of the church within his jurisdiction. Petrine Primacy would come to full fruition only two centuries later through the spurious Donation of Constantine" (de Kock, *666*, vol. 1, p. 194).

As detailed in the remarks on Daniel 7, Justinian sent his general Belisarius in AD 533 to fight the Vandals in North Africa, conquering them by March of AD 534 and marking the end of Germanic Christianity in North Africa. Then proceeded a push against the Ostrogoths in AD 535, with the result that on March 12, 538, the Ostrogothic king Vitiges withdrew his Roman siege and later abandoned Germanic Christianity in favor of Catholicism. This marked the end of the Germanic threat to papal superiority, enabling Justinian's decree to go into effect. The papacy was now the counterfeit high priest ("head of all the churches") for the 3.5 times, or 1,260 years, of Daniel 7:25.

Justinian is the particular party who was "outraged against the holy covenant" in verse 30. He would "identify with those who desert the holy covenant" by linking up with the Roman papacy; he would also employ "arms" (i.e., military strength) to achieve his ends.

How did this "pollute the sanctuary," also identified in verse 31 as the "stronghold"? The rest of the verse provides the answer. By elevating the papacy and squelching those who adhered to biblical Christianity, Justinian and his forces were removing Christ's continual ministration in the heavenly sanctuary by establishing the detestable idol that desolates (i.e., Satan's earthly counterfeit, the papacy). This false system leaves its adherents destitute of Christ's purifying work in the life.

The Papacy's 1,260 Years

According to verse 32, the papacy is directly antagonistic to God's covenant, the everlasting covenant established with Abram in Genesis 15 and 17. Since this is a covenant of righteousness by faith, Satan's goal through the papacy is to prevent the restoration of the divine image with which mankind was originally endowed in Genesis 1:26–27. The papacy will "defile with smooth [words]," the Hebrew word for "smooth" signifying deceitful and/or flattering talk (see Prov. 2:16; 5:3; 7:5, 21; 26:28; 28:23; 29:5). Thus, we learn that the papacy is pleased to tell the lie that God's covenant in 10 Commandments (see Exod. 34:28; Deut. 4:13; 1 Kings 8:9, 21) is done away. Conversely, those who take hold of God's covenant are strengthened to withstand the boldest lies and strongest persecution that any earthly power can put forth. One need only read a history of the Waldenses to learn what people can endure when strengthened by God's grace (see, e.g., Wylie, *The History of Protestantism: Protestantism in the Waldensian Valleys*, vol. 16, ch. 5, "Persecutions and Martyrdoms" and ch. 11, "The Great Massacre").

Tertullian noted that the blood of martyrs in the days of the Roman emperors was seed for the spread of the gospel. Therefore, in the days of papal persecution, the immovability of the faithful martyrs caused the multitudes to understand the power of God's sustaining grace. Loving not their lives unto the death, all of Satan's coercive tactics (sword, flame, captivity, pillage) were shown to be utterly impotent when a person is devoid of self-interest, whole-heartedly serving Jesus.

The "[many] days" of verse 33 are not specifically stated to be the 1,260 years (AD 538–1798), but verse 35 does make plain that these days continue "until the end time" (i.e., 1798 onward). The less specific "[many] days" may refer to the fact that the papal persecution ended before the 1,260 years were completed:

> The persecution of the church did not continue throughout the entire period of the 1260 years. God in mercy to His people cut short the time of their fiery trial. In foretelling the "great tribulation" to befall the church, the Saviour said: "Except those days should be shortened, there should no flesh be saved: but for the elect's sake those days shall be shortened." Matthew 24:22. Through the influence of the Reformation the persecution was brought to an end prior to 1798. (White, *GC*, pp. 266, 267)

We are reminded of the deliverance from Egypt in verse 34. In Exodus 12:38, a mixed multitude of certain Egyptians joined themselves to the Israelites, with the *apparent* intent of joining in the worship and service of *Yahweh*. However, as the designation "mixed" indicates, some wished to serve *Yahweh*, while many more joined up out of a sense of self-preservation or idle curiosity:

> In this multitude were not only those who were actuated by faith in the God of Israel, but also a far greater number who desired only to escape from the plagues, or who followed in the wake of the moving multitudes merely from excitement and curiosity. This class were ever a hindrance and a snare to Israel. (White, *PP*, p. 281)

Similarly, in the days of the Reformation, there were those of the German princes who provided the necessary protection for the Reformation to get under way, while there were numbers of people who pretended to join up with the Reformation, yet had no genuine attachment to the movement.

Some who favored the Reformation posted placards all around France in a single night, attacking the mass. A placard was posted on the king's private chamber, which led him to declare, "Let all be seized without distinction who are suspected of Lutheresy. I will exterminate them all." A poor craftsman was seized, ordered to disclose the locations of all suspected Lutherans in Paris on pain of instant death, and tragically, the man yielded to the threat to spare his own life. He led Morin around Paris, giving a sign at each Lutheran home. As captives were added to the death train, "Morin made all the city quake" (d'Aubigne, *History of the Reformation in Europe in the Time of Calvin*, bk. 4, ch. 10, pp. 58, 60). Like this craftsman, some who joined the Reformation were like the seed in Matthew 13:5–6: They had no depth of root to enable them to stand firm when faced with persecution.

The experience of God's people in verse 35 is to be repeated during the end time (the "appointed time," which began in 1798). Comparison with Daniel 12:10 reveals that those in the end time will be "purified, whitened, and refined":

> The prophecy in the eleventh of Daniel has nearly reached its complete fulfillment. Much of the history that has taken place in fulfillment of this prophecy will be repeated. In the thirtieth verse a power is spoken of that "shall be grieved, and return, and have indignation against the holy covenant: so shall he do; he shall even return, and have intelligence with them that forsake the holy covenant." [Verses 31–36, quoted.]
>
> Scenes similar to those described in these words will take place. (White, *13MR*, p. 394)

Throughout history, God has strengthened people to stand nobly for Him despite persecution. Those in the very end who will face the fiercest persecution ever to come to God's people will not lose heart, but will recall these former episodes of sacred history and His sustaining grace.

Having outlined the career of the papacy during the 1,260 years in verses 32–35, verse 36 refers to papal Rome as a "king" that "will do according to his own will." This very description was used of Medo-Persia, Alexander the Great, and Rome in the days of the Republic (see 8:4; 11:3, 16). Along with these prior kings, the king of verse 36 manifests the character of Satan—self-exaltation.

This king is said to "raise himself up," which on the surface might appear to refer to a sort of resurrection, following the infliction of the mortal wound received in 1798 at the hands of General Berthier (see Rev. 13:3). However, Daniel 11:36 explains "raising himself up" as "exalting himself above every god," which the papacy has been doing ever since its installation back in AD 538 as it carries forward Satan's plan to displace Christ as supreme Judge (see Isa. 14:13, 14; compare 33:5, 10, 22).

Having sought to exalt himself above God, the king will speak "wonderful things," blasphemous words against the God of gods (i.e., the Most High God). The papacy's "wonderful" words against the Most High hearken back to the "wonderful" work of corruption of pagan Rome in Daniel 8:24, standing in marked contrast with the Wonderful Numberer (Jesus) of Daniel 8:13. Great, blasphemous words and exalting self above God are attributed to the horn from insignificance, the sea beast, and the man of sin, all designations for the antichrist, papal Rome (see Dan. 7:25; Rev. 13:5; 2 Thess. 2:3, 4). Therefore, there is no question that the king of Daniel 11:36 is none other than the papacy.

The apparent triumph of the papal king is not permanent, for the text states that "this outrage" will conclude, "for that which has been decreed must be done." Our study of Daniel 8:19 showed that "the outrage" referred to the horn's rebellious attempt to take Jesus' place as Judge and High Priest and its ruthless slaughter of millions of Christians who steadfastly refused such papal arrogance. This outrage concluded when the papacy received its mortal wound in 1798, to be followed in 1844 by the commencement of the end-time judgment, during which Jesus cleanses the heavenly sanctuary, vindicating Himself and those who (apparently) died in vain.

What is meant by "the God of his fathers"? Scripture is replete with references to "the God of your fathers: the God of Abraham, the God

Isaac, and the God of Jacob"[135] in connection with the fulfillment of His covenant. The God of Israel cries out concerning His people's "wickedness which they have done, in provoking Me to anger, in going to burn incense in the service of other gods, whom they have not known—they, you, nor your fathers" (Jer. 44:3). Hence, in giving no consideration to the God of his fathers, the papal king *disregards God's everlasting covenant* entered into with Abraham, Isaac, and Jacob.

Does "the desire of women" refer to a "desire for women," "that which women desire," or something altogether different? To answer, let us survey the Scriptures. The Hebrew verb *chamad* ("desire, esteem"), along with its derivatives *chemed*, *chemdah*, *chamudot*, *machmad*, and *machmod*, occur 68 times in 67 verses, 8 of them in Daniel. Table 17 summarizes the usages most relevant to our discussion:

Table 17: *Chamad* ("desire," "esteem") in Scripture

REFERENCE	VERSE QUOTED	SUMMARY
Gen. 3:6	"The **woman** saw that ... the tree was **desirable** for making [one] wise."	Woman desires [inappropriate] wisdom.
Dan. 10:3	"**Desirable** food I did not eat."	Points back to Eve's desire for wisdom in the garden of Eden.
Exod. 20:17; Deut. 5:21	"You will not **desire** your neighbor's **wife** ["woman"]."	Tenth commandment: God's people will not desire anything that is not their own.
Song of Sol. 2:2, 3	"Like a lily among the briars, so is My companion among the daughters." "Like an apple tree among the trees of the forest, so is my Beloved among the sons. In His shade, I took great **delight**, so I sat down. His fruit is sweet to my palate."	Jesus states that His bride stands out among the daughters [of Jerusalem]. Bride's delight is to sit in Jesus' shade.

(*continued*)

---

[135] The first is when Jacob blesses Joseph (see Gen. 48:15). The phrase is also used to identify God as *Yahweh* when the time for covenant deliverance (see Gen. 15:13) has come (see Exod. 3:15, 16; 4:5; Acts 7:32). Further, it is used in relation to the grant of land in the covenant promise of Genesis 15:18 (see Deut. 6:10; 9:5; 30:20).

Table 17: *Chamad* ("desire," "esteem") in Scripture (*continued*)

REFERENCE	VERSE QUOTED	SUMMARY
Song of Sol. 5:16	"All of Him [my Beloved] is supremely **desirable** ... daughters of Jerusalem."	Bride tells daughters of Jerusalem that Jesus is most desirable.
1 Sam. 9:20	"For whom is all the **desire** of Israel? Is it not for you, and for all the house of your father?"	Desire of Israel is for their first king [Saul, who typifies Jesus], and His father's house [typifies house of God the Father, His sanctuary].
Hag. 2:7	"I will shake all the nations, and the **Desire** of all the nations will come. I will fill all this house with glory."	Jesus is the Desire of all nations. God promises to fill His house (His sanctuary) with glory.
Isa. 53:2	"When we see Him, there is no appearance that we should **desire** Him."	When Jesus came, His own people did not desire Him.
Dan. 9:23	"For you [Daniel] are of **high esteem**."	Daniel held in high esteem because of his Christ-like character.
Dan. 10:11	"Daniel, man of **high esteem**."	Daniel held in high esteem because of his Christ-like character.
Dan. 10:19	"Do not fear, man of **high esteem**."	Daniel held in high esteem because of his Christ-like character.
Ps. 68:16	"Why envy, mountain peaks, the mountain God has **desired** to dwell in?"	God desires to dwell in Mt. Zion, the location of His sanctuary.
Lam. 1:10	"The adversary has put his hand upon all her **desirable things**, for she has seen the nations enter her sanctuary."	Jerusalem's desirable things are inside her sanctuary.
Lam. 2:4	"His right hand killed all who were **desirable** to the eye in the tent of daughter Zion."	Desirable people are those in Zion, location of the sanctuary.
Ezek. 24:21	"I am about to pollute My sanctuary ... the **desire** of your eyes."	God's sanctuary is the desire of the house of Israel.

(*continued*)

Table 17: *Chamad* ("desire," "esteem") in Scripture *(continued)*

REFERENCE	VERSE QUOTED	SUMMARY
Ezek. 24:16, 18	"Son of man, behold, I am about to take from you the **desire** of your eyes with a blow. ... My **wife** ["woman"] died that evening."	Ezekiel's wife = the desire of his eyes. Her death typified what would happen to God's earthly sanctuary = desire of the house of Israel.
Dan. 11:8	"Their gods (along with their molded images and **esteemed** implements of silver and gold) he will bring into captivity in Egypt."	Esteemed implements = objects of false worship.
Dan. 11:38	The papal king "will give glory ... with **articles of high esteem**."	Articles of high esteem employed in false worship.
Dan. 11:43	"He will rule over ... the **articles of high esteem** of Egypt."	Articles of high esteem employed in false worship.
Dan. 11:37	"Concerning the **desire** of **women** and concerning every god he will give no consideration, for above every [god] he will exalt himself."	End-time papacy exalts itself above the desire of women and every god. End-time papacy exalts itself above the heavenly sanctuary and Jesus.

Table 17 indicates that the "desire of women" points primarily to, 1) on the negative side, the inappropriate desire of the first woman, Eve, for a position beyond what God appointed her and wisdom that He forbade her to have, and 2) on the positive side, Christ Himself and His sanctuary. In manifesting Satan's character on earth, the papacy's desire for supremacy evidences a complete disregard of this biblical counsel: "Casting down imaginations, and every high thing that exalteth itself against the knowledge of God, and bringing into captivity every thought to the obedience of Christ" (2 Cor. 10:5, KJV). The papacy shows no fear of *Yahweh*, which is true wisdom (see Ps. 111:10; Prov. 9:10). Indeed, the papacy exalts itself above Christ and has instituted its own earthly counterfeit of His heavenly sanctuary.

One may still wonder about the qualifier "of women" in the phrase "desire of women." God's people, Israel, are collectively likened to a woman/wife in Scripture (see Jer. 6:2; Rev. 19:7), while Jerusalem's occupants individually may be called daughters (see Song of Sol. 5:16 in Table 17 above).

Hence, the papacy disregards the object of true desire for all those who collectively make up God's bride, Israel.

Instead of honoring God, the papacy gives "glory to a god of strongholds." The following texts make plain that the covenant-keeping God *Yahweh* is the only true stronghold:

> 2 Sam. 22:32, 33: Who is God except *Yahweh*? ... *The* God is my mighty stronghold.
>
> Neh. 8:10: For the joy of *Yahweh*, that is your stronghold.
>
> Ps. 27:1: *Yahweh* is the stronghold of my life—of whom should I be afraid?
>
> Ps. 31:4: Bring me out of the net which they have hidden for me, for You [*Yahweh*] are my stronghold.
>
> Prov. 10:29: The way of *Yahweh* is a stronghold to the perfect.
>
> Jer. 16:19: *Yahweh*, my strength, my stronghold, and my refuge in the day of distress.
>
> Joel 3:16: *Yahweh* will be a refuge for His people, a stronghold for the sons of Israel.
>
> Nah. 1:7: *Yahweh* is good, serving as a stronghold in the day of distress; He knows those who take refuge in Him.

The precious metals and stones in the remainder of verse 38 might suggest to the reader the earthly wealth that the papacy has accrued to itself. To an extent, this is true, for the only other text in which these particular riches appear is 2 Chronicles 32:27, where it is related that Hezekiah stored these items up in great abundance. He erred greatly in showing these items to the Babylonian envoys (see 2 Chron. 32:31; Isa. 39:2), who saw and coveted them. This ultimately led to the Babylonian deportation recorded at the beginning of Daniel (see Isa. 39:7). Since the end-time Babylon is papal Rome, it makes sense that it would covet these items as did Babylon of old.

However, the focus of Daniel 11:38 is the papacy's relation to *worship*. In Scripture, to "give glory" unto God is to worship him: "Ascribe unto

Yahweh the glory due His name; worship *Yahweh* in the splendor of holiness" (Ps. 29:2). "Fear God, and give glory to him; for the hour of his judgment is come: and worship him that made heaven, and earth, and the sea, and the fountains of waters" (Rev. 14:7, KJV). By giving glory to "a god whom his fathers did not know," the papacy *worships* a false god. This "god whom his fathers did not know" encompasses all manner of idolatry and demon worship:

> Deut. 28:36: *Yahweh* will bring you and your king whom you will raise up over you to a nation whom you have not known—you nor your fathers—and there you will serve other gods, tree and stone.
>
> Deut. 28:64: *Yahweh* will scatter you among all the peoples from [one] end of the earth unto [the other] end of the earth, and there you will serve other gods whom you have not known—you nor your fathers—tree and stone.
>
> Deut. 29:13: That He may raise you up today to be His people, and that He may be your God, just as He told you, and just as He swore to your fathers, to Abraham, Isaac, and Jacob.
>
> Deut. 29:25, 26: Then they will say, "Because they forsook the covenant of *Yahweh*, the God of their fathers, which He cut with them when He brought them out of the land of Egypt, and they went and served other gods and worshipped them, gods whom they did not know, and [whom] He had not appointed for them.'
>
> Deut. 31:16: This people will rise up, and act the harlot with other gods of the strangers of the land, into whose midst he ["this people"] is going. He ["this people"] will forsake Me and break My covenant which I cut with him ["this people"].
>
> Deut. 31:20: For when I have brought him to the land which I swore to his fathers—flowing with milk and honey—and he has eaten, been satisfied and grown fat, then he will turn to other gods—they will serve them and shun me—and he will break my covenant.

> Deut. 32:17: They slaughtered [sacrifices] unto demons—not God—gods they did not know, new ones who came in from nearby. Your fathers were not acquainted with them.

The gold, silver, precious stone, and articles of high esteem of verse 38 indicates that the papacy's false worship of idols and demons is a counterfeit of God's sanctuary service:

> 1 Chron. 29:2: According to all my strength, I have prepared for the house of God the gold for that which is to be of gold, the silver for that which is to be of silver, the bronze for that which is to be of bronze, the iron for that which is to be of iron, the wood for that which is to be of wood, onyx for inlay, a variety of antimony stones, every precious stone, and an abundance of marble stone.
>
> 2 Chron. 36:10: King Nebuchadnezzar sent, and brought him to Babylon with the esteemed vessels of the house of *Yahweh*.

The god advanced by the king is here referred to as "foreign." Let us examine each occurrence of this phrase in the Hebrew Scriptures:

> Ps. 81:9, 10: There will not be among you a strange god, nor will you bow down in worship to a foreign god. I am *Yahweh* your God who brought you up out of the land of Egypt. Open your mouth wide, and I will fill it.
>
> Deut. 32:12: *Yahweh* alone led him [Israel during the wilderness wanderings], a foreign god was not with him.
>
> Mal 2:11: Judah has acted faithlessly, an abomination has been committed in Israel, even in Jerusalem, for Judah has defiled the sanctuary of *Yahweh* which He loves, and married the daughter of a foreign god.

The foregoing passages each deal with Israel's unfaithfulness in departing from *Yahweh*, the one true God who faithfully led Israel out of Egypt and through the wilderness, to follow after other false gods, thereby breaking covenant with Him. Of particular interest is Malachi 2:11, in which *Yahweh* charges His people with marrying the "daughter of a foreign god." Reference to the "covenant of our fathers" in verse 10 and the "God of judgment" in verse 17 suggest that verse 11 is not limited to earthly marriage. On the whole, Malachi 2 points back to God's covenant with the Levites (the priestly class) in Exodus 32, when all the other tribes proved unfaithful to *Yahweh* by worshipping the golden calf. In Malachi 2, the priests as a whole are faithless to the covenant (a feminine noun in Hebrew), marrying the daughter (feminine) of a foreign god. In other words, by indulging idolatry, they have broken covenant with *Yahweh*, who is a jealous God according to the second commandment forbidding image worship (see Exod. 20:4–6).

What has this to do with papal Rome? Recall that the Catechism of the Catholic Church completely removes the second commandment prohibiting image worship (idolatry), hence the papal system *encourages* idolatry in the lives of its adherents. These idols obtain a stronghold that draws its followers out of covenant relationship with *Yahweh* and into captivity to Satan, the foreign god.

"The land he will divide for a price." Notice how Scripture equates the *land* of the covenant with the *people* of the covenant: "He [*Yahweh*] will provide atonement for His land, His people" (Deut. 32:43). A prime catalyst for Luther and the Protestant Reformation was the indulgence. For the price of an indulgence, the Roman Catholic Church promised remission of *all future sins* for the certificate holder, without any need for repentance. Indulgences could even be purchased on behalf of those who had already died. Johann Tetzel, the German Grand Commissioner for indulgences, is credited with the blasphemous ditty, "As soon as the gold in the casket rings, the rescued soul to heaven springs."[136,137]

---

[136] "Johann Tetzel," Wikipedia, https://1ref.us/z2 (accessed January 22, 2020).

[137] This promise is faulty on several counts: 1) It extorts money, 2) it teaches that one can secure another person's salvation, 3) it teaches that souls can be rescued from purgatory, a place of cleansing taught nowhere in the Bible, and 4) it teaches spiritualism, the unscriptural belief that at death, people's spirits live on without a body.

Hence, papal Rome treats God's people and their salvation, which was purchased at infinite cost, as nothing more than property. History records that the papacy martyred millions during the 1,260 years while it led countless others to perdition with the false hope that they can have salvation while continuing to live in sin. To this day, papal Rome continues to make merchandise of God's covenant, even though He freely offers salvation "without money and without price" (Isa. 55:1, KJV). This is so serious in God's sight that this is the very reason He gathers the wicked in the end for judgment:

> Joel 3:2, 3: I will gather all the nations, and I will bring them down to the valley of Jehoshaphat ["*Yahweh* judges"]. I will enter into judgment with them there concerning My people, My inheritance Israel, whom they have scattered among the nations. My land they have divided; for My people, they have cast lots.

Kings of South and North Unite Against God's People

Gabriel now comes to the final events of his prophetic outline. In verse 40, we meet once again with the kings of the south and north. Who are these entities, and what is their relation to each other and the papal king of verses 36–39? Are either of them identical with the papal king? To avoid mere speculation, we need to gather the biblical evidence that bears on the end-time conflict.

Nearly all translations and commentators identify the first "him" of verse 40 as the king of verses 36–39, and the second "him" as the just-mentioned king of the south. However, the present commentary holds that *both* mentions of "him" in verse 40 refer to "the God of gods" and "God of his fathers" in verses 36 and 37. Why such a different interpretation? Let us consider two main lines of evidence.

First, we noted a similar phenomenon in Daniel 9:27: The word "he" did *not* refer to the immediately preceding person, the agent, in verse 26. Rather, "he" referred to Messiah even earlier in verse 26. Such a phenomenon also appears in Exodus 34:28, which reads: "And he [Moses] was there with *Yahweh* 40 days and 40 nights. Bread he did not eat, and water he did not drink. And he wrote upon the tablets the words of the covenant, the 10 Words." To the English reader, the "he" in the last sentence of this verse suggests that Moses wrote the 10 Commandments the second time, following the golden calf episode of chapter 32. In fact, *Yahweh* wrote the 10 Commandments not only the first time, but the second as well: "*Yahweh* said to Moses, 'Carve out for yourself 2 tablets of stone like the first [tablets of stone], then I will write upon the tablets the words which were upon the first tablets, which you broke.'" (34:1). We have two very clear examples, including one from the book of Daniel itself, in which the pronoun "he" does not refer back to the immediately mentioned party, but to God Himself.

Second, observe that Revelation 19:19 describes Babylon's attempt to destroy God's faithful remnant as waging war against *Jesus*. Again, Psalm 83:3 and 5 declares that those who conspire to destroy God's people enter into covenant against *God*. This second line of evidence suggests that both occurrences of "him" in Daniel 11:40 refer to God Himself, in the person of His saints.

Let us move on to the king of the north. It is said that he will "overflow and pass over," while in verse 45, he comes to his end. Earlier in verse 10, the king of the north, Antiochus III, was said to "sweep over flood-like and pass over" in his work of reclaiming Seleucia and Syria. The flood imagery ultimately hearkens back to Isaiah 8:7–8, in which the king of Assyria (associated with the north in Zephaniah 2:13) is equated with the Euphrates river, overflowing its banks as it brought the northern kingdom of Israel to its end. The king of Assyria models the archenemy of God in that he alone, of all the wicked kings of earth, is termed "the great king" (2 Kings 18:19, 28; Isa. 36:4, 13), a title elsewhere used of God (see Ps. 47:2; 95:3; Mal. 1:14). All who relied on earthly alliances in Isaiah 8 were taken by the king of Assyria; so it will be with the king of the north in the end time. His strength will be so great that one's only hope is to rely on *Yahweh*. Anyone who yields to the temptation to rely on any earthly deliverance is sure to be lost.

The destruction of Jerusalem in AD 70 by the Roman army is described in Daniel 9:26 as the work of an overwhelming flood. Again, the flood description was applied to Roman emperor Tiberius as he came to his end, and Rome's army swept over flood-like against Antony (see 11:22, 26). The work of Satan in persecuting God's people during the 1,260 years of papal Rome is described as a flood (see Rev. 12:15, 16). We conclude that the end-time king of the north is once again Rome—papal Rome.

In verse 40, we learn that "the king of the south will engage in butting with Him." The only other occurrence of "butting" in Daniel is in 8:4, describing the aggression of the Medo-Persian ram. Further, the king of Persia, Cyrus, is called both a shepherd and messiah (see Isa. 44:28; 45:1), identifying him as a type of Christ. Are we then to picture the king of the south as some sort of shepherd, a *messianic* figure? To answer, we do a word search on *nagach*, the word translated "butting." Apart from both occurrences in Daniel, the word is used another eleven times (see Exod. 21:28–36 (six times); Deut. 33:17; 1 Kings 22:11; 2 Chron. 18:10; Ps. 44:5; Ezek. 34:21). The following texts provide interpretive keys for Daniel 11:40:

> Ps. 44:4, 5: You are my King, God. Command complete victory for Jacob. Through You, we will butt at our adversaries. Through Your name, we will trample those who rise up against us.

> Ezek. 34:20–24: Therefore, thus says *Adonai Yahweh* to them: "Behold, I Myself shall judge between fat sheep and lean sheep. Since with side and shoulder you have thrust, and with your horns you have butted all the weak until you have scattered them abroad, I will save My flock, and they will no more be a prey—I will judge between sheep and sheep. I will raise up over them one Shepherd, and He will shepherd them—my servant David. He will shepherd them, He will be their shepherd. I, *Yahweh*, will be their God, and My servant David [will be] Prince among them. I, *Yahweh*, have spoken."

In Ezekiel 34:21, the enemy of God's people butts against them, while His people butt against their enemy in Psalm 44:5. This butting between God's enemies and His people is highlighted in Daniel 11:40, in which *nagach* appears not in its common Piel or Qal stems (six and four occurrences, respectively), but the Hithpael stem (the *only* Hithpael occurrence of *nagach* in the Hebrew Bible), a stem often employed for reciprocal, back-and-forth behavior. The passage in Ezekiel 34:20–24 highlights God's concern for the flock of His people. Those who butt against them are identified in verse 2 as the unfaithful "shepherds of Israel," the religious leaders (just as the modern "pastor" shepherds God's people).

We conclude that the king of the south who butts back and forth with God's people is a religious entity. Does Scripture elsewhere depict an end-time religious leader, employing the imagery of a ram with horns? Yes, indeed. Following the description of the papacy as a beast in Revelation 13:1–10, verse 11 mentions a second beast that has 2 horns like a lamb, yet speaks as a dragon. The rest of the chapter indicates that this second beast eventually forces the world to worship the papacy. Indeed, this second beast is of a religious, persecuting nature—at full maturity, one aptly described as a butting ram and false shepherd. In fact, this second beast is a false messiah. Its designation as a lamb connects it with Jesus, the "Lamb slain from the foundation of the world" (Rev. 13:8). Its rise in power from the uninhabited "earth" (verse 11), versus the populous "sea" (verse 1) from which the papacy arises, coincides temporally with the deadly wound of the papacy in 1798. Hence, the king of the south is none other than the United States of America, specifically apostate American Protestantism, which employs the strong arm of civil government to enforce its agenda of false worship. The Unites States began as a distinctly Protestant nation, but as the second coming draws nearer, its likeness to Christ grows ever dimmer. Ultimately, it will exhibit the character of Satan as it employs the dragon power—the kings and rulers of the world[138]—to enforce false papal worship.

---

[138] "Kings and rulers and governors have placed upon themselves the brand of antichrist, and are represented as the dragon who goes to make war with the saints—with those who keep the commandments of God and who have the faith of Jesus" (White, *TM*, p. 39).

Why does the king of the *north* have chariots and horsemen, though Scripture routinely ascribes chariots and horsemen to Egypt,[139] described as the *south* in Daniel 11? The key is to review the history already delineated in this chapter. The daughter of the south attempted a union with the north in verse 6, so in the end time, it is to be expected that the daughter of the south will again propose a union with the north. We just noted from Revelation 13 that the second beast (apostate Protestantism in the United States) will force the world to worship the sea beast (the papacy). Further, Revelation 17 refers to a woman (the papacy) who rides a scarlet beast (apostate Protestantism in the United States) with 10 horns (the kings of the world and their military might). Finally, Revelation 19:17–21 refers to the beast (the papacy), the false prophet (apostate Protestantism in the United States), and the kings and military leaders of the world. In each of these prophetic scenarios, American Protestantism is subservient to the papacy. Hence, the king of the *north* in Daniel 11:40 comes with the chariots, horsemen, and ships of the *south*, because the south willingly provides its resources to serve the papacy (compare Rev. 17:12, 13).

Before moving on, it is worth noting that this union of north and south is prophesied elsewhere in Scripture, and in harmony with the book of Daniel, the union is assured of failure. In Zechariah 10:10, God promises to gather His people out of end-time, spiritual Egypt (the south) and spiritual Assyria (the north).[140] In verse 11, He foretells that the depths of the Nile will dry up (support for spiritual Egypt; compare Revelation 16:12, in which support for end-time Babylon is represented as the Euphrates drying up), the pride of Assyria will be brought down, and the scepter of Egypt will turn aside.

---

[139] See Exod. 14:9; 15:19; Josh. 24:6; 2 Kings 18:24; 2 Chron. 12:3; Isa. 31:1; 36:9.

[140] Babylon and Assyria are used interchangeably in prophecies of the king of the north. There is no inconsistency here: Assyria's capital city, Nineveh, became known as New Babylon when it conquered Babylon in 689 BC (Christopher Klein, "Hanging Gardens Existed, but not in Babylon," History, https://1ref.us/z3 [accessed January 22, 2020]). In 612 BC, Babylon raided Nineveh and transferred power to Babylonia under Nebuchadnezzar's father, Nabopolassar.

Let us consider how the papacy and United States have come to work closely together already. Since the deadly wound in 1798, the papacy has been rebuilding its authority, particularly during the 20th century. A particular boon was the creation of Vatican City in 1929 as a result of the Lateran Treaty between the Holy See of Rome and Italy. Nevertheless, that did not mark when the U.S. and papacy began working closely together. As recently as 1960, in which John F. Kennedy was the Democratic presidential candidate, many Americans were wary of a Roman Catholic in the Oval Office. In a bid to alleviate public concern about how his Catholicism might negatively impact his decision-making, Kennedy affirmed the foundational principle of separation of church and state and assured those present that his Catholicism would not influence his presidency:

> I believe in an America where the separation of church and state is absolute; where no Catholic prelate would tell the President—should he be Catholic—how to act, and no Protestant minister would tell his parishioners for whom to vote; where no church or church school is granted any public funds or political preference, and where no man is denied public office merely because his religion differs from the President who might appoint him, or the people who might elect him.
>
> I believe in an America that is officially neither Catholic, Protestant nor Jewish; where no public official either requests or accept instructions on public policy from the Pope, the National Council of Churches or any other ecclesiastical source; where no religious body seeks to impose its will directly or indirectly upon the general populace or the public acts of its officials, and where religious liberty is so indivisible that an act against one church is treated as an act against all. ...
>
> I am not the Catholic candidate for President.
>
> I am the Democratic Party's candidate for President who happens also to be a Catholic.

I do not speak for my church on public matters; and the church does not speak for me.[141]

However, the religious climate changed before the close of the 20th century during charismatic John Paul II's tenure as pope (October 16, 1978–April 2, 2005) and Ronald Reagan's presidency (January 20, 1981–January 20, 1989). Both men were avowedly anti-communist, viewing its hold upon Russia, Eastern European countries, and even Cuba under Fidel Castro as a significant threat to the planet. Behind the scenes, Ronald Reagan and Pope John Paul II cooperated to bring down this common enemy. On June 12, 1987, in an effort to end the so-called Cold War, President Reagan issued his famous challenge to General Secretary Mikhail Gorbachev: "Mr. Gorbachev, open this gate! Mr. Gorbachev, tear down this wall!" Those assembled at the Malta Summit declared on December 3, 1989 that the Cold War was over, and the Soviet Union effectively ended on August 24, 1991 with the resignation of Gorbachev as President and the dissolution of Communist party segments of the government. *Time Magazine* recognized the joint effort of Reagan and Pope John Paul II in bringing down communism, for the cover of the February 24, 1992 issue featured photos of the men facing each other, with the words "HOLY ALLIANCE—How Reagan and the Pope conspired to assist Poland's Solidarity movement and hasten the demise of Communism."

One more observation on the kings of south and north. In Daniel 10:20–21, there is a conflict between the ruler of Persia and the Ruler, Michael, to be followed by a contest between the ruler of Hellas and the Ruler, Michael. The rulers of Persia and Hellas are one (Satan), while the Ruler, Michael, is Jesus. The war is fought on earth between their representatives: the *kings* of Persia and Greece on the one hand, and Michael's representative, Gabriel, on the other. So it is with the final conflict outlined in Daniel 11:40: Satan's king of the south (apostate American Protestantism controlling the civil

---

[141] John F. Kennedy, "Address to the Greater Houston Ministerial Association," American Rhetoric, https://1ref.us/z4 (accessed January 22, 2020).

government) wages war against "Him" (God's people on earth), and then Satan's king of the north (the papacy) wages war against "Him" (again, God's people on earth). This explains why it is that Michael reappears in Daniel 12:1, standing up for the sons of Daniel's people. Michael is the "Him" who has been attacked in the person of His people! Hence, the earthly conflict at the close of Daniel 11 is but the earthly manifestation of the greater cosmic battle between Christ and Satan.

In verse 41, the papal king of the north enters the beautiful land, begging the question, What is the beautiful land? In verse 16, it was prophesied that Roman general Pompey would "stand in the beautiful land" when he intervened in the contest for high priest in Judea. The result was that Judah was conquered and made a Roman province. The same event was referred to in Daniel 8:9, when the horn from insignificance (Rome) pushed toward the "beauty" (short for "beautiful land"). Judah's Roman subjugation typifies Daniel 11:41.

In the end time, south and north refer to very real, identifiable entities—just not geographic Egypt and Assyria/Babylon. The king of the south is apostate American Protestantism controlling the civil government, and the king of the north is the papacy. In like manner, the beautiful land refers to a very real entity—just not geographic Israel. The Bible makes the identification for us:

> <u>Deut. 32:36, 43</u>: For *Yahweh* will vindicate His people ... and provide atonement for His land, His people.
>
> <u>Mal. 3:12</u>: All the Gentiles will call you blessed, for you ["sons of Jacob" = Israel, verse 6] will be a delightful land.
>
> <u>Joel 2:18, 21, 23</u>: *Yahweh* was jealous for His land, He had compassion on His people. ... Do not fear, land! Rejoice, be glad, for *Yahweh* will do great things. ... Sons of Zion, rejoice, be glad in *Yahweh* your God, for He has given you the early rain for righteousness; He will bring down for you rain: early rain, and latter rain in the first month.

In these verses, *Yahweh* equates His people with the land. His aim is to complete atonement for His parched land by pouring out rain (the Holy Spirit, per Joel 2:28–29 and Acts 2:1–18) upon His remnant people in the last days. Satan's purpose in entering in among God's remnant people—the beautiful land—is to prevent Him from completing His work of atonement by filling His people with the Holy Spirit.

Satan will not succeed entirely in overthrowing God's people, yet verse 41 does indicate that many of His remnant church "will be overcome." This same description was used in verses 33–35 to refer to those who yielded up their lives rather than their faith. However, while many will die for their faith, those styled "Edom, Moab and the foremost of the sons of Ammon" are delivered from the papacy's hand. Edom refers to the descendants of Jacob's brother Esau (see Gen. 36:1), while Moab and Ammon are descended from the union of Abraham's nephew Lot with each of his daughters, following their escape from Sodom (see Gen. 19:36–38). How is it that these groups are delivered? In Psalm 83:1–7, these same 3 groups conspire against God's people, while verse 8 states Assyria joins with them, serving as the arm (strength) for the sons of Lot. Recalling that Daniel 11:40 describes the papacy as Assyria by allusion to Isaiah 8:7–8, we understand Daniel 11:41 to say that Edom, Moab, and the foremost sons of Ammon join with the papacy in its attempt to rout God's faithful remnant church in the end time. These peoples aim to save themselves by turning on the true Israel of the last days.

What does their description as Edom, Moab, and Ammon tell us about these turncoats? Edom (Esau, twin brother of Jacob, the father of the 12 tribes of Israel) rejected his birthright, consequently forfeiting the covenant privilege of being forebear of the Messiah (see Gen. 25:34). Hence, Edom refers to those who once knew and rejoiced in the truth, but later reject it.

The brief book of Obadiah describes Edom's rejection of the truth. In verse 7, we learn that Edom has entered into covenant with the forces of darkness with the intent of securing peace (i.e., avoiding the end-time persecution of God's faithful remnant—economic sanctions and even death itself; see Rev. 13:15, 17). According to verses 8–16, the papacy merely uses Edom to gain information to persecute God's faithful people. Following this treachery, Edom is destroyed by God Himself. As Jesus says, "Whoever wishes to save his life will lose it" (Matt. 16:25).

As for Moab and Ammon, their illegitimate births are the key to understanding their reference in Daniel 11:41. According to Deuteronomy 23:2–4, no child by incest shall enter the assembly of *Yahweh*, specifically the Ammonite or Moabite because they did not provide bread or water to the Israelites when they emerged from Egypt, and they hired a false prophet to curse them. There is a clear parallel in the end time. As Lot's daughters played the harlot with him, so apostate Protestant churches in the end time are harlot daughters of the papacy (see Rev. 17:5). Apostate Protestantism coerces the United States government to persecute God's faithful people in Revelation 13:15, for which cause this union of Protestantism and civil government is styled the false prophet (see 19:20).

This still leaves open what is meant by the "foremost of the sons of Ammon." Observe that 1 Chronicles 19:3 refers to the "rulers of the sons of Ammon." When Nahash of the Ammonites died, his son Hanun became king. King David decided to send a delegation to comfort Hanun, but the "rulers of the sons of Ammon" falsely accused David of a plot to conquer their land. Since Daniel has used the terms "foremost" and "rulers" synonymously, describing Michael as "[number] 1 of the foremost rulers" (10:13), we conclude that the "foremost [rulers] of the sons of Ammon" in the end time will behave just as the "rulers of the sons of Ammon" did in David's day: They will lead out in misconstruing the motives of those who are faithful members of God's remnant church.

This deception by the foremost of the sons of Ammon leads the Protestant churches to unite in pressuring the U.S. government to pass laws against Sabbath-keepers. This is clear from Revelation 13:17, in which those who lack the mark of the beast cannot buy or sell. Such a sanction is a perversion of Nehemiah 10:31 and 13:15–22 (see also Amos 8:5), in which God prohibits buying and selling on the Sabbath. Protestant churches will distort the fourth commandment to prohibit such activity on *Sunday*, the pagan day of the sun. The following gives a very plain description:

> As the storm approaches, a large class who have professed faith in the third angel's message, but have not been sanctified through obedience to the truth, abandon their position and join the ranks of the opposition. By uniting with the world and partaking of its spirit, they have come to view matters in nearly the same light; and when the test is brought, they are prepared to choose the easy, popular side. Men of talent and pleasing address, who once rejoiced in the truth, employ their powers to deceive and mislead souls. They become the most bitter enemies of their former brethren. When Sabbathkeepers are brought before the courts to answer for their faith, these apostates are the most efficient agents of Satan to misrepresent and accuse them, and by false reports and insinuations to stir up the rulers against them. (White, *GC*, p. 608)

Blue laws, many of them dormant, are still on the books in many states today. Revival of enforced Sunday observance in America is hastening on apace:

> In a speech on the state Senate floor during a debate over HB2320, which would allow the carrying of firearms in public buildings by those holding a concealed carry permit, Sen. Sylvia Allen, R-Snowflake, said: "Probably we should be debating a bill requiring every American to attend a church of their choice on Sunday."
>
> However, she quickly added, "That would never be allowed."
>
> "It is the soul that is corrupt," Allen commented, "and how we get back to a moral rebirth in this country, I don't know, since we are slowly eroding religion at every opportunity that we have."

> Allen later told the AZ Capitol Times that it was a "flippant comment," but refused to back off and stuck to her guns while recalling her childhood.
>
> "People prayed. People went to church. I remember on Sundays the stores were closed. The biggest thing is religion was kicked out of our public places, out of our schools."[142]

Notice the reference to stores being closed on Sunday and that the reason for a call to enforced Sunday church attendance is the undeniable erosion of morals in the country and the equally true expulsion of religion from the schools. For every problem Satan creates, he stands ready to supply a solution—one employing *force* and tainted with his nefarious hatred for the law of God.

Protestant churches are the children of the Reformation, but sadly they no longer solidly uphold the reforms their founders advocated. Rather, they are a blend of biblical truth and the pagan errors that Roman Catholicism has adopted from Greek philosophy. They are a corruption of the holy seed, illegitimate children who are labeled the offspring of the mother of harlots (see Rev. 17:5). Please note, though, that it is not *individual* Protestants, but Protestant *churches*, that are illegitimate children. God has His faithful children in *all* churches. Nevertheless, He calls them *out* of such churches, that they not be irreversibly corrupted by the errors that these churches teach (see Rev. 18:1–4).

Before moving on to a consideration of verse 42, a final observation concerning Sabbath-keepers and God's remnant church is in order. Some may find it a fanciful stretch to suggest that the Bible prophesies a death decree against Sabbath-keepers and that those in the end who stand fully vindicated by God will be Sabbath-keepers—every last one of them—and not Sunday-keepers. Note that Daniel 11:41 refers to the "beautiful land," which we equated earlier with the "delightful land" of

---

[142] John Blosser, "Arizona State Senator: Make Sunday Church Attendance Mandatory," *Newsmax*, March 27, 2015, https://1ref.us/z5 (accessed January 22, 2020).

Malachi. 3:12. The word translated "delightful" is the same as "pleasure" in Isaiah 58:13–14 (KJV). This passage contrasts those who enjoy God's approbation in restoring the Sabbath to its rightful position and observing it reverently with those who do their own "pleasure" on His holy day. Hence, the "beautiful land" of Daniel 11:41 implicitly refers to faithful members of God's remnant church in the end time as Sabbath-keepers.

The companion to the present volume, *THE WEDDING: Jesus Stands for His Bride in the Book of Revelation*, furnishes more evidence for the identity of this group, but at this point, we assert without further proof which church the Bible identifies as the true remnant church: the Seventh-day Adventist Church. This is not to say that all of its current members are as pure as the wind-driven snow (there will be "Edomites" who fall away from the remnant church when persecution comes), but the Seventh-day Adventist Church is the one church whose doctrinal teachings are sound, and it is the only church that will stand in the end-time judgment when God vindicates Himself and His faithful people.

Having secured the treachery of some Seventh-day Adventists, as well as some members of other churches, the papacy expands its dominion against other "lands". Since the "beautiful land" is the Seventh-day Adventist church, the remaining lands represent all other religious bodies. Satan is determined to bring *all* under his sway, so special mention is made that even Egypt will not serve as a refuge, for in the days of Joseph, Egypt *did* provide a "great escape" (Gen. 45:7) during the 7-year famine. In Isaiah 20:5–6, those who sought Egypt as a refuge from Assyria were disappointed. In Jeremiah 46:24–26, those who sought Egypt as a refuge from Babylon were delivered into the hand of Babylon.

What hope do people have in the end? Mount Zion offers deliverance, for "it will be a sanctuary" (Obad. 17). Heavenly Mount Zion is the location of God's heavenly sanctuary (see Ps. 20:2), so on earth, Mount Zion refers to those faithful members of the remnant church that enter (and remain) by faith into the heavenly sanctuary. The biblical truths they live out will testify of the only true deliverance available to anyone—the exercise of unwavering faith in the God who sent His Son to die in our place and grants grace sufficient to overcome *all* trials without indulging sin (see 2 Cor. 12:9).

All through Scripture, God warns against going to Egypt for succor. In fact, He delivers His people *from* Egypt, as stated in the introduction to the law of liberty, the 10 Commandments (see Exod. 20:2; Deut. 5:6; James 2:12). During the wilderness wanderings following the exodus from Egypt, God expressed great displeasure when the Israelites murmured, expressing a desire to return to Egypt (see Num. 11:1–10).

The futility of Egypt to deliver is brought out forcibly in Jeremiah 42–44. In this passage, a small group, led by Johanan, ask Jeremiah to seek *Yahweh's* counsel regarding fleeing to Egypt to escape the king of Babylon. The message comes that they are to remain in Judah and not seek refuge in Egypt, despite their fear. If they do not hearken and instead go into Egypt, *Yahweh* will bring disaster upon them. Upon hearing the message, they defiantly go to Tahpanhes in Egypt, though that city had previously delivered a crushing blow to the Israelites (see 2:16). God assures them that death will surely follow. Indeed, Nebuchadnezzar comes and decimates Egypt and the rebellious Israelites who ventured there.

So it will be in the end time. Many will see all earthly support removed as they cling fast to God's covenant. To their senses, it will appear foolish to remain loyal to *Yahweh*. All of Egypt's proffered support is nothing more than idols to those who cling to them, and the sure result is destruction for those who refuse to let go (see Exod. 20:5; Isa. 2:18–21; Hosea 4:6, 17).

With the papacy's hand (see Dan. 11:42) stretched forth against all lands, it may appear that God's people *must* forsake loyalty to *Yahweh* and His covenant. However, the truth is that *God's* hand controls all events. Everyone's breath is in His hand—the same hand that pronounced judgment upon Belshazzar. Ultimately, God will destroy the papacy and establish His kingdom via a stone cut out *without* hands (see Dan. 4:35; 5:23–30; 2:34, 45).

Since Daniel 11:40–45 deals with events in the end time, the day in which we are living, one may wonder whether current events link Roman Catholicism with Egypt (apostate American Protestantism). Astoundingly, they do. In January 2014, Kenneth Copeland hosted a Charismatic Evangelical Leadership Conference at his Eagle Mountain International Church. His special guest was Tony Palmer, South African bishop for the Communion of Evangelical Episcopal Churches, who in his address stated that he worked closely with the Roman Catholic Church and was personal friends with Pope Francis.

In his remarks, Tony Palmer, a self-described charismatic, evangelical Catholic, advocated putting an end to the protest of the Protestant Reformation and all believers coming together. He then introduced Pope Francis I, who appeared on a video recorded the week before on a cell phone. The whole video of 45 minutes, 57 seconds is readily available on the web by doing a search for "Kenneth Copeland Tony Palmer Pope."[143] At the 35:10 mark, Pope Francis refers to Joseph's brothers coming to Egypt during famine time to get bread, where they were reunited with their brother. Pope Francis then invites Protestants to come to him as "Brother" (capitalization appears in the cell phone video), making plain that he is to be viewed as Joseph, the separated brothers' deliverer. To fully appreciate the significance of this invitation, recall that Joseph was in command of Egypt, second only to the pharaoh, the king of the south. Hence, while apostate American Protestantism is the king of the south, this king willingly gives all authority into the hands of "Brother Joseph," the papacy. Hence, the papacy's own claims confirm the prophetic message of the book of Daniel, implicating it (king of the north) and modern-day apostate American Protestantism (king of the south) as cooperating in an Egyptian framework, with "Brother Joseph" (the papacy) in control of the relationship, of course.

Following the Pope's message, Kenneth Copeland ascended the platform once more and led the group in a tongue-speaking episode from 40:01 to 41:00. In summary, at a meeting of Charismatics (those who seek to be filled with the Spirit), a prominent Protestant urges fellow Protestants to

---

[143] "Pope Francis Sends Video Message to Kenneth Copeland—Let's Unite," YouTube, February 21, 2014, https://1ref.us/km (accessed January 22, 2020).

acknowledge an end to the Reformation. He then displays a video from Pope Francis urging all Protestants to return to him as Brother. This is followed by a period of ecstatic utterance (people worked by a spirit). With this in mind, read solemnly the following description of end-time events:

> The Protestants of the United States will be foremost in stretching their hands across the gulf to grasp the hand of spiritualism; they will reach over the abyss to clasp hands with the Roman power; and under the influence of this threefold union, this country will follow in the steps of Rome in trampling on the rights of conscience. (White, *GC*, p. 588)

The reference to gold, silver, and articles of high esteem of Egypt parallels the gold, silver, precious stone, and articles of high esteem that the papacy used to honor its false god in verse 38, pointing to its counterfeit earthly sanctuary, which embraces idolatry and demonic worship. A comparison of both verses, along with our analysis of verses 40–42, indicates that apostate Protestantism (Egypt) and Roman Catholicism worship in lockstep under the papacy's false sanctuary system.

What is the significance of the Libyans and Ethiopians? To answer, we turn to Noah's descendants in Genesis 10. Table 18 presents the family tree:

Table 18: Family Tree for Egypt, Libya, and Ethiopia (Genesis 10)

FIRST GENERATION	SECOND GENERATION	THIRD GENERATION	FOURTH GENERATION
Noah	Japheth		
	Ham	Ethiopia (Hebrew *Kush*)	Nimrod (founded Babylon in Shinar, built Nineveh in Assyria).
		Egypt (Hebrew *Mitzraim*)	Libya (Hebrew *Ludim* = *Luvim*)
		Put	
		Canaan	
	Shem		

Note that when the Libyans and Ethiopians appear together in Scripture, it is always in connection with Egypt and Assyria. In Nahum 3, God issues a solemn prophecy against Nineveh (capital of Assyria). In verses 8 and 9, God asks Nineveh (who has Libya as its help) whether she is better than the Egyptian city No-Amon, which had the Ethiopians (Egypt's brother) and Egypt as her strength. The chapter makes clear that just as Assyria destroyed No-Amon in 663 BC, so Assyria would in turn be devastated (Nineveh fell in 612 BC). This is highly significant in Daniel 11:40–45, in which the kings of south and north unite to enforce the papal agenda. Their past destruction suggests that their end-time reunion is doomed.

Again, in 2 Chronicles 12:3, Shishak, the king of Egypt, comes against Jerusalem because under Rehoboam's influence, God's people have forsaken His Torah. Shishak brings with him not only chariots and horsemen, but a horde of people from Egypt, including the Libyans and Ethiopians. In 2 Chronicles 16:8, Hanani the seer points out to King Asa that, though the Ethiopians and Libyans were a huge army (the Ethiopian army was a million strong, per 2 Chronicles 14:9), it was Asa's reliance on *Yahweh* that gave these enemies into his hand. In Daniel 11:43, the papacy has the backing of the Libyans and the Ethiopians (who support Assyria and Egypt, respectively, per Nahum 3:8–9), indicating an incredibly large army—worldwide, since all the world will wonder after the papacy (see Rev. 13:3). However, like King Asa, the faithful remnant will emerge victorious, for they will rely completely on *Yahweh*. Conversely, in spite of the enormous military support of the Libyans and Ethiopians, the papacy will have no helper in the end (see Dan. 11:45).

The papacy's plans unravel with reports from the sunrise and north. What are these reports? Some suggest military opposition from the far east, noting that Japan is called the "land of the rising sun." This can be ruled out easily, as nowhere does the Bible discuss Japan, and the focus of Daniel is *religious* conflict. Some suggest that Islam or Arabs are in view, for the Bible refers to those east of Palestine as "sons of the east." This is immediately ruled out, for the Hebrew word for "east" (*qedem*) in that phrase is *not* the same as "sunrise" (*mizrach*) in Daniel 11:44. Other speculative guesses such as Russia need not be considered.

Where to begin? Since Daniel 11:40 describes the papacy as the antitype of the king of Assyria, it is reasonable to ask whether Scripture records the ancient king of Assyria as ever hearing reports from the sunrise and north that greatly agitate him, particularly in his quest to conquer God's people in Jerusalem. An examination of 2 Kings 18 and 19 (and the parallel passage in Isaiah 36 and 37) provides a resounding "Yes!" Hezekiah paid Sennacherib, king of Assyria, a princely sum to back away from the cities of Judah. Sennacherib then sent emissaries from Lachish to Jerusalem, telling him not to trust *Yahweh* for deliverance, for Sennacherib asserts that *Yahweh* directed him to destroy Judah. Through Isaiah, *Yahweh* states, "I will put a spirit in him. He will hear a report, and return to his own land. I will cause him to fall by the sword in his own land." Sennacherib is troubled by these reports from Libnah—northeast of Lachish—and goes to war in Libnah. Sennacherib later returns to Nineveh and is slain while worshipping in the temple of his god Nisroch. This name is likely an altered spelling of either Marduk or Nusku. Marduk was a Babylonian god that Sennacherib led away and brought to Assyria, while Nusku was a solar deity (TWOT and BDB, entries on *Nisroch*).

In summary, the ancient king of Assyria heard a troublesome report from Libnah, northeast of him. Dealing with this troublesome report prevented him from destroying the remnant in Jerusalem. He meets his demise clinging to sun worship. Up through Daniel 11:43, the papacy has been on a quest to rid the world of the faithful, end-time remnant, but in verse 44, reports from the sunrise and north divert his attention. He goes "forth in a great rage to exterminate, devoting many to annihilation." The history of Sennacherib informs us that this signals the death knell for the papacy, the antitype of the "great king" of Assyria.

Before moving on to verse 45, let us now examine the biblical significance of "sunrise" and "north" to properly understand the content of these reports. Most translations render "sunrise" as "east," for the simple reason that the sun rises in the east. While no one would dispute the direction of sunrise, a careful distinction between these terms is essential to a proper understanding. The first mention of "sunrise" is Exodus 27:13, which refers to the east side of the courtyard surrounding the sanctuary as "eastward, toward the sunrise." The following texts connect sunrise with salvation:

> Isa. 60:1–3: Arise, shine, for your light has come, the glory of *Yahweh* has risen upon you. For behold, darkness will cover the earth, cloud-like darkness the peoples; but upon you, *Yahweh* will arise; upon you, His glory will be seen. Gentiles will come to your light, kings to the brightness of your dawning.
>
> Mal. 4:2: But for you who fear My name, the Sun of righteousness will arise with healing in its wings. You will go forth, leaping like calves [released] from the stall.

The Hebrew word for "sunrise," *mizrach*, comes from the same root as the Hebrew verb *zarach* (translated "risen" and "arise") and the Hebrew noun *zerach* (translated "dawning"). The revelation of God's glory—His character in the lives of His people—is plainly likened to the sun rising in Isaiah 60:1–3. This sunrise has the effect of drawing Gentiles, hitherto ignorant of God's great plan to restore His perfect image in mankind, to learn of and experience this transformation.

Malachi 4:2 provides a mixed metaphor for Jesus. Just as the sun provides vitamin D for the skin and aids in warding off depression, so Jesus rises like the sun with healing. Just as a mother bird protects her chicks with her wings, so Jesus describes Himself in Matthew 23:37. In the very end, He will rise upon His people so that others will take note of this unmistakable "sunrise" and choose salvation for themselves. This is vital, for Malachi 4:1 makes plain that destruction awaits the rebels. Furthermore, verses 4–6 equate this righteousness with remembering the Torah of Moses and love for one's fellowman. The new-covenant experience is having God's law (His character) written upon the heart and sealed in the forehead—and this seal comes from the sunrise (see Jer. 31:33 and Rev. 7:2, 3).

It is evident that Satan and his papal agents are alarmed as they recognize the full development of God's character in the faithful remnant of the Seventh-day Adventist Church, who cling to Jesus despite every act of persecution. This character development has come about as a result of *understanding* the plan of salvation as outlined in the sanctuary services of ancient Israel, and *cooperating* with Jesus as He implements the fullness of the plan of salvation in believers by finishing His work of judgment in the heavenly sanctuary. Simply put, the message from the sunrise is "righteousness by faith." Satan knows full well that as the world beholds the glory of *Yahweh* risen upon the remnant—which observation requires that the world turn its back to the sun, the idol *par excellence* throughout history—the world will likewise be transformed into Jesus' image, so he launches one last furious effort to stamp out the remnant and take the world as his prey.

The message from the sunrise is that righteousness comes only by faith, not works on our part. However, *living faith* brings true *righteousness* into our lives, not merely a spiritual whitewashing away of our past and present sins, as though it were impossible for God to produce victory over sin in our lives. Indeed, "faith works through love" and "*all* things are possible with God" (Gal. 5:6; Matt. 19:26). The message from the sunrise does away with both the false security of "once saved, always saved," popular in some evangelical circles, and the equally false teaching of salvation by works in the papal system and pagan religions. The truth is that we must die daily to self, and Jesus must abide in us, strengthening us for every need and enabling us to realize the incredible promise to be perfect, even as our Father who is in heaven is perfect (see 1 Cor. 15:31; John 15:4; Phil. 4:13; Matt. 5:48).

This message of a living faith transforms people, making them prepared to meet the Judge of all the earth at His coming, which is also from the sunrise (see Matt. 24:27). As we will see in our study of Revelation (see *THE WEDDING: Jesus Stands for His Bride in the Book of Revelation*), this message from the sunrise is the three angels' messages of Revelation 14:6–12, a message that the judgment hour is in session and immediately precedes the second coming; all people must come out of Babylon (Roman Catholicism, apostate Protestantism, and any other religious system tainted by paganism) or be destroyed; all must and may procure the faith of Jesus, which results in perfect obedience to His 10 Commandments. This message prepares people for the harvest of the earth described in Revelation 14:14–16. Probation closes when the harvest is ready, and then Jesus comes to claim His own.

> The tares and the wheat are to grow together until the harvest; and the harvest is the end of probationary time. (White, *COL*, p. 72)

> The breach [in the law of God, especially the Sabbath] is to be repaired, and the foundation of many generations to be raised up. And this message is the last to be given before the coming of the Lord. Immediately following its proclamation, the Son of Man is seen by the prophet coming in glory to reap the harvest of the earth. (White, *ST*, February 8, 1910)

Reports also issue from the north. We have already seen that Lucifer sought God's position as Judge on the sides of the north (see Isa. 14:12–15). The Bible refers to the south-to-north extent of Israel as "from Beersheba to Dan [Judge]" (1 Chron. 21:2). Furthermore, God's judgment issues from the north country (see Jer. 1:14; 6:22; 10:22). Satan knows Scripture well enough to recognize when the 7 last plagues, God's final judgment upon an impenitent world, begin to fall. As people recognize that the world is deteriorating exponentially under the papacy's sway, support for the papacy dries up, "that the way for the kings from the sunrise might be prepared" (Rev. 16:12). Satan knows this signals the nearness of deliverance at the second coming.

Since the remnant cannot be brought to yield to his temptations, he turns to his last resort—spiritualism. He sends forth demons from the mouths of the dragon (the 10 kings), beast (papacy), and false prophet (apostate American Protestantism controlling the civil government), meaning demons lead these powers to enact legislation—a universal death decree to blot the faithful remnant from the earth (see Rev. 16:13, 14). Should this prove successful, Satan would claim the planet as fully under his control. Casting the blame for the terrible plagues upon those faithful to God's covenant (i.e., loyal Sabbath-keepers), these demons gather the kings of the whole world to the battle of the great day of *Yahweh* of hosts. The dissolution of Babylon during the seventh and final plague (see Rev. 16:17–21) and its destruction at the second coming (see 19:17–21) inform us of the outcome in Daniel 11:45—the final demise of the papacy.

In confronting the message from the sunrise and north, the papacy will "pitch the tents of his ephod between the seas, in lieu of the beautiful mountain of the sanctuary." To understand the significance here, one must recognize the allusion to Israel's crossing of the Red Sea during the exodus from Egypt. Specifically, the act of "pitching" (sometimes rendered "planting") is very significant:

> Exod. 15:17: You will bring them and plant them in the mountain of Your inheritance, the place You established to serve as Your dwelling, *Yahweh*; the sanctuary, *Adonai*, which Your hand established.

Note that God's goal is to plant His people in His dwelling, the mountain of His inheritance, which is *His sanctuary*. This is why the present translation of Daniel 11:45 refers to "the beautiful mountain of the sanctuary," rather than the more common "the beautiful holy mountain." Either rendering is possible from a purely grammatical point of view ("sanctuary" and "holiness" are the same word in Hebrew), but the allusion to Exodus 15:17 points to "sanctuary" as correct in this context.

The equality of the beautiful mountain with God's sanctuary is of the highest importance. The Bible refers to the beautiful mountain, Mount Zion, as God's people (see Isa. 51:16). Our study of Daniel 8:14 showed that as God cleanses the heavenly sanctuary, He simultaneously cleanses the hearts of His people on earth, replicating His character in them. This is what finally makes them beautiful. As the world witnesses the faithful remnant in the end time, it gets a glimpse of heaven.

In planting his tents before this mountain, one is reminded of Lucifer, who sought to "sit on the mount of assembly, in the farthest reaches of the north" (Isa. 14:13). This mountain is "Mount Zion, the farthest reaches of the north, the city of the great king" (Ps. 48:2). Hence, the action of Satan's puppet, the papacy, in Daniel 11:45 points to his desire to sit as supreme judge in the north, his last act to counter the reports from the north in verse 44. The great irony is that this final push is the papacy's very undoing.

The present translation refers to the "tents of his ephod," departing from the traditional reading, "tents of his palace." The Hebrew word *'appeden* appears only here in the Hebrew Bible, so linguists have looked outside the Bible for cognate words in other languages to determine its meaning. Most lexica accept that this is a Persian loan word signifying "palace" (e.g., BDB and TWOT, entries for *'appeden*), which on the surface sounds reasonable. The present commentary presents an alternative, based on biblical evidence, that seems to better suit the context.

The Hebrew word *'appeden* consists of four Hebrew letters: the first three spell the word "ephod," a part of the high priest's garment, and the final character is a *nun*, pronounced as "n." It is not impossible that *'appeden* may represent a variant spelling of "ephod." Others have noted the same: "It seems to be derived from the same root as the ephod, a curious garment worn by the high priest among the Jews; hence Saadiah interprets it here a covering figured and wrought very artificially; and it is by some rendered 'the tents or tabernacles of his tunic or clothing'" (Gill, *Exposition of the Old Testament*, comments on Dan. 11:45, citing Fuller and Cocceius as the "some" with this understanding.).

What reasons can be brought forth for considering our word as a variant spelling of "ephod"? One simple reason is that while the Hebrew Bible does typically spell "ephod" as a masculine noun, it does, in three instances, employ an alternative feminine spelling that adds a final "h" consonant. The alternative would be pronounced as "aphuddah" (see

Exod. 28:8; 39:5; Isa. 30:22). Hence, Scripture provides at least one alternative spelling.

Another consideration is that this effort of Satan to make his last stand through the papacy corresponds to the well-known battle of Armageddon (see Rev. 16:16), the final gathering of the wicked to stamp out the faithful remnant (see 19:17–21). The Hebrew spelling of Armageddon is *har megiddon*, meaning "mountain of Megiddon." What is important for us to consider is that the Hebrew word *megiddon* appears only once in Scripture (see Zech. 12:11), while the more common spelling *megiddo* occurs 11 times.[144] The difference in spelling for *megiddon* and *megiddo* comes down to a final *nun*—the very character that distinguishes "ephod" from *'appeden* in Daniel 11:45.

Commentators have speculated for centuries as to why the word "Armageddon" translates as "mountain of Megiddon," since Megiddo/Megiddon in Scripture is a valley, not a mountain (see 2 Chron. 35:22; Zech. 12:11). The connection with Daniel 11:45 seems to make it plain. Satan, through the papacy, seeks to pitch the tents of his *'appeden* ("ephod" with a final *nun*) on the mount of Megiddon ("mount of Megiddo" with a final *nun*) because he is trying desperately to establish his false sanctuary in lieu of the true sanctuary, which is on the beautiful mountain, Mount Zion. These unique spellings of "ephod" and "Megiddo," each with a final *nun*, serve to aid the Bible student in linking these passages.

That said, how does "ephod" harmonize with the overall message of Daniel, specifically 8–12? The ephod was to be worn by the high priest in Exodus 28, and of course, the papacy attempts to take the place of Jesus as High Priest in chapters 8–12, displacing His continual ministration in the heavenly sanctuary with its own continual counterfeit, a pagan earthly sanctuary. Further, the ephod was put to idolatrous use later in Israel's history, as with Gideon and Micah (see Judges 8:27; 17:5; 18:14–20). It is also referred to among a list of idolatrous items in Hosea 3:4. This matches

---

[144] Josh. 12:21; 17:11; Judges 1:27; 5:19; 1 Kings 4:12; 9:15; 2 Kings 9:27; 23:29, 30; 1 Chron. 7:29; 2 Chron. 35:22.

the papacy, whose counterfeit earthly sanctuary is built entirely on pagan idolatry.

With this understanding, the papacy in Daniel 11:45 makes a last-ditch effort to interpose itself between the seas in lieu of the true sanctuary. Why between the seas? According to Zechariah 14:8, Jerusalem (with its sanctuary on Mount Zion) will send forth living water toward the eastern (Dead) sea and the sea behind (the Mediterranean). As a counterfeit of the true, Satan's false system stands in lieu of the true, hence between the same seas. Of course, Satan will fail. This is confirmed by Joel 2:20, which states, "The northerner I will put far away from you; I will drive him into a dry and desolate land, with his face toward the eastern [Dead] sea, and his backside to the sea behind [the Mediterranean]. His stench will ascend, his foul odor will ascend, because he has attempted great things." The Assyrian "northerner" in this verse is none other than the end-time king of the north, the papacy.

Three key observations are in order here: 1) The papacy's position between the seas coincides with the location of earthly Jerusalem; 2) according to Joel 2:20, the northerner faces east, which means he is facing the sun, harmonizing with papal sun worship[145]; 3) in facing east, he also faces the Dead Sea, looking death in the face, as it were. Each of these characterizes his last, desperate attempt to establish the papal sanctuary "in lieu of" the true sanctuary, toward which the faithful, end-time remnant is directing the world's attention. The papacy's false sanctuary is based on false sun worship, and the attempt to establish it simply assures his soon demise, for "he will come to his end."

The phrase "he has no helper" makes plain that the papacy will lose all support at the end. However, the precise wording employed points to the following Scriptures, which portray the papacy's situation more vividly:

> Ps. 72:4, 12: [God] will judge the poor of the people, He will save the sons of the needy, but He will crush the oppressor. ...

---

[145] Compare with Ezekiel 8:16, in which religious leaders face the east, worshipping the sun.

For [God] will rescue the needy when he cries for help; the poor also—he has no helper.

2 Kings 14:26: For *Yahweh* saw the affliction of Israel ... and there was no helper for Israel.

Isa. 63:4, 5, 8: For the day of vengeance is in My heart, the year of My redeemed ones has come. I looked carefully, and there was no helper ... My arm brought salvation for Me, My wrath supported Me. ... He said, "Surely they are My people, sons who do not deal falsely," so He became their Savior.

Lam. 1:7: Jerusalem remembered ... all of her articles of high esteem that she had in days of old, when her people fell into the hand of the adversary, and she had no helper. The adversaries saw her, they laughed at her Sabbaths.

Ps. 107:11, 12: Because they rebelled against the words of God, and despised the counsel of the Most High, He humbled their heart with toil. They fell, and there was no helper.

Ps. 22:11: Do not be far from Me, for distress is near, for there is no helper.

Of the above verses, only the Hebrew of Psalm 72:12 is identical to Daniel 11:45. There, God makes it clear that He will help His people who have no helper. In connection with this, verse 4 also says He will "crush the oppressor." Similarly, 2 Kings 14:26 and Isaiah 63:5 promise that *Yahweh* will help His people who have no helper. In Lamentations 1:7, God's people once again have no helper, but an additional detail emerges. Her adversaries mock at her because she observes the Sabbath. By contrast, Psalm 107:12 refers to Israel's falling (i.e., dying) in the wilderness due to their disobedience, when God stepped back and did not act as their helper. Finally, Psalm 22:11 pictures Jesus on the cross, when He became sin for us, and there was no helper; no one to save Him from all the agony of separation from the Father.

Putting these verses together, the phrase "he has no helper" informs us that the end-time papacy is the oppressor of God's people who mocked them for keeping His Sabbath holy. On the flip side, just as the oppressor is to be crushed, so God Himself will be His people's helper in their greatest extremity.

The papacy's rebellion results in an ironic change of place with the persecuted. The system must fall, as did the impenitent rebels in Psalm 107:12. Indeed, the religious leaders are massacred by the enraged multitudes at the second coming and thrown into the lake of fire (see Rev. 19:20), confirming that there is indeed no helper for the papacy:

> The people see that they have been deluded. They accuse one another of having led them to destruction; but all unite in heaping their bitterest condemnation upon the ministers. Unfaithful pastors have prophesied smooth things; they have led their hearers to make void the law of God and to persecute those who would keep it holy. Now, in their despair, these teachers confess before the world their work of deception. The multitudes are filled with fury. "We are lost!" they cry, "and you are the cause of our ruin;" and they turn upon the false shepherds. The very ones that once admired them most will pronounce the most dreadful curses upon them. The very hands that once crowned them with laurels will be raised for their destruction. The swords which were to slay God's people are now employed to destroy their enemies. Everywhere there is strife and bloodshed. …
>
> … The work of destruction begins among those who have professed to be the spiritual guardians of the people. The false watchmen are the first to fall. There are none to pity or to spare. (White, *GC*, pp. 655, 656)

The End of the Controversy

Daniel 12 opens "at that time." Is this the time when the papacy comes to its end, with no helper? No. In verse 1, we come to the close of human probation, which coincides with the outpouring of the 7 last plagues in Revelation 15 and 16. The reports from the north in Daniel 11:44 mark the beginning of the falling of the 7 last plagues, to which Daniel 12:1 takes us back. With every case decided for time and eternity, Michael stands. As noted in the comments for Daniel 10, Michael ("Who is like God?") is a name for Jesus, in His role as [number] 1 of the foremost rulers, or equivalently, Ruler of rulers (i.e., the High Priest and Supreme Judge).

Jesus stands as Ruler. The investigative portion of the end-time judgment commenced when the Ancient of days sat in Daniel 7:9–10 and ends when He stands. This recalls the story of Stephen's stoning in Acts 7:55–60. As he was dying, Stephen looked heavenward and saw Jesus as the Son of man standing at the right hand of God, identifying Him as the victorious Judge portrayed in Daniel 7:13–14. When Jesus stood at Stephen's death, it marked the *end* of the 70-week (490-year) probationary period granted the Jewish nation in Daniel 9:24. Here in 12:1, probation closes for humanity as a whole.

One might grow alarmed, fearful of the consequence of indulging sin beyond this time. However, Jesus "is longsuffering to us-ward, not willing that any should perish, but that all should come to repentance" (2 Peter 3:9, KJV). Marvelous grace! He has already pledged His existence with an oath that His covenant *will* be fulfilled in His people (see Heb. 6:17, 18; 7:22; 9:15–17) by writing His law in the minds, hearts, and foreheads of His followers (see Jer. 31:33; Rev. 7:3; 14:1). He has promised to *finish* developing His obedience in His people (see Heb. 12:2; Phil. 1:6). Hence, Jesus will not stand until He knows that those who have been growing into His likeness are *able* to remain standing with Him! "If the human agent consents, God can and will so identify His will with all our thoughts and aims, so blend our hearts and minds into conformity to His word, that when obeying His will we are only carrying out the impulses of our minds" (White, *10MR*, p. 295).

This is a critically important promise to remember, for when Jesus stands, there commences "a time of distress such as has not been since becoming a nation until that time." This language hearkens back to the seventh plague upon Egypt: "Then there was hail, and fire flashing here and there in the midst of the hail, very severe, such as has not been its like in all the land of Egypt since it became a nation" (Exod. 9:24). Just as the seventh plague fell only upon Egypt, and *not* upon the Israelites in Goshen (see Exod. 9:26), so the 7 last plagues of Revelation 16 fall only upon those who cling to *any* idol, worshipping as the papacy dictates, not upon those who have remained faithful (see Psalm 91:10).

As bad as the plagues are for the wicked, the distress of Daniel 12:1 is that of *God's people*. The cause of distress is not the threat of death on every side, for they hold to the promise of Psalm 91 that God will protect them. Their overwhelming concern is whether there may be any unconfessed sin in their lives that brings reproach upon God. It is what Jeremiah 30:7 refers to as the time of Jacob's distress/anguish:

> Though God's people will be surrounded by enemies who are bent upon their destruction, yet the anguish which they suffer is not a dread of persecution for the truth's sake; they fear that every sin has not been repented of, and that through some fault in themselves they will fail to realize the fulfillment of the Saviour's promise: I "will keep thee from the hour of temptation, which shall come upon all the world." Revelation 3:10. If they could have the assurance of pardon they would not shrink from torture or death; but should they prove unworthy, and lose their lives because of their own defects of character, then God's holy name would be reproached. (White, *GC*, p. 619)

What is absolutely fascinating here is that the word for "distress" or "anguish" is identical to that found in Psalm 22:11, detailing Jesus' experience on the cross: "Do not be far from Me, for distress is near, for there is no helper." For Jesus, it seemed that all hope and help were cut off, and so it will appear for His faithful followers. Yet, however bleak it looked for Jesus, His sole desire was to honor His Father by obeying Him: "Behold, I come. In the scroll of writing it is written concerning Me, 'My God,

I delight to do Your will; Your Torah is in the midst of My inmost being'" (Ps. 40:7, 8). To disobey in any particular would dishonor the Father. This was unthinkable for Jesus, and so it is for those who have His Torah written in their hearts. They would rather yield their life than dishonor their Maker by disobedience.

The devil will recognize the development of Christlike character in God's people, but he does not know for sure that their cases have already been forever decided in the sanctuary above, and nothing can prevail against them. He will do everything possible to get them to fall from their steadfastness:

> He sees that holy angels are guarding them, and he infers that their sins have been pardoned; but he does not know that their cases have been decided in the sanctuary above. ... He claims them as his prey and demands that they be given into his hands to destroy.
>
> As Satan accuses the people of God on account of their sins, the Lord permits him to try them to the uttermost. (White, *GC*, p. 618)

No matter how hard Satan tries to discourage God's followers, with the aim of destroying them, those written in the Lamb's scroll of life are delivered. The saints' escape here does include temporal deliverance from the intense persecution, but it also includes their eternal salvation from the power of sin. This permanent deliverance contrasts with the failed attempt at self-preservation by Edom, Moab, and the foremost of the sons of Ammon who were delivered, for a short time, from the papacy's wrath.

The longstanding dispute underlying the great controversy between Christ and Satan, namely, "Who is like God?" will be answered to the satisfaction of the onlooking universe in the lives of Christ's professed followers. It is during the seventh plague that God crowns His work of judgment by resurrecting those who trusted in the three angels' messages of Revelation 14:6–12. This is not to be confused with the general resurrection, in which the righteous are raised at the beginning of the 1,000 years, and the wicked at its end (see Rev. 20:4, 5). This is a special resurrection, in which two classes are raised *simultaneously*: individuals whose lives demonstrated God's work of character perfection via the three angels' messages, as well as those who most directly participated in Jesus' death:

> There is a mighty earthquake ... Mountain chains are sinking. Inhabited islands disappear. ... Great hailstones, every one "about the weight of a talent," are doing their work of destruction. ...
>
> ... Graves are opened, and "many of them that sleep in the dust of the earth... awake, some to everlasting life, and some to shame and everlasting contempt." Daniel 12:2. All who have died in the faith of the third angel's message come forth from the tomb glorified, to hear God's covenant of peace with those who have kept His law. "They also which pierced Him" (Revelation 1:7), those that mocked and derided Christ's dying agonies, and the most violent opposers of His truth and His people, are raised to behold Him in His glory and to see the honor placed upon the loyal and obedient. (White, *GC*, pp. 636, 637)

We can positively identify these wicked people as those who crucified Jesus, because the key word "reproaches" (see verse 2) points us back to Psalm 69, the crucifixion psalm:

> <u>Ps. 69:7–20</u>: For on Your account I have borne reproach; disgrace has covered My face. ... For the zeal of Your house has eaten Me up, the reproaches of those who reproached You have fallen upon Me. I myself wept with fasting, yet this incurred reproaches for Me. ... You have known My reproach, My shame, and My disgrace; before You are all My enemies. Reproach has broken My heart. I was sick, waiting for someone to sympathize, but there was no one; for comforters, but I did not find [any].

What do the righteous do at this time? According to verse 3, they will light up like stars, literally, as did the faces of Moses and Stephen before them (see Exod. 34:29; Acts 6:15). "Their countenances are lighted up with His glory, and shine as did the face of Moses when he came down from Sinai" (White, *GC*, p. 640). These are the seed of Abram who have partaken fully of the everlasting covenant, for *Yahweh* told him, "Look heavenward, and count the stars if you are able to count them. ... So will your seed be" (Gen. 15:5). Further, those heavenly luminaries serve as signs and mark seasons (see Gen. 1:14). Therefore, the lighting up of God's people (who are as stars) signals that probationary time is past. Further, the Bible repeatedly associates deliverance with nighttime,[146] so this lighting up signals the imminent return of Jesus for the midnight deliverance of His people (see Matt. 25:6).

At this point, Daniel is directed to seal up his scroll of prophecy until the end time. This means the book of Daniel would not begin to be understood in its fullness until the end time was reached. This would occur after the 3.5 times, or 1,260 years, coincident with the capture of Pope Pius VI on February 10, 1798.

At that time, knowledge would increase—not just any knowledge, but a knowledge of God through His Word, for lack of which "My people are destroyed" (Hosea 4:6). In Matthew 24:15, Jesus lays particular emphasis upon understanding the book of Daniel, specifically the detestable idolatry that desolates ("abomination of desolation," 12:11, KJV). The focus of the third and final part of the book of Daniel is Jesus' work of atonement, beginning with His sacrifice at the cross (see Dan. 9:24–27), and culminating in His closing work of judgment in the Holy of Holies in the heavenly sanctuary (see Dan. 8:9–14; 10:5, 6; 12:13). In fact, the phrase "many will go to and fro" in Daniel 12:4 appears in this same inflection only four other times in Scripture and suggests that it is a knowledge of Jesus' work in the heavenly sanctuary that will increase in the end time:

> <u>Amos 8:11–14</u>: "Behold, days are coming," declares *Adonai Yahweh*, "when I will send a famine upon the land—not a famine of

---

[146] Midnight deliverances: Exod. 12:29; Judges 7:19; Matt. 25:6; Acts 16:25; 27:27. Nighttime deliverances: Josh. 2:2; Acts 9:25; 12:6; 23:23.

> bread, nor a thirst for water, but rather of hearing the words of *Yahweh*. They will wander from sea to sea, and from the north even unto the sunrise; they will go to and fro to seek the word of *Yahweh*, but they will not find [it]. … Those who swear by the guilt of Samaria and say, "Your god lives, Dan!" and "The way of Beersheba lives!" will fall—and they will not rise up anymore."
>
> Zech. 4:10: They are the eyes of *Yahweh*, going to and fro throughout all the earth.
>
> 2 Chron. 16:9: For the eyes of *Yahweh* go to and fro throughout all the earth to show Himself strong on behalf of those whose heart is in harmony with Him.
>
> Jer. 5:1: Go to and fro in the streets of Jerusalem. Look, take notice, search her public squares, whether you find a man, whether there is one who executes judgment, who seeks to be faithful, that I should pardon her.

Note that Amos 8:12 identifies those who seek the word of *Yahweh* as going from the north to the sunrise. This was explained in the remarks on Daniel 11:44 as referring to judgment (north) and righteousness by faith in relation to the sanctuary (sunrise). Those who fail to procure this knowledge and continue to swear by the life of pagan gods and ways will fall when probation closes, never to rise again. The texts in Zechariah 4:10 and 2 Chronicles 16:9 refer to the eyes of *Yahweh* going to and fro, investigating the hearts of people to see whether they are in harmony with Him. While this has been true throughout this world's history, it is especially true of Jesus' closing work in the sanctuary since the end-time judgment commenced in 1844. He is now probing the depths of people's hearts to see if there is *any* secret sin that needs to be brought to light and purged for them to be in harmony with their Maker. The text in Jeremiah 5:1 is *Yahweh's* command to the people to scour the public squares of Jerusalem to see if anyone executed judgment (i.e., acted justly). In the remarks on Daniel 9:25, the public square was noted for its association with judgment.

Question and Answer: Jesus and Gabriel by the Nile

Now Daniel's attention is arrested by 2 heavenly beings on either side of the Nile, one dressed in linen, the other asking the question "Until what point [until one finally reaches] the end of these wonders?" These "wonders" allude to Rome's ability to "corrupt wonderfully" spoken of in Daniel 8:24. Rome, in both its pagan and papal phases, has corrupted wonderfully, crucifying Jesus at the cross and slaughtering millions during the Dark Ages. Until what point will the papacy be permitted to carry on its wicked work? This hearkens back to Gabriel's question at the Ulai, "Until what point does the vision concerning the continual ministry and the desolating rebellion extend, to give over both sanctuary and host to be trampled?" In response, Jesus commanded Gabriel to give understanding. Again, in chapter 10, Daniel was beside the great river, the Chiddeqel. At that time, Jesus was dressed in linen, and Gabriel came to strengthen Daniel by his touch. Comparison with these passages from Daniel 8 and 10 leads us to conclude that the beings in 12:5 are once again Jesus and Gabriel.

Many translations refer to a "river" in Daniel 12:5, while some favor "stream" (e.g., ESV). However, a survey of the term *yə'or* in Scripture shows that it is used most often of the Nile or its tributaries.[147] The Chiddeqel in Daniel 10:4 pointed back to creation, while the Ulai in 8:2 pointed to Abram and Sarai's attempt to carry out God's covenant in their own strength (see Gen. 16:1, 2) and Abraham's intercession with God prior to investigative and executive judgment on the cities of the plain in Genesis 18:22–32. What is the significance of the Nile in Daniel 12:5? To answer, we turn to Genesis 41:1–32 and Exodus 7:14–25.

In Genesis 41:1–32 is the record of Pharaoh's dreams, which Joseph interpreted regarding the 7 years of plenty and 7 years of famine. In verse 1, Pharaoh has a dream in which he is standing by (literally "upon") the Nile. Later in verse 17, as he relates the dream to Joseph, Pharaoh clarifies that

---

[147] The plainest identifications of *yə'or* as the Nile are Genesis 41:1–3, Exodus 1:22 and 7:15, Jeremiah 46:8, Ezekiel 29:3, and Amos 8:8 and 9:5.

he was standing on the side of the Nile, rather than upon the Nile itself. Joseph informs Pharaoh that the 7 sickly cows that he sees standing by the healthy cows on the side of the Nile represent 7 years of famine to succeed the 7 years of plenty. Further, Joseph informs Pharaoh that his other dream about 7 good ears of grain and 7 bad ears of grain represents the same 7 years of plenty and 7 years of famine. He concludes by noting in verse 32 that the message to Pharaoh was repeated twice to indicate that the coming famine was established by God and would be brought to pass soon.

In Exodus 7:14–25 is the record of the first of the 10 plagues culminating in the exodus from Egypt. It begins by noting that Pharaoh's heart is hard, and thus he will not release the Hebrews. God directs Moses to stand upon the side of the Nile to meet Pharaoh. Furthermore, He directs him to have Aaron strike the waters so that they turn to blood. According to Exodus 12:12, the final plague (and by implication, all 10 plagues) are to execute judgment on Egypt's false gods. The first plague showed God's superiority over *Khnum* (Nile guardian), *Hapi* (spirit of the Nile), and *Osiris* ("Nile is his blood").[148]

Now let's put these passages together to understand Daniel 12:5–7. The beings standing upon the side of the Nile in Daniel 12:5 are antitypes of Moses and Aaron standing upon the side of the Nile. Just as Moses was to be as God to Pharaoh (see Exod. 7:1), so Jesus is the answer to the question inherent in Michael's name, "Who is like God?" Aaron was Moses' prophet and mouthpiece, and Gabriel has been God's mouthpiece in Daniel and is called a prophet (see Rev. 19:10; 22:9). Here in Daniel 12:6, Gabriel inquires of Jesus as to "the end of these wonders," mirroring the question that he asked of the Wonderful Numberer, identified as Jesus in our study of Daniel 8:13.

The message given by Moses and Aaron to Pharaoh was one of judgment against the false gods of Egypt. This would seem to imply that Daniel 12:5–7 is a message of judgment against the false gods of

---

[148] *Andrews Study Bible*, chart detailing the Egyptian gods affected by the 10 plagues in comments on Exodus 7.

end-time (non-geographic) Egypt. To better appreciate this, consider Jeremiah 46:25:

> <u>Jer. 46:25</u>: Thus says *Yahweh* of hosts, the God of Israel, "Behold, I am about to pay a visit to Amon of No, that is:
> against Pharaoh, against Egypt,
> against her gods and against her kings,
> against Pharaoh and against those who trust in him."

Notice how this verse seems to equate the pharaoh with Amon of No. This makes sense, for the pharaoh was considered a god in Egyptian thinking, and Amon of No was the sun god worshipped in upper Egypt at Thebes (see, e.g., notes for Jeremiah 46:25 in NKJV and NAB). Thus, God was going to visit judgment against the sun-god of Egypt in the person of the pharaoh. Hence, Daniel 12:5–7 hints that God will do the same against end-time Egypt and its chief ruler as well.

To better understand Egypt and its chief ruler, we turn to Ezekiel 29:3, which equates Pharaoh with the great dragon of the Nile, called Leviathan in Psalm 74:13–14, the serpent and dragon whom God slays in Isaiah 27:1. Of course, the serpent and dragon is none other than Satan (see Rev. 12:9), with the dragon also encompassing Satan's earthly agency (the papacy) through whom he works to destroy the remnant (see Rev. 12:17). Hence, the message of Daniel 12:5–7 is one of doom against Satan and the papacy, the sun-worshipping head of end-time Egypt.

Jesus raises His right and left hands to heaven when announcing the 1,260-year prophecy. The twice-repeated message to Pharaoh indicated the certainty of the coming famine (see Gen. 41:32). For the end time, Amos 8:12 predicts a famine for the word of *Yahweh*, so Jesus' double-handedness points to the certainty of the 1,260-year prophecy.

To properly understand the oath in Daniel 12:7, it is imperative to consider Deuteronomy 32:35–43. Here we read that *Yahweh* will vindicate (Hebrew *din*, the verb from which we get the "Dan" in Daniel) His people when their hand (might) is gone, raising *His* hand to heaven and swearing by the fact that He lives forever, pledging that He will avenge His faithful servants and provide atonement for His land and people, while His other hand takes hold of judgment. One could not find a more perfect parallel passage for Daniel 12:7, perhaps even the entire book of Daniel. God is not a tyrant, seeking to quash sinners. Rather, He longs to vindicate His people, though He will mete out justice upon the unrepentant wicked, including the papal king of spiritual Egypt.

Scripture uses "right hand" and "left hand" as a warning not to turn into paths divergent from the narrow way to which Jesus points in Matthew 7:14. Of special interest is the following:

> <u>Deut. 17:18–20</u>: When he [a new king] sits upon the throne of his kingdom, he shall write for himself a duplicate of this Torah upon a scroll from [the Torah] before the priests of the Levites. It shall be with him, and he shall read aloud from it all the days of his life, that he may learn: to fear *Yahweh* his God; to keep all the words of this Torah and these statutes—to do them; not to lift up his heart above his brothers; not to turn aside from the commandment, right or left, so that he may prolong [his] days over his kingdom—he and his sons in the midst of Israel.

Hence, the 1,260-year prophecy of Daniel 12:5–7 warns of an earthly king, purporting to represent God's people, who does *not* read from and meditate upon the Scriptures daily, and in consequence has *not* learned to fear *Yahweh*, does *not* obey His Word, *is* proud over his brothers, and *does* deviate right and left from God's commandment. The result is that the days of his kingdom are not prolonged, but are instead numbered. In fact, they are precisely 3.5 times, or 1,260 prophetic days. Given the papacy's Egyptian description in Daniel 12 and collusion with the king of the south (i.e., king of spiritual Egypt; see 11:40), how ironic it is that France, which is called spiritual Egypt (see Rev. 11:8), deals the papacy its deadly wound in Revelation 13:3!

Observe that Jesus is dressed in the linen of the high priest upon the Day of Atonement. This is most appropriate, for at the completion of the

1,260 days in 1798, the end time commences, and He prepares to move into the Holy of Holies to begin the end-time judgment.

Jesus swears by "him who lives forever." This alludes to God's eternal existence, as well as the permanence of the covenant of righteousness by faith, which He established with Abram. To see this, note that *Yahweh* promised Abram that He would deliver his seed when the 400 years of affliction in Egypt were to close (see Gen. 15:13, 14). As the close of the 400 years drew near, He revealed Himself to Moses at the burning bush with the statement that *Yahweh* is "My name forever, My memorial from generation to generation" (see Exod. 3:15). No matter how hard the papacy attempts to stamp out truth, God will ultimately fulfill His covenant with His people.

Daniel Does Not Understand, Questions "My Lord"

Daniel says he does not understand and addresses Gabriel as *'adoni* ("my Lord," differing by one vowel point from God's title *Adonai*, which Daniel uses when addressing God in his prayer of Daniel 9:3–19). He does not ask *when* the wonders will end (contrast with Gabriel's questions in Daniel 8:13 and 12:6), but *what* will be their end result.[149]

Gabriel's Timeline Explains Latter Part of Vision

In response to this question, Daniel is told "these words are shut up and sealed until the end time," nearly replicating Gabriel's words a few verses prior: "shut up the words and seal the scroll until the end time" (12:4). What does this mean? First, "these words" concern the 1,260 days just spoken of in verse 7. That they are to be shut up until the end time is reached

---

[149] Daniel's observation that he does not understand is common to Bible prophets. Zechariah, Ezekiel, and John each voiced similar perplexity (see Zech. 4:4; Ezek. 37:3; Rev. 7:14). Peter indicates that prophets and even angels have desired a deeper understanding of the things God has revealed through them (see 1 Peter 1:10–12). Further, Daniel's question extends beyond himself; it typifies the question to be asked by those in the end time (see Rom. 15:4; 1 Cor. 10:11), just as in Revelation 10, where John's bittersweet experience typifies the experience of the Millerites in 1844.

establishes a link with 8:26, in which Daniel was told to "shut up the vision, for it pertains to many days [hence]." The end-time judgment would not commence until the 2,300 evening-mornings closed in the fall of 1844.

Of course, the 1,260 days ended in 1798, not 1844. To meet this apparent difficulty, recall that the "appearance" (the 70-week portion of the 2,300 evening-mornings) for the Jewish nation involved a sealing up of vision and prophet (see 9:24), referring to the death of Stephen, which marked its fulfillment. In like manner, we should expect a death to mark the end of the 1,260 years. The papacy's own deadly wound on February 10, 1798 (when French general Berthier took Pope Pius VI captive) marked the close of this great prophetic period. This death marked the beginning of the end time, which in turn was to usher in the end-time judgment.

Verse 10 hearkens back to Daniel 11:33 and 35, reminding us of the papacy's extermination of tens of millions of people faithful to Scripture. This confirms that verse 9 was indeed referring to the 1,260-day prophecy. The remaining verses of Daniel help us discern more closely the relationship between the 1,260 years and the 2,300 evening-mornings.

Gabriel now introduces a new prophetic period, the 1,290 days, which commences with the removal of the continual ministration, permitting the establishment of the detestable idolatry that desolates. One does not find explicit reference to the 1,290 days elsewhere in Scripture, so how does one determine *when* this time period begins? The key is to recognize the heavy emphasis that Daniel 8–12 places on the covenant made with Abram and the subsequent exodus from Egypt alluded to in Daniel 12:5–7.

In Genesis 15:13–14 Abram is told that there would be 400 years of affliction upon his people. The fulfillment of this time in the days of Moses is recorded in Exodus 3:7–8. We go on to read that "the dwelling of the sons of Israel in Egypt was 430 years. Then, at the end of the 430 years— indeed, on that very day—all the hosts of *Yahweh* left the land of Egypt" (12:40, 41). Paul informs us that "the covenant, having been ratified in advance by God through Christ, the law, having appeared after 430 years, does not invalidate so as to void the promise" (Gal. 3:17). Paul's statement makes clear that the 430 years date from the covenantal promise given to

Abram. The giving of the law at Sinai occurred a mere 7 weeks after the date of the exodus from Egypt, well within the 430th year.

The key is that the 400 and 430-year periods end co-terminally, hence the 430 years began 30 years before the 400 years. This 30-year difference, in the context of the fulfillment of the promise of deliverance from Egypt made to Abram in Genesis 15:14, suggests very strongly that the 1,290 and 1,260-year prophecies bear the same relation to each other (i.e., the 1,290 years begin 30 years prior to the 1,260 years).

What happened during the 30 years leading up to AD 538, the start of the 1,260 years? To answer, let us first note those events during the initial 30 years of the 430-year prophecy:

1: Abram is 75 years old when God announces the covenant with him (see Gen. 12:1–4).
2: Twenty-five years later, Abraham is 100 years old when his son Isaac is born (see Gen. 21:5).
3: The 400 years commence 5 years later when Ishmael is driven away. Isaac's place as heir of covenant promise is sure (see Gen. 21:8–14).

Note the similar breakdown for the 30 years preceding the 1,260 years of papal supremacy:

1: AD 508. King Tato and Lombards annihilate Heruli (covenant keepers) for resisting papal supremacy.
2: AD 533. 25 years later, Emperor Justinian declares the pope to be head of all the churches.
3: AD 538. The 1,260 years commence 5 years later, when remaining Germanic church resistance (Ostrogoths) is put down. The pope is now installed as head of all the churches, and Christ is effectively displaced as High Priest.

According to Numbers 4:47, the minimum age for those working in the temple, including priests, was 30 years. Jesus was about 30 years old when he began his 3.5-year ministry (see Luke 3:23). As a counterfeit of Jesus in every way, the papacy undergoes a 30-year period prior to its appointment as head of all the churches for 3.5 prophetic years (1,260 literal years).

At the end of his 3.5-year ministry, Jesus died. At the end of its 3.5 prophetic years, the papacy experienced a deadly wound (see Rev. 13:3). The 400 years for the Israelites concluded on the day when all of the firstborn in Egypt, including Pharaoh's own son, were killed. Since Christ is the firstborn son (see Rom. 8:29; Col. 1:15), and the papacy claims to be vicar of the Son of God, it follows that the papacy's deadly wound answers to the death of the firstborn son. Hence, the conclusion of the 1,260 years marks the beginning of the exodus from spiritual, end-time Egypt.

Now it is clear why Daniel 12 employs so much Egyptian imagery. The papacy is not only to be king of the north (spiritual Assyria/Babylon), but like Joseph in Egypt, whom the pharaoh installed as second-in-command, while acting with all the authority of pharaoh himself (see Gen. 41:40–43), he is to serve as acting ruler for the king of the south (Egypt).

When do the 1,335 days begin and end in relation to the 1,260 and 1,290 days? The key is the phrase "blessed is he who waits." Scripture uses the Hebrew verb "wait" 14 times. Note the following texts:

> Ps. 33:13, 14, 20: From heaven, *Yahweh* looks; He sees all the sons of men. From His dwelling place, He gazes upon all who dwell on the earth. ... Our soul waits for *Yahweh*—He is our strength and our shield.
>
> Isa. 30:18: Therefore *Yahweh* will wait, that He may be gracious to you. Therefore, He will be high to show you mercy, for *Yahweh* is a God of judgment. Blessed are all those who wait for Him.
>
> Zeph. 3:8: "Therefore, wait for Me," declares *Yahweh*, "unto the day I arise as Witness, for My judgment is to gather the nations, to assemble the kingdoms, to pour upon them My indignation, all My burning anger. For with the fire of My jealousy the whole earth will be devoured."

The foregoing verses admonish God's people to wait for the One who "gazes" upon everyone (i.e., scrutinizes everyone's hearts)—the God of judgment, who also serves as Witness on behalf of those faithful to Him. In other words, waiting upon God amounts to awaiting His judgment. Therefore, the 1,335 days would appear to deal with those waiting for the commencement of God's end-time work of judging and witnessing. In order to nail down the time brought to view in Daniel 12:12, we need something more. Note that the prophetic periods in Daniel 12 are expressed as 1,260 and 1,290 prophetic *days*, while the parallel periods in the exodus account are 400 and 430 literal *years*, respectively. To that end, we seek an event occurring 45 literal *years* (i.e., 1,335 – 1,290 = 45) after the exodus from Egypt. Note Caleb's statement following his entry into the promised land:

> Josh. 14:7–10: I was a son of 40 years when Moses, the servant of *Yahweh*, sent me from Kadesh-Barnea to scout out the land. I brought him a report, just as it was in my heart. Yet my brothers who went up with me caused the heart of the people to melt; but I followed *Yahweh* my God fully. So Moses swore on that day, saying, "Surely the land on which your foot has trodden will be an inheritance for you and for your sons forever because you have followed *Yahweh* your God fully." Now, behold, *Yahweh* has preserved me, just as He said, these 45 years, from the time *Yahweh* spoke this word unto Moses, when Israel journeyed in the wilderness. Now, behold, I am today a son of 85 years.

Sure enough, we have our 45-year period, but note that Caleb reckons 45 years from his initial glimpse of the promised land, which commenced *well over a year after he left Egypt at the conclusion of the 400 and 430 years*. Hence, Joshua received his inheritance *more than 46 years after* the exodus from Egypt. Returning to our end-time antitype, we should expect the 1,335 prophetic days to terminate, not 45 years, but *more than 46 years after* the 1,290 prophetic days (i.e., sometime after February 10, 1844).

To home in on a precise date, we investigate the exodus account to determine *when* Joshua scouted out the Promised Land. A most helpful clue is from another instance of the Hebrew verb for "wait":

> Ps. 106:11–15: Waters covered their adversaries, not one of them was left. They believed His words, they sang His praise. They quickly forgot His works; they did not wait for His counsel. They gave into insatiable craving in the wilderness and tested God in the desert. He gave them their request, and sent a wasting disease among them.

Following their deliverance from Egypt at the Red Sea, observe that God's people did *not* wait for His counsel, but instead yielded to their cravings, resulting in many deaths. Table 19 enables us to chart key exodus events, especially the relationship between the grumbling and scouting out the Promised Land:

Table 19: Chronology of Events in the Exodus

REFERENCE	EVENT	YEAR	MONTH	DAY
Exod. 12:6–8, 41; 13:4	Passover lamb killed.	1	1	14
	Passover meal eaten on first day of Unleavened Bread. Firstborn killed.	1	1	15
Exod. 40:17	Wilderness tabernacle set up.	2	1	1
Num. 10:11, 12	Israel leaves Sinai.	2	2	20
Num. 10:12, 33	Arrival at Taberah (see also Num 11:3, 34).	2	2	23
Num. 11:18–20	**Quail sent for 30 days starting day 24 of month 2.**	2	3	23
Num. 13:17–20	**Twelve spies sent into Canaan during first-fruits of grape harvest.**	2	≈5	?
Num. 13:25–34	**Twelve spies return from Canaan 40 days later. Forty years given.**	2	≈6	?
Deut. 1:3	Moses speaks at Jordan.	40	11	1
Josh. 4:19	Israel crosses Jordan.	41	1	10
Josh. 14:7, 10	**Caleb receives inheritance 45 years after being sent as spy.**	47	?	?

Observe from Table 19 that a precise date for the spies' entry into Canaan is not available, only an approximate season (first-fruits of the grapes). However, shortly before, there is an event with specific dates: the 30 days when God gave the quail. It was at this point that the people grumbled. From Numbers 11, we learn that it was the mixed multitude who encouraged the rest of the Israelites to grumble in favor of the food of Egypt.

From the 24th of the second month to the 23rd of the third month, and reckoning inclusively, this event began 1 year and 40 days and concluded 1 year and 69 days following the exodus. Moving ahead 1 year and 40 days (inclusive) from February 10, 1798 extends to March 21, 1799. From this date, moving ahead the additional 45 years extends to March 21, 1844 (more precisely, sunset March 20 to sunset March 21). Repeating this same exercise, but moving ahead 1 year and 69 days (inclusive) plus an additional 45 years gets us to April 19, 1844 (more precisely, sunset April 18 to sunset April 19).

Having computed this 30-day stretch as marking the end of the 1,335 days, we ask the question, Did March 21 or April 18/19, 1844 mark important prophetic events? Did these dates correspond to a trial of some kind, which led unconsecrated multitudes to grumble, expressing a desire to return to spiritual Egypt, while a few continued to wait? Incredibly, the answer is an unqualified "Yes!" The Millerites heralded the second advent of Jesus, initially believing that He would return sometime between the spring equinox of 1843 and the spring equinox of 1844 (March 21, 1844), which time period they thought equated with biblical 1843 (in biblical reckoning, years commence in the spring). They understood this year to be the last of the 2,300 evening-mornings of Daniel 8, and in common with other believers of that era, they thought that the cleansing of the sanctuary foretold was the cleansing of the earth by fire when Jesus returned. Hence, to their understanding, Jesus should return to earth in biblical 1843. When March 21, 1844 passed uneventfully, subsequent study revealed that biblical 1843 closed not with the spring equinox, but as computed via Karaite reckoning, at sunset on April 18, 1844.[150]

Hence, March 21, 1844 was the first disappointment of the Millerites. The true end of biblical 1843 coincided with sunset, April 18, 1844. Since Jesus did not return, this date proved a disappointment as well. While the Millerites were disappointed that the 2,300 evening-mornings had apparently come and gone without any eventfulness, what they did not realize at the time was that these very disappointments were in fact a fulfillment of prophecy, though not of the 2,300 evening-mornings. They had just experienced the fulfillment of the 1,335 days!

According to Daniel 12:12, the end of the 1,335 days was to prove a blessing. In what way could the first disappointment be considered a blessing? The study led the faithful Millerites to Habakkuk 2:3: "For the vision is yet for an appointed time. It will breathe on to the end, it will not lie. If it tarries, wait for it, for it will surely come, it will not be delayed." In light of this verse, the Millerites understood the first disappointment as an assurance that the true fulfillment was certain. Significantly, this verse employs the same word for "wait" as in Daniel 12:12. The Millerites were comforted, for indeed the vision *seemed* to tarry, though truly it did not.

At the August camp meeting in Exeter, New Hampshire, Samuel Snow proclaimed the date October 22, 1844 as the tenth day of the seventh month by Karaite reckoning based on his study of types in the Hebrew calendar. He held that the cleansing of the sanctuary referred to Jesus' cleansing of the earth by fire at His return on the Day of Atonement. This led to the very bitter experience of the Great Disappointment of 1844. Intense Bible study following the Great Disappointment made clear that the cleansing of the sanctuary referred to the *heavenly* sanctuary, not the earth (notice how Habakkuk 2:20 refers to Christ in His sanctuary).

---

[150] Froom, *PFF*, vol. 4, pp. 449, 784, 786, 796. The Bible calls the first month of the new year *Aviv*, which means that the barley has reached the ripe but soft stage of its development. Karaites watched for this stage of barley development, rather than following the rabbinic calendar, which was simply a mathematical calculation meant to approximate the agricultural calendar.

To make it the more trying, Revelation 10:11 made clear that they had to proclaim the truth *yet again*.

The 1,335 days led to the end of biblical 1843, rather than to judgment commencing on October 22, 1844. Would the Bible really prophesy an incorrect understanding of such a momentous event? There is biblical precedent for such disappointment. Jesus' disciples were enormously disappointed when their King was crucified, dashing all hope of an earthly kingdom. However, three days later, their hopes were revived, and they went forth once again proclaiming the King and His kingdom, but now with a *proper understanding*.

Also, the *apparent* 45-year difference between the 1,335 and 1,290 prophetic days suggests that prophetic time was to come short of the commencement of the end-time judgment, for the Bible associates the establishment of God's temple with 46 years, not 45 years: "Then said the Jews, Forty and six years was this temple in building, and wilt thou rear it up in three days?" (John 2:20, KJV). Again, Moses spent 46 days preparing to meet God before receiving instruction regarding the construction of the earthly sanctuary (see Exod. 24:12–18).

Now we reach the closing statement of the book of Daniel. A cursory reading suggests that God informs Daniel that he will be resurrected at the end of days. However, the entire book of Daniel equates standing with the end-time judgment, not resurrection. Furthermore, the phrase "according to your lot" points back to the initial use of "lot" in Scripture (see Lev. 16:8–10), in which lots were cast on the Day of Atonement to determine which goat went to *Yahweh* and which one went to *Azazel* (Satan). The "end of the days" in Daniel 12:13 is not the end of the 1,260, 1,290, or 1,335 days, but the end of the very last of the Bible's great time prophecies—the 2,300 evening-mornings of Daniel 8:14, reaching to October 22, 1844:

> "Daniel has been standing in his lot since the seal was removed and the light of truth has been shining upon his visions. He stands in his lot, bearing the testimony which was to be understood at the end of the days" (White, *1SAT*, p. 225).

INVITATION

The book of Daniel closes as it began: A young man prepared in childhood to stand "10 hands above all" before the king was able to do so for the rest of his life by faithfully adhering to God and His covenant. Through his prophecies, Daniel now stands during the end-time Day of Atonement, the judgment hour of earth's history (see Rev. 14:7). His life and book show that Jesus can and will prepare each willing person to stand perfectly for Him now at the close of the end-time judgment (see Eph. 5:27; Jude 24).

Dear reader, is it your decision to:

- Relinquish every sin, known and unknown?
- Believe that *no* sin is too great for Jesus to remove from your life?
- Accept the fact that Jesus truly can make *you* stand perfectly faithful in the judgment?
- Surrender and permit Jesus' grace to enable you to live above the power of sin?
- Let your life declare before the world, "God is my Judge—He will vindicate me!"?

SUMMARY: DANIEL 10–12

DANIEL 10–12: JESUS

In Daniel 10:5–6, Daniel sees the appearance of Jesus dressed as High Priest on the Day of Atonement. Jesus is also Michael, number 1 of the foremost rulers, Ruler of Daniel's people, the One who stands up for the persecuted remnant when probation closes, and raises the dead (see Dan. 10:13, 21; 12:1, 2). Finally, He is the Man clothed in linen, standing upon the waters of the Nile, who raises both hands heavenward and swears an oath by Him who lives forever that all of the wonders will finish after 3.5 times.

DANIEL 10–12: THE STAND

In Daniel 10:11, Daniel is once again enabled to stand by the touch of Gabriel. He has been overwhelmed by the appearance of Jesus as High Priest and Judge. Once again, Daniel's experience models our own. When we get a complete picture of Jesus, as revealed in the book of Daniel, and lose all confidence in our own strength, God provides us His own strength to enable us to stand.

In Daniel 11, a number of kings stand for a season, only to be shattered, caused to no longer stand, or be replaced by others who stand in their place. In verse 31, arms stand on behalf of the burgeoning papacy, polluting the heavenly sanctuary by their effort to establish the papal, counterfeit, earthly sanctuary. While this system continues 1,260 years, it receives a deadly wound in 1798 and finally has no helper in verse 45 when Jesus returns.

In Daniel 12:1, Jesus stands guard over His people during the falling of the 7 last plagues; and He stands when He makes His oath, pledging to fulfill His covenant for His people (see verses 5–7). Finally, Daniel is promised that he (through his book) will stand during the end-time Day of Atonement. A proper knowledge of this book will enable all willing readers to stand during the end-time Day of Atonement, honoring Jesus and prepared to meet Him at His soon return.

DANIEL 10–12: RAISED HANDS

Through His angel Gabriel, God extends His hand to strengthen Daniel when he is overwhelmed by the appearance of Jesus (see Dan. 10:10). By contrast, in 11:11, 16, 41, and 42, the hand of the king of the south and the hand of Rome refer to their use of force to secure their aims. Finally, in 12:7, Jesus raises His right and left hands in an oath, pledging to deliver His people. This will be accomplished without the use of military strength, but by laying down His life as a willing sacrifice and the convicting power of the Holy Spirit on the hearts of those who are delivered. His kingdom will be established "without hands" (see 2:34, 45).

DANIEL 10–12: JUBILEE AND DAY OF ATONEMENT

In Daniel 10:5–6, Jesus appears as the high priest would dress on the Day of Atonement (see Lev. 16:4). In Daniel 12:5–7, Jesus appears once more, dressed in linen for the Day of Atonement. The closing verse of the book alludes to the casting of lots for the two goats on the Day of Atonement (see Lev. 16:8) when it says that Daniel would "stand according to your lot at the end of the [prophetic] days."

Numerous hints of the Jubilee fill Daniel 8, suggesting it as a major theme of Daniel 8–12. The Jubilee is the great day of deliverance, which occurred every 49 years in ancient Israel on the Day of Atonement (see Lev. 25:8–55). The great Jubilee will occur when Jesus returns, for then His people will be forever free. Not only will they have overcome sin by His grace prior to His return, but at His return, they will be transformed physically, their nature will no longer be subject to temptation, and they will no more be persecuted by Satan or his followers. The joy expressed by His people at the great Jubilee deliverance is expressed in Daniel 12:1–3, when Michael stands on their behalf, raises the dead, and delivers the everlasting covenant. At this time, the eternally saved cry out, "Lo, this is our God; we have waited for him, and he will save us: this is the LORD; we have waited for him, we will be glad and rejoice in his salvation" (Isa. 25:9, KJV).

DANIEL, PART 3: THE KEY POINTS

DANIEL 8–12: JESUS, THE STAND, GOD'S HAND, ATONEMENT, AND JUBILEE

The primary themes in Daniel 8–12 are:

- Jesus' perfect atoning sacrifice in AD 31.
- Jesus' installation as High Priest at His ascension.
- Jesus' people enabled to stand in the judgment, not indulging sin in thought, word, deed, or neglect of duty.
- Jesus' all-powerful hand that can save to the uttermost.
- Jesus as Judge, cleansing the heavenly sanctuary and believers' hearts in the end-time Day of Atonement.
- Ultimate Jubilee deliverance (from both persecution and temptation) for eternity at the second coming.

DANIEL 8–12: CHAPTER SUMMARIES

Chapter 8 focuses on Rome's effort to do away with Jesus, first at the cross, then later by substituting His work in the heavenly sanctuary with an earthly counterfeit headed by the Roman papacy. The entire chapter is couched in sanctuary references. The end time began when the papacy received its deadly wound, marking the close of its 1,260 years of earthly sanctuary "service." The heavenly sanctuary is to be restored to its righteous condition at the close of the 2,300 evening-mornings, when the end-time judgment begins.

Chapter 9 details Daniel's plea to understand the appearance portion of the 2,300 evening-mornings. Gabriel arrives at the time of the evening grain offering, explaining that the beginning of the 2,300 evening-mornings is a period of 70 prophetic weeks, or 490 years. The name *Adonai* appears 10 times (once preceding Daniel's prayer, 9 times in the prayer), and the Hebrew words for "seven," "seventy," and "week(s)" appear a combined 7 times in Daniel 9:24–27. These culminate in a final week of 7 years, in the midst of which Jesus the Messiah is crucified in our place. His death simultaneously serves as the very sacrifice and grain offering needed to inaugurate Him as High Priest in the heavenly sanctuary at Pentecost, 7 weeks after His resurrection.

Chapter 10 provides Daniel an appearance of Jesus Himself, dressed in the white linen of the high priest on the Day of Atonement. Jesus' description is rich in Abrahamic covenant language. This makes clear that Jesus' High Priestly work of cleansing the heavenly sanctuary during the Day of Atonement has as its sole aim the *complete* restoration of God's character in His people via the fulfillment of His everlasting covenant.

Chapter 11 provides a detailed history of the rise and fall of Rome, highlighting Jesus' perfect atoning sacrifice in verse 22 as Agent of the covenant. In Daniel 11:40–45 is described Satan's final effort to secure the world for himself. Daniel 12:1–3 culminates in the close of human probation when Michael (Jesus) stands up for His faithful remnant, those who have permitted Him to fulfill His everlasting covenant, completing His work of atonement in their lives. This faithful remnant is sealed, and along with the resurrected righteous, they blaze forth Jesus' glory before the world just before He comes.

Chapter 12 is rich in imagery drawn from the exodus from Egypt. It refers again to the 1,260 years, describing it in terms of Pharaoh, Moses, Aaron, and the plagues that befell Egypt. New prophetic periods are introduced, the 1,290 and 1,335 prophetic days. The 1,290 days co-terminate with the 1,260, but begin 30 years prior. This 30-year period was the period necessary to prepare the papacy for her 1,260 years as a counterfeit, earthly high priest. The 1,335 days extend to the initial Millerite disappointments of March 21 and April 18, 1844. The book closes with Daniel standing according to his lot at the close of the 2,300 evening-mornings, marking the commencement of the end-time judgment on October 22, 1844.

Structure of Daniel 8–12

Table 20: Simplified Structure of Daniel 8–12

	REF.	MATCHES		REF.	
A_1	8:1, 2	Introduction: Daniel by the stream Ulai	Introduction: Daniel by the great river, the Chiddeqel	10:1–4	A_1'
A_2	8:3–12	I lifted my eyes, looked, and behold: One ram	I lifted my eyes, looked, and behold: One man	10:5, 6	A_2'
		A vision focusing on the "appearance"	The "appearance" of Jesus		
B_1	8:13, 14	Question and answer: Jesus and Gabriel by the Ulai	Question and answer: Jesus and Gabriel by the Nile	12:5–7	B_1'
B_2	8:15–26	Daniel faints, Gabriel's touch, Daniel stands.	Daniel faints, Gabriel's touch, Daniel stands.	10:7–12:4	B_2'
		Gabriel's explanation of vision.	Gabriel's explanation of vision.		
C_1	8:27–9:19	Daniel does not understand, pleads with *Adonai*	Daniel does not understand, questions *'adoni* ("my lord")	12:8	C_1'
C_2	9:20–27	Gabriel's timeline explains early part of vision	Gabriel's timeline explains latter part of vision	12:9–13	C_2'

Pictorial representation of Structure of Daniel 8–12:

Daniel 8 and 9: A_1 A_2 B_1 B_2 C_1 C_2

Daniel 10–12: A_1' A_2' B_1' B_2' C_1' C_2'

Lessons from the Structure of Daniel 8–12:

- Sections A and A' complement each other. Section A takes place by a stream (the Ulai), section A' by the great river (the Chiddeqel). The relative sizes of the water bodies harmonize with the relative sizes of the visions. The smaller Ulai is associated with the "appearance," the 70 weeks at the start of the vision; the greater Chiddeqel with the latter part of the 2,300-evening-morning vision.

- Sections *A* and *B'* form a chiasm, highlighting this portion of Daniel 8–12. Section *B* concludes with Gabriel's words, "Now, the appearance portion of the evening and the morning which was mentioned is truth, but you are to shut up the vision, for it pertains to many days [hence]." Section B_1' begins with Daniel's statement that he "saw the appearance by myself," an appearance of Jesus as High Priest clearly linked to the appearance of Daniel 8 and 9, which culminated in Jesus' death on Calvary. Further, Gabriel states in Daniel 10:21 that he will "inform you of what is inscribed in the document of truth," hearkening back to Daniel 8:26: "the appearance portion of the evening and the morning ... is truth." The chiastic arrangement of *B* and *B'* highlight Gabriel's message in Daniel 10–12 as a continuation and amplification of his message in Daniel 8 and 9.
- Sections *C* and C_1' parallel each other perfectly. In C_1, Daniel pleads with the great Judge, *Adonai*, for understanding of the appearance, referring to the early portion of the vision. In C_1', Daniel asks *'adoni* (a title of respect for *Adonai's* emissary, Gabriel) for understanding of the latter portion of the vision. In C_2 and C_2', both pleas for understanding are answered with timelines that lead to a disappointment. In the appearance (early part of the vision) of C_2, Christ's death in the middle of the 70th week was a terrible disappointment for the disciples, and Stephen's death half a prophetic week later at the end of the 70 weeks marked the close of probation for the Jewish nation as a whole. In the latter part of the vision of C_2', the Millerites' first disappointment was in the middle of the final evening-morning, coincident with the end of the 1,335 days. The 2,300 evening-mornings concluded half a year later with the Great Disappointment when Jesus did not return as expected, but it also marked the beginning of the end-time judgment, which will culminate in deliverance for those who allow Jesus to humble them completely and work out His everlasting covenant in their lives.

Table 21: Detailed Structure of Daniel 8–12

	REF.	MATCHES		REF.	
A_1		**INTRODUCTION: DANIEL BY THE STREAM ULAI**	**INTRODUCTION: DANIEL BY THE GREAT RIVER CHIDDEQEL**		A_1'
	8:1	Year 3 of King Belshazzar. Vision appeared unto Daniel.	Year 3 of King Cyrus. Matter revealed to Daniel.	10:1	
A_2		**THE VISION: CHRIST'S SANCTUARY**	**THE APPEARANCE: JESUS AS HIGH PRIEST OF SANCTUARY**		A_2'
	8:2	I was by the stream Ulai.	I was by the side of the great river, i.e., the Chiddeqel.	10:4	
	8:3	I lifted my eyes, looked, and behold: One ram standing.	I lifted my eyes, looked, and behold: One Man clothed.	10:5	
B_1		**QUESTION AND ANSWER: JESUS AND GABRIEL BY THE ULAI**	**QUESTION AND ANSWER: JESUS AND GABRIEL BY THE NILE**		B_1'
	8:13	One holy being speaking; 1 holy being said	Two others standing, 1 on this side of the Nile, 1 on that side	12:5	
	8:13	One holy being said to the Palmoni	He said to the Man clothed in linen	12:6	
	8:13	"Until what point … continual ministration and desolating rebellion?"	"Until what point … the end of these wonders?"	12:6	
	8:14	"Until 2,300 evening-mornings—then the sanctuary will be restored."	"For [3.5] appointed times … these [wonders] will finish."	12:7	
B_2		**DANIEL STANDS: THE VISION EXPLAINED**	**DANIEL STANDS: THE VISION EXPLAINED**		B_2'
	8:15	One standing before me with the appearance of a man.	I, Daniel, saw the appearance by myself.	10:7	

(continued)

Table 21: Detailed Structure of Daniel 8–12 (*continued*)

	REF.	MATCHES		REF.	
	8:16	"Gabriel, makes this particular one understand the appearance."	I saw this great appearance.	10:8	
	8:17, 19	"Understand … the vision pertains to the end time. … what will occur in the latter part of the outrage, for at an appointed time is the end."	"Understand what will confront your people in the last days, … still a [part of the] vision pertinent to those days."	10:14	
	8:18	As he was speaking with me, I was unconscious upon my face toward the ground.	As I heard the sounds of His words, I was unconscious upon my face, and my face was toward the ground.	10:9, 15	
	8:18	He touched me, enabling me to stand where I had been standing.	… touched me. "Stand … where you were standing."	10:10, 11	
	8:20–22	Kings of Media and Persia. Great horn = first king. 4 kingdoms stand.	Darius the Mede, Persian kings. Mighty king. Kingdom divided unto the 4 winds.	11:2–4	
	8:23–25	A king, goat-faced. … Corrupt many through sense of peace. Stands against Ruler of rulers—without hand he will be shattered.	He will stand in beautiful land … enter peaceably. Shattered—as well as the Agent of the covenant.	11:16–22	
	8:26a	The appearance portion of the evening and the morning … is truth.	The appearance. … what is in the document of truth.	10:7, 21	
	8:26b	Shut up the vision, for it pertains to many days [hence].	Shut up words and seal scroll until the end time.	12:4	
C_1		**DANIEL DOES NOT UNDERSTAND, PLEADS WITH *ADONAI***	**DANIEL DOES NOT UNDERSTAND, QUESTIONS *'ADONI***		C_1'
	8:27	There was no one to give understanding.	I heard, yet I did not understand.	12:8	

(*continued*)

Table 21: Detailed Structure of Daniel 8–12 (*continued*)

	REF.	MATCHES		REF.	
	9:3–19	I set my face toward *Adonai* God to seek Him by prayer and petitions.	"*'adoni*, what is the end result of these [wonders]?"	12:8	
		GABRIEL'S TIMELINE EXPLAINS EARLY PART OF VISION	**GABRIEL'S TIMELINE EXPLAINS LATTER PART OF VISION**		
	9:22	I have come to make you wise with understanding.	The wise will understand.	12:10	
	9:24	Seventy weeks cut off to seal up vision and prophet.	These words are sealed till the end time.	12:9	
C_2	9:25	From going forth of decree to restore and to rebuild Jerusalem until Messiah the Agent, there are to be 7 weeks, then 62 weeks.	From time continual ministration taken away to establish detestable idolatry which desolates until end of wonders, there are to be 1,290 days [30 days, then 1,260 days].	12:11	C_2'
	9:26a, 27a	In middle of 70th week, Messiah cut off. [Disciples' disappointment half a week before end of 70 weeks.]	Blessed is he who waits and arrives at the 1,335 days. [First Millerite disappointment half a year before 2,300 evening-mornings end.]	12:12	
	9:26b	The end of war.	The end of the days.	12:13	

CONCLUDING MATTER

BIBLIOGRAPHY

"Absolution." *Wikipedia.* n.d. https://1ref.us/yt (accessed January 22, 2020).

"Agathocles of Egypt." *Wikipedia.* n.d. https://1ref.us/z0 (accessed January 22, 2020).

"Alexander the Great." *Wikipedia.* n.d. https://1ref.us/yv (accessed January 22, 2020).

Barnes, Albert. *Notes on the Old Testament.* London: Blackie & Son, 1884.

Blayney, Benjamin, ed. *The Holy Bible, King James Version.* Oxford: Oxford University Press, 1769.

Blosser, John. "Arizona State Senator: Make Sunday Church Attendance Mandatory." *Newsmax.* March 27, 2015. https://1ref.us/z5 (accessed January 22, 2020).

Brown, Francis, S. R. Driver, and Charles A. Briggs. *The Brown-Driver-Briggs Hebrew and English Lexicon with an Appendix Containing the Biblical Aramaic.* Oxford: Clarendon Press, 1907.

Catechism of the Catholic Church. 2nd ed. Vatican: Libreria Editrice Vaticana, 2016.

Catholic Mirror. "The Christian Sabbath: The Genuine Offspring of the Union of the Holy Spirit and the Catholic Church His Spouse. The Claims of Protestantism to any Part Therein Proved to be Groundless, Self-Contradictorry, and Suicidal." September 2, 9, 16, 23, 1893.

Common English Bible. Common English Bible, 2011.

"Constantine the Great." *Wikipedia.* n.d. https://1ref.us/z1 (accessed January 22, 2020).

d'Aubigne, J. H. Merle. *History of the Reformation in Europe.* 1867. Vol. 2. Rapidan, VA: Hartland Publications, 1999.

Davidson, Richard. *A Song for the Sanctuary.* As yet an unpublished manuscript.

de Kock, Edwin. *7 Heads and 10 Horns in Daniel and the Revelation.* Edinburg, TX: Self-published, 2011.

—. *Christ and Antichrist in Prophecy and History.* 4th ed. Edinburg, TX: Self-published, 2013.

—. *The Truth About 666 and the Story of the Great Apostasy.* 2nd ed. Vol. 1. Edinburg, TX: Self-published, 2013.

—. *The Use and Abuse of Prophecy.* Edinburg, TX: Self-published, 2007.

Doukhan, Jacques. *Secrets of Daniel.* Hagerstown, MD: Review and Herald Publishing Association, 2000.

Durant, Will. *The Story of Civilization: Part III—Caesar and Christ.* New York: Simon and Schuster, 1944.

—. *The Story of Civilization: Part II—The Life of Greece.* New York: Simon and Schuster, 1939.

Dybdahl, Jon L., ed. *Andrews Study Bible.* Berrien Springs, MI: Andrews University Press, 2010.

Eck, Johann. *Enchiridion Locorum Communium Adversus Lutheranos.* Venice: Antonius & Fratres de Sabio, 1533.

"Egypt (Roman province)." *Wikipedia.* n.d. https://1ref.us/yp (accessed January 22, 2020).

English Revised Version. Oxford: Oxford University Press, 1885.

"Etemenanki." *Wikipedia.* n.d. https://1ref.us/yr (accessed January 22, 2020).

Ferraris, Lucius. *Prompta Bibliotheca.* 4th ed. Vol. 6. Venice: Gaspar Storti, 1763.

Freedman, David Noel, ed. *Eerdmans Dictionary of the Bible.* Grand Rapids, MI: William B. Eerdmanns Publishing Company, 2000.

Friberg, Barbara, ed. *Analytical Lexicon of the Greek New Testament.* Grand Rapids, MI: Baker, 2000.

Froom, LeRoy Edwin. *The Prophetic Faith of Our Fathers—Early Church Exposition, Subsequent Deflections, and Medieval Revival.* Vol. 1. Washington, D.C.: Review and Herald Publishing Association, 1950.

—. *The Prophetic Faith of Our Fathers—New World Recovery and Consummation of Prophetic Interpretation.* Vol. 4. Washington, D.C.: Review and Herald Publishing Association, 1954.

—. *The Prophetic Faith of Our Fathers—PART I Colonial and Early National American Exposition & PART II Old World Nineteenth Century Public Awakening.* Vol. 3. Washington, D.C.: Review and Herald Publishing Association, 1946.

—. *The Prophetic Faith of Our Fathers—Pre-Reformation and Reformation Restoration, and Second Departure.* Vol. 2. Washington, D.C.: Review and Herald Publishing Association, 1948.

Geiermann, Peter. *The Convert's Catechism of Catholic Doctrine.* St. Louis, MO: B. Herder Book Co., 1946.

Gibbon, Edward. *The History of the Decline and Fall of the Roman Empire.* Vol. 4. London: Strahan & Cadell, 1776–1789.

Gill, John. *Exposition of the Old Testament.* 6 vols. 1748–1763.

God's Word Translation. Ada, MI: Baker Publishing Group, 1995.

Groves, J. Alan, ed. *Groves-Wheeler Westminster Morphology and Lemma Database [The Hebrew Scriptures].* n.d.

Guiness, H. Grattan. *The Approaching End of the Age.* 8th ed. London: Hodder and Stoughton, 1882.

Hardinge, Leslie. *Jesus is My Judge: Meditations on the Book of Daniel.* Harrisburg, PA: American Cassette Ministries, 1996.

Harris, R. Laird, ed. *Theological Wordbook of the Old Testament.* Chicago: Moody Press, 1980.

His Holiness John Paul II. *Crossing the Threshold of Hope.* New York: Alfred A. Knopf, 1994.

Hodgkin, Thomas. *Italy and Her Invaders.* 2nd ed. Vol. 1. London: Oxord University Press, 1892.

"Johann Tetzel." *Wikipedia.* n.d. https://1ref.us/z2 (accessed January 22, 2020).

Johnson, Paul. *A History of Christianity.* New York: Simon and Schuster, 2012.

Josephus, Flavius. *Complete Works of Flavius Josephus.* Translated by William Whiston. Grand Rapids, MI: Kregel Publications, 1960.

Keil, Johann Carl Friedrich, and Franz Delitzsch. *Keil & Delitzsch Commentary on the Old Testament.* Edinburgh: T. and T. Clark, 1866–1891.

Kennedy, John F. "Address to the Greater Houston Ministerial Association." *American Rhetoric.* n.d. https://1ref.us/z4 (accessed January 22, 2020).

Klein, Christopher. "Hanging Gardens Existed, but not in Babylon." *History.* n.d. https://1ref.us/z3 (accessed January 22, 2020).

Leeser, Isaac. *Jewish Bible*. Philadelphia: Self-published, 371 Walnut Street, 1853.

Liddell, Henry George, ed. *A Greek–English Lexicon*. Oxford: Oxford University Press, 1843.

"Macedonia (Roman province)." *Wikipedia*. n.d. https://1ref.us/yn (accessed January 22, 2020).

"Marduk." *Wikipedia*. n.d. https://1ref.us/ys (accessed January 22, 2020).

Margolis, Max, ed. *JPS Holy Scriptures 1917*. Jewish Publication Society, 1917.

Maxwell, C. Mervyn. *The Message of Daniel: God Cares Volume One*. Boise, ID: Pacific Press Publishing Association, 1981.

"Mitra." *Wikipedia*. n.d. https://1ref.us/yq (accessed January 22, 2020).

New American Bible. Washington, D.C.: Confraternity of Christian Doctrine, Inc., 2010.

New English Translation. Biblical Studies Press, L.L.C., 2006.

New Jewish Publication Society of America Tanakh. Jewish Publication Society of America, 1985.

New Living Translation. Tyndale House Foundation, 2007.

Nichol, Francis D., ed. *The Seventh-day Adventist Bible Commentary*. Vol. 4. Washington, D.C.: Review and Herald, 1955, revised 1976.

Owusu-Antwi, Brempong. *The Chronology of Daniel 9:24–27*. Berrien Springs, MI: Adventist Theological Society Publications, 1995.

Oxentenko, Michael. *The Two Distinct Visions of khazon and mar'eh in Daniel 8 and the Relationship of the 2300 Evenings and Mornings of Daniel 8:14 to the Seventy Weeks of Daniel 9:24–27*. Draft no. 172, September 2, 2015. As yet an unpublished manuscript.

Plutarch. "L 245 Plutarch Moralia III Kings Commanders Romans Spartans." *The Internet Archive*. n.d. https://1ref.us/yu (accessed January 22, 2020).

"Pope Francis Sends Video Message to Kenneth Copeland—Let's Unite." *YouTube*. February 21, 2014. https://1ref.us/km (accessed January 22, 2020).

"Population and Vital Statistics Report." *United Nations Department of Economic and Social Affairs Statistics Division*. n.d. https://1ref.us/yy (accessed January 22, 2020).

"Presentation of the Pontifical Yearbook 2019 and the Annuarium Statisticum Ecclesiae 2017, 06.03.2019." *Holy See Press Office*. n.d. https://1ref.us/yx (accessed January 22, 2020).

Rahlfs, Alfred, ed. *Septuaginta (Old Greek Jewish Scriptures)*. Stuttgart: Deutsche Bibelgesellschaft (German Bible Society), 1935.

Revised Standard Version. 2nd ed. Division of Christian Education of the National Council of the Churches of Christ in the United States of America, 1971.

Revised Version, American Standard Edition. New York: Thomas Nelson & Sons, 1901.

Robinson, Maurice A. and William G.Pierpont, ed. *The New Testament in the Original Greek: Byzantine Textform*. Southborough, MA: Chilton Book Publishing, 2005.

"Roman Syria." *Wikipedia*. n.d. https://1ref.us/yo (accessed January 22, 2020).

"Rome." *Wikipedia*. n.d. https://1ref.us/yw (accessed January 22, 2020).

Rotherham, Joseph B. *Rotherham's Emphasized Bible*. London: H. R. Allenson, 1902.

Singer, Isidore, ed. *The Jewish Encyclopedia of 1906*. 12 vols. New York: Funk & Wagnalls, 1901–1906.

Smith, Uriah. *Daniel and the Revelation*. Battle Creek, MI: Review and Herald Publishing Company, 1897.

Stern, David H. *Complete Jewish Bible*. Clarksville, MD: Jewish New Testament Publications, Inc., 1998.

Strachey, Lytton. *Eminent Victorians: Cardinal Manning, Florence Nightingale, Dr. Arnold, General Gordon*. New York and London: G.P. Putnam's Sons, 1918.

Strong, James. *The New Strong's Exhaustive Concordance of the Bible*. Nashville, TN: Thomas Nelson Publishers, 1990.

The Great Encyclical Letters of Pope Leo XIII. New York: Benziger Brothers, 1903.

The Holy Bible, English Standard Version. Wheaton, IL: Crossway Bibles, 2011.

The New American Standard Bible. La Habra, CA: The Lockman Foundation, 1995.

The New International Version (2011). Grand Rapids, MI: Zondervan Publishing House, 2011.

The New King James Version. Nashville, TN: Thomas Nelson, Inc., 1982.

Treiyer, Alberto R. *The Apocalyptic Times of the Sanctuary*. Self-published, 2014.

Wansbrough, Henry, ed. *New Jerusalem Bible*. London: Darton, Longman & Todd Limited, 1985.

What Does the Bible Really Teach? Brooklyn, NY: Watchtower Bible and Tract Society of New York, 2014.

White, Ellen G. *Christian Temperance and Bible Hygiene.* Battle Creek, MI: Good Health Publishing Co., 1890.

—. *Fundamentals of Christian Education.* Nashville, TN: Southern Publishing Association, 1923.

—. *Manuscript Releases.* 21 vols. Silver Spring, MD: Ellen G. White Estate, 1981–1993.

—. *Patriarchs and Prophets.* Washington, D.C.: Review and Herald Publishing Association, 1890.

—. *Prophets and Kings.* Mountain View, CA: Pacific Press Publishing Association, 1917.

—. *Sermons and Talks.* Vol. 1. Silver Spring, MD: Ellen G. White Estate, 1990.

—. *Testimonies to Ministers.* Mountain View, CA: Pacific Press Publishing Association, 1923.

—. *The Desire of Ages.* Mountain View, CA: Pacific Press Publishing Association, 1898.

—. *The Great Controversy.* Mountain View, CA: Pacific Press Publishing Association, 1911.

—. "Dear Brethren and Sisters." *The Review and Herald*, November 1, 1850.

—. "The Power of the Word of God." *The Review and Herald*, November 10, 1904.

—. "The Return of the Exiles—No. 5 Loss Through Delay." *The Review and Herald*, December 5, 1907.

—. *The Sanctified Life.* Washington, D.C.: Review and Herald Publishing Association, 1889.

—. "The Dragon Voice." *The Signs of the Times*, February 8, 1910.

—. "Nebuchadnezzar's Humiliation." *The Youth's Instructor*, March 28, 1905.

—. "Nebuchadnezzar's Second Dream." *The Youth's Instructor*, November 1, 1904.

—. "The Resurrection of Lazarus. VIII." *The Youth's Instructor*, May 18, 1899.

—. "The Unseen Watcher.—No. 1." *The Youth's Instructor*, May 19, 1898.

—. "The Unseen Watcher.—No. 2." *The Youth's Instructor*, May 26, 1898.

—. "Them That Honor Me, I Will Honor." *The Youth's Instructor*, December 31, 1907.

—. "They Shall See His Face." *The Youth's Instructor*, August 20, 1896.

Wilkinson, Benjamin. *Truth Triumphant: The Church in the Wilderness.* Reprint of original 1944 edition. Fort Oglethorpe, GA: TEACH Services, 2015.

Wylie, James Aitken. *The History of Protestantism: Protestantism in the Waldensian Valleys.* Vol. 16. 1878.

"Xerxes I." *Wikipedia.* n.d. https://1ref.us/yz (accessed January 22, 2020).

Young, Robert. *Young's Literal Translation of the Holy Bible.* 1862.

THE WEDDING: JESUS STANDS FOR HIS BRIDE IN THE BOOK OF REVELATION

Revelation picks up where Daniel leaves off. The prophet glimpses Jesus dressed in the plain white linen, which Israel's high priest wore on the Day of Atonement. The book details Jesus' work as High Priest during the Day of Atonement, culminating in His return for His collective bride—the faithful remnant who are translated without tasting death (see 1 Thess. 4:13–17), as well as the faithful throughout the ages who are raised from the grave at the sound of His voice (see John 5:25–29).

ABOUT THE AUTHOR

Scott Burgess was baptized as a Seventh-day Adventist April 1, 2006. He has been on fire to serve the Lord and share the end time message with people ever since. He is married to Karen, and God has blessed them with 3 beautiful children: Elijah Matthew, Faith Eve, and Dinah Ruth. Their names are symbolic: all who receive the *Elijah* message as the *gift of Yahweh*, exercising a *living faith* therein, will experience *vindication* during the end time judgment, having developed the steadfastness of *Ruth*.

From 2008–2011, the author was privileged to be sent to the Seventh-day Adventist Theological Seminary at Andrews University in Berrien Springs, Michigan by the Carolina Conference of Seventh-day Adventists. His love of the biblical languages developed there while preparing for pastoral ministry. Since then, he has taught a variety of courses including Daniel, Revelation, and the biblical languages at Ouachita Hills College, a Seventh-day Adventist institution in Amity, Arkansas that prepares students for full-time service for the Lord.

THE STAND: Jesus in the Book of Daniel and its sequel, *THE WEDDING: Jesus Stands for His Bride in the Book of Revelation*, provide commentary on the books of Daniel and Revelation, respectively. They elucidate the meaning of the biblical text by adhering to four key principles: using the "line upon line" method of Bible study to locate explanatory texts for each verse under consideration; working directly from the original languages; employing the historicist method of prophetic interpretation; and noting the biblical use of every number that appears in both books.

It is the author's desire that this book and others that issue from his pen will open people's understanding to the truths of God's Word. Perhaps more importantly, he hopes to demonstrate for readers *how* they too can understand the Bible for themselves by prayerfully seeking the Holy Spirit's guidance, applying the "line upon line" method of Bible study, and persevering until the solution is apparent. Armed with this knowledge, may all readers be led to share the beautiful truth of the end time judgment with everyone God puts in their path.

TEACH Services, Inc.
P U B L I S H I N G
www.TEACHServices.com • (800) 367-1844

We invite you to view the complete
selection of titles we publish at:
www.TEACHServices.com

We encourage you to write us
with your thoughts about this,
or any other book we publish at:
info@TEACHServices.com

TEACH Services' titles may be purchased in
bulk quantities for educational, fund-raising,
business, or promotional use.
bulksales@TEACHServices.com

Finally, if you are interested in seeing
your own book in print, please contact us at:
publishing@TEACHServices.com

We are happy to review your manuscript at no charge.

www.ingramcontent.com/pod-product-compliance
Lightning Source LLC
Chambersburg PA
CBHW052050230426
43671CB00011B/1855